The 2012 Nomination and the Future of the Republican Party

The 2012 Nomination and the Future of the Republican Party

The Internal Battle

Edited by William J. Miller

LEXINGTON BOOKS
Lanham • Boulder • New York • Toronto • Plymouth, UK

Published by Lexington Books
A wholly owned subsidiary of The Rowman & Littlefield Publishing Group, Inc.
4501 Forbes Boulevard, Suite 200, Lanham, Maryland 20706
www.rowman.com

10 Thornbury Road, Plymouth PL6 7PP, United Kingdom

Copyright © 2013 by Lexington Books

All rights reserved. No part of this book may be reproduced in any form or by any electronic or mechanical means, including information storage and retrieval systems, without written permission from the publisher, except by a reviewer who may quote passages in a review

British Library Cataloguing in Publication Information Available

Library of Congress Cataloging-in-Publication Data

The 2012 nomination and the future of the Republican Party: the internal battle / edited by William J. Miller
pages cm
Includes bibliographical references and index.
ISBN 978-0-7391-7592-7 (cloth) — ISBN 978-0-7391-7593-4 (electronic)
1. Republican Party (U.S. : 1854-) 2. Presidents—United States—Election—2012. 3. Presidential candidates—United States—History—21st century. 4. Romney, Mitt. I. Miller, William J., 1984-
JK2356.A17 2013
324.2734--dc23
2013023002

∞™ The paper used in this publication meets the minimum requirements of American National Standard for Information Sciences Permanence of Paper for Printed Library Materials, ANSI/NISO Z39.48-1992.

Printed in the United States of America

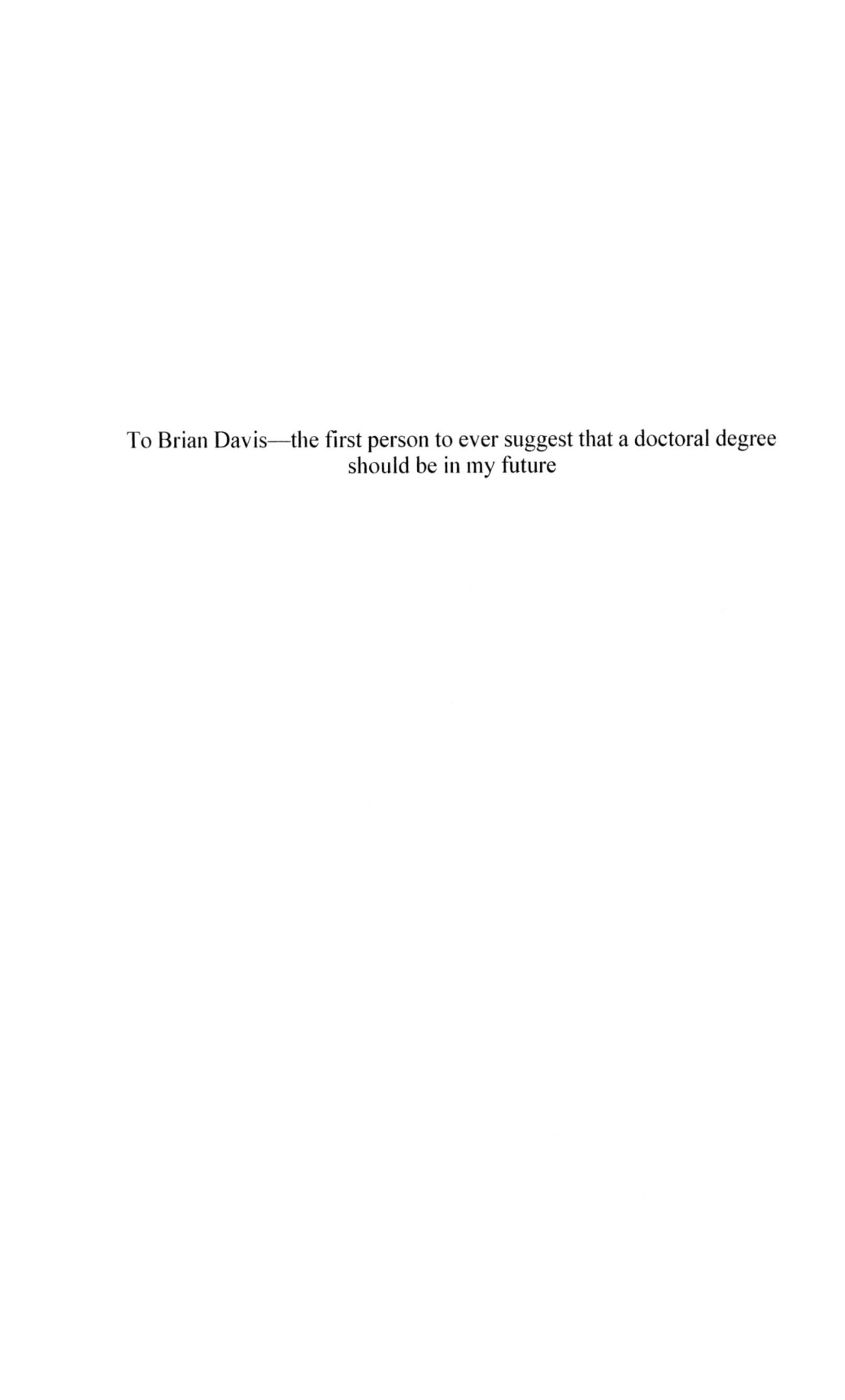

To Brian Davis—the first person to ever suggest that a doctoral degree should be in my future

The Republican Party is experiencing an existential crisis, born of its own misguided incongruity with modern American culture and its insistence on choosing intransigence in a dynamic age of fundamental change.
—Charles M. Blow, *The New York Times*, March 22, 2013

How did the party of Lincoln allow itself to be taken over by the claque of crazies who now define it?
—Don Wycliff, *The Chicago Tribune*, September 27, 2009

I was always raised to think that Republicans were about limited government, about individual liberty, about fiscal responsibility, about balanced budgets, about a wariness of military adventures abroad, about responsible encouragement to business. There's a whole list of things I thought the Republican Party was all about, and these guys that presently occupy the White House, are categorically against every single one of those things. So if they're Republicans, I'm not.
—John Perry Barlow, *Planet JH Weekly*, July 28, 2005

When the chips are down and the decisions are made as to who the candidates will be, then the 11th commandment prevails and everybody goes to work, and that is: Thou shalt not speak ill of another Republican.
—Ronald Reagan, June 17, 1982

I would not speak with disrespect of the Republican Party. I always speak with great respect of the past.
—Woodrow Wilson, 1915

Contents

Preface		ix
1	The 2012 Republican Nomination Season: A Clown Car or Feuding Conservatives? *William J. Miller*	1
2	The Impact of Rules Changes on the 2012 Republican Presidential Primary Process *Joshua T. Putnam*	21
3	White Knights to the Rescue! The Non-Candidates of 2012 *William Cunion*	35
4	The Curious Candidacy of Jon Huntsman *David F. Damore and Kenneth J. Retzl*	61
5	Early to Rise, Early to Fall: The Short Lived Hope of Michele Bachmann *Jason Rich and Brandy A. Kennedy*	77
6	The Hermanator: Anti-Elitism and the Rise of Herman Cain *Andrew L. Pieper*	103
7	Rick Perry: The Quickly Fading Star of Texas *Brian Arbour*	127
8	Newt Gingrich: It Takes More than Ideas to Win a Nomination *Joshua P. Stockley*	149
9	Ron Paul: Establishment Outsider or Radical Insider? *Jeremy D. Walling*	181
10	Of Sweater Vests and Broken Dreams: Santorum's Almost Win *Daniel J. Coffey and Terrence M. O'Sullivan*	197
11	Mitt Romney—The Republican Choice: Inevitability, Electability, and Lack of Enthusiasm *Sean D. Foreman*	219

12	The Victor's Reward and the Future of the GOP *William J. Miller*	245
About the Editor		255
About the Contributors		257
Index		261

Preface

The 2012 Republican nomination battle was not one that will be quickly forgotten. The GOP entered the period primed to select Mitt Romney to represent them against incumbent Democrat Barack Obama. After roughly two years of campaigning—including dozens of debates, stump speeches, and fundraising—and nearly a dozen individuals leading in some national poll at one time or another, they ended up exactly where they expected to be. It came at quite a cost, however. Like a boxer being asked to immediately head back into the ring after fighting through 12 rounds, Romney emerged a battered victor.

Campaign strategy tells us that a party is best served in a presidential race by quickly selecting a nominee and allowing them to immediately move toward the center—especially when they are facing a sitting incumbent at is still popular in his party. In 2012, Republican voters opted to try the exact opposite, dragging their process out nearly as long as possible without having a contested convention and forcing the candidate polling best against Obama into sounding increasingly conservative as time went on in order to win the nomination. By the time it was over and Romney took the stage in Tampa at the Republican Convention, he was a bleeding target in shark infested waters. There were no secrets left. His fellow Republicans had laid a golden strategy for President Obama and Democratic operatives to use and even forced him into saying things about policy that we still are not entirely sure that he actually believed.

Beyond potentially costing Republicans the 2012 election, the recent nomination process signaled larger problems for the GOP: structural cracks within their very foundation. Whereas in previous years the evangelical Christian wing, business wing, and Tea Party wing were able to find a candidate that seemingly worked for all, in 2012 this was not the case. And in the end that could very well be the most important takeaway from the recent presidential election cycle. Republicans—to be successful at the national level—need to take an introspective look at the present state of their party, their supporters, and their policy beliefs to determine their future direction. Demographics and internal bickering suggest there are potentially difficult times ahead. In this book, I set out to examine how the 2012 nomination demonstrates the potential trouble in the future of the Republican Party.

In the first chapter, I lay out a general overview of the GOP nomination process and how it ultimately played out. Josh Putnam follows with a discussion of how the nomination process was structured in 2012 and how it differed from 2008 and potentially impacted strategic decisions made by candidates. William Cunion discusses one of the more popular discussions from the 2012 nomination—all of the candidates who chose not to enter the race. Then we have a series of chapters devoted to each of the main candidates with David Damore and Kenneth Retzl starting off with a discussion of Jon Huntsman's short-lived presidential bid. Jason Rich and Brandy Kennedy follow with an analysis of Michele Bachmann's early rise and near immediate collapse. Andrew Pieper highlights the campaign of perhaps the most bizarre of the Republican candidates: Herman Cain of 9-9-9 fame. Brian Arbour tells us how Rick Perry went from the acclaimed savior of the party to non-entity during a single debate. Newt Gingrich's unusual campaign strategy is next covered by Joshua Stockley. Jeremy Walling discusses the consistency of Ron Paul's message and delivery, along with his ever-faithful following. Daniel Coffey and Terrence O'Sullivan show readers how Rick Santorum went from being a relative afterthought to almost pulling off the impossible through detailed messaging and strategic decisions. And then Sean Foreman highlights the steady campaign and resource dominance of the eventual winner, Mitt Romney. I conclude with a discussion of Romney's campaign against Obama and how all of this spells potential doom for the Republicans in 2016 and beyond.

In preparing this book, I have been fortunate to have had the assistance of many individuals whom we need to take time to thank. First, I would like to thank everyone at Lexington Books for making this book possible. Melissa Wilks, Lenore Lautigar, and Justin Race have been invaluable as editors. Justin has been especially helpful as a sounding board for ideas and theories. Likewise to Erin Walpole, Alison Northridge, and Alissa Parra for answering my frequent questions related to formatting and timeliness. Next, I have to thank the individuals who really made this book everything that it is—the contributing authors. While I had established relationships with some authors, others were solicited especially for this project. I appreciate their willingness to invest their time and effort to help me tell this important story. All of my authors assisted me more than they know by sending in chapters that were true to the goals of the book and only in need of minor edits. I would be remiss—if not in trouble—if I did not thank my wife, Jill. A life-long liberal Democrat, Jill often grew tired of discussions of the material of this book but still patiently listened and added commentary and feedback as necessary.

William J. Miller
St. Augustine, FL
April 25, 2013

ONE

The 2012 Republican Nomination Season: A Clown Car or Feuding Conservatives?

William J. Miller

Politics seem to happen in cycles. A candidate or party may be up one day—seemingly destined to exert political dominance for years to come—only by the next morning to have disappeared as a serious actor. At times, individual decisions or gaffes lead to such a dramatic slide. But in other situations, the mood of the populace causes such expedient alterations of opinion. The 2012 Republican nomination battle (and the four years spent building up to it) provides us with a perfect case study from which to examine the protean nature of parties and candidates in the United States. In 2008, Democrats found themselves well-positioned to exert influence over federal policy. Then in the midterm elections of 2010, Republicans came roaring back. And it was not just the typical Republican winning seats, the Tea Party had arrived. By 2012, Americans seemed genuinely dissatisfied with everything related to government—Republicans especially. As a result, we witnessed a constant ebb and flow of candidates into and out of the race to be the Republican nominee. In the end, Mitt Romney took the torch and flamed out in the general election. More than just a loss, the primary election battle and Romney's subsequent performance suggests serious concerns about the Republican Party's long-term potential to reach citizens in the new American electorate.

Chapter 1

THE SETTING

It seems like a long time ago, but in 2008 Barack Obama shook the traditional political order of our country and secured the presidency. Not only was he the first African-American to ever win the office, but he did so with a populist message and charismatic delivery that beckoned comparisons to past revered Democratic leaders Franklin Roosevelt and John Kennedy. Riding his coattails were 21 new Democratic members of the United States House of Representatives and eight United States Senators. Washington was colored blue—symbolizing Democratic dominance over the federal government for the first time since 1993-1995 (and only the second time since 1970). But then reality set in. Public attitudes dropped. Promises of hope and change were remembered by voters who became dissatisfied when their situations did not improve immediately. Guantanamo did not close down. Healthcare reform dragged on. Obama seemed to be delivering more of the same. Entering office with nearly 65 percent approval, he took less than seven months before dropping below 50 percent for the first time.

Midterm elections are never good for the party of a new president. Historically, political science has told us that the president's party always loses seats during this first election period. Thus, Democrats were well aware that November 2010 would likely not be their greatest month. But not even the strongest Republican advocate could have predicted the red tidal wave that overtook the nation. By the end of the 2010 election cycle, Republicans had gained 63 seats in the House (along with control of the body) and six Senate seats (to draw closer to even). Unified government no longer existed for Democrats and Obama's job of selling policy became exponentially more difficult. Most importantly, however, was the success of a new faction within the Republican Party—the Tea Party. Originally viewed by many Americans as a group of angry Republicans who would have little impact, instead the movement succeeded in upsetting moderate Republican loyalists. The newly elected Republicans were noticeably more conservative than their predecessors. New U.S. Senators like Marco Rubio, Rand Paul, and Mike Lee took their uncompromising positions to Washington. They stressed curbed spending and less taxes; they were the self-proclaimed anti-Obamas. Even the president had to be honest in his assessment of what happened in November 2010, referring to the election as a shellacking.

When the new Congress came together in 2011, seismic shifts within our nation's borders and politics came with it. Depending on one's personal views, activities in the Middle East and North Africa were seen as being democratic or destabilizing. Two long-term American enemies—Osama bin Laden and Muammar al-Gaddafi—were killed by American forces. Instead of celebrating such success, Americans instead engaged in a drawn out discourse regarding who (Bush or Obama) should receive credit. The constant budget fight in D.C. shook financial markets. Scott Walker (Governor of Wisconsin) pressed labor laws that led to a fight between unions and government in his state. The same battle would later occur in other similar states—mainly Ohio, led by John Kasich. And in *Citizens United*, the Supreme Court welcomed additional outside spending from Super PACs, which would alter the federal election landscape in unknown ways come 2012. For President Obama, healthcare reform was still a lightning rod issue that he had to answer to on a regular basis. It was not just the political climate that suggested potential problems for Democrats in 2012. In the middle of 2011, the national mood was depressed. Less than half of Americans reported feeling any level of optimism toward the economy. On InTrade, Obama received even odds to be reelected. In short, Democrats and Republicans seem to be as divided as ever, but Obama's downward trend in the polls and the 2010 midterm elections seemed to suggest that 2012 could be a golden opportunity for Republicans to regain the keys to the White House.

THE MAIN PLAYERS

When describing the Republican response to the political climate they found themselves in during 2011, conservative blogger Susannah Fleetwood claimed the party turned into The Clown College.[1] Going further, she publicly asked how the GOP ended up with an "endless clown car full of crazy."[2] At first take, the metaphor seems to be slightly over-stated but once we consider the volume of individuals who sought the nomination (and at one point or another was leading in the polls), it does seem to fit better than national Republicans may wish to acknowledge. Putting accusations of crazy aside, the nomination season did seem as if a very small car pulled up to the American public and Republicans began emerging out of every opening. By the end, there were more candidates than it seemed plausible to have inside the initial car.

For a Republican looking at the seemingly countless candidates they could choose from, numerous questions needed to be answered. If the political climate really was predicting an Obama defeat, Republicans could roll the dice and try to select a more conservative candidate. On the other hand, if they wanted to be safe, they could look at general electability and play to the center-right values so many Republicans hold near and dear. If more conservative candidates regularly challenged the center-right choice, the only outcome would be a significantly decreased opportunity to unseat the Democratic incumbent. Much like many voters had faced in Republican primaries in 2010, the choice ultimately came down to voting for someone dubbed most likely to win the general election or to vote for a candidate that more wholly espoused traditional conservative values. With that dichotomy in mind, we can now introduce the major players from the 2012 Republican primary presidential season.

Mitt Romney

Mitt Romney entered the primary season as former Governor of Massachusetts. He had unsuccessfully run for president in 2008 and U.S. Senate in 1994. From the beginning of the race, Romney was deemed to be the mainstream favorite to win the nomination. Four years earlier, he had been identified as the candidate too far from the political center to have a chance to defeat Senator Obama. Now, less than half a decade later, many wondered if he was too centrist to be able to energize the base enough to overcome Obama's incumbency advantage and loyal Democratic following. Over the course of the election, Romney would need to answer numerous questions. First, Romney is of the Mormon faith. This in and of itself raised questions about his electability with the party base given the strong influence of Southern evangelical Christians in recent elections.[3] Second, he had largely passed and supported a healthcare reform measure as Governor of Massachusetts that looked similar to Obama's healthcare efforts at the national level. How would he be able to speak out with authority against the single largest piece of legislation during Obama's first term if he had previously endorsed a similar measure? These two contextual issues were complicated by a series of gaffers during the course of the campaign. Romney publicly stated that he was not concerned about the very poor due to the presence of a safety net for them.[4] He did little to help himself with Southern Republicans when commenting that he has friends who are NASCAR team owners in an effort to appease the particular voting bloc.[5] He offered a $10,000 bet to show he was correct on a point made during a debate and mentioned his wife owning a couple of Cadillacs. He then fell out of favor with some voters after it was revealed that he once strapped his family dog (Seamus, the Irish Setter) to the roof of his station wagon for a twelve hour ride.[6] His alleged involvement in vulture capitalism while CEO of Bain Capital also hampered his standing with some Republicans and Democrats alike.[7] Further, he continually failed to ever fully answer to his decision to publicly state that the federal government should not bailout General Motors despite his family's strong history and ties to Detroit.[8] And to top it off, longtime Romney advisor Eric Fehrnstrom explained how campaigns were like an Etch-A-Sketch that could be shaken up and started all over as necessary.[9] Despite these gaffes, Romney spent the entire primary season largely believed to be the likely nominee. He had mainstream support, the necessary financial backing, and simply looked the most like a president. If anyone running was truly electable and looked presidential, it was him.

Rick Santorum

Rick Santorum had served two terms in the U.S. House of Representatives and a subsequent two terms as a U.S. Senator representing the state of Pennsylvania. Prior to his 2006 re-election campaign for Senate, he was cited as a possible 2008 Republican presidential nominee. Yet he polled poorly and eventually lost his Senate seat, along with any presidential aspirations at the time. In 2008, instead of running himself, Santorum supported Mitt Romney due to John McCain's pro-life voting record and moderate values. Once Sarah Palin was named as the Vice Presidential nominee, Santorum began to support McCain—albeit in a fairly lukewarm fashion. In 2012, Santorum did choose to insert himself into the race to be the Republican nominee against Obama. Early in the race, Santorum was largely considered a fringe candidate due to his extreme issue positions and personal gaffes. The most notable aspect of the Santorum campaign in the beginning was the internet attack launched by Dan Savage after a Santorum interview where he spoke out against acts of homosexuality.[10] Then there was the recounted story of the Santorum family's decision to take their deceased child's body home after he was lost to a miscarriage in 1996. The story brought attention to Santorum's Catholic faith and policy attitudes based on those religious views. Radio host Alan Colmes led the attack, accusing Santorum of grossly permitting his family to play with the corpse of their deceased child.[11] In terms of issue statements, Santorum also found himself attracting negative attention when he stated that President John F. Kennedy's famous speech on the separation of church and state made him want to throw up.[12] This is not surprising given statements Santorum made in 2008 about a potential war with Satan: "Satan is attacking the great institutions of America, using those great vices of pride, vanity, and sensuality as the root to attack all of the strong plants that has so deeply rooted in the American tradition."[13] While some Republican voters strongly agreed with Santorum's assessment, it was still an overall net negative for his campaign.[14] And how could we mention Rick Santorum in 2012 without bringing up his personal fashion statement: the sweater vest.[15] While all the candidates seemed to ebb and flow, Santorum went from being a true underdog to nearly pulling off a monumental upset given his strong support from the Christian conservatives within the Republican Party.

Ron Paul

If Romney was the favorite and Santorum was the underdog, Ron Paul was the annoying sidekick—unwilling to remove himself from the race but unable to gain enough support to truly pose a threat to either candidate. A long-time Representative from Texas, Paul first ran for president in 2008. While his push to eliminate unnecessary government bureaucracy and foreign involvement (including ending all wars and eliminating key departments and agencies), his early campaign was resonated best as a grassroots movement supported by college students and individuals who preferred cardboard campaign signs in the back windows of cars to traditional tactics. Without attracting much media attention, Paul struggled to gain traction and ultimately failed to muster a serious threat to other Republican candidates. Yet, he still made waves when he refused to endorse any of his competitors in the party and instead backed four independent presidential nominees. By the time 2012 rolled around, many felt Paul would have a better chance at being a serious candidate. The Tea Party movement, after all, had a strong impact on the 2010 midterm elections and aligned well with the views and opinions of Paul. Yet, his 2012 performance was only marginally better than he had experienced four years prior. It should be noted, however, that the general public and other Republican candidates did recognize Paul as a threat. Unlike in 2008, there was a volume of opposition research conducted against Paul. Most striking, opponents found a passage from a 1992 Ron Paul Political Report talking about the Los Angeles race riots that said: "Order was only restored in L.A. when it came time for the blacks to pick up their welfare checks."[16] Other comments pulled from Ron Paul newsletters claimed that citizens with AIDS should be banned from public restaurants because "AIDS can be transmitted by saliva" and another that was critical of President Reagan for agreeing to create a federal holiday for Martin Luther King Jr., which the newsletter referred to as "Hate Whitey Day."[17] While his presidential bid was not long-lasting, his influence was seen throughout the campaign. His call for the United States to withdraw from Afghanistan caught on among other candidates—as did his concern about the federal debt and general distrust of the Federal Reserve.[18] In the end, it became clear that much like in 2008, Ron Paul was pushing a message more than his own candidacy.

Newt Gingrich

Showing how truly wide-open the 2008 Republican primary season was, the party opted to dust off one of their old stalwarts for another attempt at electoral glory: former House Speaker Newt Gingrich. At one time, Gingrich was the hero for the GOP. He helped orchestrate the Republican takeover in 1994 and was viewed as the future of conservative thought in the country. But then he put all of his political capital into the government shutdown battle and lost to President Clinton. The final nail in his coffin was the Clinton impeachment—which ultimately went over with the American public like a lead balloon.[19] Yet in 2012, even Gingrich found himself entering the fray with a fighting chance. Yet his baggage would prove to be too much to overcome. The start of his campaign was riddled with questions. He publicly stated he was relying on Christian conservatives to support him, yet went on a family vacation rather than being in Washington, D.C. for a gathering of prominent religious conservatives.[20] Regarding policy, Gingrich regularly touted Obama as the food stamp president. This led to an early debate exchange with Juan Williams—who asked if Gingrich was trying to belittle people. Gingrich replied by stating: "The fact is that more people have been put on food stamps by Barack Obama than any president in American history. . . I believe every American of every background has been endowed by their creator with the right to pursue happiness. And if that makes liberals unhappy, I'm going to continue to find ways to help poor people learn how to get a job, learn how to get a better job and learn some day to own the job."[21] He then went before an audience and called out the NAACP in urging African-Americans to demand paychecks, not food stamps. He further wanted a new Social Security program to help African-American males who he argued received the smallest return on the current program.[22] Beyond policy, Gingrich also had to handle the loss of dozens of his senior campaign staff over disagreements regarding the direction of the campaign.[23] On the personal side, Gingrich had to answer questions regarding why he left his first two wives while both were seriously ill.[24] By the end of his time in the nomination, many Republicans were prepared to send Gingrich off to the moon—which he spent time promising to colonize during the campaign.

Rick Perry

When Rick Perry decided to enter the race, he was treated to a hero's welcome. The Texas governor basked in the attention and expectations many Republicans had for him. Yet to a non-partisan outsider, Perry's candidacy raised questions about the beliefs of mainstream conservatives. Perry, after all, was in some policy areas fairly moderate—if not liberal. First, consider his decision to implement the DREAM Act, which allows foreign-born children of illegal immigrants to pay in-state tuition.[25] And second, Perry went outside the traditional legislative process and issued an executive order that mandated the HPV vaccine for young girls.[26] In both of these policy areas, Perry appeared to buck national conservative thought. Yet he entered the race saying the right things: accusing Ben Bernanke of treason and arguing he should be subject to Texas Justice.[27] But like all of the other Republican candidates, policy issues appeared to be the least of Perry's worries. Once facing the national spotlight, numerous gaffes harmed Perry and quickly took him from front-runner status to yet another afterthought. Shortly after entering the race, the national media began questioning Perry about his hunting camp—Niggerhead. Given the name, many questioned Perry's personal beliefs and convictions and whether he was fit to be the leader of the country.[28] Then Perry and his campaign released one of the more infamous ads of the nomination, entitled Strong. In the ad, Perry states that one doesn't need to be in the pews every Sunday to know that something is wrong in the United States when "gays can serve openly in the military but our kids can't openly celebrate Christmas or pray in schools." While the ad was clearly meant to demonstrate a tie to religious conservatives in the Midwest and South, it was controversial even within the Perry campaign—let alone the nation as a whole.[29] Perry was already beginning to feel the pressure when he took the debate stage in Rochester, Michigan. By the end of the night, one-55 second sound bite would end his campaign. When discussing the three agencies he would eliminate if president, Perry blanked on the third, leading to a period of awkward silence in which even his fellow competitors seemed to take pity on their opponent.[30] With that, Perry left seemingly as quickly as he entered. Perhaps he will be president one day—of the nation of Texas, a move he had previously supported before running for President of the United States.[31]

Herman Cain

Of all the candidates for the Republican nomination, no one was quite as perplexing as Herman Cain. Cain had no previous political experience. Instead, he had served as CEO of Godfather's Pizza, Chairman of the Federal Reserve Bank of Kansas City, and President of the National Restaurant Association. Compared to other candidates, Cain was the unknown. Republicans seemed to appreciate his straightforward approach and unwillingness to play the typical political games. The cornerstone of Cain's campaign was his 9-9-9 taxation plan. This plan would eliminate the current federal tax code and replace it with three taxes—a 9 percent income tax, a 9 percent business transactions tax, and a 9 percent federal sales tax.[32] Throughout the debate season, Cain steadfastly sang the praises of his plan, answering any question possible with some reference to 9-9-9. Yet, after some investigation, many began drawing similarities between Cain's 9-9-9 plan and a similar taxation scheme that forms the cornerstone of revenue generation in the SimCity computer game.[33] But the 9-9-9 plan became an afterthought compared to Cain's three major gaffes during the campaign. First, the Cain campaign released some of the most bizarre online commercials ever recorded during the nomination process. Ranging from Chief of Staff Mark Block smoking and talking about how patriotic Cain is to the Yellow Flowers Western-style sketch, the ads were vastly different from the expected norms and led to more questions about his seriousness as a candidate than increases in support.[34] Second, Cain had an endorsement interview slip when he was asked whether he agreed with how President Obama was handling Libya by the *Milwaukee Journal Sentinel* editorial board. Cain responded with: "OK, Libya. President Obama supported the uprising, correct?"[35] While the Cain team claimed it was not a major issue, once the video went viral, Cain immediately saw his poll numbers begin to slip. And lastly, Cain faced a series of serious allegations related to sexual harassment and other various sex scandals. During his tenure as Director of the National Restaurant Association, Cain was accused by two women of a litany of inappropriate behaviors, including "conversations allegedly filled with innuendo or personal questions of a sexually suggestive nature, taking place at hotels during conferences, at other officially sanctioned restaurant association events, and at the association's offices and physical gestures that were not overtly sexual but that made women who experienced or witnessed them uncomfortable."[36] Taken together, these issues would ultimately spell the end of Cain's bizarre campaign, leading to his Pokemon-inspired exit from the race: "Life can be a challenge. Life can seem impossible. It's never easy when there's so much on the line. But you and I can make a difference. There's a mission just for you and me."[37]

Michele Bachmann

While Herman Cain may have been the most curious Republican seeking the nomination, Michele Bachmann was the most polarizing. At the start of the recognized nomination period, Bachmann was actually the surprise favorite, having won the Ames Straw Poll.[38] This surprising victory led to an aura of credibility to her campaign that had been lacking prior. Bachmann, however, seemingly set out in the immediate aftermath of the victory destined to destroy every shred of credibility she had earned. In the aftermath of the Ames Straw Poll, Bachmann announced her concerns with the HPV vaccine—going as far as to suggest that exposure to the drug could lead to mental retardation.[39] Her claims were denounced by medical professionals from across the globe and even led to a group of bioethics professors to offer $10,000 for proof that Gardasil actually could cause mental retardation.[40] While the claims themselves brought negative attention to her campaign, the bigger concern was the tendency of Bachmann to speak off-the-cuff and make comments that could easily be misconstrued or viewed as hyperbole. Bachmann's sense of history and geography also came under scrutiny. First, she mistakenly failed to realize that Libya is in Africa while denouncing Obama's plan to place troops in Uganda.[41] Then she struggled with Civil War history and discussed how Lexington and Concord took place in New Hampshire.[42] When it comes to Iraq, Bachmann gained notoriety for a series of statements about how Iraqis should reimburse the United States for assisting them.[43] Politically, Bachmann again made far-fetching claims that ruined her credibility and odds at election. Consider when she explained to an audience that "swine flu epidemics are a Democratic phenomenon."[44] Perhaps most damning however was attention devoted to discussing her husband's controversial clinic, which aimed to cure homosexuality through prayer.[45] While the provocative idea of the clinic would have likely been enough to end any aspirations for Bachmann, it also didn't help that the clinic was known for collecting Medicaid payments—which ran directly counter to her own denouncement of that program as part of her campaign platform. Of all the candidates, Bachmann went from the highest high to the lowest low the most quickly, but she definitely made herself known during her moment in the sun.

Jon Huntsman

Jon Huntsman is the seemingly forgotten candidate from the Republican nomination. He had vast political experience, having served in the Reagan administration, as a U.S. Trade Representative, Governor of Utah, Ambassador to Singapore, and Ambassador to China. Yet all of these things—which many would have viewed as strengths—came back to be mentioned as weaknesses by his detractors. His time in Utah solidified his labeling as the other Mormon in the race. And his time in China garnered him the label of communist sympathizer. Add in the fact that Obama nominated him to the post in China and Huntsman was seen as being far too liberal for the GOP. Reality, however, told a different story. He lowered taxes in Utah, supported the Ryan plan for reforming government spending, and passed lots of pro-life legislation in his state. But he was never able to differentiate himself from other candidates in the eyes of voters. Realizing their dad was struggling to gain traction, three of Huntsman's daughters (Abby, Liddy, and Mary Anne) took to social media to bolster his odds. Their snarky commentary eventually overshadowed his actual campaign.[46] In the end, he worked for Obama, was too much like Romney, and tried to be moderate in a year of revolt.[47] His daughters will likely be remembered in campaign history even more than their dad.

Synthesis

The secret to success for Republicans in the lead-up to 2012 would have been to select a candidate that best appealed to the major factions within the GOP (traditional business conservative, Tea Party, and evangelical Christians) and provided the greatest chance of defeating President Obama. These eight candidates (and the countless others who considered a run at one point in the process), however, decided to wage such a fierce primary battle that whoever emerged would be wounded before entering the general election against President Obama. The succession of candidates continued to raise the hopes of Republican voters only to ultimately dash them. As a candidate moved toward success, hope increased that they could be the candidate of choice, and then something seemed to knock them back to the pile. As the Japanese proverb predicts, the nail that stuck out was quickly pounded in.

ACT ONE: THE PRE-PRIMARY

In the pre-primary stage of the campaign, the action centered on determining which candidates were serious about actually running for the Republican nomination. Early speculation involved a series of familiar names. Talk show host and former Arkansas Governor Mike Huckabee, former Florida Governor Jeb Bush, Former RNC Chair and Mississippi Governor Haley Barbour, Tea Party favorite Marco Rubio, South Dakota Senator John Thune, New Jersey Governor Chris Christie, and Indiana Governor Mitch Daniels all decided to not even enter the fray for various reasons. At the earliest of stages, Donald Trump was actually polling as a Republican favorite—spearheaded by his obsession with Obama's birth certificate. Former Governors Gary Johnson (New Mexico) and Buddy Roemer (Louisiana) both stuck a toe in the water but quickly left the campaign trail.

Jon Huntsman's campaign got off to a rocky start with the former Utah Governor choosing to declare at the Statue of Liberty. But the camera angles were poorly thought out, there was limited attendance, and press credentials had his name spelled wrong.[48] After choosing to respond to a debate question in Mandarin Chinese early in the race, the writing was on the wall regarding his long-term chances. Another governor—Tim Pawlenty of Minnesota—was the early favorite for the presidential bid according to many pundits. Pawlenty was seen as being the perfect mix of conservative and moderate while also coming from a state bordering Iowa, which is a key gateway to early returns. But Pawlenty was also extremely low-key and many wondered if he could handle the pressure of a prolonged nomination battle. Appearing on *Fox News Sunday*, Pawlenty showed signs of being the candidate Republicans were hoping for when fusing Romney's Massachusetts healthcare plan with Obama's Care Affordable Act, referring to it as ObamneyCare. Yet he failed to utilize the saying further in the campaign—including debates—and saw poll numbers decrease before withdrawing.

Michele Bachmann had been fresh on the minds of Americans since the conclusion of the 2008 campaign cycle when she asked journalists to look into Congress to see who was pro- and anti-American. She ended up gaining 28 percent of the vote in the Ames Straw Poll to win (although with an asterisk since Mitt Romney did not participate). But she had spent all of her time, energy, and money in Iowa and showed no life anywhere else on the electoral map leading to her staffers quitting quickly before she chose to withdraw. While Bachmann was on the down swing, Rick Perry threw his cowboy hat into the ring, bringing a folksy style and a reliance on data analysis. In fact, Perry—some claim—hurt Bachmann by announcing his entrance the same day she won in Ames. Perry, much like another Texas governor turned president, was good at shaking hands but not the best at publicly debating or speaking about policy. His famous debate gaffe ultimately ended any realistic chance he had at becoming president. As Perry dropped out of sight, Herman Cain began moving up the ladder. Cain—known for always smiling—brought a directness to the campaign that had been lacking. But he quickly came unglued after finding himself as the frontrunner in the polls when he seemed surprised by allegations of sexual harassment and then had the editorial board interview gaffe. He fell out of contention almost as quickly as he found himself in it.

By the end of the pre-primary season, Donald Trump, Mitt Romney, Rick Perry, and Herman Cain had all led in the national polls while Michele Bachmann had won the Ames Straw Poll. Yet for every victory, each candidate had been dealt a fatal blow as well—with only Romney remaining stable. Unfortunately, that's the best word to describe Romney during this period. Republicans were not enthusiastic about his candidacy, but he was the best bet of everyone on the stage.

ACT TWO: CORN, GRANITE, AND PALMETTOS

For Romney, it seemed as if the campaign always came down to Romney versus "someone." Yet no matter how many "someones" he was successful in beating back, there were still more challengers coming. When it came time for the votes that would actually count in determining the Republican challenger against President Obama, attention fell squarely on Iowa. As Herman Cain quickly fell back to earth, his place atop the GOP leaderboard was taken by Newt Gingrich. For Gingrich, his rise was well-timed, placing him near the top at the perfect time. Like with all who had come before him, Gingrich immediately found himself facing intense pressure from his fellow Republicans. Romney made fun of his moon colony plan and Paul argued that he lobbied for Freddie Mac. Then advertisements in Iowa started rolling. Romney TV ads (largely funded through Super PAC money) stated that Gingrich had more baggage than an airline.[49] By the time it was over, anti-Gingrich ads were estimated to account for 45 percent of all campaign ads that ran in Iowa in the month of December.[50]

By the time January 3rd rolled around and voting occurred, a surprise result emerged. Rick Santorum had been largely ignored, opting to shake hands in the 99 counties of Iowa instead of dropping millions of dollars on television advertisements. He created direct relationships with social conservatives across the state and when the votes were cast ultimately fell only eight shy of Mitt Romney. Gingrich finished disappointingly far behind his two counterparts. While Romney technically won the state, it was Santorum who benefitted the most given the relative lack of attention that the media and fellow candidates had given him throughout the period preceding the vote. Despite not winning (at least not officially at that time), Santorum delivered a victory address and urged his supporters that it was "Game on!" Yet momentum would be difficult to maintain for Santorum with New Hampshire the next stop for the Republicans.

The Granite State is known for libertarian flare and a lack of agreement with most evangelical Christian values. Its southern media markets are shared with Boston, further hampering Santorum since that area was very familiar with Romney already. New Hampshire was not a state where Super PAC advertising would help win an election. Instead, meeting citizens and seeking key endorsements would better aid candidates in rounding up support. In November of 2011, the *Manchester Union Leader*, under publisher Joe McQuaid, chose to endorse Gingrich due to his possessing "the experience, the leadership qualities, and the vision to lead this country in these trying times."[51] Despite this setback, Romney had been seeking support in the state for years and still felt comfortable in his chances of regaining momentum on voting day. Ultimately, he was right. Romney won the New Hampshire primaries with just under 40 percent of the vote, easily distancing himself from Ron Paul and Jon Huntsman with Gingrich and Santorum both failing to muster even one out of ten votes. After the first two rounds, Romney and Santorum had both experienced victories, meaning Gingrich needed to produce or risk becoming yet another GOP afterthought.

Luckily for Gingrich, the third stop was in South Carolina, near his home state of Georgia. Much of the focus during the South Carolina primary season was on Mitt Romney's experience as CEO of Bain Capital. Rick Perry actually started the attacks by referring to Romney as a vulture capitalist with Gingrich supporters agreeing and producing a roughly thirty minute long video exposing the evils of the company. Ironically, this led to a situation where two arch-conservatives were attacking an allegedly moderate candidate for being too capitalistic while running a company. With time, the attacks diminished and Gingrich instead resorted to his typical Southern message that had served him well almost two decades before. In the end, it worked. Gingrich had little trouble gaining 40 percent of primary voters with Romney trailing with 28 percent and Santorum with 17. In other words, Romney won 28 percent and the field took over 70. After the three early states had cast ballots, we knew little more about which Republican would ultimately face Obama than we did in the beginning. All that had become clear was that the race would be between Romney, Santorum, and Gingrich, with Ron Paul coming along for the ride.

ACT THREE: GOP, MEET THE REST OF THE NATION

By the time the candidates were done in Iowa, New Hampshire, and South Carolina, theories began to surface as to why Romney was still the prohibitive favorite nationally to secure the GOP nomination. First and foremost, it was pointed out that Romney had access to a series of large donors to complement his own personal wealth. Yet with the emergence of Super PACs, it's not like Romney was alone in this regard. Jon Huntsman's father had largely bankrolled his entire campaign. Sheldon Adelson—a casino mogul—was doing the same for Gingrich while investor Foster Friess was behind Rick Santorum. As a result of these large donors, the field was relatively even despite the assumption that Romney had more cash at hand simply due to his out raising his opponents through traditional avenues. Of all the states that witnessed an influx of outside money, Florida saw more than its fair share as Romney and Gingrich pushed to claim the key battleground state and hopefully eliminate the other from contention. Even with Sarah Palin jumping in to help Gingrich, he still lost the state by 15 points. For Gingrich, this was the beginning of the end; he wouldn't win another state until his home state of Georgia on Super Tuesday.

Santorum never expected to compete well in Florida. He lacked the financial backing of Romney and Gingrich while also not espousing the conservative values most likely to resonate state-wide. Instead, he devoted his energies to middle America where he hoped to pull off the same results he saw in Iowa. The plan worked well as he exceeded expectations by winning Missouri, Minnesota, and Colorado. Then he did the unexpected and won Alabama and Mississippi with Romney coming in third behind Gingrich. Poll data was sending a mixed message; Santorum held a ten point edge over Romney in terms of candidate preference but was losing to him by 26 points in electability.[52] In this sense, Obama was Romney's best friend. Republicans preferred Santorum but seemed to feel Romney gave them the best chance to take back the White House.

The concern for Republicans was that by this point, a chosen candidate should have been moving toward the middle, attempting reach out to moderate voters (or even Democrats). Instead, they were busy proving how conservative they could be to the Republican base in a concentrated effort to even make the general election. There was no time for a national vision. What kept Romney ahead was his organization and funding. Santorum and Gingrich were simply unable to remain competitive within every state they needed to. But Romney was present everywhere; and this helped him gain delegates far more quickly. As Santorum began to slip on the campaign trail and Gingrich fizzled out, Romney was able to start consolidating victory on Super Tuesday. Like many general elections, it seemingly hinged on Ohio. If Santorum could win the Buckeye State, Romney would be in serious trouble. But Santorum was simply spread too thin and Romney's resources and organization proved to be too much. By the end of Super Tuesday, Santorum was out of contention. In the following weeks Gingrich and Santorum would exit, Romney would win states, and support began to swing. The primary was over. But it took a heavy toll on both the candidates and the party as they moved toward November.

THE REVIEWS

To quickly recap the nearly two-year lead-up to Mitt Romney securing the GOP nomination, one would need to remember the following events. Twenty debates (enough for network syndication if the Republicans desired) featuring a combination of ten different candidates. Five different nominees leading the national polls at certain points (Romney from February through August 2011 and then late February 2012 through the end, Perry from August through September 2011, Cain for a brief period in early November 2011, Gingrich from November 2011 through early January 2012, and Santorum from mid-February through mid-March 2012). And the gaffes and mistakes were nearly uncountable. Just to reiterate a few of the highlights[53] :

- To begin, Republicans seriously considered Donald Trump as a legitimate candidate.
- Jon Huntsman apparently felt the Republican base was looking for a bilingual candidate and seemed surprised when there was an angry response to his speaking in Mandarin during a debate.
- Michele Bachmann during an interview confused John Wayne (the movie hero) with John Wayne Gacy (the serial killer). She then used the politically incorrect term retarded when discussing potential side effects of HPV.
- Tim Pawlenty created the buzzword Obamneycare and then refused to use it in debates.
- Newt Gingrich killed his early momentum by heading off to visit the Greek Isles in the middle of his campaign.
- Herman Cain could not remember exactly where Libya is or what President Obama thinks about them. Nor could he remember sexually harassing multiple women. All he knew was 9-9-9.
- Rick Santorum pushed voters in Michigan toward Romney by openly attacking sex, the value of college, and former President Kennedy. Overall, he failed to have the necessary funding or organization for his sweater vests to carry him permanently into the lead.
- Rick Perry—hot in the polls at the time—was too excited about getting into the White House and slashing government bureaucracy. Sadly, during the debate, he could not remember exactly which

agencies he was looking to get rid of. However, he did remember his version of the DREAM Act and his support for the HPV vaccine.
- The entire field of Republican candidates seemed unwilling to fully attack Romney for his support of RomneyCare as a model for the nation or for his statements related to the auto bailout.
- And Ron Paul, was well Ron Paul. Full of ideas a large number of Republicans seemingly agree with but unable to aggregate the necessary support to win.

Based on this list, it becomes clear how Mitt Romney won the nomination. He entered as the front-runner and never made an error quite as serious as the ones listed above; he was steady. In the end, Romney was a clear victor at the convention, securing over 10 million popular votes (for 52.13 percent) and winning 37 states along with five territories. Santorum was a distant second with just short of 4 million votes (20.43 percent) and 11 states; Gingrich was third (with two states and approximately 14 percent of the vote); and Paul was fourth, winning the Virgin Islands and more than one out of ten popular votes cast.

Republicans rejoiced. A candidate had been chosen, and it was the one that they thought would fare the best against President Obama all along. Yet pundits were not convinced that Romney would ultimately match-up well with the sitting incumbent Democrat after having been exposed to the two years of battles leading up to it. Part of this was Romney's fault. Throughout the campaign, he had failed to sufficiently highlight his actual strengths. He rarely talked about his chief executive experience, instead choosing to talk about being pro-life and pro-gun. Unfortunately, those were beliefs he had realized later in life. To moderates, he was too conservative. To conservatives, he was too moderate. And to those just looking at him, his issues of choice did not match the persona he presented. At the end of the day, it seemed that his political ambition guided his every move and statement.

But concerns about Romney's general election chances were also fanned by the actions of his GOP counterparts. Gingrich started the attacks by questioning his honesty. Perry piled on by asking him to disclose more of his tax returns. And they both wanted to hear more about his time at Bain Capital. The Obama campaign pounced. Taking the calculated risk that Romney would win the nomination, Obama began expending large amounts of money into shaping voter opinion of Romney as an individual who preferred outsourcing and had no sympathy about firing workers. Even with all of his former primary opponents ultimately endorsing him, it felt like it could be too little too late. After all taking a turn at attempting to unseat him as well, the endorsements felt and appeared less genuine than in years past.

But Romney's campaign actually came out of the primary season stronger than it had started. He had successfully survived early disappointments, high expectations, and resilient opponents. His field organization learned invaluable lessons, fundraisers were able to reach out to voters across the country, and he had practice working a national strategy. More than anything, Romney learned what his identified weaknesses were and had plenty of opportunities to begin practicing rebuttals. Regardless of what happened in November, however, the 2012 nomination battle exposed a growing problem for Republicans nationwide: a fractured party base. While the Democrats have long been regarded as the big tent party—willing to accept anyone who was willing to support the party's beliefs, Republicans were no longer able to agree on a single candidate. Traditional business conservatives, Tea Party supporters, and evangelical Christians each had a chosen candidate in the nomination and the entire process led to speculation on whether the GOP would come together in November or not. Romney, after all, had to spend more time throughout the primary moving further and further to the right when traditional campaign strategy suggested that he should have been moving even closer to the middle.

NOTES

1. Susannah Fleetwood, "Romney Lost Because Republicans Behaved Like Undisciplined Clowns," *Right Wing News* 2012, http://www.rightwingnews.com/election-2012/romney-lost-because-republicans-behaved-like-undisciplined-clowns/ (accessed March 8, 2013).
2. Fleetwood, "Romney Lost."
3. Thomas Burr and Peggy Fletcher Stack, "Mitt Romney on the Verge of Making Major Mormon History," *Huffington Post* 2012, http://www.huffingtonpost.com/2012/04/11/mitt-romney-mormon-history_n_1419126.html (accessed February 17, 2013); Matthew Philibin, "Networks Obsessed with Labeling Romney Mormon," *News Busters* 2012, http://newsbusters.org/blogs/matthew-philbin/2012/04/12/networks-obsessed-labeling-romney-mormon (accessed January 29, 2013); Tresa Edmunds, "Mormons are Proud of Mitt Romney's Success—but Fear what Comes Next," *The Guardian* 2012, http://www.guardian.co.uk/commentisfree/cifamerica/2012/apr/12/mitt-romney-mormons-election-campaign (accessed January 4, 2013); Peggy Fletcher Stack, "Before Politics, Mitt Romney was a Mormon Bishop," *USA Today* 2012, http://www.usatoday.com/news/religion/story/2012-03-28/mitt-romney-mormon-bishop/53836844/1 (accessed February 14, 2013).
4. Stack, "Before Politics"; Maggie Haberman, "Limbaugh Questions Romney's Comment on Fixing 'Safety Nets'," *Politico* 2012, http://www.politico.com/blogs/burns-haberman/2012/02/limbaugh-questions-romneys-comment-on-fixing-safety-113192.html (accessed December 18, 2012); Rachel Weiner, "Romney, Citing Safety Net, Says He's 'Not Concerned about the Very Poor'," *Washington Post* 2012, http://www.washingtonpost.com/blogs/the-fix/post/romney-im-not-concerned-with-the-very-poor/2012/02/01/gIQAvajShQ_blog.html (accessed December 13, 2012).
5. Dino Grandoni, "Romney's NASCAR Comment is Rich," *The Atlantic Wire* 2012, http://www.theatlanticwire.com/politics/2012/02/romneys-nascar-comment-rich/49185/ (accessed December 14, 2012).
6. Lauren Fox, "'Dogs Against Romney' Upset Again," *U.S. News & World Report* 2012, http://www.usnews.com/news/blogs/washington-whispers/2012/04/12/dogs-against-romney-upset-again (accessed January 1, 2013).

7. John Bussey, "How Race Slipped Away from Mitt Romney," *Wall Street Journal* 2012, http://online.wsj.com/article/SB10001424127887324073504578105340729306074.html (accessed November 9, 2012).

8. Mitt Romney, "Let Detroit Go Bankrupt," *New York Times* 2008, http://www.nytimes.com/2008/11/19/opinion/19romney.html?_r=3& (accessed December 1, 2012).

9. Jeff Zeleny and Jim Rutenberg, "Romney's Day to Relish is Marred by Aide's Gaffe," *New York Times* 2012, http://www.nytimes.com/2012/03/22/us/politics/jeb-bush-endorses-romney-aide-makes-etch-a-sketch-gaffe.html?_r=1&hp (accessed November 7, 2012).

10. Stephanie Mencimer, "Rick Santorum's Anal Sex Problem," *Mother Jones* 2010, http://www.motherjones.com/politics/2010/08/rick-santorum-google-problem-dan-savage (accessed July 14, 2011).

11. John Hayward, "Alan Colmes Accuses Rick Santorum of 'Playin With' his Son's Corpse," *Humane Events* 2012, http://www.humanevents.com/2012/01/03/alan-colmes-accuses-rick-santorum-of-playing-with-his-sons-corpse/ (accessed March 13, 2012).

12. Luke Johnson, "Rick Santorum on JFK 'Throw Up' Comments: 'I Wish I Had that Particular Line Back.'" *Huffington Post* 2012, http://www.huffingtonpost.com/2012/02/28/santorum-throw-up-jfk-kennedy-speech_n_1307214.html (accessed April 14, 2012).

13. "Rick Santorum Defends Satan Comments," *Huffington Post* 2012, http://www.huffingtonpost.com/2012/02/22/rick-santorum-satan-_n_1293658.html (accessed March 29, 2012).

14. Mark Trumbull, "Does it Help Rick Santorum to Slam JFK on Religion's Role in Politics?," *Christian Science Monitor* 2012, http://www.csmonitor.com/USA/Elections/President/2012/0227/Does-it-help-Rick-Santorum-to-slam-JFK-on-religion-s-role-in-politics (accessed June 22, 2012).

15. Robin Bravender, "Rick Santorum Campaign a Boon to Sweater Vest Maker," *Politico* 2012, http://www.politico.com/news/stories/0312/74322.html (accessed August 2, 2012).

16. Jim Rutenberg and Richard A. Opel, Jr., "New Focus on Incendiary Words in Paul's Newsletters," *New York Times* 2011, http://www.nytimes.com/2011/12/20/us/politics/bias-in-ron-pauls-newsletters-draws-new-attention.html?_r=0 (accessed January 22, 2012).

17. Rutenberg and Opel, Jr., "New Focus."

18. Micah Cohen, "A Living Autopsy of the Ron Paul Campaign," *New York Times* 2012, http://fivethirtyeight.blogs.nytimes.com/2012/04/09/a-living-autopsy-of-the-ron-paul-campaign/ (accessed January 3, 2013).

19. Brian Bolduc, "Why Newt Left the House," *National Review* 2012, http://www.nationalreview.com/content/why-newt-left-house (accessed June 16, 2013).

20. Tom Hamburger, "Where's Newt? Post-Announcement Vacation Raises Questions about Gingrich's Candidacy," *Los Angeles Times* 2011, http://www.latimes.com/news/politics/la-pn-newt-gingrich-20110603,0,4491031.story (accessed April 14, 2013).

21. Rachel Weiner, "Newt Gingrich Doubles Down on 'Food Stamps'," *Washington Post* 2012, http://www.washingtonpost.com/blogs/the-fix/post/newt-gingrich-doubles-down-on-food-stamps/2012/01/17/gIQAjMZM6P_blog.html (accessed April 14, 2013).

22. Suzanne Gamboa, "Newt Gingrich Says He Would Urge Blacks To Demand Paychecks, Not Food Stamps In Front Of NAACP," *Huffington Post* 2012, http://www.huffingtonpost.com/2012/01/06/newt-gingrich-naacp-food-stamps_n_1189005.html (accessed March 23, 2012).

23. Jeff Zeleny and Trip Gabriel, "Gingrich's Senior Campaign Staff Resigns," *New York Times* 2012, http://thecaucus.blogs.nytimes.com/2011/06/09/gingrich-senior-campaign-staff-resigns/ (accessed June 14, 2012).

24. Karol Markowicz, "Newt's New Marriage Problem," *New York Post* 2012, http://www.nypost.com/p/news/opinion/opedcolumnists/newt_new_marriage_problem_OeG8a497TJpURr1XlczdIO (accessed January 2, 2013).

25. Mallie Jane Kim, "Rick Perry Stands By Texas DREAM Act," *U.S. News & World Report* 2011, http://www.usnews.com/news/articles/2011/07/25/rick-perry-stands-by-texas-dream-act (accessed March 29, 2012).

26. Benjy Sarlin, "Rick Perry's Vaccine Push Sparked Backlash From Left And Right Alike," *Talking Points Memo* 2012, http://tpmdc.talkingpointsmemo.com/2011/08/rick-perrys-vaccine-push-sparked-backlash-from-left-and-right-alike.php (accessed July 21, 2012).

27. "Rick Perry's 'shocking' gaffe: Ben Bernanke is 'treasonous,'" *The Week* 2011, http://theweek.com/article/index/218350/rick-perrys-shocking-gaffe-ben-bernanke-is-treasonous (accessed March 21, 2012).

28. Stephanie McCrummen, "At Rick Perry's Texas hunting spot, camp's old racially charged name lingered," *Washington Post* 2011, http://www.washingtonpost.com/national/rick-perry-familys-hunting-camp-still-known-to-many-by-old-racially-charged-name/2011/10/01/gIQAOhY5DL_story.html (accessed October 21, 2011).

29. Sam Stein, "Rick Perry's Anti-Gay Iowa Ad Divides His Top Staff," *Huffington Post* 2011, http://www.huffingtonpost.com/2011/12/08/rick-perry-anti-gay-iowa-ad-divides-top-staff_n_1136587.html (accessed December 2, 2011).

30. Brad Knickerbocker, "After his debate gaffe, Rick Perry goes into full spin mode," *Christian Science Monitor* 2011, http://www.csmonitor.com/USA/Elections/Vox-News/2011/1111/After-his-debate-gaffe-Rick-Perry-goes-into-full-spin-mode (accessed December 1, 2011).

31. "Gov. Rick Perry: Texas Could Secede, Leave Union," *Huffington Post* 2011, http://www.huffingtonpost.com/2009/04/15/gov-rick-perry-texas-coul_n_187490.html (accessed December 22, 2011).

32. Glenn Kessler, "Herman Cain's 999 plan: a misleading pitch," *Washington Post* 2011, http://www.washingtonpost.com/blogs/fact-checker/post/herman-cains-misleading-pitch-for-the-999-plan/2011/10/12/gIQAHszPgL_blog.html (accessed October 29, 2011).

33. Amanda Terkel, "Herman Cain 999 Plan: Did It Come From SimCity?," *Huffington Post* 2011, http://www.huffingtonpost.com/2011/10/13/herman-cain-999-simcity_n_1008952.html (accessed October 22, 2011).

34. Dan Amira, "Five Theories About the Bizarre New Herman Cain Campaign Ad," *New York Magazine* 2011, http://nymag.com/daily/intel/2011/10/herman_cain_ad_smoking_cigarette.html (accessed December 3, 2012).

35. Ewen MacAskill, "Herman Cain Libya blunder casts doubt on fitness to be president," *The Guardian* 2011, http://www.guardian.co.uk/world/2011/nov/15/herman-cain-libya-blunder-doubt (accessed March 13, 2012).

36. Jonathan Martin, Maggie Haberman, Anna Palmer, and Kenneth P. Vogel, "Herman Cain accused by two women of inappropriate behavior," *Politico* 2011, http://www.politico.com/news/stories/1011/67194.html (accessed November 2, 2011).

37. Andy Kouhri, "Herman Cain Suspends Campaign, Confesses Pokemon Inspiration," *Comics Alliance* 2011, http://www.comicsalliance.com/2011/12/05/herman-cain-pokemon-suspending-campaign/ (accessed March 13, 2012).

38. Chris Cillizza, "Michele Bachmann wins the Ames Straw Poll," *Washington Post* 2011, http://www.washingtonpost.com/blogs/the-fix/post/michele-bachmann-wins-the-ames-straw-poll/2011/08/13/gIQApgnoDJ_blog.html (accessed March 14, 2011).

39. Chris McGreal and Ian Sample, "Michele Bachmann HPV row prompts fears for vaccine programme in US," *The Guardian* 2011, http://www.guardian.co.uk/world/2011/sep/14/michele-bachmann-hpv-vaccine (accessed October 14, 2011).

40. Chris Moody, "Professors offer more than $10,000 for proof that Bachmann's story about HPV is true," *Yahoo* 2011, http://news.yahoo.com/blogs/ticket/professors-offer-more-10-000-proof-bachmann-story-132647843.html (accessed March 2, 2013).

41. Amanda Terkel, "Michele Bachmann: Obama 'Put Us In Libya. He Is Now Putting Us In Africa,'" *Huffington Post* 2011, http://www.huffingtonpost.com/2011/10/18/michele-bachmann-libya-africa_n_1018814.html (accessed December 29, 2012).

42. "Bill O'Reilly: Michele Bachmann 'Doesn't Know Where Lexington And Concord Are,'" *Huffington Post* 2011, http://www.huffingtonpost.com/2011/03/25/bill-oreilly-michele-bach_n_840744.html (accessed January 22, 2013).

43. Lucy Madison, "Michele Bachmann: U.S. got "kicked out" of Iraq," *CBS News*, http://www.cbsnews.com/8301-3460_162-20124360/michele-bachmann-u.s-got-kicked-out-of-iraq/ (accessed February 14, 2013).

44. Rachel Weiner, "Michele Bachmann Links Swine Flu To Democrats, Gets History Wrong," *Huffington Post* 2011, http://www.huffingtonpost.com/2009/04/28/michele-bachmann-links-sw_n_192493.html (accessed January 14, 2012).

45. Mariah Blake, "'God Has Created You for Heterosexuality': Clinics Owned by Michele Bachmann's Husband Practice Ex-Gay Therapy," *The Nation* 2011, http://www.thenation.com/article/161883/michele-bachmann-husband-ex-gay-therapy (accessed March 14, 2012).

46. Michelle Cottle, "We'll Miss the Hunstman Daughters the Most," *The Daily Beast* 2012, http://www.thedailybeast.com/articles/2012/01/16/jon-huntsman-s-daughters-what-we-ll-miss-most-about-his-campaign.html (accessed August 12, 2012).

47. Michael Brendan Dougherty, "The Myth About The Jon Huntsman Campaign," *Business Insider* 2011, http://articles.businessinsider.com/2011-12-01/politics/30462185_1_huntsman-campaign-jon-huntsman-mitt-romney (accessed March 1, 2012).

48. Maggie Hagerman, "Jon with no 'H' declares in N.J., not N.Y.," *Politico* 2011, http://www.politico.com/news/stories/0611/57498.html (accessed May 1, 2013).

49. Joe Johns, Paul Steinhauser, and Erika Dimmler, "Candidates Turn Negative in Multimillion Dollaw Iowa Television Ad Blitz," *CNN* 2011, http://www.cnn.com/2011/12/27/politics/iowa-ad-wars (accessed January 4, 2012).

50. Jonathan D. Salant, "Iowa Campaign Ads Show Power of Negativity in Republican Race," *Bloomberg* 2012, http://www.bloomberg.com/news/2012-01-02/gingrich-standing-falters-as-negative-advertising-dominates-iowa-airwaves.html (accessed January 14, 2012).

51. Joseph W. McQuaid, "An Editorial: For President, Newt Gingrich," *New Hampshire Union Leader* 2011, http://www.unionleader.com/article/20111127/NEWS0605/711279999 (accessed February 13, 2012).

52. Frank Newport "Santorum expands lead, but Romney gains electability vote," *Gallup*, http://www.gallup.com/poll/152840/Santorum-Expands-Lead-Romney-Gets-Electability-Vote.aspx (accessed February 22, 2012).

53. List adapted from Keith Boykin, "The 10 Biggest Republican Mistakes of the 2012 Primary Campaign," *Huffington Post* 2012, http://www.huffingtonpost.com/keith-boykin/the-10-biggest-republican_b_1322230.html (accessed March 26, 2012).

TWO

The Impact of Rules Changes on the 2012 Republican Presidential Primary Process

Joshua T. Putnam

THE 2012 RULES: PAST IS PRELUDE?

If there has been one consistent "law" of the presidential nomination process in the time since the McGovern-Fraser reforms fundamentally altered the way in which Americans nominate candidates for the two major parties starting in 1972, it is that lessons are learned from one nomination cycle to the next. The 2012 nomination process was no different. What was witnessed over the first half of 2012 was in part—whether large or small—attributable to what happened in 2008. In other words, both the set up—in terms of the rules governing the delegate selection process—and the way in which the process played out were reactionary; the extension of a dynamic quadrennial process.

To see this in full contrast one must first look back at 2008. If the events of one cycle are in reaction to the immediately prior cycle, then what was it (or what was it that was wrong) about 2008 that laid the groundwork for what happened in 2012? It should be noted that the process of nominating a presidential candidate is a party function. The rules governing the election of delegates on the state level are the domain of, first, the national parties but then with some input from the state parties as well. If a problem is perceived to have arisen in the process, the remedy to that issue for the next iteration—if any ultimately arise—will find its nexus from within the national parties. Typically, it has been the Democratic Party in the post-reform era that has been the most active in tinkering with its presidential nomination rules; forming commissions every four years to refine the method of choosing the party's nominee. Whether limiting delegate allocation to proportional methods, instituting a de facto quota system to ensure the representativeness of state delegations, or adding "superdelegates" as a means of balancing elite and rank-and-file party member influence over a nomination, it has been the Democratic Party that has tinkered more with the process that selects its standard bearer every four years. However, with no competitive race in 2012, the Democrats only slightly tweaked the rules the party utilized during the Obama-Clinton race in 2008.

It was, instead, the competitive Republican environment that proved the more hospitable to any form of system change. In fact, partly in coordination with the Democratic Party and partly in response to the longevity of and enthusiasm behind the 2008 Democratic nomination battle, the Republican National Committee took the unprecedented step of examining its 2012 delegate selection rules outside of the confines of the national convention.[1] The Republican Temporary Delegate Selection Committee saw the same problem in 2008 that its counterpart commission on the Democratic Party side saw: the process started too early and there were too many contests too early on the primary calendar during that cycle.

Iowa kicking the process off on January 3, 2008 placed, in the eyes of those within the national parties crafting the 2012 delegate selection rules, a seemingly unnecessary burden on the candidates, campaigns, and voters over the holiday season. Additionally, having over half of the country voting on the same date just a month later theoretically gave an advantage to either the frontrunner candidate—as measured by the polls and fundraising—or to an upstart candidate from outside of the party establishment who could win early and establish enough momentum to carry said candidate through the early series of contests.[2] Though the parties view the latter as more problematic, the former has become progressively truer as the frontloading of primaries and caucuses has intensified in the time since reform.[3] Still, the national parties—acting through their respective rules-making bodies—foresaw the potential for the type of retail politics both parties attempt to nurture through early contests in small states like Iowa and New Hampshire to be reduced. Worse, that further opened the door for the parties to lose even more control over their sometimes-tenuous grasp on the presidential nomination process.

To deal with the Iowa issue (starting too early), some members of the rules making committees in both parties informally agreed that the starting point of the process should be pushed back into February.[4] For both parties that meant Iowa, New Hampshire, Nevada, and South Carolina—the so-called "carve out" states—holding February contests with all other states granted the ability to caucus or conduct primaries on the first Tuesday in March or thereafter.

In order to deal with the crowding problem—other states/state parties positioning their contests early and close enough to the carve out states as to push them to even earlier than intended spots on the calendar—the Democratic National Committee (DNC) and Republican National Committee (RNC) had different approaches. The Democrats opted to provide a carrot to states willing to shift back the dates of their primaries or caucuses. States with contests later than March got progressively larger "bonus" delegates tacked onto their delegations the later their respective contests were. A state with an April contest received a 10 percent boost, a May state garnered a 15 percent bump, and a June state, a 20 percent increase.[5] Additionally, as a new recommendation handed down from the Democratic Change Commission, the DNC also rewarded states that attempted to cluster their primaries or caucuses with neighboring states. The incentive in that instance was also a boost in delegates (15 percent), but states could also benefit from a series of regionally proximate states better able to attract candidates than if the state held a lone contest or a primary or caucus concurrent with a large number of regionally diverse contests.[6] Together, both types of bonuses were intended to entice state-level decision makers to move or consider moving their state's contests to points later on the calendar.

The RNC, on the other hand, approached the crowding problem in a different manner. Embedded in the Republican rules were both carrots and sticks. Gone were the days when the Republicans introduced—but did not stick with—the bonus delegate concept.[7] Instead, the RNC, on the recommendation of the Temporary Delegate Selection Committee, took the unprecedented step of restricting the customary freedom of states/state parties in deciding the method of delegate selection. Early states were restricted while later states maintained the state-level latitude to decide how national convention delegates would be chosen in later states.[8] In practice, this meant that states with contests on or after April 1 could allocate delegates in any way the state party deemed fit.[9] During the 2012 cycle, the most common response to these rules changes in later states was to maintain the status quo.[10] The path of least resistance was for state parties to simply keep the same delegate allocation rules used in 2008 and before.

For early states, however, the restrictions laid out in the augmented Rule 15 of the Rules of the Republican Party meant that there had to be some element of proportionality to the delegate allocation plan implemented by a pre-April 1 state. States could not, in other words, allocate all of their delegates to a statewide plurality winner. The mandate that came down from the RNC was not nearly as uniform as the requirements on the Democratic side. The Democrats mandate a strict proportional allocation of all of the party's delegates. A candidate who receives 55 percent of the vote in a primary or caucus would be allocated approximately 55 percent of the state's total delegates. The Republican Party in its rules change took a broader view of the definition of "proportional." Again, any resultant delegate selection plan in a pre-April 1 state had to have an element of proportionality. The reality was that the RNC prohibited a strict, electoral college-style, winner-take-all allocation of delegates in that pre-April 1 window. That was the stick.

However, there were various subtleties embedded in the Republican rules that meant the resulting patchwork of delegate selection plans in pre-April 1 states diverged from the uniform proportionality requirement on the Democratic side. Stated differently, there were "loopholes" in the RNC delegate rules that allowed states—even pre-April 1 states—some latitude in formulating delegate selection plans that were true to traditional local custom, even if that meant having the allocation of some delegates decided on a winner-take-all basis.[11] States had the option of allocating the entirety of their delegation in a manner proportionate to the primary or caucus vote in the state, but that was one end on a spectrum of many options. The most common change that pre-April 1 states made to their delegate selection plans in order to comply with the new mandate was to make the delegate allocation conditionally winner-take-all. The lowest the bar could be set according to the national party rules was 50 percent. In other words, if a candidate received a majority of the vote in any given state, that candidate could claim all of that state's delegates. If no candidate met that threshold, then the allocation would be proportional. Such was the case in the Idaho Republican caucuses.[12]

That was one such trigger option. Others made a distinction based on the sub-categorization of delegates. The Republican Party formula for determining how many delegates each state receives separates delegates into three basic types: automatic delegates, at-large delegates, and congressional district delegates. More often than not, the automatic delegates—the state party chair, the national committeeman, and the national committeewoman from the state—were free to choose a candidate of their preference.[13] But how the other two categories of delegates were allocated could have differed—and did differ—widely from one state to another among the states with primaries or caucuses prior to April 1 much less those held after that point. At a minimum, states could either, as was described above, allocate their delegates conditionally winner-take-all/proportional or merely subject the handful of statewide, at-large delegates to being proportionally allocated. Those were the easiest paths to compliance for states that were required to and willing to act in accordance with the new national party rules.

Yet, the state parties with pre-April 1 primaries and caucuses used countless other variations of delegate selection plans. The Georgia Republican Party, for example, made the allocation of their 31 statewide, at-large delegates proportional to the statewide vote and the 42 congressional district delegates—three per congressional district—proportional based on the percentage of each congressional district vote.[14] Republicans in Ohio, on the other hand, used a similar formula for allocating statewide delegates while allocating all three congressional district delegates to the winner in each congressional district.[15] The result was that there was not one uniform definition of proportionality under the Republican rules. That created an array of plans occupying space between the Democratic Party definition of proportional and a true winner-take-all allocation of delegates. The intent was for these delegate allocation changes along with the changes to the primary calendar to slow down the accumulation of delegates for each candidate, stretch out the nomination race, and capture some of the positive mobilization developments the Democratic nomination race—and ultimately its nominee—benefitted from in 2008.

There were, then, various new sticks involved in the altered Republican Party rules for states that also affected candidate and campaign strategy. The carrot—or partial carrot if one was to be found—was that states still had the freedom to choose any method of allocating delegates. The catch was that states only had this freedom if their contests were after March. Those wanting to avoid the aforementioned penalties or desiring a shift to—or to continue with—winner-take-all rules could move back to a later date, thus protecting a winner-take-all method of allocation or the freedom to choose any method of allocation. The Republican delegate selection rules in 2012 were less about carrots than about new sticks to keep states in line in terms of scheduling their delegate selection events.

What did not happen in the commission and committee meetings that ultimately set the overall national party delegate selection rules for 2012 was anything to fix the Florida/Michigan problem that arose in 2008. Both states in 2008 gambled that 1) the early and noncompliant dates of their respective primaries were more valuable than the 50 percent reduction in penalties associated with the violation of rules and 2) the national parties would ultimately reinstate the delegates for the late summer national conventions. The parties attempted in the ways described above to incentivize the movement of states to later dates (or to deter their continued movement forward), but did nothing to augment the penalties associated with rogue states.[16] Despite a new level of rules coordination across national parties, the penalties stemming from the rules changes were never sufficiently robust as to prevent a repeat of or growth in the type of behavior Florida and Michigan exhibited in 2008. That had the effect of undermining the efforts both parties had undertaken to back up the date of the first contest (the caucuses in Iowa) or to prevent the type of crowding that might force Iowa or any of the other carve out states to earlier and non-compliant dates. The door was opened, then, to continued or increased rogue activity in 2012, but states/state parties were not necessarily willing or able to pull the trigger on such a move.

2011: IMPLEMENTATION OF THE RULES IN THE STATES AND FALLOUT FROM PENALTIES

Heading into 2011, there were 20 states that had to make some change to either state election law or state party bylaws to alter the dates on which their primaries or caucuses were scheduled for 2012.[17] By and large, the bipartisan coordinated calendar was effective in shifting most states back. The threat of reducing by half a non-compliant state's delegation was a seemingly sufficient penalty coming down from the national party level to keep most states in line. That both parties were on board with the changes meant that partisanship or negative partisan motivations behind primary date-setting had been largely removed from the decision-making calculus. It was not absent, but reduced with both national parties presenting the closest thing to a united front in the post-reform era.

While the national parties did present something approximating a united front in terms of the adoption of a relatively uniform set of rules governing the presidential primary calendar, the method of sanction for breaking those rules continued to differ across parties. That, in turn, has the impact of undermining the intent of the overall rules changes. Under the 2012 rules, both the DNC and RNC penalized a state in violation of the timing rules—that is, when a state can schedule its nominating contest—half its delegation. Additionally, the Democratic Party rules sanction candidates who campaign in rogue states in an attempt to keep them from campaigning in those states.[18] The DNC delegate selection rules also grant the Rules and Bylaws Committee the latitude to increase the penalties for violating states on a case-by-case basis. The Republican Party rules reduced a state delegation by half for a violation of either the timing rules or the aforementioned proportionality requirement, but do not have the authority to double penalize a state or increase the level of that penalty in any way. The 50 percent delegate reduction could be used in response to a violation of one rule but not both. The RNC rules do include an option to ramp up the penalties via a demotion in hotel assignments or convention floor seating assignments as well as a stripping of some delegate VIP passes, but that is a smaller overall sanction from both the candidates' and states'/state parties' perspectives than those penalties aimed at the size of the delegations.

With the Democratic Party idle in 2012, primary calendar movement—or lack thereof—was more a function of the Republican Party rules than anything else.[19] Most states were threatened enough by the potential loss of half a delegation or willing enough regardless to move back to a date that was compliant with national party rules or were deterred from moving up to a non-compliant date. Of the previously cited 20 states that had to shift back the dates on which their primaries or caucuses were held, 17 moved into compliance or maintained their previous level of compliance.[20] The three that did not—Arizona, Florida, and

Michigan—forced the hands of decision makers in the four carve out states, initially pushing each into January.[21]

In so doing, those three rogue states created three tiers of states on the primary calendar: 1) Carve out states willing to break the rules in order to protect/maintain a calendar position codified in national party rules (i.e., New Hampshire and South Carolina); 2) States willing to break the rules in order to be early but not necessarily earlier than the carve out states (i.e., Arizona, Florida, and Michigan); and 3) States willing to follow the rules (i.e., every state with a contest on or after the first Tuesday in March). That small group of rules-breakers in the second tier wreaked havoc on the carefully constructed calendar the national parties had assembled, forcing a repeat of the January 3 start to primary season from the 2008 cycle. That tier of states not only rendered the parties' efforts to rein in the Iowa problem moot, but it also reignited the Florida/Michigan problem that arose in 2008. The crux of that latter problem is that there is/was no one size fits all approach to effectively penalizing states in violation of delegate selection rules. What Alabama and Connecticut, for example, view as strong and effective penalties, Florida, Michigan, and now Arizona do not. That second (rogue) tier of states valued influence on the nomination race and the resulting attention to the state from it over potentially losing half of their delegates to the national convention. Conversely, the states that shifted back the dates on which their 2012 primaries and caucuses were held valued a full delegation at the national convention over going early. Both the second and third tiers of states were willing to roll the dice, but the latter wagered that the Republican nomination race would still be competitive by the time the contest entered March and later points on the calendar. The former tier, on the other hand, gambled, wagering that first, early influence over the nomination was of preeminent importance and that, furthermore, the delegations were likely to be reinstated in full at the national convention.

Much of the talk in the press around the time the calendar was taking its final form during the fourth quarter of 2011 revolved around the domino effect the Florida decision had on the first part of the primary calendar. Members of the Republican-controlled date selection committee in Florida, mindful of the impact the state had on the 2008 contest, were motivated to place the Sunshine state primary in a similarly decisive role in the 2012 Republican race. The pattern of movement exhibited by other states was just as instructive. Republican-controlled states—whether state governments or state parties—tended to move back less than Democratic-controlled states.[22] The Republican states tended to shift back into March positions while more Democratic states occupied April and later dates when they moved. That created a calendar that was regionally and ideologically diverse at its outset, but one that was more southern and more conservative in March and more mid-Atlantic/northeastern and less conservative in April.

This was motivated by a confluence of factors. First of all, compliant and Republican-controlled states were deterred from holding February or earlier contests, but simultaneously wanted to influence the competitive phase of the Republican nomination race in 2012. Based on the bulk of Republican-controlled state movement, March was as much of a gamble as decision makers in most of those states were willing to take. In the frontloaded era, earlier was and is better in terms of guaranteeing voters a voice in the presidential selection process. Over time however, occupying that early space on the calendar has translated into sharing any given date with enough other states to render that voice nearly mute. That reality, in concert with later states playing a role in the 2008 process, had a handful of states reconsidering the combination of an early but crowded primary or caucus date. In 2012 that left states with a desire to be early enough, but to also seek out a position that maximized the attention a state would receive from the candidates and the media.

As alluded to above, though, this movement had a partisan element to it as well. Republican-controlled states—Tennessee and Virginia, for example—were less likely to inch back too far on the calendar for fear of holding a contest outside of the window of decisiveness—when a presumptive nominee would emerge with half plus one of the available delegates. Democratic-controlled states had a choice of whether to maintain the status quo (if the state was compliant at the outset) or move back and take advantage of the late-contest delegate bonuses and/or the clustered-states bonuses available to states under the Democratic National Committee rules. Several, like Massachusetts and Vermont, remained consistent with what state law had originally mandated in terms of the primary dates while other states, such as Connecticut, Delaware, New York, and Rhode Island, opted to move their respective primaries back into late April time slots. What this latter group lost in influence over either nomination race they collectively gained back in bonus delegates. That is a trade off that works in a year in which the party in control in the state has no active presidential nomination race. The calculus is different in competitive years (as Democrats will no doubt see during the 2016 cycle).

What did not seemingly motivate states in positioning their various delegate selection events for 2012 was the new addition to the Republican rules: the rule requiring states with contests prior to April 1 to have a proportional element to their delegate allocation. The change was viewed within the RNC as both a deterrent to states moving primaries and caucuses up, but also as a reward to states that moved back. However, states that shifted back to or maintained March dates, in most cases, did the bare minimum necessary to comply with the strictures of the new rule, and states that selected dates later than April 1 merely maintained the delegate selection rules they had used in prior cycles, a nod to the continuance of local custom. Counter to that, the only post-April 1 states that altered their delegate selection rules—Connecticut and New York—adopted slightly more proportional rules than what each had previously used. The consensus within the RNC was that states that voluntarily moved to dates in April and later would gravitate toward a more winner-take-all formula of delegate allocation. That was not the case in 2012.

THE RULES' IMPACT ON THE 2012 REPUBLICAN NOMINATION RACE

That the Republican Party made seemingly significant delegate selection rules changes—and atypically, outside of the usual venue (the preceding convention)—was noteworthy, but in practice the Republican-specific rules had limited influence over the nomination race that resulted in the winter and spring months of 2012. As was described above, most states that were required to move to later dates under the informally coordinated calendar structure both parties adopted, did, in fact, move back. Arizona, Florida, Michigan, and a small group of non-binding caucus states pushed into February and only served to force an earlier-than-intended start to the process followed by a dead period throughout the middle and end of February.

At the outset of primary season, the fits and starts beginning opened the door to one candidate—presumably the nominal frontrunner and ultimate nominee, Mitt Romney—sweeping the early contests and effectively ending the race in a manner not inconsistent with the way in which a host of candidates in previous cycles had wrapped up nominations. Al Gore and George W. Bush in 2000 as well as John Kerry in 2004 and John McCain in 2008 were able to win early and often enough to signal to primary voters, if not opposing candidates, that the parties' rank-and-file were lining up behind them. The voters did fall in line, but that may have been precipitated by the withdrawal of the remaining viable candidates from those respective races.

That pattern of early wins as a springboard to massive Super Tuesday victories has been what the frontloaded era, post-reform, increasingly had moved toward up until the 2008 cycle. The flirtation with primaries and caucuses scheduled in the year prior to the election in the lead up to 2008 coupled with an early February Super Tuesday that featured enough states to constitute well over half of the total number of delegates in both parties' competitive nomination races forced some within not only the national parties but actors on the state level to reconsider the utility of such early contests (both individually at the state level and collectively on the national level through the national parties).

The Romney campaign planned for the long haul but hoped for a quick win on the order of what Bush, Gore, Kerry, and McCain were able to do following the turn of the century. Instead of that, Romney got something closer to, though not nearly like, the slower path Obama trod in winning the Democratic nomination four years earlier. Part of that slower build for Romney was a function of the early split of contests: Santorum narrowly winning Iowa, Romney winning New Hampshire, Gingrich winning South Carolina, Romney winning Florida, Maine, and Nevada, and Santorum winning Colorado and Minnesota in the contests prior to the dead period in February.

The early calendar split decision worked in conjunction with a couple of other factors to draw out the Republican nomination contest. One was rules-based and the other was more psychological in nature. Obviously, the 2012 presidential primary calendar was much more evenly dispersed—in terms of the contests—than was the case with the hyper-frontloaded 2008 calendar. January contests in 2012 did not feed into a de facto national on the first Tuesday in February as in 2008. By its nature, that shift fundamentally altered the way in which delegates would be accumulated by candidates from contest to contest. The earliest point that a candidate could have won the requisite number of pledged/bound delegates to clinch the nomination moved back from February 5 during the 2008 cycle to March 20 in 2012. Mitt Romney wrapped up the Republican nomination in early April with the withdrawal of Rick Santorum from the race, but did not reach the 1,144 delegates plateau until his victory in the May 29 Texas primary.

Logically, it may also be assumed that the new proportionality requirement would also slow down the pace of delegate accrual. If, after all, states are changing from more winner-take-all rules to rules that have an increased level of proportional allocation embedded in them, then the seemingly obvious conclusion would be that the process would be slower. It was not, and that was due in large part to where states were located on the calendar and the percentage of evangelicals in a given state.[23] Southern and/or more highly evangelical states were more likely to split their support among Mitt Romney, Newt Gingrich, and Rick Santorum with the latter two candidates usually outpacing Romney in the resulting delegate counts from those states. However, the shift to slightly more proportional rules kept Romney closer than the former Massachusetts governor otherwise would have been in past years. Without the proportionality requirement and under the 2008 rules, Rick Santorum would have gained not only victories, but a greater delegate advantage coming out of some of the mid-March southern contests; pulling closer to Romney and drawing out the process even further than was actually the case in 2012.[24]

While the impact of the proportionality rule for states with contests prior to April 1 paled in comparison to the calendar changes overall, the new rule did factor into the greater psychology—and resultant candidate/campaign strategy—of the 2012 primaries. What the proportionality requirement along with the influx of Super PAC money into a presidential nomination context collectively did was to alter the approach of candidates—particularly those who were attempting to break Mitt Romney's seemingly tenuous hold on the frontrunner mantle. Both served as strategic lifelines. Gingrich had casino magnate Sheldon Adelson fueling the Gingrich-aligned Winning Our Future Super PAC and Rick Santorum had investor Foster Friess serving in a similar role with the Santorum-aligned Red White and Blue Fund Super PAC. Alternately, the reality was that the delegate accumulation was not fundamentally different in 2012 than it had been in previous cycles, but the candidates were behaving as if it was.[25] The change in rules seemingly, though not really, opened the door to candidates competing not for contest wins alone but for delegates in more proportional states.[26] Similarly, Super PAC money allowed candidates who had one or more big-money donors to keep a campaign alive even if small donors had largely disappeared or stopped contributing to the campaigns. Those two lifelines kept the Santorum and Gingrich candidacies afloat financially and rife with messages of the next battleground for delegates—no matter how far-fetched.[27]

CONCLUSION

Yet, the end result was much the same as what has been witnessed with rare exception throughout most of the post-reform era. Mitt Romney—a better financed, better positioned (polling), but perhaps not as heavily establishment supported candidate (endorsements)[28] —entered primary season in January 2012 with certain measureable, though tenuous, advantages and emerged at the end with more than enough delegates to secure the Republican nomination. The grinder through which the campaign and its candidates went may have been different, but the outcome was not.

Still, the 2012 cycle was marked by a host of on-the-surface significant rules changes to both parties' sets of delegate selection rules. As usual, those rules had a hand in affecting the course of the nomination race, but not necessarily in the ways that the parties may have intended. The spreading out of the calendar of contests played a larger role than anything else. This was particularly true relative to the expectations versus reality of the newly instituted proportionality requirement on the Republican side. The intention was for that rule to draw out the point at which the Republican nomination was clinched and as a result bring additional states into the window of decisiveness. That goal was not realized through the proportionality rule but rather by the resulting spreading out dates on which the various primaries and caucuses were scheduled. The result was that—even though the race took a different route to get there—the frontrunner won the Republican nomination.

That means neither that the rules did not matter in 2012 nor that how they were implemented and affected the race in real-time will not affect what the rules look like in 2016 and beyond. The 2012 rules may not have altered the outcome, but they once again affected the way in which the candidates campaigned and strategized about the race. The patchwork of not only state contests but how those state parties allocated delegates— newly changed in 2012—opened doors to strategizing about this race that may not be open or opened as widely in future cycles following this first run of the rules. Future office-seeking candidates (or those supporting them) may not be able to effectively line up Super PAC funders or make the case that the delegate math will work out in certain ways with one iteration of the new rules now having set a precedent. Of course, that assumes that Republicans will stand pat with their current rules regime (something the party has already signaled ahead of its 2012 convention when those rules decisions for 2016 will be made), that the calendar will remain the same, and that the party will have a competitive nomination race in 2016. None of that is assured at this point. The only thing that is assured is that the impact of the rules will once again be broadly discussed then as now regardless of the conditions.

NOTES

1. In the years following the McGovern-Fraser reforms to the Democratic nomination process, the Republican National Committee moved at a slower pace of reform. That changes to the delegate selection rules occurred early on was more a function of changes being made through state legislatures affecting primary contests in both parties. From within, there was far less structural change to the Republican process. First, the national party left the delegate selection process up to the states. But secondly, the party also set its rules—in every cycle in the post-reform era—at the immediately prior convention. This differed from the more deliberative, intra-cycle rules-making sequence within the Democratic National Committee that had the party settling on rules typically during mid-term election years; two years instead of four out from the next presidential election.

2. William G. Mayer, "Forecasting Presidential Nominations," in *In Pursuit of the White House: How We Choose Our Presidential Nominees*, ed. William G. Mayer (Chatham, NJ: Chatham House, 1996); Barbara Norrander, "Presidential Nomination Politics in the Post-Reform Era," *Political Research Quarterly* 49, no. 4 (1996): 875-915.

3. William G. Mayer and Andrew E. Busch, "The Front-loading Problem in Presidential Nominations" (Washington, DC: Brookings Institution Press, 1993).

4. Don Means, "'National Caucus for 2012 Reform' Yields New Bi-Partisan Agreement," http://www.nationalcaucus.com/blog/2008/08/20/%2526quot%3Bnational-caucus-2012-reform%2526quot%3B-yields-new-bi-partisan-agreement (accessed August 1, 2012).

5. Delegate Selection Rules for the 2012 Democratic National Convention, 2010, http://wfc2.wiredforchange.com/o/8787/images/
DNC%202012%20Delegate%20Selection%20Rules.pdf (accessed August 1, 2012).

6. Report of the Democratic Change Commission, 2010, http://s3.amazonaws.com/apache.3cdn.net/c52190b72ce1a37ccc_yem6be4xg.pdf (accessed August 1, 2012).

7. Andrew E. Busch, "New Features of the 2000 Presidential Nominating Process: Republican Reforms, Front-loading's Second Wind and Early Voting," in *In Pursuit of*

the *White House 2000: How We Choose Our Presidential Nominees*, ed. William G. Mayer (Chatham, NJ: Chatham House, 2000).

8. The environment that existed for post-April 1 states in 2012 was the same environment that existed for all states in previous cycles. Put simply, states—all states—were free to determine how they would allocate national convention delegates. That same freedom was only afforded to post-April 1 states in 2012.

9. The Rules of the Republican Party, 2010, http://www.gop.com/images/legal/2008_RULES_Adopted.pdf (accessed August 1, 2012).

10. The only states after March to make changes to their delegate selection rules compared to 2008 were the Republican Parties in Connecticut and New York. Counterintuitively, both moved not toward a more winner-take-all system of allocating delegates, but toward a more proportional method of allocation.

11. Josh Putnam, "An Update on the 2012 Republican Delegate Selection Rules," *Frontloading* 2011, http://frontloading.blogspot.com/2011/02/update-on-2012-republican-delegate.html (accessed August 1, 2012); Josh Putnam, "Republican Delegate Allocation Rules: 2012 vs. 2008," *Frontloading* 2011, http://frontloading.blogspot.com/2011/12/republican-delegate-allocation-rules.html (accessed August 1, 2012).

12. Josh Putnam, "2012 Republican Delegate Allocation: Idaho," *Frontloading* 2012, http://frontloading.blogspot.com/2012/03/2012-republican-delegate-allocation.html (accessed August 1, 2012).

13. In this capacity—free to choose whichever candidate they please—the so-called automatic delegates are analogous to the Democratic Party superdelegates, though not nearly as great in number to their Democratic counterparts.

14. Josh Putnam, "2012 Republican Delegate Allocation: Georgia," *Frontloading* 2012, http://frontloading.blogspot.com/2012/02/2012-republican-delegate-allocation_8092.html (accessed August 1, 2012).

15. Josh Putnam, "2012 Republican Delegate Allocation: Ohio," *Frontloading* 2012, http://frontloading.blogspot.com/2011/10/delegate-allocation-rules-hinged-on.html (accessed August 1, 2012).

16. A rogue state is defined as one that was undeterred by national party penalties and not sufficiently enticed by the promise of additional delegates awarded for later primary or caucus dates.

17. Josh Putnam, "The 2012 Presidential Primary Calendar (6/30/10)," *Frontloading* 2010, http://frontloading.blogspot.com/2010/06/2012-presidential-primary-calendar.html (accessed August 1, 2012).

18. In a personal interview with the author, Democratic Rules and Bylaws Committee members Jim Roosevelt (co-chair) and Carol Fowler (former chair) were both dubious as to how this 2008 addition to the sanctions was implemented. Both indicated that it was a combination of the 2008 candidates agreeing to abide by the sanctions, and the carve out states threatening candidates who would potentially campaign elsewhere (in states other than the carve outs). This was the first time that such an action had been in any way codified in national party rules. Up to 2008, the carve out states were left to—admittedly effectively—police themselves.

19. This was true despite the unprecedented level of informal coordination between and across the two national parties.

20. Colorado and Minnesota, for instance, held seemingly non-compliant caucuses on February 7, 2012. However, since no delegates to the national convention were directly selected or bound in those precinct caucuses, neither incurred penalties under the RNC delegate selection rules for the decisions (Josh Putnam, "Is This Deadline in Minnesota a Big Deal for the 2012 Primary Calendar?," *Frontloading* 2011, http://frontloading.blogspot.com/2011/02/is-this-deadline-in-minnesota-big-deal.html (accessed August 1, 2012); Josh Putnam, "Colorado Precinct Caucuses Shifted Up to February 7," *Frontloading* 2011, http://frontloading.blogspot.com/2011/09/colorado-republican-precinct-caucuses.html (accessed August 1, 2012).).

21. The Nevada Republican Party originally moved the date of its precinct caucuses from February 18 to January 14 in response to the Florida Presidential Preference

Primary Date Selection Committee decision to schedule the Florida primary for January 31 (Josh Putnam, "Nevada Republican Caucuses Set for January 14," *Frontloading* 2011, http://frontloading.blogspot.com/2011/10/nevada-republican-caucuses-set-for.html (accessed August 1, 2012).). That decision in Nevada severely curtailed the ability of the Iowa Republican Party and New Hampshire Secretary of State, Bill Gardner, to comply with respective state laws requiring a certain amount of time between each of the two earliest states' contests and any other similar contest. The move granted neither Iowa nor New Hampshire the space necessary to follow state law and still schedule the primary or caucus in the calendar year 2012. The resultant standoff between New Hampshire and Nevada culminated with the Nevada GOP moving the caucuses in the Silver state back to February 4, the Saturday following the Florida primary (Josh Putnam, "Housekeeping: Caucuses for Both Nevada Parties Moved Back," *Frontloading* 2011, http://frontloading.blogspot.com/2011/10/housekeeping-caucuses-for-both-nevada.html (accessed August 1, 2012).). That placed Nevada fifth instead of third in line—the rules-implied position—in the primary calendar shuffle.

22. Josh Putnam, "[2012 Presidential Primary Calendar in Review] Part Two: How We Got Here—The Motivation," *Frontloading* 2012, http://frontloading.blogspot.com/2012/01/2012-presidential-primary-calendar-in.html (accessed August 1, 2012).

23. Ryan Lizza, Joshua T. Putnam, and Andrew Prokop, "The Delegate Predictor: Is It Over?," *The New Yorker* (2004), http://www.newyorker.com/online/blogs/newsdesk/2012/04/the-delegate-predictor-is-it-over.html (accessed August 1, 2012).

24. Josh Putnam and John Sides, "Republican Rules Are Not to Blame for Primary War," *Bloomberg* 2012, http://www.bloomberg.com/news/2012-03-22/republican-rules-are-not-to-blame-for-primary-war.html (accessed August 1, 2012).

25. There were only six strictly winner-take-all states in the Republican process in 2012, a number just four less than the number of states with similar rules in 2008.

26. Barbara Norrander, "The End Game in Post-Reform Presidential Nominations," *Journal of Politics* 62, no. 4 (2000): 999-1013; Audrey A. Haynes, Paul-Henri Gurian, Michael H Crespin, and Christopher Zorn, "The Calculus of Concession: Media Coverage and the Dynamics of Winnowing in Presidential Nominations," *American Politics Research* 32, no. 3 (2004): 310-337.

27. Josh Putnam, "Santorum Super PAC Doubles Down on Ludicrous Delegate Count Claim," *Frontloading* 2012, http://frontloading.blogspot.com/2012/03/santorum-super-pac-doubles-down-on.html (accessed August 1, 2012).

28. Romney held the overall advantage in endorsements—whether elected officials or automatic delegates—but lagged behind where other previous eventual nominees had been at a similar point.

THREE

White Knights to the Rescue! The Non-Candidates of 2012

William Cunion

In the first week of January 2012, just days after the first two contests of the nomination season, a CBS poll asked Republican voters if they were satisfied with the field of candidates. A stunning 58 percent of them indicated that they wanted more choices. More incredibly, that number had actually *increased* by 12 points since October 2011.[1] The more the primary electorate learned about their candidates, the less they liked them. Pundits started identifying the White Knights who would ride in to save the party, pleading with governors Chris Christie of New Jersey, Mitch Daniels of Indiana, and Bobby Jindal of Louisiana to reconsider their decision not to run. Movements to draft candidates seemed to pop up everywhere, ranging from the familiar names, such as former Florida Governor Jeb Bush, to the recent upstarts, such as Wisconsin Congressman Paul Ryan. The narrative that soon emerged would dominate the early months of the election: A conservative Republican candidate could defeat Barack Obama, but that candidate was not in the race. Would a mysterious White Knight come to the rescue? If so, who?

In this chapter, we will explore "what might have been" by taking a brief look at the Republican field of non-candidates. Why didn't they run? It has been said that every politician, right down to the dog catcher, imagines himself taking the presidential oath of office from the Chief Justice at the Capitol Building; surely, those who have achieved so much in politics to be called upon to "save the country" must be tempted to do so. We'll also loosely place this election in a broader context. While the frustration of the 2012 Republican electorate was undoubtedly high, there is nothing unusual about voters hoping for someone new, someone different, someone perfect. Just...*someone else*. Trouble is, that someone else has to be *someone else*.

THE PERFECT CANDIDATE WHO WASN'T

On paper, Mitt Romney appeared to be the perfect candidate at exactly the right time. A safe, disciplined candidate with a prodigious organization, Romney had never really stopped running for president since dropping out of the race for the Republican nomination in 2008. He had spent the four years in between slowly but steadily building a vast network of relationships that would translate into endorsements and contributions. At a time when voters of all stripes were fed up with Washington insiders, but fearful of the unknown, Romney represented the unique combination of executive experience without the Beltway baggage. He had been an effective governor of a liberal state, as well as an extremely successful businessman; at a moment of great economic uncertainty, he seemed to be the one who knew how to put the country back on the path to prosperity. Voters looking for a family values candidate couldn't ask for more: Mitt and Ann Romney have known each other since grade school; their forty-year marriage has produced five handsome sons, and survived bouts with serious challenges, including her battle with multiple sclerosis and breast cancer. On top of it all, in Mitt Romney, Republicans had a candidate with an unquestionable presidential presence, with broad shoulders, perfect hair, and a strong chin. He was almost too good to be true.

But from the start, something was missing from the Romney candidacy—that same indescribable enthusiasm that propelled Barack Obama four years earlier was wholly lacking from Romney's campaign. In a crowded field of candidates throughout 2011, Romney's support remained a steady, respectable 30-35 percent—no more, no less. Other candidates carved out more narrow portions of the Republican base, but Romney's problem wasn't so much about them as about himself. The downside of a safe candidate is that he is probably also a boring one. While his opponents sometimes presented visions of the future that bordered on science fiction (most notably, Newt Gingrich's plan for an American colony on the moon), Romney's approach seemed so carefully designed not to offend that it couldn't possibly inspire. Republicans debated more than twenty times during this process, and in most of those debates, Romney emerged unbloodied, but also without landing many real blows. To mix sports metaphors, he was playing "prevent defense" throughout the early campaign—a strategy better suited for a candidate with 60 percent support than one with half of that.

He made his share of gaffes. In this era, no candidate will escape without doing some damage with a slip of the tongue. But for Romney, his slip-ups played right into his core weakness: He was a multi-millionaire trying to be a regular guy. Fed up with a baseless repeated claim from his opponent Rick Perry, Romney offered to wager a cool ten grand if Perry could prove him wrong. He also quipped that he liked "firing people"—a perfectly appropriate concept when one receives poor services (which was the context of his remark), but a politically poor one for voters who saw in him the boss who really did fire them. Even when trying desperately to "connect" with voters, Romney struggled: at the Daytona 500, he alluded to the NASCAR *owners* he knows; and to prove his support for the American auto industry, he offered that his wife drives *two* Cadillacs. Fair or not, his extraordinary wealth made him inaccessible to many voters on a personal level; he could roll up his sleeves and wear blue jeans on the campaign trail, but his were tailor-made shirts and designer jeans. Even his Republican opponents seized the opportunity to use his wealth against him. The day before the Ohio primaries, Rick Santorum delivered a thinly-veiled shot at Romney, "We need . . . someone who knows you can't buy it, you've got to earn it, that you've got to fight for America."[2] The same day, Newt Gingrich was characteristically more direct when asked about Romney's plan for rising gas prices: "if you're Mitt Romney and you're rich enough, maybe you don't get it."[3] With bank bailouts and corporate greed very much on the public radar, perhaps a perfect candidate just can't be worth $200 million.

Romney's clumsiest error revealed the full scope of the problem with his candidacy. In a live interview shortly after his victory in the Florida primary, Romney said:

> I'm in this race because I care about Americans. I'm not concerned about the very poor. We have a safety net there. If it needs repair, I'll fix it. I'm not concerned about the very rich, they're doing just fine. I'm concerned about the very heart of the America, the 90 percent, 95 percent of Americans who right now are struggling.

The reporter, CNN's Soledad O'Brien, immediately recognized the misstatement, and offered Romney an opportunity to clarify, or even backpedal. But he persisted:

> Well you had to finish the sentence, Soledad. I said, 'I'm not concerned about the very poor that have a safety net but if it has holes in it, I will repair them.' The challenge right now—we will hear from the Democrat party the plight of the poor. And there's no question it's not good being poor and we have a safety net to help those that are very poor. But my campaign is focused on middle-income Americans. We have a very ample safety net, and we can talk about whether it needs to be strengthened or whether there are holes in it. But we have food stamps,

we have Medicaid, we have housing vouchers, we have programs to help the poor.[4]

Although Romney was trying to communicate a message of concern about the struggling middle class, he came across as a heartless patrician, missing only the dismissive, "Let them eat cake." But somehow, the comment even revealed his weakness to core conservatives, who might otherwise be sympathetic to this message. By emphasizing his support to "repair" the "safety net," Romney manages to remind these voters that he may not be a real conservative at all. Any real conservative would know to say that a thriving economy with full employment is the only answer to poverty. That he didn't even think to say that—even after being given a second chance to do so—only confirmed their suspicions. Romney's record as governor of Massachusetts was already toxic to the most conservative wing of the Republican electorate, many of whom believed that "Romneycare" was the model for "Obamacare"—a government takeover of the health care system in America that dominated the Republican victories in the 2010 midterm elections. That he couldn't even articulate the most fundamental message of conservative economic ideology was yet another frustrating example of why the "perfect candidate" was anything but.

AN IMPERFECT FIELD

The 2012 Republican field was a crowded one from the start. In June 2011, the first debate in New Hampshire[5] featured seven candidates: Besides Romney, the stage included Minnesota Congresswoman Michele Bachmann, businessman Herman Cain, former Speaker of the House of Representatives Newt Gingrich, Texas Congressman Ron Paul, former Minnesota Governor Tim Pawlenty, and former Pennsylvania Senator Rick Santorum. The first Iowa debate (in August) saw the addition of an eighth contender, former Utah Governor Jon Huntsman. Texas Governor Rick Perry jumped in the race in September. If we include minor candidates who have held high office,[6] no fewer than a dozen Republicans officially sought the Party's nomination for president. Many of them had a moment (or two) in the spotlight, but none of them were able to live up to the impossible ideal of the perfect candidate.

The main problem was one of logic. Although the Democratic Party is typically seen as the more diverse—the one with the "big tent"—the contemporary Republican Party actually consists of a wide variety of factions. Each faction adheres to its own brand of conservatism, and the top priorities for each differ widely. The fiscal conservatives focus mainly on stimulating the economy with policies that favor business interests. They are the most vocal advocates for lower taxes, especially on those in higher tax brackets. Many of them have moderate or even liberal views on social issues, which puts them squarely at odds with the social conservatives. These voters are concerned primarily with social and cultural issues, often identify as Evangelical Christian, and prefer candidates who are strongly opposed to abortion and same-sex marriage. While there is much overlap in the two groups, their regional appeal underscores their differences. Fiscal conservatives tend to appeal to Republican voters in the Northeast, while social conservatives fare well in the South.

But there are many other factions in the Republican Party that further complicate the ability to find a candidate that the entire party can support. The libertarian wing advocates the view that government (especially at the federal level) should be much less involved in people's lives—both fiscally and socially. Some in this camp also hold that the Constitution has been ignored not only at home, but also in our foreign affairs, and they would like to see the American military presence abroad reduced dramatically. This is in stark contrast to the neoconservative faction, which prioritizes national security as the most important issue; they believe that an aggressive foreign policy is the best approach to advancing American interests and promoting stability in the world.

In addition, there are numerous moderate Republicans, who may hold some conservative economic principles or disapprove of same-sex marriage...but only to an extent. Besides all of these factions, there are various single-issue groups within the Party, most formidably gun owners and immigration opponents.

And this is only a small slice of a very complex mix of people that make up the Republican Party. To be sure, there is much overlap here. Many social conservatives also prefer lower taxes, as do most neoconservatives. And in theory, nearly all can agree that the federal government has become too large, virtually ignoring the limits established by the 10th Amendment. But in practice, their differences can matter tremendously, and the upstart Tea Party movement that shook up the 2010 midterm elections[7] are only the most visible effect of these intraparty disparities.

The problem, then, is fairly obvious. With so many candidates to choose from, such a divided party is likely to splinter in numerous directions. Oversimplifying a bit, the social conservatives quickly lined up behind Rick Santorum and Michele Bachman, and briefly flirted with Rick Perry. Some neoconservatives found something to like in Newt Gingrich, while others supported John Huntsman. Mainstream fiscal conservatives favored Romney, while the outsider fiscal conservatives latched onto the unlikely candidacy of Herman Cain. The libertarian faction passionately promoted Ron Paul. All of these candidates (and others) are explored more fully by the other contributors in this volume. Suffice to say here that the very thing that made each of them attractive to one portion of the party is what drove them away from other Republican voters.

During the early months of the election cycle, it became clear that none of them would pull away as the candidate who could bridge the various gaps within the party. But even if the factional divides weren't so stark, the same outcome was likely, due to some new rules Republicans had instituted regarding the allocation of delegates to the nominating convention. At its core, the new rules provided for a proportional number of delegates pledged to candidates within states, as opposed to the winner-take-all rules that applied to previous election cycles. The combined effect was predictable: Even as the field winnowed, an unusually high number of candidates remained in the race. Indeed, even after Romney's nomination became a virtual certainty following Super Tuesday in the first week of March, three other candidates (Santorum, Gingrich, and Paul) soldiered on. In the age of an endless news cycle, the media narrative that emerged may have been inevitable: Republicans didn't like their choices, and they needed a new candidate.

THOSE WHO DIDN'T

That would have been a short media obsession, except that there were a lot of names on the list of non-candidates. Then again, how could it be otherwise? The list of non-candidates is necessarily artificial, constrained only by the constitutional eligibility requirements and the imagination of a journalist, blogger, or author of this book chapter.

Somewhat unsystematically,[8] I've identified about twenty non-candidates worth mentioning. A number of them made public statements about running (or not running, as the case may be), and a few even took some credible steps in that direction. But most were simply fantasy White Knight candidates, the ones who could come in and quickly unite the factions, and then handily defeat Barack Obama in November. Tellingly, not a single one of these individuals even declared an official candidacy.

THE LONG SHOTS

Congress has always been a steady source of presidential candidates. One suspects that nearly every member of Congress has imagined that he or she could eventually move to the other end of Pennsylvania Avenue — and do a much better job than the incumbent, no doubt. Even in this era of abysmally low approval ratings for Congress itself, a number of senators and representatives found themselves the subject of speculation about a possible presidential run.

South Dakota Senator John Thune was an early favorite among many conservatives. He had successfully defeated then-Majority leader Tom Daschle to win his Senate seat back in 2004, and was so popular in his state that he was re-elected without opposition in 2010 — the only uncontested Senate race in the country during the year of the Tea Party. Moreover, Thune was popular among his Senate colleagues; even Senate Minority Leader Mitch McConnell of Kentucky publicly suggested that Thune seek the Party's nomination: "He's a very sharp, capable individual, [and has] good leadership qualities which I see on display every week in the Senate. I'm a big John Thune fan."[9] In February 2011, though, Thune passed on the opportunity, posting a note to his Facebook page which read in part: "There is a battle to be waged over what kind of country we are going to leave our children and grandchildren and that battle is happening now in Washington, not two years from now. So at this time, I feel that I am best positioned to fight for America's future here in the trenches of the United States Senate."[10] Some concluded that Thune simply didn't have the national reputation to mount a credible run—at least not yet. At just 51 years old, his name may surface again.

Another Senator who was widely discussed as a possible candidate was South Carolina's Jim DeMint. Like Thune, DeMint first came to the Senate in 2004, and was easily reelected in 2010 with more than 60 percent of the vote. Unlike Thune, DeMint courted controversy by staking out strongly conservative positions, often in strident tones. Advancing the conservative cause more broadly, DeMint even founded a political action committee, the Senate Conservatives Fund, which has helped to finance candidates like Rand Paul in Kentucky and Marco Rubio in Florida, in their successful challenges against establishment Republicans. Although he had solidly confirmed his conservative credentials with Republican primary voters across the country, DeMint ultimately chose not to run so that he could continue to attract and support conservative candidates to run for the Senate. In March 2011, a spokesman for the Senate Conservatives Fund explained simply, "He's said all along that he isn't running for President and his role in the primary is to encourage the candidates to embrace conservative principles."[11] One can't help but wonder if that strong base of support might someday translate into a ready-made organization to make an eventual run at the White House.

At the other end of the Republican ideological spectrum, Massachusetts Senator Scott Brown heard the call to run following his historic victory in the special election in 2009 to fill the vacancy created by the death of Ted Kennedy. Brown was the first Republican elected to the Senate from Massachusetts in almost 40 years, and some Republicans reasoned that a Republican who could win in Massachusetts could win anywhere. Brown himself has claimed to be a genuine conservative (though he began to hedge a bit as his 2012 reelection bid approached), and liberal activist groups have shared that view.[12] His record, though, more fully supports the claim that he is a pretty moderate Republican; according to the *National Journal*, his voting record is similar to other New England Republicans, such as Olympia Snowe of Maine.[13] He was one of only eight Republican senators to vote to repeal the ban on gays in the military, for example. Fueled by the quick rise of Barack Obama, many Republicans and other pundits began hinting at a Scott Brown candidacy within hours of his election to the Senate.[14] But with little explanation, Brown stopped all speculation in April 2010, unequivocally rejecting the idea in an interview on *The Today Show*: "Yes, absolutely, 2012, I'm ruling it out."[15] He added that he would be endorsing Mitt Romney. Brown is the unusual case in which the national exposure is there, but the rationale for the candidacy is not. His early endorsement of Mitt Romney clearly places their many similarities in focus. Why would we need two?

Some possible candidates have a rationale, but lack "something else." Tennessee Senator Bob Corker comes to mind. Corker has been a steady voice of criticism against Barack Obama from the beginning, especially on fiscal matters. Like the others, he is a fairly new senator, first elected in 2008 (defeating the popular Harold Ford, Jr., in a close race). But he quickly established himself on Capitol Hill as a thoughtful conservative. With his business background to complement his voting record, he certainly fits the times, at least on paper. And it's no secret that he has entertained the idea of running for president. In April 2011, he explained his decision not to run for president with an acknowledgement that he thought he had much to offer: "Do I think that I have a vision for our country that would be one the American people would support? Yes. Do I think I have the ability to lead and to be an executive and to get good people that you could trust . . . ? Yes." But like the others, he cited his preference to continue working within the Senate as a way to advance his vision. Still, he did not rule it out forever: "Maybe someday, but it's just not on my plate. I just don't have the fire in the belly to do that . . . right now."[16] One could speculate that Corker recognized early some challenges that he might face in developing a national reputation, but given the rigors of running for president, it might be best simply to take him at his word. It takes too much to run for president to do it without being fully devoted to doing so.

On the House side, only one representative generated any serious discussion as a possible presidential candidate, Mike Pence of Indiana, a solid conservative with ten years of House votes to prove it. In September 2010, Pence delivered a powerful speech to the influential Values Voters Summit, which led to his surprise victory in their presidential straw poll, defeating better-known candidates like Mike Huckabee and Sarah Palin. Shortly thereafter, the America's President Committee, a group of conservatives that included former Reagan administration officials and members of Congress, publicly called upon voters to urge Pence to seek the nomination: "Grass-roots conservatives, Republicans, the tea party and populists are looking for a man or woman of principle who can champion and unite the newly energized and engaged citizenry. Mike Pence is the best choice to lead us into a new era of peace and prosperity."[17] Their goal was to demonstrate to Pence himself that he had the kind of enthusiastic support among Republican voters needed for a successful candidacy. But Pence made his decision not to run even before these efforts could fully take shape, announcing instead that he would seek to become his state's next governor: "In the choice between seeking national office and serving Indiana in some capacity, we choose Indiana."[18]

Perhaps his interest in the governorship is a hint that he will eventually make a run for the presidency. After all, governors can most effectively combine the two competing qualities that voters seem to prefer: experience and lack of connection to Washington. Going back a generation, we see more presidents who were governors (Carter, Reagan, Clinton, and George W. Bush) than presidents who weren't (George H.W. Bush and Obama). One unusual sign of the preference for governors was the suggestion by influential Republican anti-tax activist Grover Norquist that Puerto Rico Governor Luis Fortuño should consider running[19] — despite the fact that Puerto Rico does not vote in the presidential election!

Governors and former governors from more traditional places consumed much of the speculation about possible candidacies. One name that has floated around this discussion for many years is former New York Governor George Pataki, who served three terms as the chief executive of one of the country's biggest states. Pataki stunned the political world by defeating incumbent Governor Mario Cuomo in 1994, and governed as a moderate throughout his tenure, advancing significant tax reductions, but also supporting union rights and stronger environmental regulations. Following his governorship, Pataki continued working on a variety of political issues, creating a non-profit advocacy group, No American Debt, and even securing a Senate-confirmed appointment as a delegate to the United Nations in 2007. Frequent public appearances in Iowa and New Hampshire starting in 2009 fueled suspicions that he was prepared to run for president. His own spokesman confirmed the Governor's interest as late as mid-August 2011.[20] But polls throughout 2011 consistently showed that Pataki was not registering as a national candidate. Between his liberal record on social issues and his support for unions, Pataki was simply unable to find a receptive niche among the many Republican factions. On August 26, he ended the speculation: "I remain committed to the advancement of real, politically viable reforms to entitlements and rolling back the size and cost of the federal government. At this time, I will continue to do this as the leader of No American Debt and not as a candidate for president."[21] With little hope of winning New York in the general election in the foreseeable future, it is extremely difficult to envision any scenario in which Republicans would nominate a moderate New Yorker for the presidency, even if he was a popular, effective governor.

However, they might nominate a popular, effective governor of Mississippi. In Haley Barbour, they seemed to have it all: unblemished conservatism, a long record of bipartisan results, prodigious fundraising abilities, and a national base of support. Barbour had built that base during the 1990s, when he served as Chair of the Republican National Committee. Though much of the credit (rightly) belongs to Newt Gingrich, Barbour's work helped to secure the Republican takeover of the House of Representatives during the 1994 midterm elections. He then served as Mississippi's governor from 2004 through 2012, most notably seeing the state through the recovery from Hurricane Katrina to widespread praise. As governor, Barbour had to work with a legislature dominated by Democrats (albeit many of the more conservative Southern variety), managing to secure substantial budget cuts, tax reductions, and tort reform. In addition, the state added restrictions to abortion access during his tenure. Between his work with Republicans at the national level and his successes in Mississippi, the headline for the profile of Barbour in *Politico* was quite apt: "The Most Powerful Republican in Politics."[22] Like so many others, Barbour was coy about his interest in running for president, but he certainly didn't deny it. Like Pataki, Barbour may have simply found the early polls too discouraging. His name was consistently included among the options, but also consistently ignored by voters; through 2010 and 2011, he failed to hit the 5 percent threshold even once. In most polls, just 1-3 percent of voters indicated that Barbour was their preference. Though it's hard to know for sure, it seems likely that many Republican voters feared how Barbour's image would play in a general election. Could a "Good Ol' Boy" defeat Barack Obama in November? For much different reasons, Pataki and Barbour were simply the wrong men at the wrong time. Barbour's statement, in April 2011, announcing that he would not run for president offered no explanation.[23]

Sometimes, no explanation is necessary. If he had any other last name, we might well be seeing bumper stickers that read, "Jeb 2012." As a moderately conservative governor of a key swing state who resonates strongly with Latino voters, former Florida Governor Jeb Bush would seem to be top tier candidate for the Republican nomination, perhaps even the frontrunner — except for that last name he shares with his brother, George, who left the White House with an approval rating of 22 percent. A Jeb Bush candidacy would be saddled with his brother's political baggage, and he consistently denied any interest in running in 2012. Even so, some pushed hard for Jeb to make a run. His own son publicly urged Jeb to reconsider, but in so doing, immediately drew upon the comparisons to his uncle: "'Make no mistake about it, I think a lot of people sorely miss and would relish some sort of return of that type of approach to leading our country.'"[24] That might be a selling point within the family, but unlikely to make the sale with the public. In February 2011, asked again whether the door remained firmly shut on a 2012 bid, Jeb Bush answered with a single word: Yes.[25] Even so, calls for Bush to reconsider continued well into 2012.[26] But his one-word answer really says it all.

Several other governors were on the outskirts of the presidential conversation, as well. A quick Google search will find columns proposing presidential runs for Wisconsin's Scott Walker,[27] Florida's Rick Scott,[28] and Virginia's Bob McDonnell[29] —among others. This group consists mainly of new governors with recent, high-profile achievements, such as Walker's successful effort to reduce the power of public unions in his state. Such actions naturally generate much enthusiasm for those looking for someone new who can "get things done." But a limited record is a major liability when a core Republican criticism of Barack Obama is that he was too inexperienced to be president. In that light, it isn't surprising that most of this type of speculation begins—and ends—with the newspaper column or Facebook fan page. Ultimately, these governors didn't make a run for the same reason as the more experienced group: They stayed out because they couldn't win.

THE OUTSIDERS

Frustration with the establishment is an increasingly common theme in American politics. On both the Right and the Left, we've seen this frustration reach the boiling point in recent years. There may not be much connecting the Tea Party movement to the Occupy Wall Street protests, but they can agree that the country needs to move in a vastly different direction. That sentiment has typically favored governors, who can play the role of Washington outsider. But in 2012, it also led to some speculation about presidential runs from a handful of individuals outside of electoral politics, including one semi-serious bid from a genuine outsider—if a mega-high profile celebrity businessman with his own television show and line of hotels can be considered an "outsider."

Although so much of the political spotlight focused on domestic issues due to the long economic recession, presidential elections often revolve around foreign affairs. At least three potential candidates brought vast foreign policy expertise to the table, even without any political experience. David Petraeus was a four-star Army general who came to national prominence as commander of all multinational forces in Iraq during the surge of 2007, and then as commander of U.S. forces in Afghanistan from July 2010 through July 2011. One supporter made the obvious comparison perfectly explicit: "Not since 1952, when a certain Dwight Eisenhower, Supreme Commander of Allied Forces in Europe during the Second World War, was elected President, have the chances of a military man winning the White House been more propitious."[30] Petraeus himself has consistently denied any interest in seeking political office, but to his supporters, this only serves to confirm his image as a modern-day Eisenhower, one who would ultimately succumb to the call of duty. But his denials were more reminiscent of another general of the past; William

Sherman famously announced in 1884 that he "would not accept if nominated and [would] not serve if elected." Petraeus sounded equally emphatic: ""I thought I'd said 'no' about as many ways as I could. I really do mean no . . . I will not ever run for political office, I can assure you."[31] Needless to say, his later sex scandal revelation confirmed his decision.

Another foreign policy expert who heard the call to run in 2012 was former Secretary of State Condoleezza Rice. In the 1800s, secretaries of state were nominated for president numerous times (six won the election), but none for nearly a century. Rice had been the subject of much speculation four years prior, and in many ways, seemed a natural Republican successor to George W. Bush, given Dick Cheney's decision not to run. After passing on the opportunity in 2008, Rice took a faculty position at Stanford University and wrote her memoir. Her 2012 buzz was considerably quieter, though she fueled speculation when she casually answered, "You never know," when asked about running for political office.[32] Her name would surface from time to time in discussions that emphasized the weak foreign policy credentials of the Republican field. But just as often, the attention seemed to focus less on her experience and more on her demographic qualities:

> As a black woman—her family has roots in the Deep South stretching back to before Civil War era, and worked as sharecroppers after emancipation—she would mute Democrats' charges of racism among conservatives, especially tea party members. And her sex would likely prompt moderate women to take a serious look at the Republican ticket.[33]

It isn't hard to see why an accomplished diplomat and scholar might find such "qualifications" beneath her. She chose instead to remain on the faculty at Stanford.

However, another Bush Administration foreign policy official was interested. At first glance, John Bolton seems a very unlikely candidate for president, having never run for political office, and most shockingly, sporting a mustache![34] But at a time when voters want something new, perhaps his non-political qualities would play well. Trouble is, Bolton spent most of the previous decade as a lightning rod as one of the most controversial members of the George W. Bush administration. He served as Bush's Ambassador to the United Nations only after a recess appointment, and was unable to secure a confirmation from the Senate, even after serving in that position for over a year. Even so, there was no confusion about his interest in seeking the Republican nomination for president, offering several interviews in which he discussed voter frustration with the field of candidates, and his own frustration in their lack of foreign policy experience. But his real motivation was directed not at fellow Republicans, but at the Democrat in office: "[Obama's] policies come from a foundation of near-disinterest in national security, influenced by his view, which he expressed many times during the campaign, that he doesn't see real threats and challenges to the United States in the world as a whole. The consequence of those two views is that he portrays a weak and indecisive presidency."[35] Bolton announced in September 2011 that he would not run for president, offering a refreshingly straightforward explanation: "I kept coming to the conclusion that I couldn't possibly win the nomination and I didn't like that answer."[36]

The inability to win the election seems a compelling reason not to run; indeed, some research has suggested that active candidates withdraw from presidential primaries as the certainty of losing increases.[37] But at least one potential candidate may have been indifferent to his chances of winning the office. When celebrity businessman Donald Trump began floating the idea that he might seek the presidency, most pundits chalked it up to the latest publicity stunt, a way to promote the next season of *Celebrity Apprentice*. Regardless, there was no denying that Trump had some qualities that might play well with a frustrated electorate. Former CBS executive Bernard Goldberg cautioned against those who would dismiss Trump, and summarized nicely Trump's formidable strengths:

> What they don't understand, even the journalists that I have lot of respect for, what they don't understand is that millions of Americans who live between Manhattan and Malibu think that Donald Trump's greatest asset is that he is not a politician, that he doesn't talk like politician or think like a politician. And that he is a businessman and most politicians couldn't run a lemonade stand. That's the disconnect between the journalists who will be covering Donald Trump and the people they're reporting for. The people who live in the United States of America.[38]

Polls in spring 2011 seemed to validate Goldberg's claims. Trump consistently ranked near the top of the field, even leading the pack in a CNN poll in mid-April. With so many possible candidates splitting the vote, Trump's numbers never exceeded 17 percent, but he was clearly in the mix. Further, he already had very high name recognition, proven ability to self-promote, and very deep pockets. At one point, he stated that he was willing to spend $600 million on his own campaign.[39] Alas, such qualities can take a candidate only so far—and name recognition can sometimes be a double-edged sword. A *USA Today* poll at the end of April 2011 found that 50 percent of Americans thought Trump would make a "poor" or "terrible" president, and 63 percent (including 46 percent of Republicans) indicated that they would *never* vote for Trump.[40] Two weeks later, Trump announced his decision not to run, with characteristic lack of humility:

> After considerable deliberation and reflection, I have decided not to pursue the office of the Presidency. This decision does not come easily or without regret; especially when my potential candidacy continues to

be validated by ranking at the top of the Republican contenders in polls across the country. I maintain the strong conviction that if I were to run, I would be able to win the primary and ultimately, the general election.[41]

We'll never know.

THEIR TIME WILL COME

Nearly all of the possible candidates discussed above share a core problem: They identify so closely with one faction of the Republican Party that they may be unable to appeal more broadly to the others. Fiscal conservatives might wonder how Petraeus or Bolton would manage the economy, while moderates would bristle at the social conservative messages of DeMint or Barbour. And it's hard to see many establishment Republican leaders in any faction warming to the prospect of a Trump candidacy, no matter the grassroots desire for an outsider. But there were at least three possible candidates waiting in the wings who seemed to appeal to numerous factions within the Party: Wisconsin Congressman Paul Ryan, Louisiana Governor Bobby Jindal, and Florida Senator Marco Rubio.

In 2008, Paul Ryan was serving his fifth term in the House of Representatives when he emerged as a Republican leader by proposing a comprehensive plan to reform entitlement spending and reduce taxes, a plan he called, "The Roadmap for America's Future." Ryan became Chair of the House Budget Committee when Republicans took control of the House in 2011, and in that role, he led the coordinated effort to provide an alternative to the President's agenda with updated versions of his original Roadmap. "The Path to Prosperity" lays out a clear vision for the nation's economic future, one characterized by a much smaller federal government, including an end to Obama's health care reform legislation. Ryan became the most visible spokesperson for the opposition, frequently appearing on Sunday morning news shows and talk radio. Why not take that opposition to the next level, and present voters with a clear alternative in the 2012 election? Ryan himself acknowledged as much in an interview with a Milwaukee radio host in August 2011: "Look, the way I see 2012—we owe it to the country to let them choose the path they want our country to take. And I just have yet to see a strong and principled articulation of the kind of limited government, opportunity society path that we would provide as an alternative to the Obama cradle to grave welfare state."[42] Rumors flew that Ryan met with House Speaker John Boehner in August 2011 to discuss plans for a run.[43] But by the end of August, Ryan was out, announcing that he would prefer to continue to work on fixing the country's economic problems from his (important) position in Congress. However, that didn't end matters. Speculation about a Paul Ryan candidacy continued to flourish well into 2012, as conservatives continued to worry about Mitt Romney's ability to capture voter frustration with Barack Obama—some continued to argue that Obama's main congressional adversary was the one best suited to take the case against the President to the American people. The idea made sense also because Ryan held the "right" positions on social issues and matters of foreign policy, enough to be acceptable to those wings of the Party, as well.

Another possible candidate who held all the right views was Louisiana Governor Bobby Jindal. In 2007, during his second term in the U.S. House of Representatives, Jindal was easily elected governor, winning a majority of votes in a crowded field of candidates.[44] Still reeling from Hurricane Katrina two years prior, Louisiana was badly in need of new leadership when Jindal took office. But Jindal wasn't merely offering himself as a technocratic, non-partisan executive. Across the board, Jindal took very conservative positions on nearly every issue, and quickly became a national favorite for social conservatives and fiscal ones. A clear sign of his wide appeal, he was selected to provide the Republican response to President Obama's first State of the Union Address. It was a challenging opportunity, given Obama's high approval ratings at the time, and Jindal simply could not compete with the new President's star power, and his message of "too much government" fell flat. Even the otherwise supportive pundits on Fox News were sharply critical of Jindal's speech.[45] But he continued to shine as governor, earning wide praise for his response to the BP oil spill in the Gulf in June 2010.[46] By the end of that year, Jindal had unequivocally rejected the idea that he would run for president in 2012, and he turned his energies to his gubernatorial reelection efforts. In October 2011, two-thirds of Louisiana voters opted to give him another term in office.

Perhaps the only matter of universal agreement in contemporary American politics is that the rising star in the Republican Party is Florida Senator Marco Rubio—and with good reason. The son of Cuban immigrants, Rubio exploded onto the national stage in 2010 as the veritable face of the nascent Tea Party movement by soundly defeating then-governor Charlie Crist for Florida's vacant U.S. Senate seat.[47] Rubio was no political neophyte, however; he had served in the Florida Legislature for ten years, including a term as House Speaker. But it wasn't his experience that put him over the top—indeed, he campaigned for office as an outsider, emphasizing the need to return to basic conservative values across the board, and ran very much against the establishment. Instead, Rubio's success turned on his exceptional ability to articulate the conservative message, his incredible charisma, his wonkish attention to policy detail, and his confidence and ease with a variety of audiences. Modest beginnings, exceptional intelligence, a rapid rise, the ability to energize a crowd. Rubio may be the mirror image of Barack Obama. In that light, it isn't surprising that within days of taking office, Rubio was asked if he would challenge his political doppelganger in 2012. He dismissed the question as part of the media circus, and his decision to focus on building a record in the Senate seems wise in the long run.

All three of these men are probably thinking more about the long run, in fact. All are in their early forties, all with small children, and all with a very bright political future—one that could be destroyed quickly. Any potential candidate has to weigh the consequences of losing, and those with the brightest future clearly have the most to lose. By 2016, Ryan will (presumably) have additional evidence about the nation's fiscal health, Rubio will have completed a full term in the Senate, and Jindal will be looking for a job, having been term-limited out of the governor's mansion. One suspects that their stories are to be continued.

THE A-LIST

One argument in favor of any of those young Republican leaders to enter the fray is to set themselves up for next time. Republicans, in particular, have routinely nominated the previous runner-up. From Reagan in 1980, Bob Dole in 1996, and John McCain in 2008, failing to win the Republican nomination has been something of a long-term strategy to win it next time. In 2012, the nomination of Mitt Romney repeats that cycle—sort of.

It isn't always easy to determine who has finished in second place in the nomination process. Is it measured by delegates won? States won? Popular votes? Last date of withdrawal? By most of these measures, Romney qualifies as the 2008 runner-up, but the last (competitive) candidate to drop out of the race was former Arkansas Governor Mike Huckabee. A strong favorite among social conservatives, Huckabee is a Baptist minister who surprised everyone by winning the Iowa caucuses in January 2008, but then had trouble sustaining that momentum throughout the primary season. By the time he ended his candidacy in March, John McCain had already wrapped up the nomination. But instead of retreating from public life, Huckabee used the experience to build his brand, hosting a television program and later a talk radio show. The formats suited Huckabee well, allowing him to demonstrate his amiable personality; as a candidate, his wry humor was best captured in a memorable campaign ad featuring Chuck Norris. Following McCain's defeat, Huckabee immediately became a frontrunner for 2012. Throughout 2009, 2010, and the first half of 2011, he was at or near the top of every major poll listing potential Republican candidates, *far* ahead of everyone else discussed in this chapter. With his campaign experience, ability to connect with voters, and his media savvy, Huckabee might have been the candidate to beat in 2012. Yet his inclusion on this "A-list" seems awkward, since his name so rarely surfaced during the frantic search for a non-

Romney candidate in the early months of 2012. Maybe that can be attributed to his unique explanation for staying out of the race. At the end of his television show in May 2011, he said, "All the factors say go, but my heart says no and that's the decision I have made. . . . The external signs . . . point strongly toward running. But only when I was alone, in quiet and reflective moments, did I have not only clarity but an inexplicable inner peace."[48] A year later, he elaborated just a bit, alluding to the ugliness of politics: "It's easier to walk away from a job that you want than to walk away from your own integrity and character."[49] That sounds like someone closing the door permanently.

One could also argue that neither Romney nor Huckabee was the *real* runner-up in 2008. Perhaps the next in line was Vice Presidential nominee Sarah Palin. Enough has been written and said about Sarah Palin that I don't need to pile on here. Her liabilities and weaknesses are well known, and public opinion polls confirm the conventional wisdom. The same poll that doomed Donald Trump's candidacy had even worse news for Palin; while 63 percent of Americans said they would never vote for him, *65 percent* said they would never vote for her.[50] Still, Palin has her fervent supporters, too—a lot of them. Even while she had the highest negatives among the Republicans, she continued to poll remarkably well all the way through the end of 2011, even leading the pack from time to time. Frustrated voters were practically begging for someone to "go rogue" against the establishment, and Palin struck a perfect chord with the Tea Party conservatives. And she earned that respect. It is easy to forget just how exciting Palin was upon landing the number two spot on the 2008 ticket; her acceptance speech at the Republican Convention brought down the house. Speculation about a possible 2012 run turned on whether she could recapture that initial magic, or whether her reputation was permanently damaged. In October 2011, she ended the speculation with a long letter that read in part, "I believe that at this time I can be more effective in a decisive role to help elect other true public servants to office—from the nation's governors to Congressional seats and the Presidency."[51] If those candidates are successful, she may yet reemerge as a major political figure. She is still in her forties, so there is time. But that time is not 2012.

One of the most even-handed criticisms of Palin is that she resigned as governor of Alaska before her term was finished, thereby disqualifying her for the nation's highest office. That's a bit ironic in light of the fact that the last two non-candidates on this long list are current governors who have been *begged* to step down from their posts to seek the presidency. The first is Mitch Daniels of Indiana. In January 2012, at the peak of the Republican pining for a White Knight, Daniels delivered the response to the President's State of the Union Address to rave reviews. *Washington Post* columnist Charles Krauthammer summarized the moment: "I could hear sighs all over the country from Republicans [about] what might have been."[52] A widely-circulated cartoon from the *Indianapolis Star* portrayed Daniels as a reluctant Obi Wan Kenobi, a hooded elephant pleading with him, "Help me, Mitch Daniels . . . You're my only hope!" The message was nothing new. In fact, Daniels had been a favorite among Republican strategists and Party leaders since the beginning of Obama's term. He had amassed considerable executive experience, both as OMB Director in the Bush administration (both an asset and a liability) and as governor of a swing state. His record won him the attention of party leaders, having demonstrated a rare ability to seek innovative solutions to public problems without sacrificing core conservative principles. While some social conservatives were concerned that he had called for a "truce" on social issues due to the urgency of the country's economic woes, his record again stood on its own—having actually governed as a social conservative. But perhaps most importantly, Daniels had become a thoughtful, vocal critic of the administration—talents that were on full display following the State of the Union Address. In the early weeks of 2012, calls for Daniels to enter the race bordered on the obnoxious—as if he were being rude for sitting it out.

But Daniels never blinked. Despite expressing some interest in the position in 2010 and early 2011, even winning a straw poll in Oregon in March, he never wavered from his decision in May 2011 not to run. In an email to his staff and supporters, he said, "In the end, I was able to resolve every competing consideration but one... the interests and wishes of my family, is the most important consideration of all."[53] Candidates frequently cite "family concerns" as a generic reason for withdrawing from a race or resigning a position, but in Daniels' case, it was probably real. He and his wife had divorced in the early 1990s and remarried several years later, but only after she had married another man in the interim. As scandals go, it seems almost quaint, but nearly every article discussing his possible run alludes to it—case in point right here. Daniels may have wanted to spare her from the overwhelming media scrutiny that comes with running for president.[54] His email was almost plaintive in acknowledging how the decision would be received: "If I have disappointed you, I will always be sorry. If you feel that this was a non-courageous or unpatriotic decision, I understand and will not attempt to persuade you otherwise. I only hope that you will accept my sincerity in the judgment I reached."[55] Daniels had all of the qualities of a top candidate—but his heart was elsewhere.

If we're counting down the field of non-candidates, number one with a bullet is New Jersey Governor Chris Christie. Elected to lead the Garden State in 2009, Christie quickly emerged as a national figure, and a clear favorite among those looking for an alternative to the Republican presidential field. Much is made of Christie's weight (he does not disclose the specifics, but it is clear that he is well over 300 pounds), both as a political liability as well as a health issue of public concern.[56] But it is the size of his personality that puts him at the top of this list. His style is almost stereotypically New Jersey—direct, blunt, and unapologetic. But also fiercely honest and candid, and holding everyone to the same high standards. As a U.S. Attorney, he secured well over one hundred convictions of public officials (of both parties) for corruption and fraud, never losing a single case.[57] He took the same no-nonsense approach to the Statehouse, bringing order to the state's budget woes within months. He handled the state's economy as a crisis, and employed emergency measures to restore fiscal health. The appeal to national Republican leaders was obvious: Here was a man who would not only shout "Fire!"—but would also extinguish the flames.

Perhaps it was that same candor that led him to assess his own situation more realistically than some of his supporters. Easily overlooked in the frenzy was the fact that Christie had so little experience. Like some of the other governors mentioned above, he had been in major public office for less than a full term. Characteristically, Christie himself offered the clearest succinct analysis of the problem: "I am not arrogant enough to believe that after one year as governor . . . that I am ready to be president of the United States."[58] He later added, "You don't make a decision to run for president of the United States based on impulse. I don't feel ready in my heart to be president. Unless I do, I don't have any right offering myself to the people of this country. It's much too big a job. And so you have to first feel in your heart that you're ready."[59] He is smart to be cautious, because in the spotlight of a presidential bid, voters would take close stock of his record, and some factions might be puzzled. On the one hand, he kept his campaign promise to veto a bill that would allow for same-sex marriage, but on the other, he appointed an openly gay man to the state Supreme Court and has made somewhat disparaging remarks about social conservatives. As a non-candidate, that is largely a non-issue. But as many others before him have learned the hard way, voters are fickle, and they often love the idea of a candidate a lot more than they love the actual candidate. It seems likely that Christie will remain on the national scene for the foreseeable future, as his articulate, confrontational style will continue to appeal to conservatives looking for a straight shooter—especially one with a good sense of humor. In one public statement denying his interest in running for president, Christie quipped, "I threatened to commit suicide . . . to convince people I'm not running. Apparently I actually have to commit suicide to convince people I am not running."[60] He may have it backwards: it's safe not to run; it's often suicidal to do so.

RECENT HISTORY ADVISES CAUTION

Voter discontent with the field of candidates isn't that unusual, historically speaking. Particularly when a party is split into numerous factions, the narrative can quickly turn sour, spurring the search for an alternative. The handful of true "Dark Horse" candidates who secured presidential nominations, such as James Polk, James Garfield, and Warren Harding, emerged from badly divided parties—and the fear of a deeply disappointed electorate. These men became candidates only after the convention deadlocked; leaders settled on them as compromise candidates who were "good enough" for all factions of the party—and who could win the election. The ultimate success of their candidacies vindicated the party leaders who wanted "someone else."[61]

But in today's political environment, party leaders are less decisive in the selection of a nominee. Convention delegations are chosen mainly by voters in primary elections, and even party caucuses have become rather open affairs, where rank-and-file voters can cast meaningful votes that contribute to the nomination. Herein lies a problem that is not at all obvious. In the early stages, party leaders are far more in tune with a candidate's strengths and weaknesses than the average voter. A frustrated electorate may demand new candidates, but party leaders would be more careful to choose wisely. In recent years, we've seen candidates succumb to the public pressure to run—only to fizzle badly as actual candidates. In 2004, General Wesley Clark *seemed* to be the ideal foil to George W. Bush, until he started campaigning. A similar story could be told about Republican Senator Fred Thompson in 2008, and also Texas Governor Rick Perry in 2012. Despite their experiences and credentials, none of them were fully prepared to run a national campaign for president, and their embarrassing debate performances will live forever on the Internet to warn future potential candidates that it isn't as easy as it looks.

But even if they had performed well in debates, each of them would have quickly learned that voters love potential candidates a lot more than they love real ones. Potential candidates typically don't have to answer tough questions. They aren't asked about a public statement they made twenty years ago. They can make a slip of the tongue and no one cares. But once they declare—let the countdown begin. Is it a coincidence that these recent examples were all dreadful failures as candidates? Voters, it seems, like the idea of someone a lot more than they like that someone. On this view, perhaps we should not be asking why Paul Ryan, Chris Christie, and the others did not run, but instead asking why *anyone* does run.

THE CONTESTED CONVENTION

Yet so many do—even beyond the point at which winning is a likely outcome. Into April 2012, four candidates continued to pursue the Republican nomination. Even though Mitt Romney had secured a significant majority of the delegates, his opponents marched on. They had their sights on the possibility of wresting the nomination from Romney at the convention itself. If Romney were unable to secure a majority of voting delegates on the first ballot, the argument goes, these voters might choose to go with one of the other candidates. When Gingrich compared himself to Warren Harding, it was a strong hint that he was banking on this strategy.[62]

But a contested convention actually seems more likely to pull a non-candidate on the stage. After all, it is difficult to see disappointed Romney delegates moving so quickly into the camp of his main opponents—the very men who prevented their candidate from winning. So we're right back to the ones who didn't run in the first place.

As if on cue, just one day after Super Tuesday, Sarah Palin hinted that she wouldn't rule out accepting the party's nomination at the Republican Convention in late August.[63] The unusual dynamics of the race[64] seem to provide a realistic context for her statement. But a closer analysis reveals just how implausible such a scenario is.

While a White Knight candidacy could conceivably provide the answer to voter discontent, it just can't happen in today's political environment. As a practical matter, one cannot mount a successful candidacy on the fly. A couple of hiccups from the primary season are instructive; recall that Santorum and Gingrich failed even to qualify for the Virginia ballot. In both Ohio and Illinois, Santorum did not submit the required paperwork to field a full slate of delegates. These are quick reminders of the massive organizational challenges of running for president. The notion that an individual—an *individual*!—could organize and mount a successful campaign in a truncated period is absurd. Since party leaders know this, they'll do whatever it takes to avoid a contested convention, which means that late entrants will have no chance to be nominated. In sum, the Dark Horse candidates are a relic of the distant past.

Anticlimactically, the Republican Convention will rally support around Mitt Romney as the nominee. No White Knights will be riding in to unite the fractured party. In fact, the party faithful—from all factions—will leave Tampa with a new hope that Romney will defeat Barack Obama. Party leaders will faithfully express their support for Romney, and many of the non-candidates will appear with him at rallies in their states and elsewhere. But some of these White Knights may quietly determine that this battle is lost, and begin preparing for the next fight in 2016. They should start now, or they will likely reappear in the new version of this chapter in four years. White Knights and Dark Horses are now figments of political imagination. Shoulda-been candidates are not.

NOTES

1. Brian Montopoli, "Poll: 58 percent of Republicans want more presidential choices," *CBS News* 2012, http://www.cbsnews.com/8301-503544_162-57355532-503544/poll-58-of-republicans-want-more-presidential-choices/?tag=cbsnewsMainColumnArea.

2. S. A. Miller, "Romney wealth clubbed," *New York Post* 2012, http://www.nypost.com/p/news/national/romney_wealth_clubbed_6C72NvlqygCSQ5hGME4ctJ?utm_medium=rss&utm_content=National.

3. Justin Sink, "Gingrich: Romney 'Rich Enough' to Not Care About High Gas Prices," *Fox News* 2012, http://nation.foxnews.com/super-tuesday/2012/03/05/gingrich-romney-rich-enough-not-care-about-high-gas-prices.

4. Mackenzie Weinger, "Mitt Romney: 'I'm not concerned about the very poor'," *Politico* 2012, http://www.politico.com/news/stories/0212/72297.html.

5. The South Carolina Republican Party had actually hosted a debate a few weeks earlier, on May 5. Five candidates participated, but neither Mitt Romney nor Newt Gingrich took part.

6. This list would include former Louisiana Governor Buddy Roemer, Michigan Congressman Thad McCotter, and former New Mexico Governor Gary Johnson. Johnson actually qualified for and participated in a Republican debate in Florida in September, before dropping out of the race to pursue the nomination of the Libertarian Party. Roemer would continue his candidacy as an Independent, or as the nominee for the Reform Party.

7. William J. Miller and Jeremy D. Walling, eds. *Tea Party Effects on 2010 U.S. Senate Elections* (Lanham, MD: Lexington Books, 2011).

8. Depending on how one assesses the scientific merits of a Google search.

9. Brian Beutler, "Thune Rejects Obama's Call For Infrastructure Investment," *Talking Points Memo* 2011, http://tpmdc.talkingpointsmemo.com/2011/01/thune-rejects-obama-call-for-infrastructure-improvements.php.

10. Jason Linkins, "John Thune: I Won't Run For President In 2012," *Huffington Post* 2011, http://www.huffingtonpost.com/2011/02/22/john-thune-president-2012_n_826572.html.

11. Chris Cillizza, "Jim DeMint won't run for president in 2012," *Washington Post* 2011, http://www.washingtonpost.com/blogs/the-fix/post/jim-demint-wont-run-for-president-in-2012/2011/03/24/ABXFrZPB_blog.html.

12. Garrett Quinn, "Scott Brown is a 'mildly conservative fellow'," *Boston.com* 2012, http://boston.com/community/blogs/less_is_more/2012/03/scott_brown_is_a_mildly_conser.html.

13. "Centrist Senators: The Most Moderate Members," *National Journal* 2012, http://www.nationaljournal.com/pictures-video/centrist-senators-the-most-moderate-members-pictures-20120302.

14. Max Fisher, "Scott Brown Presidential Campaign Already Underway," *The Atlantic Wire* 2010. http://www.theatlanticwire.com/politics/2010/01/scott-brown-presidential-campaign-already-underway/25797/.

15. Andy Barr, "Sen. Scott Brown won't run for president in 2012," *Politico* 2010, http://www.politico.com/news/stories/0410/36268.html.

16. . Clint Brewer, "Corker on a White House bid: 'Maybe someday'," *The Tennessean* 2011, http://blogs.tennessean.com/politics/2011/corker-on-a-white-house-bid-maybe-someday/.

17. Associated Press, "Rep. Pence Urged to Enter 2012 Presidential Race," *Fox News* 2011, http://www.foxnews.com/politics/2011/01/17/rep-pence-urged-enter-presidential-race/.

18. Mary Beth Schneider and Maureen Groppe, "Rep. Mike Pence closes door on White House run," *Indianapolis Star* 2011, http://www.indystar.com/article/20110127/NEWS05/110127015/Rep-Mike-Pence-closes-door-White-House-run.

19. Andrew Romano, "Absurdly Premature 2012 Watch, Vol. 2: The Governor of Puerto Rico . . . for President?," *The Daily Beast* 2009, http://www.thedailybeast.com/newsweek/blogs/the-gaggle/2009/11/25/absurdly-premature-2012-watch-vol-2-the-governor-of-puerto-rico-for-president.html.

20. Lucy Madison, "Former NY Gov. George Pataki 'seriously considering' 2012 presidential bid ," *CBS News* 2011, http://www.cbsnews.com/8301-503544_162-20095550-503544.html.

21. Mark Preston, "Pataki decides against White House run," *CNN* 2011, http://politicalticker.blogs.cnn.com/2011/08/26/pataki-decides-against-white-house-run/?hpt=po_bn1.

22. Jim VandeHei, Andy Barr, and Kenneth P. Vogel, "The most powerful Republican in politics," *Politico* 2010, http://www.politico.com/news/stories/0810/41236_Page2.html

23. Michael Muskal, "Haley Barbour will not run for president," *Los Angeles Times* 2011, http://articles.latimes.com/2011/apr/25/news/la-pn-haley-barbour-gop-nod-20110425.

24. "George P Bush wants father Jeb in the White House . . . by 2013," *Daily Mail* 2011

25. Jonathan Martin, "Jeb emails: National Review or not, it's still no," *Politico* 2011, http://www.politico.com/news/stories/0211/49078.html.

26. Glenn Thrush and Maggie Haberman, "Despite Mitt Romney wins, both sides keep eying Jeb Bush," *Politico* 2011, http://www.politico.com/news/stories/0212/73475.html.

27. Bill Murchison, "Scott Walker for President," *Town Hall* 2011, http://townhall.com/columnists/billmurchison/2011/02/23/scott_walker_for_president/page/full/.

28. Adam C. Smith, "Rick Scott for president? It's possible," *Tampa Bay Times* 2011, http://www.tampabay.com/news/politics/national/rick-scott-for-president-its-possible/1169238.

29. Lynn R. Mitchell, "Virginia Gov. Bob McDonnell for President?," *Washington Examiner* 2011, http://washingtonexaminer.com/opinion/opinion-zone/2011/04/virginia-gov-bob-mcdonnell-president/143462.

30. Toby Harnden, "David Petraeus for President: Run General, run," *The Telegraph* 2010, "http://www.telegraph.co.uk/news/worldnews/northamerica/usa/7549797/David-Petraeus-for-President-Run-General-run.html" .

31. Harnden, "David Petraeus."

32. Sam Stein, "Condoleezza Rice Opens Door On Run For Office: 'You Never Know'," *Huffington Post* 2010, http://www.huffingtonpost.com/2010/10/14/condoleezza-rice-opens-do_n_762793.html.

33. Joseph Curl, "One president, please, with a side of Rice," *Washington Times* 2011, http://www.washingtontimes.com/news/2011/dec/18/curl-one-president-please-with-a-side-of-rice/?page=all#pagebreak.

34. Neither party has nominated a candidate with facial hair since Thomas Dewey carried the Republican banner in 1948. And lost.

35. Lloyd Grove, "John Bolton for President in 2012?," *The Daily Beast* 2011, "http://www.thedailybeast.com/articles/2011/01/04/john-bolton-interview-former-ambassador-mulls-presidential-run.html".

36. Juana Summer, "John Bolton won't run for president," *Politico* 2011, "http://www.politico.com/news/stories/0911/62783.html".

37. David F. Damore, Thomas G. Hansford and A.J. Barghothi, "Explaining the Decision to Withdraw from a U.S. Presidential Nomination Campaign," *Political Behavior* 32, no. 1 (June 2010): 157-180.

38. Stephen Loebe, "Donald Trump's Run For President Is Real And The Media Should Take It Seriously," *Business Insider* 2011, http://articles.businessinsider.com/2011-04-05/entertainment/29968537_1_donald-trump-unforeseen-circumstances-celebrity-apprentice#ixzz1rGydC8cj.

39. Ashleigh Banfield, Rich McHugh, and Suzan Clarke, "Donald Trump Would Spend $600 Million of His Own Money On Presidential Bid," *ABC News* 2011, http://abcnews.go.com/Politics/donald-trump-president-trump-weighs-sheen-palin-obama/story?id=13154163.

40. Susan Page, "Poll: What kind of president would Donald Trump make?," *USA Today* 2011, http://www.usatoday.com/news/politics/2011-04-25-trump-president-poll.htm.

41. Brian Montopoli, "Donald Trump not running for president," *CBS News* 2011, http://www.cbsnews.com/8301-503544_162-20063266-503544.html.

42. Stephen F. Hayes, "Ryan for President?," *The Weekly Standard* 2011, http://www.weeklystandard.com/blogs/ryan-president_590273.html.

43. David M. Drucker, "Paul Ryan Talked to Boehner About White House Bid," *Roll Call* 2011, http://www.rollcall.com/news/source_paul_ryan_talked_to_boehner_about_white_house_bid-208196-1.html.

44. Statewide elections in Louisiana compete in a nonpartisan blanket primary that includes all candidates. If a candidate wins more than 50 percent of the vote, he or she is elected to office; if not, the top two vote-getters compete in a runoff election.

45. Sam Stein, "Bobby Jindal Response Panned By Pundits, Republicans And Democrats Alike," *Huffington Post* 2009, http://www.huffingtonpost.com/2009/02/25/bobby-jindal-response-pan_n_169710.html.

46. Debbie Elliott, "Oil Spill Crisis Puts Jindal Back On Center Stage," *NPR* 2010, http://www.npr.org/templates/story/story.php?storyId=128200820.

47. Crist had effectively withdrawn from the Republican primary as Rubio's lead grew, but had remained in the race for the seat, running as an Independent. In the general election, Rubio won 49 percent of the vote to Crist's 30 percent, with the remaining 20 percent going to Democrat Kendrick Meek.

48. Jon Ward, "Mike Huckabee Not Running For President In 2012," *Huffington Post* 2011, http://www.huffingtonpost.com/2011/05/14/mike-huckabee-president-2012-announcement_n_862068.html.

49. "Mike Huckabee gives Glimpse into Why His Heart said No," *I Like Mike Huckabee* blog 2012, http://ilikemikehuckabee2012.blogspot.com/2012/01/mike-huckabee-gives-glimpse-into-why.html

50. Susan Page, "Poll: What kind of president would Donald Trump make?," *USA Today* 2011, "http://www.usatoday.com/news/politics/2011-04-25-trump-president-poll.htm".

51. "Sarah Palin Will Not Run for President," *ABC News* 2011, http://abcnews.go.com/blogs/politics/2011/10/105741/.

52. Mark Guarino, "Mitch Daniels State of the Union rebuttal makes GOP wonder: 'What if?'," *Christian Science Monitor* 2012, http://www.csmonitor.com/USA/Politics/2012/0125/Mitch-Daniels-State-of-the-Union-rebuttal-makes-GOP-wonder-What-if.

53. "Mitch Daniels Will Not Seek GOP Nomination," *Fox News* 2011, http://www.foxnews.com/politics/2011/05/22/mitch-daniels-seek-gop-nomination/.

54. Rachel Weiner, "Mitch Daniels's wife, Cheri, is in the spotlight," *Washington Post* 2011, http://www.washingtonpost.com/politics/mitch-danielss-wife-cheri-is-in-the-spotlight/2011/05/12/AFCi0c1G_story.html

55. Maggie Haberman and Jennifer Epstein, "Mitch Daniels won't run in 2012," *Politico* 2011, http://www.politico.com/news/stories/0511/55424.html.

56. Eugene Robinson, "Chris Christie's big problem," *Washington Post* 2011, http://www.washingtonpost.com/opinions/chris-christies-big-problem/2011/09/29/gIQAAL7J8K_story.html.

57. "An impressive resume," *Star-Ledger* 2008, http://blog.nj.com/njv_editorial_page/2008/11/an_impressive_resume.html.

58. Brian Montopoli, "Could Chris Christie win the Republican nomination?," *CBS News* 2011, http://www.cbsnews.com/8301-503544_162-20112283-503544.html.

59. Jonathan Karl, "Chris Christie Not Running for President," *ABC News* 2011, http://news.yahoo.com/chris-christie-not-running-president-143335342.html.

60. Montopoli, "Could Chris Christie."

61. Such candidates were not always successful. The most recent dark horse was John Davis, Democratic nominee for president in 1924. It took party delegates over 100 ballots to decide on a nominee. Their eventual choice, WV congressman Davis, won only 29 percent of the popular vote, losing to incumbent Calvin Coolidge that fall.

62. Rachel Rose Hartman, "Contested convention is Gingrich's last hope," *Yahoo* 2012, http://news.yahoo.com/blogs/ticket/contested-convention-gingrich-last-hope-162331829.html.

63. Mark Preston and Peter Hamby, "5 things we learned from Super Tuesday," *CNN* 2012, http://www.cnn.com/2012/03/07/politics/5-things-we-learned-from-super-tuesday/index.html?hpt=hp_t1.

64. Including the new delegate allocation rules that could have prevented Romney from securing a clear majority of delegates.

FOUR

The Curious Candidacy of Jon Huntsman

David F. Damore and Kenneth J. Retzl

While the 2012 Republican presidential nomination campaign featured a number of candidates and potential candidates with dubious qualifications and outsized personalities, perhaps the most curious candidate of all was Jon Huntsman. No candidate or near candidate seemed more out of step with the Republican Party circa 2012 than the former Utah Governor and Ambassador to China. On a host of issues ranging from evolution to global warming to gay rights, Huntsman's positions were antithetical to the party's ascendant conservative wing leading *New York Times*' columnist Frank Bruni to characterize Huntsman as "the brother from another Republican planet."[1]

Huntsman's candidacy was further complicated by the inevitable comparisons to the 2012 Republican frontrunner, Mitt Romney. Both Huntsman and Romney share the same faith (Mormonism), both are the sons of well-known, successful business executives who served in the Nixon administration, and both had records of moderation during their governorships. Yet, unlike Romney, Huntsman was unwilling to recalibrate his rhetoric or disavow his prior positions in hopes of appealing to the Republican base—a necessary, and at times uncomfortable, dance for any candidate seeking to negotiate the GOP fault lines that had only grown larger with the rise of the Tea Party in 2010. As a consequence, many political pundits and observers wondered if Huntsman was either 30 years behind his party or four years ahead of it. In this regard, Huntsman's 2012 bid had many of the hallmarks of a candidacy designed to raise his profile for a future presidential run.

In what follows, we develop these themes in more detail as we investigate Jon Huntsman's candidacy for the 2012 Republican presidential nomination. Specifically, we begin by discussing Huntsman's background and the long shadow cast by his father Jon Huntsman Sr. Next, we examine Huntsman's tenure as the Governor of Utah and Ambassador to China to examine his penchant for breaking with Republican orthodoxy on a number of issues. In the chapter's third section, we offer an overview of Huntsman's campaign messaging, fundraising, and strategy to focus on the New Hampshire primary. We conclude by analyzing Huntsman's decision to exit the race after the New Hampshire primary and assessing what the failure of Huntsman's candidacy means for the trajectory of the Republican Party.

IN THE SHADOW OF A GIANT

Born in northern California on March 26, 1960, Jon Meade Huntsman Jr. is the oldest of Jon and Karen Huntsman's nine children. When Jon Huntsman Jr. was born his father was serving in the United States Navy. Soon after, Jon Huntsman Sr. left the military and took a job as the Vice President of operations for Olson Egg Farms in Los Angeles where his primary responsibility was developing better packaging to transport eggs. Utilizing the knowledge he acquired at Olson Egg Farms, Huntsman Sr. founded the Huntsman Container Corporation in 1970. This company was best known for supplying the containers for McDonald's Big Mac sandwiches. After selling the Huntsman Container Corporation to Keyes Fiber Company in 1976, Huntsman Sr. founded the Huntsman Chemical Corporation (which later became the Huntsman Corporation). In addition to his business successes, which by 2010 resulted in the senior Huntsman being the 937th wealthiest person in the world with a net worth of $1 billion,[2] Huntsman Sr. has been active in Republican Party politics. Most notably, the elder Huntsman served in the Department of Health, Education and Welfare and then as the Staff Secretary and Special Assistant to the President under President Richard Nixon.

Because of his father's business and political pursuits, the junior Huntsman's childhood was one of frequent relocations. After living in California, the family moved to Maryland while his father worked in the Nixon Administration. Eventually the family settled in Salt Lake City, where Huntsman Jr. attended high school. It was here that Huntsman Jr. first demonstrated a willingness to deviate from expectations as he dropped out of high school to play keyboard in his band "Wizard." After a quick change of heart, Huntsman earned his G.E.D. and enrolled at the University of Utah in 1978. While in high school, Huntsman met Mary Kaye Cooper whom he would wed at the age of 23. Eventually, Jon and

Mary Kaye would become parents to seven children including two children who were adopted from China and India.

Just as Huntsman Jr. had interrupted his high school career to pursue his interest in music, his college career was interrupted in 1979 to fulfill his commitment to the Church of Jesus Christ of Latter-day Saints via a two-year mission to Taiwan. In Taiwan Huntsman would learn the language skills that would help him to advance his subsequent diplomatic career in the administrations of Presidents George H.W. Bush and Barack Obama. Upon returning from his mission, Huntsman continued his education at the University of Utah but again his studies were interrupted when he left college to work as an intern for Senator Orrin Hatch and then as a staff assistant to President Ronald Reagan.

Although Huntsman completed his mission and grew up in the church, his devotion to Mormonism is an open question. Huntsman had added to this uncertainty by, for instance, answering an interviewer's question if he was a member of the church by responding, "[t]hat's tough to define" and then asserting that "I'm a very spiritual person and proud of my Mormon roots."[3] Elsewhere, Huntsman suggested that "I can't say I'm overly religious" and "I get satisfaction from many different types of religions and philosophies."[4] At the same time, the Huntsman family, much like the Romneys, has long standing ties to the Mormon Church. Huntsman's grandfather was a church apostle and Jon Huntsman Sr. is a prominent Mormon lay leader. Still, during the 2008 Republican presidential nomination campaign while Utah and Mormon political leaders overwhelmingly supported Mitt Romney, Huntsman Jr. did not. Instead, he backed John McCain for whom he bundled $500,000 in campaign contributions.[5]

As a consequence of his early forays into politics, Huntsman did not complete his undergraduate education until 1987 when he earned a degree in International Relations from the University of Pennsylvania. Throughout the 1980s and 1990s, Huntsman alternated between various government positions and working in his family's businesses (e.g., the Huntsman Chemical Corporation and the Huntsman Family Holdings Corporation) and philanthropic (e.g., Huntsman Cancer Foundation) enterprises. Most notably, between 1983 and 1988, he worked at the Huntsman Chemical Corporation where he helped to take the company global. As part of this expansion, Huntsman and his family resided briefly in Taiwan. Huntsman also worked in the family business from 1993 to 2001 in the position of the vice-chairman of the board.

Eased by his family's connections and his father's history of donating to various Republican candidates, committees, and causes, Huntsman secured a series of diplomatic and trade positions in between his stints in the family companies. In 1989 he was named the Deputy Assistant Secretary for the Trade Development Bureau of the Commerce Department and in 1990 he was appointed the Deputy Assistant Secretary of Commerce for East Asia and the Pacific. From 1992 to 1993 Huntsman served as the United States Ambassador to Singapore; the youngest person to lead a diplomatic mission in a century. During George W. Bush's first term, Huntsman was Deputy U.S. Trade Representative. Huntsman would, however, leave this position in 2003 to return to Utah and explore a gubernatorial run.

A RINO IN THE MAKING?

Aided by his family's deep pockets and high levels of name recognition, Huntsman was easily elected governor in 2004 with the support of 58 percent of the Utah electorate. In 2008, he was reelected with better than three-quarters of the vote. Because Utah is as close to a one party state as there is, Huntsman faced little Democratic opposition in pushing his legislative agenda. As a consequence, he accrued an impressive record of policy accomplishments during his tenure including recognition for overseeing the best managed state by the Pew Center on the States. [6]

Central to Huntsman's policy successes were tax cuts and simplifications to Utah's tax code that sought to improve the state's business climate. The perceived success of these policies was aided by the fact that Huntsman, like many governors who served during the boom years of the prior decade, held office during a period of tremendous job growth. Huntsman also signed into law the Parent Choice in Education Act that offered vouchers to help offset the costs for parents who wanted to send their children to private school and he signed a number of bills restricting access to abortion. In 2008, Huntsman successfully proposed a tax credit for families to purchase health insurance in the open market, a notable contrast to the government run program instituted by then Massachusetts Governor Mitt Romney.

While much of Huntsman's gubernatorial record was in-line with his party's economic priorities, some of his other initiatives ran counter to prevailing Republican doctrine. For instance, Huntsman drew the ire of the libertarian Cato Institute for his willingness to increase government spending. Huntsman also drew criticism for supporting the Western Climate Initiative, a memorandum of understanding among western governors that sought to establish a framework for limiting greenhouse gases across the region. Central to the pact was a regional cap-and-trade agreement whereby limits were set on emissions emanating from specific jurisdictions. If companies exceeded these limits, they were required to purchase credits to offset their industrial pollutants.

Like many governors at the time, Huntsman also used the 2009 Recovery Act (e.g., the stimulus) to promote a number of Utah specific projects. Although Huntsman couched his support in terms of job creation, Chris Chocola, a Republican former member of Congress from Indiana, criticized Huntsman's acceptance of federal funds by noting that "he [Huntsman] took the money and didn't even kind of pretend he didn't want it. Regardless of what the stimulus was made up of, thinking you need more of it from the government is not exactly a limited government view."[7] Huntsman responded by contending that while he took stimulus funding, he wished it was administered with more of a focus on businesses and infrastructure. He also noted that all governors, even those who vehemently criticized the legislation, took stimulus funding.[8]

In addition to breaking with GOP views on climate change and the stimulus, Huntsman's stance on civil unions was at odds with the social conservative wing of the Republican Party. Although he endorsed a constitutional amendment to ban same-sex marriage in 2004 while campaigning for the governorship, Huntsman supported a 2009 initiative to recognize civil unions in Utah.[9] His support for the initiative ran counter to citizen sentiment as indicated by a *Salt Lake Tribune* poll suggesting that 70 percent of Utahans opposed civil unions.[10] In speaking to ABC News' George Stephanopoulos, Huntsman stated, "I think, in the case of civil unions, I think it's a fairness issue. I believe in traditional marriage. But subordinate to that, I think we probably can do a better job when it comes to fairness and equality."[11] Huntsman continued to support civil unions during his campaign for the 2012 Republican presidential nomination, stating as much when asked at a campaign stop in South Carolina.[12]

Huntsman also made national headlines in 2009 for his rebuke of the GOP's congressional leadership. In his remarks, he noted that he does not read or listen to commentary from his party's leadership in Washington, which he deemed "inconsequential." And while many in his party criticized Democratic spending initiatives, Huntsman was quick to note that the Republican "moral soapbox was completely taken away from us because of our behavior in the last few years. For us to now criticize analogous behavior is hypocrisy."[13]

Huntsman's decision to not just break from some of his party's core policy principles, but to openly call out Republican duplicity left many of his supporters in Utah scratching their heads. For instance, Huntsman's then 2004 campaign manager and now U.S. House member Jason Chaffetz, noted that candidate Huntsman presented himself to voters far more conservatively than he would actually govern.[14] This disjuncture caused many to speculate that Huntsman was using his record as governor to lay the groundwork for a future bid for national office. Huntsman's decision in August of 2009, less than a year into his second term, to resign his governorship to serve as the Ambassador to China under Democratic President Barack Obama provided additional fodder for such conjecture.[15]

CANDIDATE HUNTSMAN

Huntsman's stay in China was short-lived. In early 2011, Huntsman notified the Obama administration that he would be resigning his ambassadorship, a decision that set off immediate speculation that Huntsman was preparing to run for president in 2012. Perhaps weary of facing a moderate Republican with strong record of job growth as governor and more experience on the international stage than all of the other GOP candidates and potential candidates combined, President Obama used the opportunity of Huntsman's resignation to sow further doubts about his former ambassador's conservatism by stating, "I couldn't be happier with the ambassador's service, and I'm sure he will be very successful in whatever endeavors he chooses in the future. And I'm sure that him having worked so well for me will be a great asset in any Republican primary."[16]

After establishing an exploratory committee in May of 2011, Huntsman officially announced his candidacy for the 2012 Republican presidential nomination in a June 21st speech staged at Liberty State Park, New Jersey—the same location where Ronald Reagan had kicked off his presidential candidacy in 1980. With the Statue of Liberty and Ellis Island in the background, Huntsman used his announcement speech to frame his campaign's themes of fiscal conservatism, foreign policy moderation, and the need to restore civility and trust in politics. Unfortunately for Huntsman, the campaign's roll-out was marred by the distribution of press passes that misspelled the candidate's name ("John Huntsman for President") and early campaign spots that were parodied by his rivals.

By pressing the notion that "Americans are suffering from a deficit of trust,"[17] Huntsman's campaign had echoes of John McCain's 2000 candidacy. Perhaps not coincidentally two of Huntsman's top advisors were longtime McCain campaign hands John Weaver and Fred Davis. According to Huntsman, the erosion of citizen confidence was not only found in the economy, but also in the government. To boost citizen trust, Huntsman, like many would be reformers before him, advocated a number of measures that played to popular disdain towards the process of politics.[18] For instance, he supported a constitutional amendment to limit representatives to six two-year terms and senators to two six-year terms[19] and restrictions that would prohibit former members of Congress and cabinet members from lobbying their former government employers for four years after they leave office and would prohibit in perpetuity former members of Congress and cabinet members from lobbying on issues over which they had significant responsibility.[20]

To restore trust in the financial system, Huntsman proposed significant regulatory reform to the banking and financial sector. Most prominently, he wanted to limit "too-big-to-fail" banks by setting a cap on bank size based on assets as a percentage of gross domestic product (GDP), set a similar cap to limit a bank's total borrowing capacity, and impose a fee for those banks that exceed the authorized bank size or leverage cap to cover any future bailouts.[21] At the same time, Huntsman called for the repeal of the Dodd-Frank Act, a regulatory overhaul that was passed in response to the bank bailouts in 2008. In Huntsman's view, Dodd-Frank, which aimed to reduce the government's dependence on big banks, as well as to avoid future bail-outs, was an inappropriate response to the crisis. In an opinion piece in the *Wall Street Journal*, Huntsman wrote that Dodd-Frank was a failure because three years after the crisis the country's major financial institutions were larger than they ever were and continued to pose a threat to the nation's economic well-being.[22]

As he had done as governor, Huntsman also proposed simplification of the tax code as a means to increase economic growth. Specifically, he supported eliminating all tax deductions and credits and lowering existing individual rates to 8 percent, 14 percent, and 23 percent.[23] He also supported the elimination of the alternative minimum tax, as well as taxes on capital gains and dividends.[24] Like many Republicans, Huntsman argued that because the United States has the second highest corporate tax rate in the world American companies were increasingly uncompetitive in the global economy.[25] To level the playing field, Huntsman proposed lowering the corporate tax rate from 35 percent to 25 percent. Huntsman's plan was applauded by small business owners for reducing their tax rates, but the plan was likely to raise taxes on multinational corporations that utilize tax loopholes to pay effective tax rates much less than the current 35 percent rate.[26]

On the spending side, Huntsman, like virtually every other presidential candidate of either party, vowed to cut wasteful federal expenditures "in every corner of the government, leaving no sacred cow untouched."[27] The reductions Huntsman directly targeted were subsidies to agricultural and energy programs, as well as many entitlement programs that rely on too few workers to support a growing number of retirees. And while Huntsman would not commit to cuts in military spending, he claimed that "being the best will not simply be a function of spending the most"[28] and that the military must adapt to twenty-first century security concerns.

Following a long, protracted conflict in Afghanistan, Huntsman believed it was time to return American troops home. Specifically, he called for a continued intelligence presence in Afghanistan, as well as a small cadre of Special Forces to carry out counter-terrorism measures. Huntsman also viewed Pakistan as an on-going threat to both the Afghani government and the United States. To this end, he proposed tying American aid to Pakistan's efforts to fight terrorism.[29] In this regard, Huntsman's foreign policy prescriptions largely followed those of President Obama and stood in contrast to the hawkish campaign rhetoric of Mitt Romney.

In relation to another form of security, energy security, Huntsman campaigned on the well-worn theme of reducing America's dependency on foreign oil. To do this, he proposed cutting subsidies and regulations that support foreign oil companies and that hinder the development of domestic alternatives. To boost energy production in the United States, Huntsman favored increased exploration and drilling in the Gulf of Mexico and off of the coast of Alaska and the extraction of shale oil and gas.[30] According to Huntsman finding alternatives to foreign oil would not be difficult, as "the nation is drowning in competitive energy supplies from domestic sources."[31] In addition to increasing the production of domestic energy, Huntsman believed his energy policy would create jobs for Americans.

In sum, while Huntsman had developed a reputation of breaking with his party, many of the policy positions underlying his presidential bid drew on traditional Republican themes (i.e., energy exploration, and tax reform) mixed with a helping of populism (i.e., cutting government waste and reforming governmental processes). Where Huntsman did diverge with some of his more conservative competitors was in advocating for regulation of Wall Street and embracing a more internationalist and moderate vision of foreign policy; a world-view that had fallen out of favor among Republicans during George W. Bush's administration. Not surprisingly, many of the issues that had caused some in his party to question his conservatism (e.g., gay rights, evolution, and climate change) got little attention by candidate Huntsman.

Unfortunately for Huntsman, his policy proposals largely fell on deaf ears as his campaign struggled to raise the requisite campaign funds needed to finance a national campaign operation. Fundraising problems began almost immediately. By October of 2011, Huntsman's campaign had expended over $4 million, roughly the same amount of money that his campaign had raised.[32] By the time that Huntsman withdrew from the race, his campaign carried nearly $5.5 million in debt; of that, $2.6 million was owed to Huntsman himself who had used his own money to keep his campaign afloat.[33] Data from the Center for Responsive Politics website (OpenSecrets.org) indicate that Huntsman raised $7.8 million, less than 10 percent of the total that eventual nominee Mitt Romney would raise and significantly less than other candidates who made early exits such as Michele Bachmann ($10.3 million), Herman Cain ($16.3 million), and Rick Perry ($19.8 million).[34]

The cause of Huntsman's lackluster fundraising stemmed from his inability to develop a broad base of small donors to whom he could return to over the course of the campaign. Specifically, only 6 percent of Huntsman's total fundraising came from donations of $200 or less; the second lowest total (Perry = 5 percent) among the GOP candidates. Instead, Huntsman relied heavily on large contributions from a small pool of donors as 30 percent of the 2,267 donors who contributed more than $200 to the Huntsman campaign gave the maximum.

Huntsman's failure to develop the fundraising network needed to sustain a nomination campaign made it difficult for his campaign to expand his name recognition and attract voter support. A Pew Research Center survey completed at the end of May 2011, reported that only 35 percent of the GOP voters sampled had heard of Huntsman.[35] More troubling, no national poll conducted between the summer of 2011 through the time that Huntsman dropped out of the race in the middle of January indicated support for Huntsman that exceeded the poll's margin of error. In most instances, Huntsman polled between one and four percent among national samples of likely Republican primary voters.[36] Perhaps the ultimate indicator that 2012 was not going to be Huntsman's year was a poll of South Carolina Republican primary voters commissioned by Public Policy Polling that placed Huntsman behind non-candidate and Comedy Central mock-pundit Stephen Colbert.[37] As a consequence, it was not uncommon at early campaign stops for members of the press corps to outnumber voters, sometimes by great numbers.[38] There were even reports of voters who came to Huntsman rallies to catch a glimpse of their favorite national news correspondent.[39]

Huntsman's struggles with donors and voters, however, stood in marked contrast to the positive media coverage that he received from the national media throughout the summer and fall of 2011. Most notably, in June Huntsman was the subject of an extensive profile in *The New York Times Magazine* and in July he was the focus of a *Weekly Standard* story entitled "The Rethinking Man's Candidate." More generally, analysis conducted by the *Pew Research Center's Project for Excellence in Journalism* suggests that throughout the summer and fall of 2011 Huntsman's coverage tended to be significantly more positive than negative. However, after the roll-out of his campaign in June, except for the week that he withdrew, Huntsman's share of the total coverage of the campaign exceeded 10 percent in just one week.[40]

Still, conservatives, such as Rich Noyes, the research director of the Media Research Center, argued that the divergence between Huntsman's media profile and his poor polling numbers stemmed from media bias. In a *Politico* story, Noyes asserted that Huntsman "represents what I think a lot of liberals think is a better perspective than conservatives. They [the mainstream media] are trying to find a candidate that they can tolerate more than the others."[41] Others suggested that Huntsman's positive coverage reflected the media's tendency to latch on to candidates with little prospects of winning but who are perceived as willing to go against the grain. Or as Noyes put it, "Every campaign, they [the mainstream media] adopt one of these candidates who can't win but they like, and give a little extra boost, partly because they know it doesn't matter. It was bias they could indulge in without messing everything up."[42]

Some of the limitations of Huntsman's cash-strapped campaign were offset by the efforts of a Super PAC, Our Destiny PAC, which was organized independently of his campaign to promote his candidacy. In particular, Our Destiny PAC bought airtime to run pro-Huntsman campaign spots in the crucial early primary state of New Hampshire.[43] The fact that Huntsman had a Super PAC was not all that surprising given that many of the 2012 GOP candidates had outside groups working on their behalves. What distinguished Huntsman's Super PAC from those of the other candidates was the source of much of Our Destiny PAC's funding. Specifically, Federal Election Commission records indicate that during the final quarter of 2011 Our Destiny PAC received $2,680,560 in contributions. Of that amount, Jon Huntsman Sr. contributed $1,887,040 (or approximately 70 percent).[44]

Once again, the long shadow of Jon Huntsman Sr. hung over another of his son's endeavors.[45] Indeed, the large contributions of his father to Our Destiny PAC coupled with Huntsman's limited fundraising prowess raised a new round of questions about Huntsman's independence from his father. To this end, an MSNBC.com article detailing the contributions of Huntsman Sr. to Our Destiny PAC was entitled "Sugar Daddy: Huntsman's Father Gave $1.9 Million to Super PAC."[46] Huntsman sought to sidestep the issue by taking cover behind the legal fig-leaf that prohibited outside groups from coordinating with a campaign. In a CNN interview in November he responded to a query about his father's support for Our Destiny PAC by offering that "[H]e can do whatever he wants to do. We don't talk about those things; we can't. I'm just delighted that we've actually got some outside assistance from wherever it might come from that believes in our cause."[47]

The reality was that because of weak fundraising, Huntsman needed Our Destiny PAC to sustain his campaign. The first ad run by Our Destiny PAC sought to increase Huntsman's name recognition. In it, citizens discussed the problems facing America and one commented "No one has shown up we can trust as a conservative." The commercial then highlighted the achievements of Jon Huntsman, and concluded by asking, "Why haven't we heard of this guy?"[48] Subsequent spots produced by Our Destiny PAC attempted to contrast Huntsman's record of consistent conservatism to Mitt Romney, whom the group labeled a "chameleon."

While Our Destiny PAC relied on traditional forms of campaigning to raise Huntsman's profiles, Huntsman's daughters utilized social media to promote their father's candidacy. Huntsman's three oldest daughters, Mary Anne, Liddy, and Abby, branded themselves the Jon2012Girls and posted regular Twitter updates and YouTube videos to connect with younger voters and generate media buzz. Perhaps their effort that received the most attention was a YouTube video that parodied Justin Timberlake's song "Sexy Back." Their version ("Huntsman's Back") utilized sound bites from the other Republican candidates to highlight why their father was a better candidate.[49] In another YouTube video, the Jon2012Girls parodied a Herman Cain ad that featured his mustached chief-of-staff asking viewers to support his candidate while taking a long drag on a cigarette. In the parodied version, the Jon2012Girls wore taped on mustaches and highlighted Huntsman's governmental service record. In place of the cigarette, the trio ended the video by blowing bubbles toward the camera.[50] To some degree the Jon2012Girls were successful as by early January they had over 23,000 Twitter followers[51] and their "Smoking Ad" and "Huntsman's Back" ads on YouTube had approximately 350,000[52] and 300,000[53] views respectively.

Nonetheless and despite the efforts of three generations of Huntsmans, heading into late 2011 the campaign had failed to gain any traction. As a consequence, Huntsman made the decision to forgo competing in the Iowa caucuses in hopes of a strong showing in New Hampshire. Huntsman's decision to focus exclusively on New Hampshire was based on three factors. First, with little money, his campaign did not have the luxury of campaigning in multiple early states. Moreover, New Hampshire's small size and expectation for retail politics was a good match for a campaign that could do little more than hold town hall meetings and canvass door-to-door. Second, given the outsized role that social conservatives play in the Iowa GOP caucuses, it was unlikely that Huntsman and his reputation for moderation would have much resonance in an environment where abortion and gay marriage were emerging as key issues. Third, because New Hampshire allowed unaffiliated voters to participate in the state's primary, the state's electorate provided the best chance for a Huntsman breakthrough as it had for John McCain in 2000.

In hopes of currying favor with New Hampshire's electorate, Huntsman even went so far as to opt out of an October debate in Las Vegas. At the time, Nevada and New Hampshire were feuding over when each state was going to hold its nominating event in light of Florida's decision to move its primary up to the end of January. While Huntsman's decision to ignore the Las Vegas debate was eased by the fact that Romney was poised to dominate the Nevada caucuses, it was unclear why a candidate desperate to increase his name recognition would skip a nationally televised debate. More generally, while some of the second and third tier Republican hopefuls were able to use the campaign's numerous debates to elevate their profiles, Huntsman's cool style got him little attention in the debates and because he posed no threat to any of the other candidates, he remained on the periphery of the action. A rare exception to this was an early January debate in New Hampshire where Huntsman, in an exchange with Romney over China's currency policy, infused Mandarin into his response—a ploy that garnered some media hits, but did little to move the needle for Huntsman.

In the end, Huntsman finished a disappointing third in the New Hampshire primary. Capturing just 17 percent of the vote, he ran more than 20 points behind the winner, Mitt Romney. With no way to spin any plausible measure of success from his New Hampshire performance, Huntsman's only path forward was to cobble together enough money to muddle through subsequent contests in hopes that other candidates would exit the race first and allow him to emerge as the alternative to Romney. Instead of taking this course and plodding on to South Carolina and what surely would have been a poor showing, on January 16th Huntsman dropped out of the battle to take on Obama.

HUNTSMAN 2016?

In the aftermath of Huntsman's departure there was much handwringing among political analysts and pundits—perhaps his biggest supporters—about why Huntsman had fared so poorly. Some suggested that his past breaks with the party and his unwillingness to run to the right created an insurmountable chasm between his candidacy and the base voters who determine nomination campaigns. For others it was his decision to emphasize civility that created doubts about Huntsman's willingness to take the fight to his former boss in November. Some in the Huntsman camp argued that the culprit was a lack of funds as suggested by an anonymous aide's claim that "[i]f he doesn't prevail, it's going to be for lack of resources."[54]

Yet, for each explanation put forth there was ample evidence to the contrary. As compared to Romney, Huntsman did possess a record that was more consistently conservative including on such touchstone issues as abortion and taxes. And while Huntsman may have been hesitant to use tough-talk about Obama to demonstrate his fortitude to the fateful, he was more than willing to engage in uncivil politics towards Romney whom he pilloried with a number of clever metaphors ("pretzel candidate" and "a perfectly lubricated weather vane") playing off of the front-runner's proclivity to flip-flop. The website BuzzFeed even went so far as to catalogue the "Top Eight Jon Huntsman Attacks on Mitt Romney."[55] As for the campaign's perpetual money shortfall, with an estimated net worth between $16 and $70 million, certainly Huntsman could have thrown in more than the $2.6 million that he contributed to his campaign to keep it going. After all, in 2008 Mitt Romney loaned his campaign more than $44 million to stay in the race until the first week of February; just three week longer than Huntsman lasted in 2012.

In the end, perhaps the manner in which Huntsman departed the race was the most telling indicator of what his campaign was actually all about. In this regard, Huntsman acted like the consummate profile-raiser.[56] By using his run in hopes of raising his visibility both nationally and within the Republican Party, Huntsman sought to build political capital that could be used for another presidential run in either 2016 or 2020 (when he would be just 60 years old) or to gain considerations for an appointment in a future administration. Yet, because Huntsman never broke through nationally to command the media attention needed to burnish his standing, he opted to exit before incurring any long-term damage to his reputation. Moreover, clearly, Huntsman behaved like someone who cared about his ties to his party as he immediately endorsed Mitt Romney, something that none of the other early exiting candidates did. Otherwise, why would a candidate who just the week before had railed against Romney's fickleness so quickly get inline unless he valued what party allegiance meant for the realization of his future political pursuits?

But of course what the Republican Party will be and who will be leading it in the near term is, in many ways, the defining, if unspoken, question encompassing the 2012 Republican nomination campaign. Huntsman's poor showing coupled with the difficulty that Mitt Romney had putting away a weak field to secure the nomination despite commanding financial and organizational advantages does not bode well for the party's diminishing ranks of moderates. Yet, Huntsman's record of competent governance, economic conservatism, and social moderation mixed with an acceptance of climate change and evolution has a number of parallels to many of the other names being bandied about as up and coming GOP leaders and likely future presidential candidates such as Governors Chris Christie (New Jersey), Mitch Daniels (Indiana), and Brian Sandoval (Nevada). Indeed, with respect to Huntsman, perhaps the only point that the political class could agree upon is that it is unlikely that 2012 was Jon Huntsman's swan song from politics.

NOTES

1. Frank Bruni, "Embracing the Pretzel," *New York Times*, January 18, 2012.
2. "The World's Billionaires," *Forbes* 2010, http://www.forbes.com/lists/2010/10/billionaires-2010_Jon-Huntsman_FETQ.html (accessed February 20, 2012).
3. Melinda Henneberger, "Jon Huntsman: The Potential Republican Candidate Democrats Most Fear," *Time* 2011, "http://www.time.com/time/magazine/article/0,9171,2071150,00.html#ixzz1uy4thU00" (accessed May 15, 2012).
4. Dan Gilgoff, "Understanding Jon Huntsman's Distinct Brand of Mormonism," *CNN* 2011, http://religion.blogs.cnn.com/2011/06/21/understanding-jon-huntsmans-distinct-brand-of-mormonism/ (accessed April 27, 2012).
5. Michael Beckel, "http://www.opensecrets.org/news/2009/06/obamas-new-ambassador-nominees.html" (accessed April 27, 2012).
6. "Measuring Performance: The State Management Report Card for 2008," *Governing* 2008, http://www.pewcenteronthestates.org/uploadedFiles/Grading-the-States-2008.pdf (accessed March 5, 2012).
7. Jackie Kucinich, "Huntsman's Utah Record Will Face Increased Scrutiny," *USA Today* 2011, http://www.usatoday.com/news/politics/2011-06-20-Huntsman-GOP-presidential-race-Obama-administration_n.htm (accessed February 27, 2012).

8. "Transcript: Exclusive Interview with Jon Huntsman," *ABC News* 2011, http://abcnews.go.com/blogs/ politics/2011/05/exclusive-interview-with-jon-huntsman/ (accessed February 27, 2012).

9. "People in the News: Jon Huntsman," *The Washington Post* 2011, http://www.washingtonpost.com/politics/jon-huntsman/gIQARSRx9O_topic.html (accessed February 27, 2012).

10. Rosemary Winters, "Guv, at Odds with Most Utahans, Backs Civil Unions for Gays," *Salt Lake Tribune* 2009, http://www.sltrib.com/ci_11666928 (accessed February 27, 2012).

11. "Transcript: Exclusive Interview with John Huntsman"

12. Anne Christnovich, "Huntsman Pushes Term Limits, Balanced Budget During Hilton Head Visit," *The Island Packet* 2012, http://www.islandpacket.com/2012/01/14/1928154/huntsman-pushes-term-limits-balanced.html (accessed March 7, 2012).

13. "GOP Governor: Congressional Leadership 'Inconsequential,'" *The Washington Times* 2009, http://www.washingtontimes.com/news/2009/feb/24/utah-governor-ignores-top-gop-legislators/ (accessed February 28, 2012).

14. Kucinich, "Huntsman's Utah Record Will Face Increased Scrutiny."

15. Kucinich, "Huntsman's Utah Record Will Face Increased Scrutiny."

16. Peter Wallsten and Anne E. Kornblut, "Jon Huntsman Leaving Administration Soon," *The Washington Post* 2011, http://www.washingtonpost.com/wp-dyn/content/article/2011/01/31/AR2011013106271.html?sid=ST2011020102680 (accessed February 24, 2011).

17. Huntsman2012HQ, "Restoring Trust," *YouTube Video File*, December 7, 2011, http://www.youtube.com/ watch?v=OfHdg2O4rgw (accessed March 6, 2012).

18. John R. Hibbing and Elizabeth Theiss-Morse, *Stealth Democracy* (Cambridge: Cambridge University Press, 2002).

19. "Jon Huntsman President 2012: Restoring Trust in Government," *Jon Huntsman: President 2012*, http://jon2012.com/trust/plan (accessed February 15-March 6, 2012).

20. "Jon Huntsman President 2012: Restoring Trust in Government."

21. Connor Friedersdorf, "Jon Huntsman's Detailed Plan to End 'Too Big to Fail,'" *The Atlantic* 2011, http://www.theatlantic.com/politics/archive/2011/11/jon-huntsmans-detailed-plan-to-end-too-big-to-fail/249144/ (accessed March 6, 2012).

22. Jon Huntsman, "'Too Big to Fail' Is Simply Too Big," *The Wall Street Journal* 2011, http://online.wsj.com/article/SB10001424052970204346104576635033336992122.html?mod=WSJ_Opinion_LEADTop (accessed March 6, 2012).

23. "Jon Huntsman President 2012: Jobs and the Economy," *Jon Huntsman: President 2012*, http://jon2012.com/ index.php/issues/jobs-economy-tax-reform (accessed February 15-March 6, 2012).

24. Joe Deaux, "Huntsman Outlines Sweeping Tax Reform," *The Street* 2011, http://www.thestreet.com/ story/11235622/1/huntsman-outlines-sweeping-tax-reform.html (accessed March 7, 2012).

25. "Jon Huntsman President 2012: Jobs and the Economy," *Jon Huntsman: President 2012*.

26. Merrill Goozner, "How Huntsman Would Reform Corporate Taxes," *The Fiscal Times* 2011, http://www.thefiscaltimes.com/Articles/2011/09/01/How-Huntsman-Would-Reform-Corporate-Taxes.aspx#page1 (accessed March 7, 2012).

27. "Jon Huntsman President 2012: Restoring Trust," *Jon Huntsman: President 2012*, http://jon2012.com/trust (accessed February 15-March 6, 2012).

28. "Jon Huntsman President 2012: National Security," *Jon Huntsman: President 2012*, http://jon2012.com/ issues/national-security (accessed February 15-March 6, 2012).

29. "Jon Huntsman President 2012: National Security."

30. "Jon Huntsman President 2012: Energy Security," *Jon Huntsman: President 2012*, http://jon2012.com/issues/ energy-security (accessed February 15-March 6, 2012).

31. "Jon Huntsman President 2012: Energy Security."

32. Peter Hamby, "Huntsman Campaign Nearly Broke as GOP Campaign Heats Up," *CNN* 2011, http://politicalticker.blogs.cnn.com/2011/10/14/huntsman-campaign-nearly-broke-as-gop-campaign-heats-up/ (accessed March 7, 2011).

33. Robin Bravender, "Jon Huntsman Campaign Owed $2.6 to Him," *Politico* 2012, http://www.politico.com/news/stories/0212/73090.html, (accessed March 7, 2012).

34. "2012 Presidential Candidate Fundraising Summary," *Center for Responsive Politics*, "http://www.opensecrets.org/pres12/index.php" (accessed May 18, 2012).

35. "Republican Candidates Stir Little Enthusiasm," *Pew Research Center* 2011, http://www.people-press.org/2011/06/02/republican-candidates-stir-little-enthusiasm/ (accessed March 7, 2012).

36. See PollingReport.com (http://www.pollingreport.com/wh12rep.htm).

37. Alexander Abad Santos, "In South Carolina Poll, Stephen Colbert Leads Jon Huntsman," *Atlantic Wire* 2012, http://www.theatlanticwire.com/politics/2012/01/south-carolina-poll-stephen-colbert-leads-jon-hunstman/47215/ (accessed May 16, 2012).

38. Joshua Green, "Huntsman's Paltry Crowds," *The Atlantic* 2011, http://www.theatlantic.com/ politics/archive/2011/06/huntsmans-paltry-crowds/240812/ (accessed March 7, 2012).

39. Matt Bai, "Huntsman Steps Into the Republican Vacuum," *New York Times* 2011, http://www.nytimes.com/2011/06/26/magazine/jon-huntsman-steps-into-the-republican-vacuum.html?pagewanted=all (accessed March 7, 2011).

40. Campaign 2012 in the Media, *Project for Excellence in Journalism* 2012, http://www.journalism.org/commentary_backgrounder/pejs_election_report (accessed May 16, 2012).

41. Keach Hagey, "Rick Perry and Jon Huntsman Prove Media Wrong," *Politico* 2012, http://www.politico.com/news/stories/0112/71694.html (accessed May 16, 2012).

42. Hagey, "Rick Perry and Jon Huntsman."

43. Jim Rutenberg, "Huntsman Campaign Gets Aid from Group Tied to Father," *New York Times* 2011, http://www.nytimes.com/2011/12/04/us/politics/jon-huntsmans-cash-poor-campaign-gets-help-from-father.html?pagewanted=all (accessed February 20, 2012).

44. FEC Form 3x Schedule A – Itemized Receipts: Our Destiny PAC, *Federal Election Commission* 2011, http://query.nictusa.com/cgi-bin/dcdev/forms/C00501098/763217/ (accessed February 20, 2012).

45. . Exactly how willing Jon Huntsman Sr. was to work on behalf of his son's candidacy is unclear. For instance, a *New York Times* story in early January reported that Huntsman's campaign was based on the premise that "he would tap his father's resources and connections to have one of the best-financed operations in the Republican presidential field" and that from "the start, Mr. Huntsman's father was prepared to press his network of high-flying associates — and underlings — into the service of raising money for the campaign." The reason why this did not occur, however, was because of "a stand-off between two headstrong Huntsmans, one unwilling to help greatly if he is not asked, the other unwilling to ask" that was further complicated by the two's differing devotions to the Mormon Church and Huntsman's Jr. desire not to have his election bought for him (see, Jim Rutenberg, "Huntsman, Out of Options, Bets It All on New Hampshire," *New York Times* 2012, http://www.nytimes.com/2012/01/08/us/politics/ready-or-not-huntsman-faces-his-moment-in-new-hampshire.html?pagewanted=all (accessed May 17, 2012).

46. Bill Dedmen and Lisa Riordan Seville, "Sugar Daddy: Huntsman's Father Gave $1.9 Million to Super PAC," *MSNBC* 2012, http://nbcpolitics.msnbc.msn.com/_news/2012/01/31/10280176-sugar-daddy-huntsmans-father-gave-19-million-to-super-pac?lite (accessed May 17, 2012).

47. CNN Political Unit, "Huntsman's Dad Gave Big to His Super Pac," *CNN* 2012, http://politicalticker.blogs.cnn.com/2012/01/31/huntsmans-dad-gave-big-money-to-his-super-pac (accessed may 17, 2012).

48. OurDestinyPAC, "Someone," *YouTube Video File*, November 14, 2011, http://www.youtube.com/watch?v=eWMmPu0OKiU (accessed March 7, 2012).

49. Jon2012Girls, "Huntsman's Back," *YouTube Video File*, November 30, 2011, http://www.youtube.com/watch?v=h94iTnGQ0oI&context=C31754f6ADOEgsToPDskKvHpPk_bI289rMAIQG6005 (accessed February 28, 2012).

50. Jon2012Girls, "Jon2012Girls Smoking Ad," *YouTube Video File*, October 28, 2011, http://www.youtube.com/watch?v=iOYVB2hc0HA&feature=related (accessed February 28, 2012).

51. Emily Steel, "Obama Tweeted More Often Yesterday than any of the Republican Candidates," *Washington Wire* 2012, http://blogs.wsj.com/washwire/2012/01/11/obama-tweeted-more-often-than-any-of-the-republican-candidates-yesterday/ (accessed February 28, 2012).

52. Jon2012Girls, "Jon2012Girls Smoking Ad."

53. Jon2012Girls, "Huntsman's Back."

54. Rutenberg, "Huntsman, Out of Options, Bets It All on New Hampshire."

55. Andrew Kaczynski, "Top Eight Jon Huntsman Attacks on Mitt Romney," *BuzzFeed* 2012, http://www.buzzfeed.com/andrewkaczynski/top-eight-jon-huntsman-attacks-on-mitt-romney (accessed May 17, 2012

56. See David F. Damore, Thomas G. Hansford and A.J. Barghothi, "http://faculty.unlv.edu/dfdamore/Publications/Explaining%20the%20Decision%20to%20Withdraw%20from%20a%20U.S.%20Presidential%20Nomination%20Campaign.pdf" *Political Behavior* 32, no. 1 (June 2010): 157-180.

FIVE

Early to Rise, Early to Fall: The Short Lived Hope of Michele Bachmann

Jason Rich and Brandy A. Kennedy

At the end of 2010, Republicans likely had high hopes of capturing the White House. Unemployment was still above nine percent nationally, growth in jobs and the economy was modest at best, the president continued to have an approval rating below 50 percent, and the GOP had picked up an impressive 63 seats in the House of Representatives to regain the majority. It seemed all the party needed to do was find the right candidate to ride this momentum to the nomination and then the presidency. This, however, would prove to be a daunting task, as the field became crowded with hopeful candidates. One of the more memorable hopefuls was Congresswoman Michele Bachmann from Minnesota. A Tea Party favorite, fund raising machine, and conservative media stalwart, Bachmann quickly established herself as a potential rival to Mitt Romney. She captured the positions early of fiscal hawk and anti-"Obamacare," which helped propel her to an Iowa Straw Poll victory in August. Although Bachmann would eventually fade as a credible and serious candidate, her campaign ultimately helped shift the entire GOP nomination process farther to the right and made the repeal of health care reform a central issue for any Republican nominee.

CANDIDATE BACKGROUND

Michele Amble (Bachmann) was born in Waterloo, Iowa in 1956. After her parents divorced, she moved with her mother and siblings to Anoka, Minnesota where she later graduated high school. She went on to attend

Winona State University where she met her husband, Marcus Bachmann and graduated in 1978. Bachmann earned a J.D. in 1986 from the O.W. Coburn School of Law at Oral Roberts University and an L.L.M. in Tax Law at the College of William and Mary in 1988.[1] Before pursuing a political career, Bachmann was a tax litigation attorney.

While Bachmann is well known for her strong conservative views, in college she was a registered Democrat and worked on Jimmy Carter's campaign. It was during this campaign that Bachmann initially became dissatisfied with the Democratic Party, based on what she perceived to be a lack of family values. Shortly after working on the Carter campaign, she changed her political affiliation to Republican.[2] Bachmann has held political office since 2000, serving in the Minnesota State Senate from 2000-2006 and the U.S. House of Representatives from 2006-present.

In 1999, Bachmann entered her first campaign, running for a seat on the local school board. Her campaign was controversial and garnered more attention than the average school board race, characteristics emblematic of later campaigns. While school board races are traditionally nonpartisan, in an unprecedented event, the Republican Party endorsed five candidates, including Bachmann, based on their vocal opposition to recently enacted state education policy. The party's unusual involvement in the race was criticized.[3] While Bachmann and the other four endorsed candidates ultimately lost the election, this first campaign set the stage for future races.[4]

Her next campaign was for Minnesota State Senate District 56 in 2000. Running in part on her continued opposition to the controversial Profile of Learning education initiative, Bachmann won a remarkable and unexpected primary victory against 28-year incumbent Gary Laidig.[5] Her primary campaign was immediately energized when the Republican Party endorsed her at their convention, snubbing the incumbent. While Bachmann ran a strong campaign that was well-financed, and well-organized with grass roots support and the backing of key interest groups, her selection as the party nominee was far from certain. The party's convention endorsement created a divide between the state Republican Party and the State Senate's more moderate Republican Caucus. The state party favored Bachmann's strong conservatism, and she used this to her advantage, accusing the incumbent of maintaining a liberal voting record.[6] Her strong conservative positions on key issues such as government spending, taxes, and abortion helped her to win favor with the state party, but members of the caucus and fellow Senators worried that her strong positions would be an obstacle toward winning over independents and ultimately succeeding in the general election.[7]

Despite the conflict with the Senate Caucus, Bachmann went on to defeat Laidig in a stunning primary victory, taking 60 percent to Laidig's 39.9 percent.[8] After securing the primary nomination, she entered into a three-way race with Democrat Ted Thompson and Lyno Sullivan of the

Independence Party. While District 56 is decidedly conservative, obstacles remained toward securing the general election victory. Her opponents quickly criticized Bachmann, accusing her of representing views on the "extreme right." Supporters of defeated incumbent Laidig crossed party lines to support Thompson.[9] Despite opposition, Bachmann won the seat with 51.5 percent of the vote compared to Thompson's 42.5 and Sullivan's 5.5 percent.[10]

As a state Senator, Bachmann was a strong and vocal advocate for conservative positions on social issues. Her social conservatism united supporters but also galvanized opponents.[11] To some extent, Bachmann was a polarizing figure even within the Republican Party, dividing moderates and strong conservatives in the party. The defeat of Republican Matt Dean is an interesting illustration of this divide. In 2003, Dean ran against Rebecca Otto for House District 52B. Bachmann endorsed Dean, which led some Republicans to cross party lines, giving their support to Otto . When asked about his endorsement of Otto, Yale Norwick, Mayor of Mahtomedi, was quoted as saying that the Republican Party in the district had been "hijacked . . . by an extremist element."[12] Norwick went on to say, "Matt Dean currently represents that extreme element . . . Matt may be a nice fellow, but does he represent himself and the views of 52B or is he the hand-picked puppet of extremist Sen. Michele Bachmann and her ultra-right-wing supporters? There were three mayors who ran in this campaign, but qualifications aren't an issue. It's whether Michele Bachmann anoints you."[13] When Dean lost 54 to 43, some Republicans blamed Dean's defeat on Bachmann's endorsement.

When Representative Mark Kennedy retired from the 6th district seat in the House of Representatives to pursue a Senate seat, Michele Bachmann entered the race for the GOP nomination along with four other Republicans. The Republican candidates avoided a heated primary by agreeing to abide by the endorsement made at the Republican convention.[14] Bachmann decisively won the endorsement with 61 percent against her challengers in the first round of voting. In the second round, the vote was unanimous in support of Bachmann.[15] In the race, she competed against well-known and well-funded Democrat, Patty Wetterling, who had narrowly lost the seat to Kennedy in 2004.

The race was extremely competitive with both candidates bringing in national figures to campaign on their behalf. Nancy Pelosi helped campaign for Wetterling while Karl Rove, Dick Cheney, and Dennis Hastert campaigned and raised money for Bachmann.[16] Even President Bush visited Minnesota during the campaign, raising half a million dollars for Bachmann's campaign in just a few hours.[17] Throughout the campaign, the race was extremely close. As late as mid-October, Wetterling had an edge in the polls.[18] The race was the most expensive on record in Minnesota history, dominated by national party funds on both sides and overwhelmed by negative advertising. Bachmann ultimately won the race 50-42 percent.[19]

Bachmann's 2008 re-election campaign against Democrat Elwin Tinklenberg reflected trends set in earlier races. It was an energetic, expensive race surrounded by controversy and conflict. Early on Bachmann established her footing in the race and became one of the fastest, earliest, and largest fundraisers in the state.[20] Her passion for conservative issues and outspoken nature led her to take the spotlight at the RNC convention in 2008, a somewhat unusual position for such a new face in the party.[21] However, controversy would come to threaten her campaign financially and her political future. During the campaign, Bachmann appeared on *Hardball with Chris Matthews* remarking that then-hopeful Presidential candidate Barack Obama may have "anti-American" views and suggesting members of Congress be investigated for the possibility of holding similar views. In the wake of the controversial remarks, the national Republican Party pulled advertising funding for Bachmann.[22] While polls showed Bachmann and Tinklenberg in a dead heat leading up to the election, she went on to win 47 percent to 43 percent with the Independence party candidate pulling 10 percent.[23]

In some ways, the conflict surrounding Bachmann's 2008 campaign benefitted her re-election race in 2010 where she competed against Democrat Tarryl Clar and Bob Anderson from the Independence Party. Due in part to the notoriety she gained from the controversial remarks made on *Hardball*, she went on to be a national figure and top fundraiser.[24] Additionally, her growing support among Tea Party voters helped propel her campaign forward. In the summer of 2010, she formed the Tea Party Caucus in the House.[25] She campaigned with Sarah Palin, also popular among the Tea Party supporters. The two drew large crowds at rallies and campaign events. While she gained supporters, she also energized the opposition. Her 2010 re-election was extremely contentious, bringing in significant funding from out of state and becoming a national event.[26] The race broke fundraising records in Minnesota. Between April and July, Bachmann raised more money than any other House candidate.[27] In the end, she took her largest margin of victory ever winning the race 52-41 percent.[28]

After winning re-election in 2010, Bachmann went on to be an influential member of the House yet remained a divisive figure. Shortly following re-election, she sought the 4th ranking position in the party—House GOP conference chair. She didn't win the bid, but the pursuit marked the divisions between the mainstream Republican Party and the Tea Party.[29]

ISSUE STANCES

Bachmann holds strong and consistent conservative views across a range of domestic and foreign policy issues. Illustrative of her strong conservatism, the American Conservative Union rated Bachmann 100 percent, putting her in the top "Conservatives in Congress." She, along with one other Senator and thirty-one House members, were named "Defenders of Liberty" for their voting records. Her strong issue positions have arguably helped her win elections by energizing her base supporters. However, these positions have also mobilized opponents and strained relationships with moderates in the Republican Party.

Economic policy played a prominent role in the 2012 Republican primary campaign. Several specific issues gained center stage including the question over raising the debt ceiling and the possibility of a balanced budget amendment. Bachmann was a leader in the movement against raising the debt ceiling in the most recent budget debates making it difficult for party leadership to reach a deal and avoid a government shutdown.[30] While some GOP contenders opposed the specific details of the debt deal, Bachmann took a stronger position, asserting absolute opposition to raising the federal government's borrowing authority under any circumstances.[31] Like many of her GOP counterparts, Bachmann also supports the passage of a balanced budget amendment.

The economic conditions also brought tax policy to the forefront of debate. As a former tax attorney, Bachmann has been outspoken about her position on tax reform including abolishing the current tax code and reducing tax rates on both individuals and corporations. As state Senator, Bachmann attended and spoke at anti-tax rallies,[32] a trend that continued during her tenure in the House of Representatives, joining Tea Party activists in protest of Obama's economic policy.[33]

Another key issue in the 2012 primary campaign was healthcare reform. Bachmann was an active opponent of the Patient Protection and Affordable Care Act. Her support for repealing the health care reform legislation was a centerpiece of her 2010 re-election campaign.[34] Labeling the legislation "the crown jewel of socialism," Bachmann joined other Republicans in the House voting to repeal the healthcare legislation, a bill that passed the House but failed to pass in the Senate.[35] Despite the lack of initial success repealing the healthcare legislation, Bachmann carried her opposition toward the healthcare reform act into the 2012 primary campaign stating in a Republican debate, "As president of the United States, I will not rest until I repeal Obamacare. . . . It's a promise, take it to the bank, cash the check—I'll make sure that that happens."[36]

Bachmann also holds strong conservative positions across a variety of social issues including marriage and abortion. As a state Senator of Minnesota, she fought for a state constitutional amendment prohibiting same-sex marriage.[37] As a member of Congress, she co-sponsored legislation proposing an amendment to the federal constitution to define marriage as the union between a man and woman and supports the continued recognition of the Defense of Marriage Act. She was also critical of the repeal of Don't Ask, Don't Tell and stated that if elected president, she would seek to reinstate the policy.[38]

While not a central topic in the primary, the issue of abortion was highlighted in the campaign due to controversy over continued federal funding of the organization Planned Parenthood. Bachmann pushed to have federal funding cut for the organization due to abortion services provided.[39] This was a key ideological conflict in the debate over raising the debt ceiling and made it difficult to facilitate a budget agreement between Democrats and Republicans.[40]

Controversy over Arizona's new legislation brought immigration to the forefront of the primary campaign. In September 2011, while campaigning in Arizona, Bachmann expressed support for Arizona's immigration laws and opposition to the federal government's pending lawsuit. Bachmann asserted her position that the most important aspect of immigration policy is securing the border.[41] Bachmann affirmed her stance on immigration by signing a pledge by the Americans for Securing the Border advocacy group to complete a fence around the border by 2013.[42]

Relative to domestic issues such as economic policy, foreign policy did not play as prominent a role in the primary campaign. While Bachmann is a member of the House Select Committee on Intelligence,[43] in general, Bachmann's foreign policy stances are less well known.[44] While she was relatively silent on specifics regarding policies in Afghanistan and Iraq,[45] Bachmann was openly critical of U.S. involvement in Libya, arguing that the United States was not attacked and it was not in the U.S. national interest to intervene.[46] Bachmann has also been vocal about the importance of continued U.S. support for Israel.[47]

Finally, energy and environmental issues were also addressed during the campaign. Bachmann expressed support for expanding domestic energy production, arguing this would help job creation.[48] During a debate, she expressed uncertainty that global warming was caused by human activity.[49] She also expressed support for abolishing the Environmental Protection Agency arguing the agency is detrimental to job growth.[50]

PRESIDENTIAL CAMPAIGN

In early 2011, Republicans lacked a consensus on who would be the eventual nominee. Congresswoman Bachmann's desire to run likely came from a perceived need for a Tea Party conservative to enter into the process. There was little doubt about her conservative credentials, having been rated as one of the most conservative members of Congress by the

National Journal and a propensity towards consistent conservative policies.[51] Bachmann was a founding member of the House Tea Party Caucus as well as a mainstay on Fox News, but more importantly she was a consistent voice for fiscal conservatism, opposing the stimulus and increasing the national debt. Mrs. Bachmann's first true attention grabber, however, was with the Tea Party's response to the President's State of the Union address.

In the speech she criticized the fiscal policies of the Obama Administration, citing an "unprecedented explosion of government spending and debt" and called for significant cuts in government. In addition, she highlighted the "job-destroying cap-and-trade system" as well as a need to repeal "'Obamacare' and support free-market solutions."[52] Overall, it was a fairly well regarded response by other Tea Party Republicans; however, it also may have been foreshadowing things to come. Specifically, during the entire speech, she was always looking into the camera of the Tea Party feed rather than that of the CNN feed. This mistake meant she always appeared to be looking off camera and left national TV viewers wondering where or what exactly she was looking at. This was a relatively modest mistake, but one in a long line of gaffes and missteps that would characterize here entire year campaigning. The more significant political misstep might have been Bachmann's defiance of the GOP, never giving a copy of the speech to Republican leadership ahead of time nor did her office let them know that it would be carried live.[53] Although no stranger to upsetting the party establishment, inevitably whomever was going to win the nomination would need that support and this was certainly a questionable way to start accomplishing that. Still, what this speech did do was grab the attention of those who were anti-tax, anti-government, and anti-spending and provided the sense that in one way or another Mrs. Bachmann would be a part of this race.

In early February, Bachmann herself was playing coy, indicating she had not yet made up her mind on running. She certainly sounded like a candidate at the annual CPAC conference, driving home what would be her signature point during the campaign, which was the repeal of health care. Bachman stated, "Obamacare is quite clearly the crown jewel of socialism, and repealing it is the driving motivation of my life. The first political breath I take every morning is to repeal Obamacare."[54] Characterizing the Obama Administration as socialist was a standard line employed by not only Bachmann but other potential Republican candidates as well. Unlike other potential candidates, however, Michele Bachmann had a tendency of perhaps overstepping the accepted norms on criticism.

In 2008, after the Obama Administration passed Wall Street reform, she referred to the president as having "anti-American views" and practicing "gangster government." These comments would reappear during a March appearance on *Meet the Press,* where she would state that she had no regrets about such characterizations and go on to say, "I think that there have been actions that have been taken by this government that I think are corrupt."[55] Language such as this, while popular at Tea Party rallies and among those anti-Obama supporters, likely had an alienating effect on moderates both inside and outside the party.

Yet, even though she was heightening the rhetoric against the president, she was able to find fuel for her fire. The Heritage Foundation, Politifact and Factcheck all confirmed her claims that a $105 billion "slush fund" existed inside of the health care legislation. During an appearance in New Hampshire she proclaimed, "We will not vote for the next continuing resolution until it contains language that would bring back that $105 billion into the treasury." Bachmann went on to say, "And we need to fight over this even if it means temporarily shutting down the non-essential services of government."[56] Of course, what she was referring to was the budget debate going on in Washington. Her words sent a strong message to potential voters on the level of her fiscal conservatism. Unfortunately, the very next day Mrs. Bachmann would follow up such a strong statement with another public gaffe that would capture more of the headlines. While in Manchester, NH, she made the statement, "You're the state where the shot was heard around the world in Lexington and Concord."[57] This was a reference made in regards to needing a revolutionary reform in government but clearly confusing the fact that these events occurred in Massachusetts and not New Hampshire where she was speaking.

By the end of March, Bachmann was beginning to be viewed as a real potential nominee and rumors began to heat up that an exploratory committee was being formed and that her paperwork would be filed sometime in June. Yet, the potential candidate herself remained noncommittal telling ABC News, "I'm in for 2012 in that I want to be a part of the conversation in making sure that President (Barack) Obama only serves one term, not two, because I want to make sure that we get someone who's going to be making the country work again. That's what I'm in for."[58] The pundits began to understand her as a legitimate candidate in April when early fundraising numbers came out and showed Bachmann taking in $2.2 million in the first 3 months of the year.[59] This large fundraising effort was impressive, yet her popularity numbers were not reflective of such efforts, particularly in the early primary state of South Carolina where she was polling at 10 percent[60] and New Hampshire where she was a more dismal 4 percent.[61]

During this same time the budget and debt ceiling debate was hitting a crescendo. At a rally outside of the Capital, Bachmann publically encouraged Republicans to keep up the firm stance and would go on to state on *MSNBC* that she could support no current deal because "it doesn't include the defunding of Obamacare."[62] Thus, she was sticking to her consistent themes of both fiscal conservatism and a repeal or defunding of health care even in the face of a possible default. This was a scary thought for many Americans. University of Minnesota political science professor Larry Jacobs explained, "For Michele Bachmann winning is important, but the policy principles and positions she takes are as important or perhaps even more important. She's a genuine true believer."[63] But that true believer mentality could also be viewed as a significant fault. Certainly when it came to the debt ceiling and budget, holding to principles could be considered heroic, but when faith to a position blinds reason, then it may become a problem. For example, this devotion to principles had created problems during her time in the House. Philip Rucker and Paul Kane for the *Washington Post* called attention to her rather meager record of having introduced over 45 pieces of legislation but most ending in only small symbolic resolutions or no success at all.[64]

Still, Bachmann was seen as defiant voice to the right, both on fiscal matters as well as the issue of health care. Thus, when Mike Huckabee announced in May that he would not be seeking the nomination, this seemed like a perfect opportunity for a Bachmann presidential run as the conservative's choice. Just days after Huckabee's announcement this seemed like it was going to be the case when a Bachmann fundraiser email blast looked to raise funds for a "fight against the liberal agenda of Barack Obama" and then stated in an appearance while in Iowa that she felt a "calling" to run.[65] What may have been the most significant signal of truly starting a campaign was when she hired former Ronald Reagan strategist Ed Rollins at the beginning of June. Rollins, who had also run Mike Huckabee's campaign just a few years earlier, was a recognizable name to many Republicans and no doubt the pending Bachmann campaign was looking to capitalize on his knowledge and experience.

One point that he and others had realized is that there was certainly a place for women in this Republican race and the polling numbers indicated such as well. In a Pew Research Center poll, only 5 percent of Republican men and 12 percent of women said they would be less willing to support a candidate for president who was a woman, which was a number down from over 20 percent in 2007.[66] Of course Bachmann was not the only woman being discussed a presidential contender, there was still the speculation that former Vice Presidential nominee and tea party favorite Sarah Palin might run.

While Bachmann was readying herself for a debate on June 13th, her newly hired strategist was busy attacking Governor Palin. Rollins stated in a radio interview that Palin was no serious candidate, going on to tell *Politico* that voters would "make a choice and go with the intelligent woman who's every bit as attractive."[67] Going a step further on Fox News, Rollins said, "[Palin] got the vice presidential thing handed to her. She didn't go to work in the sense of trying to gain more substance. She gave up her governorship." Clearly, there was a concern internally that there was likely only room for one conservative female in the race and likely one Tea Party candidate for that matter. Although a larger issue was whether she would be viewed as a viable option for not just Tea Party voters but conservatives across the board. Her first true test would come June 13 in the first Republican debate.

There is always a disagreement over who wins any given debate, but one would be hard pressed not to at least recognize that Michele Bachmann stole the show right from the onset of the evening. Bachmann, before even answering her first question, stated "I filed today my paperwork to seek the office of the president of the United States." The remainder of the debate was spent specifically highlighting her positions. She was insistent about her decision to oppose an increase in the federal debt limit and that it was indeed the responsible course of action. In fact, she reminded the audience that these were her principles, such as when she opposed the TARP legislation in 2008. Bachmann also made certain to point out she was the first to offer up legislation that would provide a full repeal of the President's health care policy, a position the others in the race would eventually adopt. Perhaps just as important, she remained measured when discussing social issues. She was even able to discuss in a clear and coherent manner national security, something many believed Bachmann would be weak on even though she had been appointed to the intelligence committee just months earlier. And most importantly she made sure the narrative of the evening also included her background of working as a tax attorney and the mother of 5 biological children and fostering 23 others.

Politico described her as "a nuanced, focused and polished politician rather than the one-dimensional firebrand she's been caricatured as in the past."[68] Even John Boehner, whom Bachmann has had a cool relationship with after her failed attempt at leadership inside the House, stated, "I think she did a really good job last night." Going on to say, "I think she's a bright member of our caucus, and it's one of the reasons I appointed her to the Intelligence Committee."[69] Overall, she exceeded expectations and appeared that she might be able to appeal to more than just Tea Party Republicans. This showed in a Rasmussen poll conducted after the debates that now had her in second place with 19 percent behind the front runner Mitt Romney's 33 percent. In addition, the performance gave her momentum just ahead of her June 27th official campaign kickoff in her birthplace of Waterloo, Iowa. In the first *Des Moines Register* Iowa Poll, she only trailed Romney by a margin of one percent, 22 to 23 percent. Just as important was that she had appeared to separate herself by a double-digit margin from the other "conservatives" in the race as well as had very low unfavorable numbers.[70] Of course, with this newfound notoriety would also mean far more scrutiny, both for what she said but also in regards to her actions.

The *Los Angeles Times* discovered that Bachmann's commitment to fiscal conservatism certainly could be questioned by her own personal experiences. Reports were that her family's farm in Wisconsin had received $280,000 in government support over a 13 year period, something she had stated she had never received any financial payments from. Yet her disclosure forms showed otherwise, having received payments up to $105,000. Bachmann's public gaffes were not finished either, making a reference during her campaign kickoff that she had the spirit of John Wayne who she said was also from Waterloo. The problem was that it was the serial killer John Wayne Gacy not the movie star. Such a mistake is relatively harmless, although as they add up would certainly call into question the capacity of any candidate. What was becoming more alarming, however, was the distortion and misrepresentations that were beginning to occur on a more frequent basis.

Bachmann had already made the claim that NATO airstrikes had killed up to 30,000 Libyan civilians and presented a number of inaccurate statements when it came to health care, but now some of her comments were beginning to border on absurd. For example, just before officially kicking off her campaign, she made the claim that "under Barack Obama the last two years the number of federal limousines for bureaucrats has increased 73 percent."[71] Now on the surface this is a staggering claim that would point to the government waste that she and other Tea Party Republicans had railed against, but the reality was far from the outlandish claim. The majority of the increase were for law enforcement and these limousines according to GSA were "vehicles equipped with sirens or lights, high-performance drivetrains or are used for surveillance or undercover operations," and there was no indication the Obama Administration were even responsible for the orders."[72] Another was her assertion, "If you threw a barbecue yesterday for the Memorial Day weekend, it was 29 percent more expensive than last year because Barack Obama's policies have led to groceries going up 29 percent," when in actuality it was a 10 percent increase.[73] Now while this rhetoric and misrepresentation might not seem all that important to the Tea Party conservative she tended to represent, the continuing questionable assertions presented a problem in attracting the moderate or independent voter. She clearly was beginning to have a credibility problem and it was just days into her nomination campaign.

At the end of June, even more negative press came out for the Bachmann campaign. The latest finding was that her husband's clinic, Bachmann and Associates, had received $137,000 from Medicaid based programs. Now while potentially a problem with some individuals that are hardline fiscal conservatives, the kind that she purported to represent, it created a problem for the average moderate as the clinic had been used to "cure" homosexuality. But as University of Minnesota political scientist Larry Jacobs, points out, "Their career in politics has always been about pursuing a social conservative agenda" and the fact is she reflected that social conservative stance to the core.[74] In early July Bachmann became the first of the GOP presidential candidates to sign a pledge that called for a Constitutional Amendment banning gay marriage. The pledge, put out by Iowa's The Family Leader, also had some rather questionable items in regards to sexual harassment in the military, slavery, and the "rejection of Sharia Islam."[75] Of course, these more socially conservative stances certainly did not hurt her in Iowa, as in the beginning of July she was leading the field with 25 percent support according to a poll *The Iowa Republican* from the Voter/Consumer Research. That was a 4-point gap over Romney. Yet, showing her difficulty bridging the gap of conservative and moderate, in New Hampshire she was only polling at 12 percent to Romney's 35 percent.[76]

Meanwhile, a more serious battle was being waged in the halls of Congress over raising the debt ceiling. Bachmann had long been a hardliner on the issue, now beginning to state that any debt ceiling raise should be met with equal cuts, particularly to the President's health care program. Thus, rather than settling for the Republican calls for cut, cap, and balance, defunding was also something she was going to push. What this position did was in many ways reflect her typical positions of either making bold statements on legislation or proposing legislation that did so. As *Politico* put it:

> Now in her third House term, Bachmann has never had a bill or resolution she's sponsored signed into law, and she's never wielded a committee gavel, either at the full or subcommittee level. Bachmann's amendments and bills have rarely been considered by any committee, even with the House under GOP control. In a chamber that rewards substantive policy work and insider maneuvering, Bachmann has shunned the inside game, choosing to be more of a bomb thrower than a legislator.[77]

This characterization, while somewhat harsh, was proving to be true again. However, on July 31 a deal was reached and by August 2, 2011 it was passed. Even though the compromise was reached, it came with a credit downgrade from the major rating agencies. Even in the face of this, Michele Bachmann still was proclaiming a moral victory for her principles, stating, "Someone had to stand up and say no, someone had to stand up and stay stop, and that's exactly what I did," Bachmann said, "I stood up and said no, I stood up and said stop and I said no more."[78] She was again painting herself perhaps as an extremist, which was not helped by the timing of her now infamous *Newsweek* cover having a bewildering wild stare and "The Queen of Rage" caption.

The height of the Bachmann campaign would come in August with a win in the Iowa Ames Straw Poll having 29 percent of the vote. However, the significance of this win is questionable at best. Bachmann did indeed win but did so without having some of the largest names in the field contesting for the prize. In addition, only a relatively small number of individuals participate in the poll, as normally it requires a lengthy drive as well as a $30 fee. Meaning if a person did vote they were likely ideologues that only represent a small, committed number in the electorate.[79] Finally, and most importantly, there was a significant individual who was not even on the ballot to consider, one who was gaining popularity and interest among the same Tea Party and evangelical voters that had sent Bachmann to an early lead in the polls. That individual was Texas Governor Rick Perry, and while up until this point he had not yet entered the race, whatever glory Bachmann could take from the victory would short lived as Perry announced his candidacy that same day.

Perry entered the race already with great popularity, forcing Bachmann to grow her populist standing by reaching for some extreme promises, the most memorable of which was the promise if elected she would get gas back down to $2 a gallon. Experts quickly jumped all over the claim, pointing out if prices were to drop then the United States would have to see a considerable drop in demand caused by an economic slowdown that could be potentially devastating. On top of this promise came another public gaffe when she said the recent natural disasters were a message from God about the growing fiscal debt of the country. Bachmann stated, "He said, 'Are you going to start listening to me here?' Listen to the American people, because the American people are roaring right now. They know government is on a morbid obesity diet, and we've got to rein in the spending."[80] She would later say she was merely joking but it was difficult to find any humor in the line.

Truly the entrance of Gov. Perry was a huge blow to the momentum that Bachmann had formed and rumors again began that Sarah Palin might be interested in running. Another significant blow was her campaign manager Ed Rollins was moving from day-to-day management to that of an advisory role, citing his health for the change. Quickly behind him was the departure of his deputy, David Polyansky. Ron Carey, a former Chief of Staff, was quoted about the departures as saying, "She loves when things are going well, and when things aren't going well, it's very tough times." He went on to say, "I think what brought this to a head was the lack of momentum coming out of Ames, and knowing Michele as I have for 10 years, she has probably been beside herself off-camera."[81] She needed to rally as well as a change in strategy.

The Republican Debate at the Reagan Presidential Library on Wednesday, September 7 was going to be her first opportunity to do so. Unfortunately, it was not one of her best performances and she did not even get an opportunity to speak until fourteen minutes in. Republican strategist Mark McKinnon noted Bachmann "was surprisingly cautious," going on to say "True, she didn't get many questions but she should have realized that the debate was going to be all about Perry and, therefore, taken him on."[82] In fact, the most interesting line of the night was when Gov. Perry referred to Social Security as a "Ponzi scheme," yet neither Bachmann nor any other hopefuls really were able to do anything with it at the time. Still between this comment and the fact that Perry had signed an executive order in 2007 requiring vaccinations of schoolgirls against HPV virus, Bachmann had plenty of jabs ready for the next debate just five days later.

By far one of the most contentious debates of the entire primary season, Michele Bachmann found herself right in the middle of the most heated exchanges. Bachmann defended Social Security and Medicare, as well as the prescription drug benefit. This is somewhat surprising as each program is often criticized for being an economic drain and certainly would call into question the fiscal conservatism she had always touted in the past. She also attacked "Obamacare," but perhaps the best moment for her campaign came when the issue of the HPV vaccinations came up. Bachmann attacked Perry, stating the executive order was "flat-wrong" and in doing so violated "a liberty interest." In addition she went on to say, "We cannot forget that in the midst of this executive order there is a big drug company that made millions of dollars because of this mandate. We can't deny that." She went on to point out "The drug company gave thousands of dollars in political donations to the governor and this is just flat-out wrong."[83] Making the argument even more compelling was that Perry's chief of staff had once been a lobbyist for Merck, the maker of the drug.

Unfortunately, the very next day Bachmann killed any momentum she might have gained from the night before, when during an interview on *Fox News* she told a story of talking to a mother whose daughter took the vaccine and then suffered mental retardation afterwards because of it. Immediately The American Association of Pediatrics criticized the statement, stating there was "absolutely no scientific validity." A GOP strategist David Welch described the impact of the statement, "It's the difference between the ready-for-prime-time political candidate and the not-ready-for-prime-time political candidate. You just don't repeat what somebody just told you."[84] Jim Dyke, former communications director for the Republican National Committee, commented, "This is the nail in the coffin in her campaign. Because you can be a cable television darling by saying provocative things, but you can't be president of the United States."[85] Clearly, the amount of unsupported claims and gaffes were adding up.

Bachmann had already fallen behind Romney in Iowa and was only maintaining a slim 1 percent lead over Rick Perry. Making matters worse, the Bachmann campaign lost their pollster and senior advisor at the beginning of October, a move thought to be reflective of her campaign's declining financial standing.[86] Money issues were confirmed October 15, when campaign finance reports showed that she had raised only $4 million whereas her competitors Perry and Romney had raised $17 and $14 million respectively. Making matters even worse, a CNN "Poll of Polls" showed Bachmann as being the preferred candidate of just 5 percent of Republican voters.[87]

The next few days and weeks would not get much better. During the October 18 debate Bachmann did not seem to realize Libya is a part of Africa. She said, "He (Obama) put us in Libya. Now he is putting us in Africa." Also captured in this statement was an insinuation that we should not have been part of an intervention to remove Moammar Gaddafi. In the days after she defended this position on *Fox News Sunday* stating, "Who will the real leadership be that takes over and runs Libya? It could be a radical element. It could be the Muslim Brotherhood. It could be elements affiliated with al Qaeda," going on to say, "This is a very bad decision, and it's created more instability in that region, not less."[88] Certainly there was concern over what a post-Gadhafi Libya would look like but the idea of leaving him in place did not sit well with many experts. On top of this potential problem, five staffers on her New Hampshire campaign quit, saying Bachmann's national team was "rude, unprofessional, dishonest, and at times cruel" and that they had been "abrasive, discourteous, and dismissive" of potential voters.[89] Then to just put a bow on what had been a disastrous month for the campaign, the president of American Majority, a Tea Party based organization, put out a statement declaring it was time for her to leave the race.

By November there was very little positivity associated with the campaign. Bachman began attacking all of her potential rivals and reminding everyone she was the one "true conservative" in the race. Her fire was not only directed at Mitt Romney and Rick Perry, although by this point Perry was on the decline, but she was also after Herman Cain who was the newest candidate to rise to frontrunner status. Bachmann attacked Cain on his changing positions on abortion, which had extended through the entire spectrum of beliefs from it should be illegal to it is a woman's choice. She reminded the audience during a speech to the Family Research Council in DC, "I am both personally and publicly pro-life. Our candidate needs to do more than just check the box, they need to have a proven record," she said. "I'll never be confused about that issue and you'll never find YouTube clips about me advocating anything else."[90] Ultimately, Bachmann was going to need more than tough rhetoric; however, that help was certainly not going to come from the debates in Michigan and then South Carolina.

The first was an uninspired performance where the most memorable moment was when Rick Perry's campaign effectively imploded after being unable to recall the three agencies he would cut, a gaffe that neither Bachmann nor any of the other candidates ever really tried to capitalize on. Of course, her reasons for not doing so were likely because she had been prone to so many public mistakes in the past herself. Greater attention came to Bachmann after the second debate, but it was not completely because of her performance. The most interesting comment Bachmann had was when she said she would reinstate waterboarding but it was one of only a handful of times she was actually addressed. As it turns out, that may have been intentional oversight by CBS. When a Bachmann spokeswoman had emailed CBS to volunteer the Congresswoman for a post-debate interview, in a reply CBS political director, John Dickerson wrote, "Okay let's keep it loose though since she's not going to get many questions and she's nearly off the charts in the hopes that we can get someone else." Of course, he never realized that the Bachmann spokeswoman was also on the email chain. In response, the congresswoman replied, "I think it's only respectful to allow the candidates to be able to speak and not intentionally ahead of time make a decision to limit candidates' opportunity to speak to the American people," going on to say "Clearly this was an example of media bias."[91]

This certainly was a case of bias against Bachmann not necessarily because of her policies but because she was falling behind in the polls. The rising star was now Newt Gingrich. At campaign stops she now was hammering Gingrich about his time as a paid "historian" offering "strategic advice" to Fannie Mae and Freddie Mac as well as still staying on Mitt Romney for flip-flopping and providing the blueprint for the president's health care bill. "Whether it's Freddie and Fannie or whether it's being against the Wall Street bailout, on every single issue, that's important to the voters in this upcoming election, I take every issue off the table with Barack Obama," Bachmann said.[92] But again she continued to struggle in debates, having just as many negative moments as she was having positive moments.

When Herman Cain dropped from the race, certainly a Tea Party favorite, the Bachmann campaign hoped that this would be a boost. But if Tea Party voters were paying attention to Congress, then it was growing less likely they would when on December 8th she received only one endorsement from House Tea Party caucus members.[93] In addition, polls just 3 weeks prior to the Iowa caucus had her well behind the frontrunners with only 7 percent support. By the time the last debate came on December 15, all she could do was go on the attack against the frontrunner, at the time Gingrich, and the other Republicans. She fared well, getting in good shots against Gingrich and Ron Paul for stances on abortion and Iran respectively.

Even with the success of her debate, it was too late and those inside her campaign headquarters clearly knew it. On Wednesday, December 28, less than a week before the caucus, her Iowa Campaign Chairman, state Sen. Kent Sorenson, defected to the Ron Paul campaign. The numbers were also getting worse with a December 30th poll from Rasmussen having Bachmann only ahead of Jon Huntsman with a meager 5 percent, which was exactly the percentage she would receive in the Iowa caucus on January 3, 2012. On January 4th, Congresswoman Bachmann bowed out of the race saying, "I have no regrets, none whatsoever. We never compromised our principles."

ANALYZING THE CAMPAIGN

The Bachmann campaign truly witnessed all of the highs and lows associated with presidential politics. Now it would be a mistake to believe that either Mrs. Bachmann had no chance of winning the nomination or that she was not a viable candidate when she entered the race. The field in January 2011 was a completely wide-open one, which in some ways would favor a relatively unknown candidate. Without names in the race like Palin and Huckabee, it would allow both the evangelical and Tea Party conservatives to be up for grabs. In fact, the Tea Party had relatively high numbers of favorability in January. According to a *USA Today*/Gallup Poll, 88 percent of Republicans and 71 percent of national adults believed that Congress should consider the ideas of the Tea Party movement and roughly 30 percent considered themselves to be a part of the movement.[94] Thus, there was clearly a significant part of the Republican Party that needed a candidate to fill that void.

In addition, she had the money to take on such a challenge. Her fundraising was second to none. Bachmann was already raising funds for her House re-election campaign and those funds could easily be transferred to a presidential campaign. She also had tremendous personal appeal. According to Gallup, congresswoman Bachmann's positivity numbers were only behind those of Former Arkansas Governor Mike Huckabee.[95] This popularity among those who supported her directly related to her ability to raise funds. Recall that in the first quarter of the year she was able to raise $1.7 million. Over 75 percent of those contributions were from individual donors giving $200 or less. Normally this number ranges between 5 and 10 percent for a member of the House and were higher than either that of Obama and John McCain's rate in the previous election cycle.[96] Therefore, there were clear indications that she could become a viable candidate. Unfortunately, future success was based on one single assumption, which was as she became better known both support and fundraising would increase. As it turns out, that did not happen and in fact her support would erode over time as she became better known.

At the start of the year, Bachmann was only recognizable to 52 percent of Republican voters, as compared to 81 percent for the presumptive frontrunner Mitt Romney and 87 and 96 percent for Mike Huckabee and Sarah Palin respectively.[97] Even by May, her name recognition remained at only 58 percent, although did still have the second highest positivity numbers. Because of this small recognition number, she was finishing no higher than fifth in polls and this was already after Mike Huckabee officially pulled his name out of the race.[98] Just prior to her official announcement in June, Bachmann improved to 62 percent recognition, a full ten points higher than where she started, but her positivity index had dropped a few points and now trailed that of Mitt Romney's.

Although Bachmann performed stellar in the first debate and it no doubt help surge her into the national spotlight, a constant theme that was present throughout this campaign was the fact that the field was never really settled. In other words, Republican voters never were really satisfied with the field. At the same time Bachmann was rising to second place in the polls after the debate, an NBC/Wall Street Journal poll showed that the majority of GOP voters were not satisfied with their choices. Contrast that with the fact that four years earlier at the same point 73 percent of GOP voters were satisfied with the candidates they had to choose from.[99] Also, the fact she had risen to second place in the polls only behind Romney was really false, as those numbers typically only included declared candidates. When non-declared candidates were included, she dropped to a tie for fourth behind eventual candidate Rick Perry as well as Sarah Palin and Rudy Giuliani.[100]

Of all of these potential names, she was clearly hurt the most by Rick Perry, largely because they filled the same space among the electorate. Palin of course would have presented difficulties as well but not nearly to the extent of Perry. Bachmann's numbers went down more significantly when only Perry's name was included. Overall she was polling at 18 percent with just declared candidates but those numbers dropped to only 13 percent with Perry in the field where as with Palin her support only dropped to 16 percent.[101] In addition, her support was regional, performing well in the Midwest and West, yet still trailing Romney in each of those regions. In the south she was fourth behind Perry, Palin, and Romney and in the more moderate based East, she was fifth trailing yet another unannounced candidate in Rudy Giuliani.[102] This ultimately indicated two important facts: that she never appeared to be a first choice candidate at any time except for a moment in Iowa and that she was clearly not appealing to more moderate voters or Southern Republicans, two clearly important groups if you want to ultimately win the GOP nomination.

Bachmann's notoriety hit its height after she won the Iowa Ames Straw Poll, but as she and her policies became better known we see a corresponding drop in her positivity numbers. The Ames Straw Poll was on August 18, at which time she had an 83 percent recognition factor but her positivity numbers had dropped below +20 for four of the previous five weeks after having scores over that number for February through June.[103] In addition, although she was doing well in hypothetical races against the president, what the polls showed again was that her campaign was faring poorly with independents and Democrats.[104] Bachmann was also having problems relating to women, with overall support at 10 percent by the end of August as compared with the frontrunner at the time Perry's 28 percent and Romney's 19 percent. In fact, in no subgroup based on gender, age, geographical location, ideology, or even church attendance did she lead and her support among Republicans nationally had dipped all the way down to 7 percent.[105] All of this was just a couple of weeks after winning the Ames Straw Poll; voters simply did not view her or her policies as their first choice.

Again right after her win in Iowa, Bachmann's poll numbers indicated that she remained the fourth preference choice of voters whether that Republican's vote was based on the economy, government spending and power, or social issues.[106] Keep in mind that the majority of her campaign and speeches surrounded issues of government spending and she had touted her conservative values as a focal point as well. Thus, what the people were hearing clearly was not resonating and it reflected in her poor polling performances and declining positivity numbers. Even over time as Perry's star faded, none of that support went to Bachmann but instead shifted to Herman Cain and others. By October, she had +80 recognition but only a 5 percent positivity factor.[107] Therefore, even though the campaign was still holding out hope, there really was none.

CONCLUSIONS

When attempting to explain why Michele Bachmann failed to win the GOP nomination, most would simply cite her numerous public gaffes. However, to do so would oversimplify, as it is only with a combination of other factors do we see these public statements make a difference. This chapter attempts to display how a drawn out nomination process, with a field that was never truly settled only served to undermine her campaign. In the early stages Bachmann had to make a name for herself in the declared field of relative unknowns while at the same time try to separate herself from the more well-known names who were constantly being pushed to run. Although she entered the race to be the Tea Party voice, the spectrum of Perry on the outside at first and then entering the race essentially halted any potential momentum and dealt a crushing blow to her campaign. Bachmann never was truly a "first choice candidate" among Republican voters, and even her straw poll victory was more about the names not on the ballot as opposed to her potential as a nominee or candidate. Although she had solid moments, it does not appear the party ever considered her a viable nominee.

A second significant issue appears to be Bachmann's personal commitment to a Tea Party-based political ideology and her inability to move beyond that specific base. Party nominees typically need to represent the entirety of the party and cannot be limited to just one portion of it. They also need to appeal to some portion of undecided, independent voters as well as across various subgroups. Bachmann, whether because of her Tea

Party fiscal conservatism or social conservatism, failed to be viewed as favorable among any of these groups even after her victory in Iowa.[108] For any candidate, sticking to principles can be seen as positive until it runs the potential of sacrificing the greater good in order for the candidate to retain their moral high ground. The debt debate is an excellent example of this. Tying her vote to the defunding of health care only helped to display that her Tea Party based principles would drive her decision-making rather than that of sound, fiscal policy. It also displayed the exact reason the country received a credit downgrade, which was the divisiveness of partisan politics. While this rhetoric and attitude may have worked to gain the House in 2010, when placed against the backdrop of a larger voting block it simply does not. This trend was evidenced further during the 2012 election when extreme conservative nominees such as Todd Akin of Missouri and Richard Mourdock of Indiana failed to win Senate races. Bachmann herself even struggled to regain her house seat, displaying more evidence that the desire for divisive Tea Party ideology is on the decline.[109]

Thus, in the end the gaffes only matter with the background of these two contributing factors. In other words, early on her public gaffes matter very little as she was a relative unknown. However, to make herself better known she needed to stake her claim to the far right voting block by sticking to her Tea Party conservatism. And as Bachmann got more attention and notoriety based on some early strong performances in the debates and willingness to engage with the media, what were once ignorable gaffes began to matter. Therefore, not only were moderates and independents not willing to back her because of her now better known policy positions, but these gaffes eventually began to undermine the seriousness of her campaign among conservative Republicans as well. Thus, by the time the Iowa caucus came around, Bachmann had already been fully vetted by the GOP electorate, and that electorate had decided to go in a different direction. Still, Bachmann made a lasting contribution to the process with her calls for the repeal of health care reform and desires to shift the process farther to the right. In the end, it may have very well been the rightward shift in tone that cost the Republicans and its eventual nominee the White House.

NOTES

1. "10 Things You Didn't Know About Michele Bachmann," *U.S. News Digital Weekly*, January 28, 2011, Vol. 3, Issue 4.

2. Kevin Duchschere, "Senator, mother, rising star; After four years in the Minnesota Senate, Michele Bachmann, 48, has become one of the state's most formidable conservatives, with a focus on low taxes, local school control and opposition to abortion," *Star Tribune*, January 1, 2005.

3. Norman Draper, "Partisan twist for school elections; GOP supporting some candidates in Stillwater and other districts," *Star Tribune*, October 30, 1999.

4. Norman Draper, "School Elections; GOP nod fails to help slate of 5 in Stillwater," *Star Tribune*, November 3, 1999.

5. Dane Smith, "Endorsement tensions plague GOP; Senate Minority Leader Dick Day is upset with GOP Chairman Ron Eibensteiner because Michele Bachmann was supported over veteran legislator Gary Laidig," *Star Tribune*, April 4, 2000.

6. Conrad deFiebre, "Primary races' internal rivalries; Battle enlivened by challenges within parties,"*Star Tribune*, September 3, 2000.

7. Mary Divine, "All Eyes Glued on Old, New GOPers; Incumbent, Endorsee Face Off in Primary," *Saint Paul Pioneer Press*, September 8, 2000.

8. Patrick Sweeney, "Overall, Few Upsets in Legislative Races; Bernardy, Kahn, Kelly Go to General Election," *Saint Paul Pioneer Press*, September 13, 2000.

9. Mary Divine, "Candidates Not Taking Anything for Granted; Education, Taxes Top Issues in 3-Way Race," *Saint Paul Pioneer Press*, October 14, 2000.

10. Mary Divine, "Conservative Bachmann Wins State Senate Seat," *Saint Paul Pioneer Press*, November 8, 2000.

11. Rachel E. Stassen-Berger, "Let the House race begin," *Saint Paul Pioneer Press*, February 15, 2005.

12. Mary Divine, "Dean's loss laid to GOP split, other factors," *Saint Paul Pioneer Press*, February 13, 2003.

13. Mary Divine, "Republican Norwick endorses Democrat Otto for House seat," *Saint Paul Pioneer Press*, January 31, 2003.

14. Patrick Sweeney, "Krinkie changes his mind, signs GOP primary pledge; Three other 6th District candidates made ceremonial pact Friday," *St. Paul Pioneer Press*, April 23, 2006.

15. Patrick Sweeney, "Bachmann wins endorsement," *St. Paul Pioneer Press*, May 6, 2006.

16. Eric Black, "Pelosi coming to Minneapolis to headline Wetterling fundraiser," *Star Tribune*, July 27, 2006.

17. Eric Black, Patricia Lopez, and Glenn Howatt, "In 4 hours, Bush packs a punch; The president pumped more than $500,000 into the campaign coffers of Republican Michele Bachmann. He also signed an executive order on health care," *Star Tribune*, August 23, 2006.

18. "Wetterling Holds Narrow Lead Over Bachmann, Poll Finds," *Congress Daily*, October 17, 2006.

19. "Michele Bachmann (R),"*The Washington Post*, November 9, 2006.

20. Kevin Diaz, "Walz, Bachmann build money for their next runs; The Democrat and Republican were involved in tight campaigns in 2006 and expect more of the same in 2008," *Star Tribune*, July 14, 2007.

21. Dennis Lien, "Bachmann grabs the spotlight," *St. Paul Pioneer Press*, September 2, 2008.

22. Dennis Lien and Rachel E. Stassen-Berger, "A bruised Bachmann loses GOP ad support," *St. Paul Pioneer Press*, October 22, 2008.

23. Pat Doyle, "Election 2008: Minnesota congressional delegation; Bachmann declares victory in Sixth District; GOP incumbent Michele Bachmann kept her edge over DFL challenger Elwin Tinklenberg. In the Second District, John Kline claimed victory over DFLer Steve Sarvi," *Star Tribune*, November 5, 2008.

24. John Fritze, "Politicians' harsh words pull in campaign funds," *USA Today*, July 2, 2010.

25. Molly K. Hooper and Jordan Fabian, "Tea Party gets official caucus on Capitol Hill," *The Hill*, July 20, 2010.

26. Kevin Diaz and Eric Roper, "Cash pours into Bachmann race; Donor from Atlanta: "Everything's national now. It affects all of us. The battle goes on across the nation," *Star Tribune*, April 18, 2010.

27. Eric Roper, "Bachmann bests the rest in fundraising; Since April, the Sixth District incumbent raised more than any other House candidate in nation," *Star Tribune*, July 17, 2010.

28. Jason Hoppin, "Bachmann prevails in costly clash in 6th Congressional District," *St. Paul Pioneer Press*, November 2, 2010.

29. Jeremy Herb, "Bachmann's bid shows GOP divide; Despite giving up on a leadership spot, she's still positioned to play a role in GOP-Tea Party conflicts," *Star Tribune*, November 15, 2010.

30. Jeremy Herb, "GOP divided over debt ceiling Debt ceiling vote could spark first GOP firefight; Bachmann, House Tea Party Caucus steadfast about not raising the debt limit. Rep. Michele Bachmann is one of the leading voices against raising the country's debt limit," *Star Tribune*, January 31, 2011.

31. Thomas Fitzgerald, "Most GOP presidential candidates blast the debt deal," *The Philadelphia Inquirer*, August 3, 2011.

32. Amy Mayron, "1,000 protest taxes at annual rally," *Saint Paul Pioneer Press*, April 7, 2002.

33. Bob Von Sternberg, "Anti-tax tea parties will be held today in 16 Minnesota cities and across U.S.," *Star Tribune*, April 15, 2009.

34. Hayley Tsukayama and Kevin Diaz, "Lawmakers face threats over votes on health care; Amid heightened rhetoric, Obama dared GOP critics to campaign on repeal this fall," *Star Tribune*, March 26, 2010.

35. Russell Berman, "House votes 245-189 to repeal health law," *The Hill*, January 20, 2011.

36. Michael Shear, "Bachmann Wins Over Some Skeptics," *The New York Times*, June 15, 2011.

37. Bill Salisbury, "Lawmakers want to bolster gay marriage ban; Minnesota: Two legislators announced they are seeking an amendment to the state constitution to prevent judges from recognizing a Massachusetts ruling," *Duluth News-Tribune*, November 21, 2003.

38. . James Dao, "'Don't Ask, Don't Tell' Has Bachmann's Support," *The New York Times*, August 16, 2011.

39. Clint Brown, "Bachmann makes visit to Pella," *Pella Chronicle*, April 15, 2011.

40. James Politi and Stephanie Kirchgaessner, "US budget hinges on ideological battle," *Financial Times*, March 8, 2011.

41. Jeremy Duda, "Bachmann says she will campaign in Arizona," *The Arizona Capitol Times*, September 14, 2011.

42. Seema Mehta,"Bachmann Draws Hard Line on U.S.-Mexico Border; She is 1st Presidential Hopeful to Sign Pledge to Build Fence by 2013," *The Baltimore Sun*, October 16, 2011.

43. Anna Fifield, "Republican foreign policy begins at home," *Financial Times*, October 7, 2011.

44. Jeremy Herb, "Pawlenty tries to be hawk in presidential field's flock," *Star Tribune*, June 29, 2011.

45. Michael O'Brien, "GOP field struggles to define its foreign policy credentials," *The Hill*, June 28, 2011.

46. Richard McGregor, "Republicans target the White House over expensive foreign wars," *Financial Times*, June 18, 2011.

47. Bill Salisbury, "Outspoken Bachmann makes case for 'bold' 2012 pick," *Saint Paul Pioneer Press*, June 26, 2011.

48. Jessica Bernstein-Wax, "GOP presidential candidate Bachmann addresses supporters in San Rafael," *Marin Independent Journal*, September 15, 2011.

49. Bill Salisbury, "In Minneapolis, Bachmann says she can attract Democrats, 'new voters'," *St. Paul Pioneer Press*, June 18, 2011.

50. David Hogberg, "GOP Rivals In Sync On Regulatory Rollback; Economic Burden Stressed; All want Obamacare out, several favor killing EPA, Dodd-Frank financial law," *Investor's Business Daily*, December 28, 2011.

51. J. Matt Barber, "Bachmann: Reagan in pumps; She's the kick the GOP presidential field needs," *The Washington Times*, January 10, 2011.

52. Bill Salisbury, "Obama gets mixed marks from State's delegation," *St. Paul Pioneer Press*, January 25, 2011.

53. Jake Sherman and Meredith Shiner, "Bachmann's fire keeps prompting cool response from GOP establishment," *St. Paul Pioneer Press*, January 26, 2011.

54. Kevin Diaz, "Bachmann spurs on 'Triple Crown'," *Star Tribune*, February 11, 2011.

55. "Transcript", Meet the Press, March 6, 2011.

56. John Distaso, "Bachmann: Demand health-care law money, " *The Union Leader*, March 11, 2011.

57. Holly Ramer, "Bachmann flubs Revolutionary War geography in NH," *Associated Press*, March 13, 2011.

58. Brian Bakst and Philip Elliott, "Advisor: Bachmann likely to enter WH race," *The Associated Press*, March 24, 2011.

59. "Minn.'s Bachmann scoops up $2.2M since Jan. 1," *The Associated Press*, April 1, 2011.

60. "Huckabee Wins York County, South Carolina county Straw Poll," *The Frontrunner*, April 4, 2011.

61. Public Policy Polling (D) survey of 384 usual New Hampshire Republican primary voters taken March 31-April 3.

62. "At Rally, Bachmann Blasts Democrats Over Budget Battle," *The Frontrunner*, April 7, 2011.

63. Daniel Malloy, "Tea Party's Bachmann is Building a Fan Base," *Pittsburgh Post-Gazette*, April 10, 2011.

64. Philip Rucker and Paul Kane, "Long on Ambition but Short on Record," *The Washington Post*, May 2, 2011.

65. Mike Glover, "Bachmann note 'calling' to run to president," *The Associated Press*, May 27, 2011.

66. Sandhya Somashekhar , "Two candidates who are just their cup of tea," *The Washington Post*, June 6, 2011.

67. Ben Smith and Maggie Haberman, "Stars collide: Michele Bachmann vs. Sarah Palin," *Politico*, June 8, 2011.

68. Jonathan Allen and Meredith Shiner, "Michele Bachmann wields national security credentials," *Politico*, June 14, 2011.

69. Jordan Fabian and Michael O'Brien, "Bachmann Steals Spotlight," *The Hill,* June 15, 2011.

70. Douglas K. Daniel, "Bachmann: 'Scare tactics' in Debt ceiling issue," *Associated Press*, June 26, 2011.

71. Robert Farley, "Michele Bachmann Claims Federal Limousines up 73 percent under Obama," *St. Petersburg Times*, June 27, 2011.

72. Farley, "Michele Bachmann Claims."

73. Steve Holland, "Bachmann's wild comments are getting more scrutiny," *Buffalo News*, June 29, 2011.

74. "Faith & Politics," *The Washington Post*, July 6, 2011.

75. "GOP candidates caught in slavery controversy," *CNN Wire*, July 11, 2011.

76. "Bachmann moves to distant 2nd place in NH poll," *The Associated Press State & Local Wire*, July 5, 2011.

77. Angie Drobnic Holan, "Tim Pawlenty Said Michele Bachmann's Legislative Record is 'Failed Amendments'," *St. Petersburg Times*, July 28, 2011.

78. Josh Nelson, "Bachmann in Waterloo raps Obama on credit downgrade," *Waterloo Courier*, August 7, 2011.

79. "Iowa straw poll gets more attention than it deserves." *USA Today*, August 12, 2011.

80. Alexander Burns, "Bachmann calls East Coast storm a political message from God," *St. Paul Pioneer Press*, August 28, 2011.

81. Trip Gabriel and Michael D. Shear, "Loss of Top Two Aides Raises Questions About Bachmann Campaign," *The New York Times*, September 7, 2011.

82. Trip Gabriel and Michael D. Shear, "Muted in Last Debate, Bachmann Looks to Rejoin Conversation," *The New York Times*, September 12, 2011.

83. "Did Bachmann wound front-runner Perry at CNN/Tea Party Debate?," *CNN Wire*, September 13, 2011.

84. Brian Bakst, "Bachmann also feels sting of shot at Perry over HPV vaccines," *Charleston Daily Mail*, September 15, 2011.

85. Trip Gabriel, "With stakes for Bachmann Higher Now, Her Words Get in the Way," *The New York Times*, September 16, 2011.

86. Brian Baskt, "More aides leave Bachmann presidential campaign," *The Associated Press*, October 4, 2011.

87. "Bachmann raises almost 4 million, but spends nearly 6 million," *CNN Wire*, October 15, 2011.

88. David Eldridge, "Obama hit on Iraq, Libya; Bachmann sees post-Gadhafi uncertainties," *The Washington Times*, October 24, 2011.

89. Holly Ramer, "Bachmann's ex-NH staff: Campaign was rude, cruel," *The Associated Press*, October 24, 2011.

90. Reid J. Epstein, "Bachmann: GOP rivals are 'frugal socialists'," *St. Paul Pioneer Press*, November 6, 2011.

91. "Bachmann cries 'bias' after Saturday debate," *CNN Wire*, November 13, 2011.

92. "Bachmann: Gingrich was paid to 'influence' Republicans for Freddie Mac," *CNN Wire*, November 16, 2011.

93. Seth McLaughlin, "Tea Party Caucus members don't back Bachmann; Romney tops in endorsements," *The Washington Times*, December 8, 2011.

94. . Lydia Saad, "Americans Believe GOP Should Consider Tea Party Ideas," *Gallup*, January 31, 2011, http:www.gallup.com/poll/145838/Americans-Believe-GOP-Consider-Tea-Oarty-ideas.aspx.

95. Frank Newport, "Huckabee, Bachmann Have Most Intense Following in GOP Field," *Gallup*, March 15, 2011, http:www.gallup.com/poll/146621/Huckabee-Bachmann-intense-following-GOP-field.aspx.

96. "Can Small-Dollar Donors Fuel A Michele Bachmann Presidential Bid?," *State News Service*, May 12, 2011,

97. Frank Newport, "Huckabee, Bachmann Have Most Intense Following in GOP Field," *Gallup*, March 15, 2011, http:www.gallup.com/poll/146621/Huckabee-Bachmann-intense-following-GOP-field.aspx.

98. Frank Newport, "With Huckabee Out, No Clear GOP Front-Runner," *Gallup*, May 17, 2011, http:www.gallup.com/poll/147584/Huckabee-no-clear-GOP-Front-runner.aspx.

99. Gary Younge, "Comment: It's not the Republican line-up but the economy that Obama must fear most: Conservative hopefuls may look weak. But what will count for voters is food on the table, clothes for the kids, and a roof," *The Guardian*, June 20, 2011.

100. Jeffrey M. Jones, "Romney Leads Field of Announced GOP Candidates," *Gallup*, July 27, 2011.

101. Jones, "Romney Leads Field."

102. Jeffrey M. Jones, "Perry is Top GOP Pick in South, Romney in West," *Gallup*, July 28, 2011.

103. Jeffrey M. Jones, "Perry Rises in Recognition and Maintains Positive Image," *Gallup*, August 23, 2011.

104. Frank Newport, "Obama in Close Race Against Romney, Perry, Bachmann, Paul," *Gallup*, August 22, 2011.

105. Jeffrey M. Jones, "Perry Zooms to Front of Pack for 2012 GOP Nomination," *Gallup*, August, 24, 2011.

106. Jeffrey M. Jones, "Tea Party Supporters Backing Perry for GOP Nomination," *Gallup*, August 26, 2011.

107. Jeffrey M. Jones, "Perry Plummets, Cain Surges in Positive Intensity," *Gallup*, October 4, 2011.

108. Jeffrey M. Jones, "Perry Zooms to Front of Pack for 2012 GOP Nomination," *Gallup,* August, 24, 2011.
109. Elspeth Reeve, "The Tea Party's National Ambitions are Finished," *The Atlantic Wire,* November 7, 2012.

SIX

The Hermanator: Anti-Elitism and the Rise of Herman Cain

Andrew L. Pieper

In the long line of actual and potential Republican presidential candidates with less experience than ambition, radio host and former pizza titan Herman Cain had perhaps the tallest climb and steepest fall from prominence. Donald Trump topped the polls for a brief week or two in March, and Michele Bachmann caused a stir when she won the Iowa Ames Straw Poll. But Cain, whose sole political experience consisted of a failed U.S. Senate run in 2004, was able to capture the attention of voters and media members at least twice, including a sustained month at the top of the polls in October and November. His star burned brightly and intensely, only to consume itself in a fiery combustion of campaign gaffes and accusations of sexual misconduct. Cain's greatest strengths as a candidate—his willingness to buck established norms, his resolve to eschew formal campaign organization, and his personal charisma and dynamic debating and speaking skills—also proved to be the fatal flaws that doomed his candidacy. However, Cain's ability to attract and invigorate disenchanted primary voters with his message of business oriented policies and anti-Washington rhetoric came to be a model other candidates would attempt to incorporate.

CANDIDATE BACKGROUND

With the rise of the Tea Party conservatism and the corresponding anti-government rhetoric of the contemporary Republican Party, Herman Cain was an appealing candidate on several dimensions. First, Cain portrayed himself as a risk-taking, job-creating, dynamic business leader whose business experience and willingness to face tough choices with courage and conviction would lead to economic recovery and prosperity. Second, Cain's rags-to-riches background and message of self-reliance helped contrast him with Mitt Romney, the other major GOP candidate who claimed the mantle of corporate competence. Finally, Cain clearly benefited from his most recent career of talk-radio host, which gave him the pedestal and practice from which to promote the Herman Cain brand of anti-Obama rhetoric and message of small government conservatism.

No phrase better captured Cain's blend of business titan and populist truth-speaker than the frequently used designation "Godfather pizza magnate." Most of Cain's campaign autobiography *This is Herman Cain!* details his rise from Morehouse College math student to Chief Executive Officer of Godfather's Pizza.[1] According to Cain, his greatest asset was that he had the tenacity and problem-solving skills to persevere during difficult times. At each stage of his corporate career Cain faced tremendous obstacles, and he succeeded (spectacularly, he would argue) at each. His first task when he moved from Coca-Cola to Pillsbury was to take over the construction of new World Headquarters in Minneapolis.[2] Although the project was behind schedule and over budget, Cain "was not afraid to take charge, make decisions, and focus on the critical things I needed to do in order to get the project moving." The project "was completed ahead of schedule and under budget."[3] After taking a voluntary (and risky) demotion to learn the ropes at Burger King, Cain took charge during a "crisis" while he was an assistant manager. Despite at least two conspiracies to get Cain fired during his climb at Burger King, his performance proved his effectiveness as a leader, and he was tapped to take over the failing Godfather's Pizza. Cain returned Godfather's to profitability, and eventually bought the company from Pillsbury.

Cain's success in the business world was the most prominent tangible selling point to potential supporters.[4] His message was one of simple and direct approaches to problems, and he argues in his book that his dynamic leadership, rather than any specific policy proposals, could cure what ills the American spirit and economy. From Cain's perspective, the obstacles to economic recovery are not based in failed policies per se (though he claims there were many), but rather from a failure of spirit and competent management. Critics of Cain argued that he may have oversold his business successes, especially the turnaround of Godfather's.[5] But Cain's appeal comes from his salesmanship of an attitude, an up-by-the-bootstraps form of self-help, rooted in his upbringing and called "CEO of Self." In his book he addresses those critics who question how he would put the United States on the road back to prominence and power: "The short answer is that I'll do what I did when I put Burger King's Philadelphia region on the right track; I'll do what I did when I helped restore Godfather's Pizza, Inc., to profitability; I'll do what I did during my presidential campaign when I defied the nay-sayers, not to mention the odds against me, and came out ahead of the field."[6]

Cain's upbringing in Atlanta played prominently in his campaign speeches, and he retold countless times the stories of his father, who worked for Coca-Cola, most prominently as the chauffer for CEO R.W. Woodruff. According to Cain, Woodruff "loved and trusted Dad more than some of his executives." Cain's father had a "Ph.D. in common sense, and . . . he had graduated with honors—cum laude."[7] Cain emphasized that he, like his father, had special qualities that drew people to him. More than once in his youth others apparently recognized his leadership potential. Sometimes these people tested him, and challenged him, and Cain argued that his work ethic, dedication, and philosophy of "CEO of Self" helped him overcome these obstacles.

One of those obstacles was racism. Cain does not ignore race, nor deny the racism of his youth (though he pointedly defends his decision to not take part in the civil rights movement of his college years). But Cain argues that black Americans need to respond to racism by persevering. He says that a "victim mentality" holds African Americans back, not racism. From his perspective, if he can make it, anyone can make it, as long as one has the right attitude. On the surface, Cain's race played little part in his campaign, though he often relished his position as a black conservative foil to President Obama, calling himself the "dark horse" of the GOP. Some liberals asserted that support for Herman Cain among conservative voters was an effort to refute accusations of racism, especially in the Tea Party movement. But Cain was unfazed by such accusations, and he mentioned race substantively only twice. The first was when he criticized as "insensitive" a racially inflammatory rock marker at Rick Perry's hunting camp, and the second was when he faced charges of sexual harassment, and invoked fellow black conservative Clarence Thomas.[8]

Cain's campaign speeches also included prominent messages about the strength and fortitude he found in his faith. He occasionally preached at his church, and in his book calls his decision to run for president as inspired by a prayerful plane ride, and that he is "inspired by God Almighty."[9] This faith not only seeps into every aspect of his life and leadership, but gives him the courage to make difficult decisions, and overcome adversity, including his battle with cancer in 2006.[10]

A final chapter in Cain's development as a public figure began in 2005 as he started hosting a local radio program in Atlanta on Saturdays. In 2008, he was given a prominent 7-10:00 pm weeknight slot, and Cain became more politicized. According to Cain, the program was "God's way of forcing me to understand the critical issues confronting our nation."[11] Cain's natural personality was well-suited to the medium of talk radio, though critics argue that the slash and burn style of conservative talk radio informed Cain's politics, and Cain's "understanding" of the issues was skewed by the disillusioned callers and right wing attacks on the Obama administration. Cain learned how to speak to this disillusioned audience, however, and developed the message and mantras that would eventually serve him well on the campaign trail.

ISSUE STANCES

Of the many idiosyncrasies of the Cain campaign for President, one of the most telling was the apparent lack of specific policy positions Cain was willing to promote with any candor. Although presidential candidates regularly ply the predictable political trade of policy vagueness, Cain's avoidance was different. His campaign book, his website, his stump speech, and his interviews—all were virtually vacant when it came to policy prescriptions. One conservative writer argues that "Cain is cautious, critics would say evasive, on a number of issues."[12] Eventually Cain came to be most identified with his tax reform proposal, which he called 9-9-9. Other than this grand proposal, Cain's policy stances were largely absent from the campaign trail. This may have been strategic—when Cain did attempt to discuss policies in detail, he frequently stumbled over even basic details, and regularly made verbal gaffes that were widely panned in the media.

9-9-9

Of all the Republican candidates, none made as spectacular policy splash as Cain did with his 9-9-9 tax reform plan. This plan had the benefit of being bold and readily marketable at the same time. As described by the Cain campaign, the 9-9-9 plan consisted of eliminating all existing personal income, corporate, capital gains, estate, and payroll taxes. They would be replaced with a flat nine percent personal income tax, a nine percent corporate tax, and a nine percent sales tax on all goods and services.[13] According to Cain, "these measures would free up capital, spur production, and incentivize risk-taking, thereby fueling the economy and creating jobs."[14]

The 9-9-9 plan received tremendous attention from both the media and fellow Republican candidates (Jon Huntsman joked that it sounded more like a pizza deal than an economic policy). Much of the debate surrounded whether the plan would bring in enough revenue to support government spending. The plan gained an important endorsement from Arthur Laffer, a conservative economist, in *The Wall Street Journal*. According to Laffer, the 9-9-9 plan "would indeed be static revenue neutral, and with the boost it would give to economic growth it would bring in even more revenue than expected."[15] Other experts from conservative think tanks the Heritage Foundation and the American Enterprise Institute claimed the plan would be revenue neutral.

However, most of the reception to Cain's 9-9-9 plan was skeptical at best, even from conservatives. An analysis by the Tax Policy Center found that most taxpayers, and the bottom 40 percent in particular, would see tax increases, while most upper-income taxpayers would see dramatic tax cuts.[16] Bruce Bartlett, a former Reagan policy advisor and Treasury Secretary under George H.W. Bush, argued that the plan would provide most of its benefits to the rich and transfer the tax burden to the poor, and that it would dramatically increase the U.S. debt. He claims that "At a minimum, the Cain plan is a distributional monstrosity. The poor would pay more while the rich would have their taxes cut, with no guarantee that economic growth will increase and good reason to believe that the budget deficit will increase."[17] One *National Review* writer asserted that "his plan's peculiarities of design, substantive flaws, and political naiveté render it unworthy of conservative support."[18] Conservative writer Kevin D. Williamson complained that the plan "is marked by Mr. Cain's most distressing hallmark: wishful thinking that borders on fantasy."[19]

Virtually all agreed, however, that the 9-9-9 plan was bold, audacious, and more concrete than any of the other Republican tax reform plans. Although Cain's strength as a campaign speaker and novelty on the conservative circuit allowed him to become known among conservative activists, it was the 9-9-9 plan that catapulted him to widespread prominence. The plan made Cain a serious contender for the nomination, or at least gained him serious media coverage.

Absence of Policy Positions

Cain's lack of political experience made positions on most policy issues difficult to decipher, as he had no track record on which to run or to point to in even the simplest of policy areas. His campaign book has three chapters totaling less than forty (short) pages that purport to educate readers about his positions. However, these words, like what remained of the Cain campaign's web presence (www.cainconnections.com) contained mostly vague platitudes. Cain's plan to promote a strong national defense: "If you mess with Israel, you're messing with the United States of America. Is that clear?"[20] Cain promoted cutting taxes to "unleash economic growth." Appendix A of *This is Herman Cain!* attempted to describe his general positions on some major issues, and most were standard Republican fare with no specific policy proposals. Cain was against "Obamacare" (he called it health care "deform"), and in favor of sweeping tort reform, health care savings accounts, and shifting "ownership of one's health care back to where it belongs, with the individual."[21] He suggested that labor union leaders are "not interested in a free society where people can think and make decisions for themselves." They have an outdated "Big Brother" mode of thinking. According to Cain, "That dog won't hunt."[22] Although he supported Wisconsin Governor Scott Walker's approach to public unions, he did not mention right-to-work laws, or any other specific policies in relation to private labor unions. He advocates a personal retirement account *option* for Social Security, which would help us move "from an entitlement society to an empowerment society."[23] Cain argued we need to "revamp our social and welfare programs," but his strategy consisted of working with Congress to achieve these goals.[24] Cain opposed subsidies or incentives for green energy, arguing instead that "We will adopt a Drill Here, Drill Now strategy. We will set this as our bold goal: zero dependence on foreign oil."[25] Most of these positions were generally shared by all of the major Republican Party candidates, and many other important issues were mentioned hardly at all by the candidate or campaign. According to a candidate profile published by www.procon.org, Cain publically took a position on only 23 of 45 (51 percent) policy issues they measure.[26]

Policy Confusion

There were some policy areas where Cain made attempts to be more specific, but these attempts frequently resulted in confusion, or worse, outright embarrassment.

Abortion

By most accounts, Herman Cain was a standard pro-life Republican. But in an October 19, 2011 interview with Piers Morgan on CNN, Cain seemed to hedge when it came to abortion-rights for rape victims. Cain said "it's not the government's role or anybody else's role to make that decision . . . it ultimately gets down to a choice that that family or that mother has to make."[27] He added "I shouldn't try to tell them what decision to make for such a sensitive issue."[28] After an outcry by pro-life activists accusing him of using the logic of pro-choice advocates, Cain attempted to quell the controversy on Twitter by stating "I'm 100 percent pro-life. End of Story."[29] For over a week Cain was forced to respond to fellow candidates' and critics' concerns that he was insufficiently pro-life.

Immigration

In his campaign book, Cain indicated that the main problem with immigration is the federal government's inability to enforce the laws. To remedy this, he suggested letting states enforce the immigration code.[30] But in campaign stops over the summer, Cain suggested installing a lethal 20 ft. electric border fence with an alligator filled moat. At October campaign rallies in Tennessee, Cain suggested using military forces with "real guns and real bullets" to prevent border crossings.[31] Cain later said that "That's a joke" and added, "That's not a serious plan." But observers complained that Cain never presented them as anything other than a serious solution to the serious problem of immigration.[32]

Muslims

Cain's position on Muslims was a distraction throughout his campaign, beginning at a conservative conference in March 2011 when he told a liberal blogger that he would not be comfortable appointing a Muslim to his cabinet or to the federal courts. Cain struggled to pinpoint his position throughout the spring and summer. At times he claimed that his comments were taken out of context, and that "I have hired good people regardless of race, religion, sex, gender, or orientation and this sort of thing."[33] In other interviews, however, he defended his position on denying Muslims positions in the cabinet. To Neil Cavuto on March 28, 2011, Cain confirmed that he would not appoint Muslims, "And here's why . . . I would have to have people totally committed to the Declaration of Independence and the Constitution of the United States. And many of the Muslims, they're not totally dedicated to this country."[34] In April, Cain repeated his position to radio host Bryan Fischer. "The Constitution does not have room for Sharia law . . . and to introduce that element as part of administration when we've got all of these other issues, I think I have the right to say that I won't."[35] In contrast, he writes in his book that "I want to make sure that anyone, of any religion, serving in my administration—who is of course, serving the people of our nation—is committed to our Constitution."[36] However, in his June interview with Beck trying to clarify his position, he explained that he would require some proof of loyalty from Muslims, adding, when asked, that he would not require such proof from Catholics or Mormons.[37] He justified his positions by claiming that "I have had one very well-known Muslim voice say to me directly that a majority of Muslims share the extremist views."[38]

Individually, the policy controversies were not likely significant factors to the decline of Cain's campaign. However, as they accumulated—and combined with other, perhaps more egregious policy stumbles discussed below—they revealed a candidate that many argued was not fully prepared for the rigors of a presidential campaign. But during the late summer and early fall of 2011, the Cain campaign was able to weather the storm, and his support climbed in spite of his often confusing positions on central issues.

CAMPAIGN STRATEGY

Herman Cain's relatively low national profile combined with his lack of political history, created a fairly unique campaign scenario. Like other business titans turned presidential aspirants before him (Ross Perot and Steve Forbes), Cain was forced to learn on the fly. As detailed above, he stumbled often. However, unlike Perot and Forbes, Cain did not spend his fortune on huge media campaigns or campaign advisors.[39] He mobilized his support almost entirely through events and speeches, and eschewed traditional campaign strategies and organizations. This emphasis on Cain's interpersonal talents helped build his support amongst survey respondents as his reputation grew, but it caused problems within the campaign itself.

Organizational Scarcity

Media accounts of Cain's campaign staff and organization were relatively rare. His campaign was unique in that most positions were named not after traditional political titles, but rather used corporate lingo. Cain was the CEO, his campaign manager was the Chief of Staff, and the top fundraiser was the Director of Development. However, coverage generally focused on two issues: an inexperienced and volatile campaign staff, and Cain's peculiar strategy choices.

By most accounts, Cain relied upon a team of relative political novices and castoffs. Cain's Chief of Staff and most trusted political advisor, Mark Block, is described by one conservative writer as "weird."[40] Block was accused of impropriety in a 2001 Wisconsin Supreme Court campaign, paid a $15,000 fine and was forced out of politics until 2004. Cain met Block while Block ran Wisconsin chapter of Americans for Prosperity, funded by the billionaire conservative donors, the Koch brothers. It was while Cain worked as a spokesperson for Americans for Prosperity that Block convinced Cain that he could be a legitimate presidential contender. Block oversaw a separate, but related group, Prosperity USA, and there is an ongoing investigation into whether Cain's campaign improperly received financial support from Prosperity USA.[41] Block starred in a bizarre internet campaign video where he stared strangely into the camera and smoked a cigarette. Other staffers created similarly strange storylines. Cain's chief economic advisor and architect of the 9-9-9 plan was Rich Lowrie, whose primary political experience was with the Ohio chapter of Americans for Prosperity. Lowrie, who had no formal economics training, was widely criticized for failing to provide answers to questions about 9-9-9, and avoiding attempts to more deeply explain its details. Prior to joining the Cain campaign, he worked as an investment advisor.[42] Another campaign consultant, Scott Toomey, was reportedly hidden from the public because he is gay.[43] Cain's vice president of national field and political preparations, Jamie Brazil, also had a sketchy past, reportedly having been "barred by the National Association of Securities Dealers in 2006 'from associating with any member in any capacity.'"[44] Cain rarely recruited staff with national political experience, and when he did, they rarely stayed long.

Cain's unique interpersonal style caused some turmoil within the staff. During June and July several major staff members resigned, including both his Iowa and New Hampshire campaign directors, who charged that he was not serious about running a successful campaign.[45] His first campaign manager left in June, and Cain went months before replacing him. This left Cain unprepared for the upsurge he experienced in October. His top two communications aides left the campaign as well.[46] According to one report, the Cain campaign distributed a "memo ordering staff not to speak to . . . Mr. Cain unless spoken to."[47] Generally speaking, Cain's campaign staff lacked the stability, experience, and professionalism to either structure the candidate's decision-making, or to deal with the inevitable ebbs and flows of a long campaign.

Questionable Strategy

One of the major complaints of disaffected staffers (and conservative journalists) was the problematic campaign travel schedule and organization. Some of these decisions were Cain's own, as part of his strategy. He apparently saw the campaign as an extension of his personality, which he viewed as casual and based on charisma. According to staffers, his campaign lacked regular meetings or even conference calls.[48] After Cain's surprising Florida Straw Poll victory, Cain was accused by staffers as overly focused on his book tour, rather than attempting to consolidate his newfound prominence. He did not appear in Iowa for nearly two months from August to November, instead visiting states like Tennessee and Virginia, states not anywhere near the front of the primary calendar. The Cain campaign's non-traditional structure prevented it from managing basic tasks, such as communicating with supporters, attracting donors, and organizing campaign events. One *New York Times Magazine* profile describes a typical incident where Cain not only kept a restless crowd waiting nearly an hour, but did so while sitting on stage with his back to the silent crowd while conducting a phone interview with Fox News' Mike Huckabee.[49] This lack of focus and attention to detail was most obvious when the candidate faced sexual harassment revelations in November (see below). Some staff questioned whether he was serious about running for president, or whether the entire exercise was simply a publicity tour.[50]

Debate Performances

Cain's charismatic performances and ability to connect with audiences at campaign stops allowed him to overcome shortcomings in staff selection and organizational sophistication. These abilities extended to debate performances. Although Cain was not a central player in many of the debates, his second rise in the polls in late September made him a focal point of a series of debates as other candidates began attacking his positions, particularly his 9-9-9 plan. Prior to his October rise in the polls, Cain was able to effectively discuss his business experiences and engage audiences with humor and attacks on President Obama. During October debates, Cain was a target of other candidates, and although he did not falter, he largely stayed out of the fray.

Cain's campaign theme was to "Let Herman be Herman" and his staffers were inclined to let Herman call the shots.[51] Cain did not think the normal rules of presidential campaign organizations applied to him. He failed to fully staff his campaign, and those he did hire did not have the experience or stature to rein in his idiosyncrasies, nor to compel him to take basic steps toward consolidating success. Although other successful nomination campaigns have undergone organizational upheaval (see John McCain, summer 2007), Cain's was unable to recover because he made decisions based on instinct rather than coherent strategies of presidential electioneering. The same personality that made him such an appealing candidate to disaffected voters around the country made him unwilling or unable to make difficult choices when faced with the inevitable obstacles that any candidate faces.

OUTCOMES

In spite of the Cain campaign's organizational difficulties and policy mishaps, and possibly because of them, he outperformed any pundit or critic's wildest imagination. Initially dismissed by many as an arrogant, wealthy, bored businessman taking advantage of his relative radio fame, Cain instead took advantage of the Republican electorate's willingness to throw their support to candidates who spoke bluntly and passionately about America's promise, and presented an alternative to Mitt Romney. In a field many decried as weak, Cain began as the longest of the long shots. But his performance in the polls belied the predictions and his nontraditional campaign. For at least a month, he could credibly be called the most prominent alternative to Mitt Romney. Ultimately Cain's campaign foundered not from vague policy positions, organizational chaos, or political inexperience, but from sexual harassment accusations and claims of an affair.

Cain's first introduction to a national audience and serious coverage by the media came with his victory in the September Florida Straw Poll. This victory was driven by a "fiery speech . . . that had the crowd on their feet for an extended standing ovation."[52] At the time, Cain was stagnating in the polls at around 5 percent, but his victory commenced a climb to GOP fame.[53] The Florida vote was a huge setback for Rick Perry and Michele Bachmann, both of whom had hoped to consolidate their respective summer polling gains with a victory in an important swing state. Cain's victory gave him exposure and opportunities that had previously eluded him.

Cain's Florida victory, and the subsequent media attention to both his campaign and his 9-9-9 tax plan, led to a nearly two month run as the top challenger to Mitt Romney in the national polls. On Saturday September 24, the day of the Florida Straw Poll, Real Clear Politics' aggregate poll put Cain's national support at only 5.2 percent, ahead of only Rick Santorum and Jon Huntsman. One week later, on October 1, Cain trailed only Perry and Romney, and by October 8, as Perry's support collapsed, Cain trailed Romney by only five percentage points, 21.8 percent to 16.2 percent. From October 20 to November 10, Cain led the national polls with approximately 25 percent of respondents' support.

During this stretch, Cain faced the scrutiny that comes with being a legitimate candidate for the presidency. Cain's 9-9-9 plan, a primary focus of the October 11, 2011 GOP debate in New Hampshire, was criticized by both the media and his fellow GOP candidates. His stump speech and sometimes simplistic policy prescriptions were mocked by other campaigns.[54] Policy misstatements (or mistakes) regarding the immigration fence and abortion were made or exacerbated during this time, and the media and his fellow candidates pounced on his inability to articulate responses to the criticism. But despite the intense scrutiny, Cain maintained his lead in the polls, as many Americans responded to his bold policy proposals, straightforward mannerisms, and engaging speaking style. As the month of October wore on, Perry's debate flubs sunk his numbers, and the polls suggested a two way race between Romney and Cain, with a resurgent Gingrich using his own debate successes to slowly climb back into the race.

Allegations of Sexual Impropriety

On October 30, *Politico* reported a story that would initiate the downfall of the Cain campaign. According to the *Politico* story, two women had accused Cain of inappropriate behavior during his time as CEO of the National Restaurant Association (NRA) in the late 1990s. The women received financial settlements, and were beholden to confidentiality agreements.[55] Cain's campaign responded that "These are old and tired allegations that never stood up to the facts" adding that *Politico* was "part of a smear campaign meant to discredit a true patriot who is shaking up the political status quo."[56]

These initial accusations did not immediately hurt Cain—on the contrary, his poll numbers increased as Cain successfully portrayed the accusers as overly sensitive and the media as driven by liberal bias and racism. Cain told PBS anchor Judy Woodruff that "I referenced this lady's height . . . saying, 'You're the same height of my wife.'" Cain argued that "obviously she thought that that was too close for comfort."[57] Cain told Woodruff that his gregarious personality and willingness to use humor may be interpreted differently by different individuals.[58] Cain's campaign dismissed the reports and accused a former Cain staffer working in Rick Perry's campaign of leaking the information, and argued in an interview with Sean Hannity on November 3 that liberal racism was behind the coverage of the allegations.[59] One of the allegations surrounded a night of drinking where Cain's flirtations escalated to suggestions that the woman accompany him to his suite.[60] One woman claimed the attitudes of her superiors became hostile after she complained to NRA officials. Joel P. Bennett, a lawyer for one of the accusers, said that in contrast to Cain's recollection, it was not a single incident that led to his client's complaints but a "series of inappropriate behaviors and unwanted advances" over a period of two months.[61] Cain appeared indignant toward the allegations, and his campaign appearances became even more enthusiastic and his campaign donations increased during the early days of the scandal.[62] The accusations seemed to galvanize conservative supporters as they rallied behind Cain against what they perceived to be an onslaught of unsubstantiated charges and liberal media attacks.

Although the initial reports of sexual harassment did little to slow the Cain surge, within a week additional developments complicated matters for Cain. On November 7, a woman claimed that in 1997 she had asked for Cain's assistance in securing employment after she had been fired from the NRA. The woman, Sharon Bailek, alleged that Cain surprised her by paying for an upgraded hotel room, and then, after dinner and drinks, he reached up her skirt and implied that if she wanted help from him, she should engage in sexual activity. When Bailek declined, she claimed that Cain said, "You want a job, right?"[63] Bailek's account was supported by her boyfriend at the time, who said the incident was disturbing for her. The following day, Karen Kraushaar, one of the women who received a financial settlement from the NRA, came forward to defend her allegations, and attempted to organize a press conference with other accusers.[64] Cain's campaign attacked both women's credibility, accusing Bailek, and her celebrity lawyer, Gloria Allred, of creating stories for financial gain, and saying that Kraushaar's accusations were found to be "baseless." Though it took place during the peak of the scandal, the November 9 debate in Michigan only briefly touched on the sexual harassment charges before being dominated by Rick Perry's blunder about which federal departments he would eliminate.

The harassment charges, and the Cain campaign's response to them, began to dominate the GOP storyline. Cain's lawyer, L. Lin Wood, told the *Atlanta Journal Constitution* that other accusers should "think twice" before coming forward, because Cain was considering legal action against those making false claims.[65] According to the Real Clear Politics aggregate polling, Cain continued to attract the support of 25 percent of the respondents on November 10. However, the poor response and negative attention began to take its toll. By Thanksgiving, Cain attracted only 18 percent support, and trailed both Romney and Gingrich, who by then topped the polls.

The week after Thanksgiving, Cain faced a final, fatal, accusation. Ginger White, an Atlanta resident, disclosed to an Atlanta area Fox affiliate that she had carried on a long-term affair with Cain. White described a casual relationship that began in the late 1990s and continued until early 2011, when Cain began considering a presidential run. She claimed he flew her to various engagements throughout the country, showered her with gifts, and helped her with financial problems.[66] After the Fox reporter texted Cain using the number on White's phone, Cain called the phone back, saying she had his number because he was "trying to help her financially."[67] Cain insisted that there was no affair, that he "had known her as a friend" and he was "a soft-hearted person" when it came to helping people financially.[68] After the revelations, Cain retreated to Atlanta to discuss his campaign with his wife, Gloria, who Cain admitted had not known about his financial assistance to White.[69]

During this difficult time, Cain suffered a separate, policy-related, setback that may have been just as damaging to his chances as the sexual harassment charges. On November 14, Cain stumbled badly during a meeting with editors and reporters for *The Milwaukee Journal Sentinel*. During the interview, which was video recorded and posted online, Cain was asked whether he thought President Obama had appropriately responded to the uprising in Libya in early 2011. Cain appeared lost, and searched for an answer, without avail. "President Obama supported the uprising, correct?" Cain said. "President Obama called for the removal of Qaddafi . . . just want to make sure we're talking about the same thing before I say 'yes, I agree,' or 'No, I didn't agree.'" During a response that included several long, uncomfortable pauses, Cain initially said he agreed with the president's approach. As he attempted to explain why, he changed course, saying "Nope, that's a different one," adding "I've got all this stuff twirling around in my head."[70] This confusion only added to a series of foreign policy misstatements during his campaign that contributed to critics' assertions that he lacked basic knowledge about international affairs. Cain's national security advisor, J.D. Gordon indicated the rambling answer was caused by fatigue, and Cain complained that the question itself was vague.[71]

Although Cain continued to defend himself against the harassment charges and denied any inappropriate relationship with Ginger White, he suspended his campaign on December 3. His support was still 14 percent at that time, but Cain claimed that "continued distractions" impaired his ability to campaign effectively, and that the accusations had hurt his family.[72] Cain declared that he would still travel the country promoting his ideas, and on January 28, 2012, he endorsed Newt Gingrich.

ANALYSIS

No scholar or pundit could have predicted in March 2011 the success of the Cain campaign. He truly came from nowhere. Of all the candidates, his stump speech was the perfect blend of anti-Obama attacks and all-American conservatism, delivered by a gifted public speaker. Early in the campaign, Cain was not well known. But those who had heard of him and heard him speak were often sold by the experience. One ABC News/Washington Post poll in October asserted that 70 percent of Republicans say, "the more they get to know about Herman Cain, the more they like him."[73] This finding helps explain his meteoric rise after the increased media attention following the Florida Straw Poll.

Although few people predicted his rise, many critics in the mainstream media and the conservative movement foresaw the shortcomings that helped lead to his eventual fall. Three common themes dominated Cain coverage, both before and after the October surge. First, many, including his own staffers, questioned the seriousness of the Cain run, and wondered openly whether he was more interested in building his personal brand than being president. Second, many critics, including his fellow conservatives, asserted that Cain was simply too unfamiliar with even basic policy knowledge to be a serious candidate for the presidency. Finally, Cain's own quirkiness and emphasis on charismatic speechmaking was both a benefit and a drawback. Though he was likely the most convincing and naturally engaging candidate in the race, critics argued that his campaign was entirely driven by his force of personality.

Questions of Seriousness

From the very beginning of his campaign, before Cain began climbing in the polls and attracting significant media attention, Cain had problems convincing people he was serious about running for the presidency. According to GOP operatives, Cain needed to "give himself over to the discipline of a national campaign."[74] At several junctures, Cain staff members left the campaign, including his Iowa and New Hampshire state directors. Staff members complained that Cain was more concerned with promoting himself than establishing the organizational framework required for a successful campaign.[75] Some aides, according to one media story, claimed "his driving motivation is publicity," and conservative commentators agreed.[76] One columnist said he "was engaged in a year-long branding experiment and wound up a serious contender for the GOP presidential nomination," left frantically hiring staff in October when it became clear that he stumbled into contention.[77] Another claimed his hyperbole made Cain sound "more like a talk-radio provocateur than a serious candidate for the Oval Office."[78] John McCormack of *The Weekly Standard* agreed, claiming that "Cain's red-meat rhetoric may have served him well as a talk radio host, but it is unpresidential."[79] Cain's detour promoting his book was particularly confusing to staffers and the national media. Both Iowa and New Hampshire are states where voters expect personal interactions with candidates, and according to Cain's former New Hampshire director, Matt Murphy, they were ideal states for a candidate, like Cain, without money or name recognition.[80] But instead of building an organization and engaging in face-to-face politicking in these states, Cain traveled to other states promoting his book. Prior to the harassment allegations, the "book tour" narrative dominated media coverage while Cain topped the polls. Because Cain dropped out of the race before Iowa and New Hampshire, it is unclear if this strategy hurt him in these states. Although he did lead the Iowa polls during this time, he never approached Romney in New Hampshire.

Cain's media campaign was largely non-existent, and even his most prominent foray into campaign commercials were confusing at best. The Cain campaign posted two "head-scratching" videos on the internet. In one, campaign advisor Mark Block exhorts volunteers to get involved—in between drags on his cigarette. Although the Cain campaign never portrayed it as anything other than a serious commercial, many commentators wondered if it was meant to be ironic. According to one, "it's weird, and therefore funny and entertaining."[81] A longer video, not produced by the campaign but was linked to its YouTube account, was actually a video short, title "He Carried Yellow Flowers." It was created by and starred Nick Searcy of the FX drama "Justified" and parodied American Western films. The short opened with the apparently meaningless line: "There was a time in America when a man was a man, a horse was a horse, and a man on a horse was just a man on a horse ... unless he carried yellow flowers." The video proceeded to criticize President Obama's use of a teleprompter, and claimed that Cain was a true leader who had success in the real world. It is not clear that these commercials had much impact on the campaign (as of April 1, 2012, the Block cigarette ad had just over 1.8 million hits on YouTube, and the "Yellow Flowers" video had around 450,000), but the ads puzzled supporters and critics alike.[82]

These organizational deficiencies were not merely cosmetic wrinkles or the complaints of those who eschewed outsider candidacies. This lack of organizational support and campaign experience hurt Cain at several points when his campaign needed such an apparatus, most glaringly when the accusations of sexual harassment emerged. Ten days before *Politico* published its report on the NRA harassment settlements, the Cain campaign was asked to respond to the allegations. Cain and his team failed to respond in any way, apparently believing the charges could simply be dismissed as delusions of hypersensitive feminists. One critic noted that "A candidate with professional campaign managers and a more sophisticated operation would have used that time to strategize, come up with a message, and perhaps even scoop Politico by revealing the sexual harassment charges on the campaign's own terms."[83] Onetime Cain sympathizer Erick Erickson at the blog *RedState* asked why "Herman Cain's consultant from 2004 uncovered it [harassment claim] in 2004 and Cain launched a presidential bid in 2011 without coming up with a damage control plan on a major issue that could destroy his campaign?"[84] Many sensed that a strategy of "Let Herman be Herman" could not effectively replace one based on crisis management and disciplined coordination.

Policy Ignorance

Aside from speculation about Cain's motives and campaign strategy, a central reality of both the campaign environment and media analysis of Cain's candidacy was his lack of policy sophistication. More candidly, Cain was accused by many in the mainstream and conservative media (not to mention liberals) of willful ignorance and policy amateurism. Much of this was driven by the policy gaffes discussed above. His confusing statements about abortion and the border moat/fence created the smoke, and his "cringe inducing" interview on Libya engulfed the campaign and, in conjunction with the allegations of sexual impropriety, directly led to Cain's collapse.[85]

Certainly Cain's 9-9-9 plan was not taken seriously by most commentators. Even Cain seemed to evade the implications when one critic complained that his sales tax combined with state sales taxes could result in a tax on goods of over 17 percent in some places. Cain asserted, without explanation, that such concerns were not warranted. "Don't combine it with state taxes" Cain said, adding "These are replacement taxes, they're not on top of anything."[86] Kevin Lowry of *National Review*, claimed that Cain's defense of 9-9-9 "relies on repetition and assertion more than detailed argument."[87]

Some critics claimed Cain's ignorance was ingrained, and disqualifying. Peggy Noonan in *The Wall Street Journal* was particularly critical, arguing that Cain's Libya brain freeze was not a brain freeze at all. According to Noonan, Cain "was desperately trying to retrieve a sound bite and not even trying to hide the fact that he was trying to retrieve a sound bite." She asserted that "To know little and to be proud of knowing little is disrespectful of the democratic process."[88] She was not alone. Lowry, of *National Review* asserted that his Libya gaffe was less forgivable than Rick Perry's executive branch debate gaffe. "Everyone has lost his train of thought" Lowry wrote, adding "Few of us have run for president knowing little about major matters of public import."[89]

The Libya gaffe was only the most prominent of several instances where Cain admitted to being ignorant of central policy issues, especially those related to foreign policy. Cain seemed to be flummoxed by a question about the Palestinian right of return and indicated that it "should be negotiated . . . I don't think they have a big problem with people returning."[90] In another exchange, he claimed he was not familiar with the term "neoconservative" and could therefore not determine whether he identified with that school of thought.[91] He either forgot or did not know that China was already a nuclear power when he stated that one of his goals would be to prevent them from getting the bomb.[92] Finally, in an apparent attempt at humor, Cain defended his foreign policy ignorance by saying that "When they ask me who is the president of Ubeki-beki-beki-beki-stan-stan, I'm going to say, you know, I don't know."[93] He said that "knowing who is the head of some of these small insignificant states around the world" was not important.[94]

Cain dismissed those who argue he does not have the experience to formulate and implement complex policy solutions, and to a certain extent, even embraced his policy ignorance. In his book, he argues that this is a compelling reason to elect him.[95] In some instances, he admits he needs to learn more about foreign policy, stating that without more information, "it's irresponsible to announce a Cain plan" to address Afghanistan.[96] He argued that "There's more that I don't know than I know" adding with candor that "I'm not going to pull a plan out of my ass."[97] His strengths, he argued during campaign speeches and his book, come from his corporate leadership. Cain is at his best, "identifying, framing, and solving problems; surrounding myself with good and great people; and giving speeches to engage the American people in my common sense solutions process."[98] Unlike President Obama, he could provide "an aggressive leadership that's courageous enough to propose and implement new economic strategies."[99] It is this courage and energy, rather than specific policies, that will put the United States on the right course, Cain argued in his campaign. "I must summon my own experiences and abilities as a well-tested corporate leader to confront and solve the myriad crises besotting the nation."[100]

Like former president George W. Bush, Cain emphasized his willingness to gather input from a range of policy advisors. Cain asserts that this is one of his selling points, arguing that he has a "well-honed instinct for identifying the right people to get the job done."[101] Critics fretted Cain's propensity to emphasize delegation, and this quality offended some, as it did when Bush ran in 2000. One conservative asserted that (among other things) "my least favorite thing about Herman Cain is that his response to every challenge is to appoint a committee of smart guys to do the right thing."[102]

Cain's familiarity with basic policy was widely questioned by writers from all ideological backgrounds, and it was often pointed. Some writers were confused and befuddled that Cain could appeal to voters with such policy gaps. Others were more hostile. According to a bracingly critical piece in *The New York Times*, T.A. Frank implied that detractors were overly coy in their denunciations of Cain's policy knowledge. He argued that "To say that Herman Cain has an imperfect grasp of policy would be unfair not only to George W. Bush in 1999, but also to Britney Spears in 1999. Herman Cain seems like someone who, quite frankly, has never opened a newspaper."[103] Though clearly hyperbolic, Frank's position summarized what had become, by the time Cain dropped out in early December, a consensus position on Cain's policy qualifications.

Personality Driven Campaign

The Cain campaign's two major shortcomings, campaign organization and policy competence, were explained by many critics to be a function of his personality. It is, of course, Cain's personality that made him so appealing in the first place. Many business leaders, political novices, and wealthy eccentrics have made attempts at the nation's highest office—few have made it as far as Herman Cain. His singular ability to appeal to the yearning amongst Republican voters for bold leadership, to develop messages that resonated with the media and masses alike, and to deliver stirring, captivating speeches, catapulted Cain from spring 2011 footnote to October 2011 frontrunner. Cain's assertiveness and self-assurance certainly fed the beast that became his compelling run for the presidency. This personality, a requirement for such an audacious run, may also have sown the seeds for its demise.

Cain's engaging public speeches frequently fed a common backhanded compliment. According to one critic, "Cain is such a winsome personality that he gets away with shameless excesses of self-promotion."[104] Another noted, that "his speeches were light on substance and heavy on bromides, which he turned into applause lines through the magic of his delivery," adding that "When he speaks to a crowd, there is a contact high between the candidates and his supporters, and it is unclear who is more pleased to be in the other's presence."[105] Some welcomed his entrance into a Republican race that, though full of interesting candidates, still seemed lackluster. Cain could fill a variety of media needs, because in "a bland field, he'd add charisma, a compelling story, and some craziness."[106] As talented as Cain was, though, it would be the craziness that would bring him down. *The New York Times* editorial page foretold the outcome of Cain's campaign in early November, arguing that "Eventually, a campaign run solely on charm and hokum tends to wind up in a ditch."[107]

The media, driven by its need for an interesting story in a race dominated by the purported inevitability of a Romney victory, embraced the "craziness." Cain's rise to the top of the polls engrossed the country for weeks, until a familiar story of sexual impropriety overtook the narrative. Cain's self-confidence, evident in his book, led many to assert that the dominant characteristics of the campaign—bold statements, brilliant campaign speeches, poor organization, lack of advisors, insufficient policy preparation, and purported sexual transgressions—were all byproducts of Cain's self-regard. Some former Cain staffers spoke "of a man so egotistical that careful self-policing would never really enter into the realm of consideration."[108] Michael Medved of *The Daily Beast* put it more succinctly than most when he wrote that "The real culprit [of Cain's demise] is Cain's bottomless vanity" adding that "his astonishing narcissism" is the real explanation of how he thought he could hide his affair with Ginger White. Medved argues that you can sense this dangerous delusion when you read Cain's book, where "The tone of self-adulation leaches so fulsomely out of every page that it practically gets on your hands."[109]

When we look back on Herman Cain's astonishing run for the GOP nomination, several lessons will likely dominate the narrative. The power and ubiquity of internet video will remind us of how poor performances, even to obscure editorial boards of small regional newspapers, can haunt political aspirants. Most likely, Cain will also join a long list of politicians whose sexual indiscretions highlight their encyclopedia entries. And finally, we'll note that the brashest, the most antiestablishment, and the most charismatic of the presidential aspirants was able, for a few weeks, to overcome substantive handicaps that most, even ideological brethren, considered disqualifying. But ultimately, these handicaps proved insurmountable, even in an election when Republican voters were looking for the brashest, most antiestablishment, and most charismatic candidate.

NOTES

1. Herman Cain, *This is Herman Cain! My Journey to the White House* (New York: Threshold Editions, 2011).
2. Before entering the corporate world, Cain briefly worked as a mathematician in the U.S. Navy.
3. Cain, *This is Herman Cain*, 47-48.
4. Cain was also on the Board of Directors of the Kansas City Federal Reserve Bank in the 1990s, but he rarely mentioned this to supporters, many of who call for the dismantling of the Fed.

Chapter 6

5. Nash Keune, "Godfather vs. Tax Man: So How Good a Businessman is Herman Cain?," *Wall Street Journal* 2011, from ABI/INFORM Global (Document ID: 2370194391) (accessed March 7, 2012).

6. Cain, *This is Herman Cain*, 164. It is also important to note that Cain writes his book from the future tense, as though he has already won the general election and is in the White House looking back on his journey.

7. Cain, *This is Herman Cain*, 16.

8. Richard A. Oppel, Jr., "Snag for Perry: Offensive Name at Texas Camp," *The New York Times*, October 3, 2011, A1; Robin Abcarian, "Cain Links Latest Controversy to Race," *Los Angeles Times*, November 5, 2011, A9.

9. Cain, *This is Herman Cain*, 151.

10. Cain also spends all of Chapter 9 explaining the significance of the number "45," providing an array of examples of how frequently it "keeps popping up" in his life and in his campaign.

11. Cain, *This is Herman Cain*, 88.

12. John McCormack, "A Cain-Do Candidate," *The Weekly Standard*, June 20, 2011.

13. The plan was clearly created quickly. The 9-9-9 plan was released around September 5, 2011, one month prior to the publication of the Cain campaign book in early October 2011. In Cain's campaign book, he does not mention 9-9-9, and simply proposes a two-step process of tax reform. First adopt Rep. Paul Ryan's tax proposals, and second, eventually adopt the FairTax, a consumption tax popular in the conservative talk radio world and among some Tea Party supporters. The 9-9-9 plan was released around September 5, 2011, one month prior to the publication of the book. It seems plausible that the plan was created sometime in August, after the book was sent to the printer.

14. John McKinnon, "Study Puts Cain's '9-9-9' Plan Under the Microscope," *Wall Street Journal*, October 19, 2011, A5.

15. Arthur Laffer, "Cain's Stimulating '9-9-9' Tax Reform," *Wall Street Journal*, October 19, 2011, A15.

16. McKinnon, "Study Puts Cain's '9-9-9' Plan."

17. Bruce Bartlett, "Economix: Inside the Cain Tax Plan," *The New York Times* 2011, http://economix.blogs.nytimes.com/2011/10/11/inside-the-cain-tax-plan/?scp=1&sq=Inside percent20the percent20Cain percent20Tax percent20Plan&st=cse (accessed March 7, 2012).

18. "Bold, Brash, and Wrong," *National Review*, November 14, 2011, 18.

19. Kevin D. Williamson, "Nein! Nein! Nein!," *National Review Online* 2011, http://www.nationalreview.com/articles/278668/nein-nein-nein-kevin-d-williamson (accessed March 7, 1012).

20. Cain, *This is Herman Cain*, 131.

21. Cain, *This is Herman Cain*, 179.

22. Cain, *This is Herman Cain*, 180-181.

23. Cain, *This is Herman Cain*, 183.

24. Cain, *This is Herman Cain*, 176.

25. Cain, *This is Herman Cain*, 175.

26. "Herman Cain," http://2012election.procon.org/view.source.election.php?sourceID=11136 (accessed March 6, 2012).

27. Sarah Wheaton, "The Caucus: Amid Abortion Questions, Cain Steps Up Iowa Game," *The New York Times* 2011, http://thecaucus.blogs.nytimes.com/2011/10/20/amid-abortion-questions-cain-steps-up-iowa-game/?scp=1&sq=Amid percent20Abortion percent20Questions&st=cse (accessed March 7, 2012).

28. The Morgan interview can be found at http://www.youtube.com/watch?v=OPKYYDefMV4 (accessed March 7, 2012).

29. Sarah Wheaton, "The Caucus: Amid Abortion Questions, Cain Steps Up Iowa Game," *The New York Times* 2011, http://thecaucus.blogs.nytimes.com/2011/10/20/amid-abortion-questions-cain-steps-up-iowa-game/?scp=1&sq=Amid percent20Abortion percent20Questions&st=cse (accessed March 7, 2012).

30. Cain, *This is Herman Cain*, 127.
31. Edward Wyatt, "The Caucus: Cain Proposes Electrified Border Fence," *The New York Times* 2011, http://thecaucus.blogs.nytimes.com/2011/10/15/cain-proposes-electrified-border-fence/?scp=1&sq=Cain percent20Proposes percent20Electrified percent20Border percent20Fence&st=cse (accessed March 7, 2012).
32. Susan Saulny and Sarah Wheaton, "The Caucus: Cain Says His Deadly Fence Plan Was 'a joke'," *The New York Times* 2011, http://thecaucus.blogs.nytimes.com/2011/10/16/cain-says-his-deadly-fence-plan-was-a-joke/?scp=1&sq=Deadly percent20Fence percent20Plan&st=cse (accessed March 7, 2012).
33. "Cain Denies Claims He Said He Would Not Appoint Muslims," *Politifact* 2011, http://www.politifact.com/georgia/statements/2011/jun/08/herman-cain/cain-denies-claims-he-said-he-would-not-appoint-mu/ (accessed March 7, 2012).
34. The Cavuto interview can be found at http://www.youtube.com/watch?v=F8jGnpbED9E&feature=player_embedded (accessed March 7, 2012).
35. The Fisher interview can be found at http://www.youtube.com/watch?v=CCwPh8n8GpY&feature=player_embedded (accessed March 7, 2012).
36. Cain, *This is Herman Cain*, 182.
37. The Beck interview can be found at http://www.youtube.com/watch?v=fhB7E7veRZc&feature=related (accessed March 7, 2012).
38. Richard A. Oppel, Jr., "Cain Stumbles in Assessing Foreign Policy," *The New York Times*, November 15, 2011, A19.
39. In reality, Cain did not have such a fortune to spend. Cain reported a net worth between $2.9 million and $6.8 million, while Perot is currently worth over $3.5 billion and Forbes is worth $450 million. According to FEC records, Cain contributed $575,000 to his own campaign.
40. Marc Ambinder, "The Real Conspiracy Against Herman Cain," *National Journal* 2011, http://decoded.nationaljournal.com/2011/11/the-real-conspiracy-against-he.php (accessed March 7, 2012).
41. Trip Gabriel, "Cain's Campaign Aide Faces Tough Questions," *The New York Times*, November 4, 2011, A16.
42. Trip Gabriel and Susan Saulny, "With Three 9s, Cain Refigured Math for Taxes," *The New York Times*, October 13, 2011, A1.
43. T. A. Frank, "On the Ropes With Herman Cain," *The New York Times Magazine*, November 6, 2011, 28-33.
44. Frank, "On the Ropes."
45. . Patrick O'Connor, and Neil King, Jr., "Cain's Gains in Polls Bring Opportunity, Challenges." *Wall Street Journal* 2011 from ABI/INFORM Global (Document ID: 2476487981) (accessed March 7, 2012).
46. Michael Crowley, "Herman Cain: Flash in the Pan or 'Serious Candidate'?," *Time Swampland*, October 6, 2011, http://swampland.time.com/2011/10/06/herman-cain-flash-in-the-pan-or-serious-candidate (accessed March 7, 2012).
47. Sarah Wheaton, "The Caucus: Discovering a Cain Campaign Sleeper Hit," *The New York Times* 2011, http://thecaucus.blogs.nytimes.com/2011/10/27/herman-cains-other-viral-vide/?scp=2&sq=Sleeper percent20Hit&st=cse (accessed March 7, 2012).
48. O'Connor and King, Jr., "Cain's Gains in Polls."
49. Frank, "On the Ropes."
50. Michael Crowley, "Herman Cain: Flash in the Pan or 'Serious Candidate'?," *Time Swampland*, October 6, 2011, http://swampland.time.com/2011/10/06/herman-cain-flash-in-the-pan-or-serious-candidate (accessed March 7, 2012); Michael Crowley, "The Cain Mutiny," *Time*, October 24, 2011, 36-41.
51. Neil King, "Cain Never Prepared for the Storm: Shifting Responses to Sexual Harassment Allegations Reflect Motto of Unorthodox Campaign, 'Let Herman Be Herman'," *Wall Street Journal*, November 4, 2011, A6.
52. Michael D. Shear, "The Caucus: Herman Cain Wins Florida Straw Poll," *The New York Times* 2011, http://thecaucus.blogs.nytimes.com/2011/09/24/herman-cain-

wins-florida-straw-poll/?scp=1&sq=Herman percent20Cain percent20Wins percent20Florida percent20Straw percent20Poll&st=cse (accessed March 7, 2012).

53. All poll numbers come from the Real Clear Politics 2012 Republican Presidential Nomination tracking poll, found at http://www.realclearpolitics.com/epolls/2012/president/us/republican_presidential_nomination-1452.html (accessed March 6, 2012).

54. Trip Gabriel, "Tested Again and Again, Cain Takes Comfort in His Rise in the Polls," *The New York Times*, October 31, 2011, A13.

55. Jonathan Martin, Maggie Haberman, Anna Palmer and Kenneth P. Vogel, "Herman Cain Accused by Two Women of Inappropriate Behavior," *Politico* 2011, http://www.politico.com/news/stories/1011/67194.html (accessed March 7, 2012).

56. Martin, Haberman, Palmer and Vogel, "Herman Cain Accused."

57. Jim Rutenberg and Michael D. Shear, "Cain Confronts Claim From '90s of Harassment," *The New York Times*, November 1, 2011, A1.

58. Rutenberg and Shear, "Cain Confronts Claim."

59. Robin Abcarian, "Cain Links Latest Controversy to Race," *Los Angeles Times*, November 5, 2011, A9.

60. Jim Rutenberg and Jeff Zeleny, "Woman Said to Have Felt Hostility at Work After Complaining About Cain," *The New York Times*, November 4, 2011, A16.

61. Michael D. Shear, Jim Rutenberg and Jeff Zeleny, "Cain Accuser Tells of Pattern, Lawyer Attests," *The New York Times*, November 5, 2011, A1.

62. According to FEC records (http://query.nictusa.com/pres/) Cain raised $2,567,499.87 the 2nd quarter of 2011, $2,813,441.52 in the 3rd quarter, and $11,480,745.35 in the 4th quarter. Cain raised $245,604.01 — the largest single day of fundraising in his entire campaign — on November 1, 2011 . . . the day after the harassment story became national news.

63. Jim Rutenberg and Michael D. Shear, "Woman Accuses Cain of Groping; He Denies Charge," *The New York Times*, November 8, 2011, A1.

64. Michael D. Shear and Jim Rutenberg, "Cain Again Denies Accusations As Second Woman Goes Public," *The New York Times*, November 9, 2011, A1.

65. Bill Torpy, "Atlanta Attorney Lin Wood Hired to Defend Cain," *The Atlanta Journal-Constitution*, November 9, 2011, A10.

66. Susan Saulny, "Woman Claims Affair With Cain, and He Denies It," *The New York Times*, November 29, 2011, A19.

67. Saulny, "Woman Claims Affair."

68. Susan Saulny, "Cain Says He Gave Money To Woman Claiming Affair," *The New York Times*, December 2, 2011, A26.

69. Saulny, "Cain Says He Gave Money."

70. The *Milwaukee Journal Sentinel* interview can be found at http://www.youtube.com/watch?v=ngmgKRnkE7M&feature=plcp&context=C350bd46UDOEgsToPDskIYoLLbssX0A1KCCGvl_bZ6 (accessed on March 7, 2012).

71. Oppel, Jr., "Cain Stumbles"; Susan Saulny, "From Cain, More on Libya," *The New York Times*, November 19, 2011, A12.

72. Susan Saulny, "A Defiant Cain Suspends His Bid For Presidency," *The New York Times*, December 4, 2011, A1.

73. John McCormack, "The Cain Surge," *The Weekly Standard*, October 24, 2011. For other analyses of this phenomenon, see Jason Riley, "Cain's Post-Racial Promise," *Wall Street Journal*, October 7, 2011, A13.

74. Neil King, "Cain's Next Test: Harnessing Surge," *Wall Street Journal*, October 17, 2011, A4.

75. Saulny, "A Defiant Cain"; Julie Jargon, "Cain's Legacy: Selling Big Ideas," *Wall Street Journal*, October 22, 2011, A4; Michael Crowley, "Herman Cain: Flash in the Pan or 'Serious Candidate'?" *Time Swampland* 2011, http://swampland.time.com/2011/10/06/herman-cain-flash-in-the-pan-or-serious-candidate (accessed March 7, 2012).

76. Michael Crowley, "The Cain Mutiny," *Time*, October 24, 2011, 36-41.

77. Peggy Noonan, "A Caveman Won't Beat a Salesman," *Wall Street Journal*, November 19, 2011, A15; Neil King, "Cain's Next Test: Harnessing Surge," *Wall Street Journal*, October 17, 2011, A4.
78. John J. Miller, "Is Cain Able?" *National Review*, June 20, 2011, 32.
79. McCormack, "The Cain Surge."
80. O'Connor and King, Jr., "Cain's Gains."
81. James Taranto, "Thanks You for Smoking; Herman Cain's Latest Ad is a Real Head-Scratcher," *Wall Street Journal*, October 25, 2011.
82. The Block video can be found at: http://www.youtube.com/watch?v=qhm-22Q0PuM and the Yellow Flowers video can be found at: http://www.youtube.com/watch?v=dSlC7BxmSqY&list=UUsRq2 PbttxbBJYK49n58L1A&index=15&feature=plcp (accessed on March 28, 2012).
83. Michael D. Shear, "The Caucus: Pundits Can Say, 'I told You So',"*The New York Times* 2011, http://thecaucus.blogs.nytimes.com/2011/11/02/pundits-can-say-i-told-you-so/?scp=2&sq=Pundits percent20can percent20say&st=cse (accessed March 7, 2012).
84. Ashley Southall, "The Caucus: Conservative Bloggers Cool to Cain," *The New York Times* 2011, http://thecaucus.blogs.nytimes.com/2011/11/02/conservative-bloggers-cool-to-cain/?scp=1&sq=cool percent20to percent20cain&st=cse (accessed March 7, 2012).
85. Rich Lowry, "Cain's Knowledge-Deficit Disorder," *National Review* 2011, http://www.nationalreview.com/articles/283454/cain-s-knowledge-deficit-disorder-rich-lowry (accessed March 7, 2012).
86. Susan Saulny and Sarah Wheaton, "The Caucus: Cain Says His Deadly Fence Plan Was 'a joke,'" *The New York Times* 2011, http://thecaucus.blogs.nytimes.com/2011/10/16/cain-says-his-deadly-fence-plan-was-a-joke/?scp=1&sq=Deadly percent20Fence percent20Plan&st=cse (accessed March 7, 2012).
87. Lowry, "Cain's Knowledge-Deficit Disorder."
88. Noonan, "A Caveman."
89. Lowry, "Cain's Knowledge-Deficit Disorder."
90. . John J. Miller, "Is Cain Able?" *National Review*, June 20, 2011, 32.
91. Saulny and Wheaton, "The Caucus."
92. "Herman Cain's Foreign Policy," *Foreign Policy* 2011, http://www.foreignpolicy.com/herman_cain/profile (accessed March 7, 2012).
93. John McCormack, "The Cain Surge," *The Weekly Standard*, October 24, 2011.
94. Steven Lee Myers, "The Caucus: Herman Cain, Hamid Karzai Knows Your Name," *The New York Times* 2011, http://thecaucus.blogs.nytimes.com/2011/10/20/herman-cain-hamid-karzai-knows-your-name/?scp=1&sq=Hamid%20Karzai%20knows%20your%20name&st=cse (accessed March 7, 2012).
95. Cain, *This is Herman Cain*, Ch. 12.
96. Miller, "Is Cain Able?"
97. McCormack, "A Cain-Do Candidate."
98. Cain, *This is Herman Cain*, 189.
99. Cain, *This is Herman Cain*, 171.
100. Cain, *This is Herman Cain*, 163.
101. Cain, *This is Herman Cain*, 163.
102. Williamson, "Nein! Nein! Nein!."
103. Frank, "On the Ropes."
104. Lowry, "Cain's Knowledge-Deficit Disorder."
105. Trip Gabriel, "Tested Again and Again, Cain Takes Comfort in His Rise in the Polls," *The New York Times*, October 31, 2011, A13.
106. Joshua Green, "Herman Cain, the GOP Wild Card," *The Atlantic*, March 2011, 17-18.
107. "The Stumbling Campaign of Herman Cain," *The New York Times*, November 3, 2011, A30.
108. Frank, "On the Ropes."

109. Michael Tomasky, "What Really Killed Herman Cain's Campaign," *The Daily Beast* 2011, http://www.thedailybeast.com/newsweek/2011/12/04/what-really-killed-herman-cain-s-campaign.html (accessed March 7, 2012).

SEVEN

Rick Perry: The Quickly Fading Star of Texas

Brian Arbour

Every April, the National Football League holds its draft, where teams pick college players to join them at the highest level of football. The marquee players each draft are the quarterbacks. Scouts sort through all the college quarterbacks to identify those with the strong arms, quick feet, agile minds, and proven leadership skills needed to succeed and win in the NFL. Many of these top prospects do succeed, becoming NFL stars like Peyton Manning, Donovan McNabb, or Aaron Rodgers. But there is an even longer list of first round quarterback busts. Ryan Leaf, Cade McNown, Tim Couch, David Carr, Joey Harrington, Matt Leinart, and Jamarcus Russell were all-star quarterbacks at the college level, and all were drafted highly by NFL teams. And, all of these quarterbacks quickly proved to be completely out of their depth in the NFL. Each of them is famous today as a "bust" in NFL circles.

This chapter focuses on Rick Perry, who is famous today as a "bust" in campaign circles. Like these NFL busts, Perry was dominant at one level, and scouting reports indicated he was an outstanding prospect for a higher level. Perry brought a raft of advantages to the 2012 Republican primary—positioning as an experienced conservative in a field that seemed to lack a candidate with both credentials, the political savvy to win statewide office in Texas six times without a defeat, a successful record on jobs growth as governor of Texas, an extensive fund raising network, and a well-regarded but hungry campaign team. When Perry joined the race in August 2011, he looked like he could lead his team to victory in the primary, and potentially the general election.

Like the famous NFL busts, Perry quickly proved to be out of his depth on a higher level. A series of gaffes in his first weekend on the campaign trail caused by belligerent and aggressive rhetoric presaged a campaign marked by rhetorical blunders and the inability to develop a coherent and effective message. Perry's initial lead in opinion polls eroded. His embarrassing "oops" moment at a November debate—when Perry could not remember the third Cabinet Department he wanted to eliminate—left Perry dead in the water for the rest of the nomination contest. Perry was felled by a lack of effort and a lack of campaign intelligence. His campaign seemed listless and uninspired, and Perry's lack of preparation on issues on which he was vulnerable (e.g., immigration and HPV vaccinations for teenage girls) raised questions not just about his conservative bona fides, but also his intelligence and political savvy.

The presidential campaign of Rick Perry presents an excellent story of the rise and fall of a particular individual. This chapter first focuses on the rise of Rick Perry, explaining the factors that made him the political equivalent of a first round draft pick to pundits and Republican Party leaders—his conservative credentials, his record as Texas governor, his perceived indomitable campaign skills, and his strong fund raising skills. The rise of Rick Perry ends when he announces his campaign for President, and I trace the events that proved him a bust as a presidential campaign—his seemingly ill-prepared debate performances, his rambling and unfocused campaign style, his disconnected campaign advertisements, and his "oops" moment in the November 9, 2011 debate. Finally, I assess why Perry's campaign failed, and what it means.

CANDIDATE BACKGROUND

Three themes emerge from Perry's biography and background which made him look to be a formidable candidate in 2012. First, Perry possesses a rural and military background. Second, Perry had a campaign record that was unmatched in the field—winning nine elections without a defeat, including six statewide elections in the nation's second largest state. Third, Perry possessed a conservative record as Governor of Texas, highlighted by Texas's strong job growth, a vital asset for a candidate running during a tepid economic recovery. This combination, especially in contrast to conventional wisdom that the Republicans had a "weak field,"[1] made Perry look like a formidable candidate when he announced his candidacy on August 13, 2011.[2]

Perry has a rural and military background, a clear asset in any Republican political contest. Paul Burka, dean of Texas political reporters, says "the first place you need to go to understand Perry is Paint Creek, where he grew up. Paint Creek is not a town. It's a watercourse that runs through the cotton fields of southern Haskell County" in rural West Texas. "Perry's parents were tenant farmers, and not just tenant farmers but dryland farmers, which is as hard as farming gets."[3] Perry's family had worked as farmers and ranchers in Haskell County for years, and while Perry's family was not well-off, Perry's father won election as County Commissioner, indicating his respect in the community.[4] As a teenager, Perry earned Eagle Scout, played on the Paint Creek High football team, and graduated third in his class of 13.[5] It is hard to imagine a more rural background for a contemporary presidential candidate.

Perry attended Texas A&M University, known for "its conservative culture, military tradition, and focus on agriculture."[6] Perry "bought all the way in" to A&M's unique culture,[7] and stood as a "staunch traditionalist" in the context of changes at the campus.[8] Perry served in the college's ROTC program, known as the Corps of Cadets. The Corps is often seen as the center of the Aggie student body, which has significant roots as a military college. In addition, Perry also served as a Yell Leader, charged with leading chants at football games and other sporting events. Aggies regard Yell Leaders with great importance, so much so that the positions are elected by the student body.[9]

After graduating from A&M in 1972 with a degree in Animal Sciences, Perry served in the Air Force reserves. He completed pilot training in 1974 and served out of Dyess Air Force Base outside of Abilene, TX. He flew cargo planes on relief missions to the nations of Mali, Mauritania, and Chad, but did not see live combat. According to the *New York Times*, Perry's military service " both expanded and narrowed him, taking him to exotic locales while cementing his Texas roots and the traditional, conservative values that have been so central to his political identity" and connected his emergence "as a muscular interventionist" in contemporary political debates to his military service.[10]

Put together, Perry's pre-political biography indicates that his campaign stances in favor of traditional values and his support for traditional institutions like the Boy Scouts were not election year conveniences, but expressions of long-standing views. As such, Perry's biography provided him credibility with conservative audiences. Further, his rural, military, and agricultural backgrounds contrasted favorably with the upper class backgrounds of Mitt Romney and Jon Huntsman, and the urban background of Barack Obama.

The second theme of Perry's background is his remarkable record of political success. Perry has run in nine elections, and won every one. Seven of those victories were statewide. Perry's first statewide race was in 1990. Like the vast majority of Texas politicians in the 1980s, Perry was a Democrat. Perry switch parties because—like many conservative Texas (and Southern) Democrats—he found the Republican Party more congenital to both his conservative policy positions and his political ambitions.[11] In Perry's case, his ambitions were for the post of Agriculture Commissioner, and he challenged incumbent Democrat Jim Hightower for the position. Few gave Perry a chance against Hightower, who combined an "awe shucks" country style with a biting wit. His populist political message gained national notoriety among liberals. But Perry campaigned on two fronts. His positive campaign advertisements emphasized his conservative background over images of him saddling and riding a horse. At the same time, his campaign attacked Hightower for using government credit cards for personal and political expenses.[12] Boosted by Texas's growing Republican affiliation, Perry defeated Hightower 49-48.

Perry was again an underdog in 1998, as he sought a promotion to Lieutenant Governor. The 1998 race attracted particular attention, as Governor George W. Bush was expected to run for President in 2000, which meant the winner might serve as Governor in the second half of the term. The Democratic candidate John Sharp had a long and successful career in politics, ranging from serving as student body president at Texas A&M (his campaign manager was his close friend from the Corps, Rick Perry),[13] state representative, and the state's Comptroller. His experience and moderate politics made him the favorite of political insiders, editorial boards, and Chamber of Commerce types. Perry emphasized conservative themes, and, in exchange for avoiding negative advertisements that would alienate moderate voters, George Bush's campaign maven Karl Rove garnered a Perry endorsement from former President George H. W. Bush.[14] Emphasizing low taxes and rural values, and aided by George W. Bush's landslide at the top of the ticket, Perry upset Sharp 50-48.[15]

In 2010, Perry faced his biggest challenge. Kay Bailey Hutchison, the state's long serving and popular Senator, challenged Perry in the Republican primary. Early polls showed that Hutchison held larger approval and favorability numbers than Perry, and many observers thought she would upset Perry.[16] Perry's campaign team quickly defined the race in terms of conservative versus moderate, and Texas versus Washington. Perry's television advertisements attacked Hutchison for being a Washington insider and for voting in favor of the TARP program. Hutchison ran a listless campaign, and never developed a message explaining why she wanted to be governor.[17] Perry crushed her, winning 51-30.[18]

Perry has won re-election as governor in three general elections. In 2002, Democrats hoped that businessman Tony Sanchez and a diverse slate of candidates would boost minority turnout. Perry's attacks on Sanchez for ties to Mexican drug lords at Laredo bank where Sanchez served as a Director combined with Sanchez's poor skills as a candidate, led to a rout. Perry won 58-40. In 2006, three candidates emerged to run against Perry in the general election—in addition to Democratic nominee Chris Bell, a former Congressman, state Comptroller Carol Keaton Strayhorn and comic author and musician Kinky Friedman ran as independents. The combination of Perry's appeal to his conservative and Republican bases and a divided opposition allowed Perry to win with 40 percent of vote (Bell finished second with 30 percent). In 2010, Democrats ran their strongest candidate, former Houston Mayor Bill White. But the conservative bent of the state, the national Republican tide, and momentum created by crushing Hutchison meant that Perry was never in trouble. He won in a landslide 55-42.

The third important theme of Perry's biography was an enviable record on jobs. As the *Washington Post* put it "[a]t the heart of Rick Perry's presidential pitch is a simple, seductive statistic. Since 2009, 37 percent of all new jobs in the United States have been created in Texas—even as the rest of the country has been limping through a weak recovery."[19] Texas "added 1.2 million net jobs since Perry took office as Texas Governor in December 2000, while the United States as a whole lost 1.1 million jobs during the same time."[20] Perry could tout the Texas Enterprise Fund and the Emerging Technology Fund for their roles in creating jobs in his state. These funds, created during Perry's tenure, enable the governor and other state officials to "award one-time financial incentives to businesses looking to relocate or expand in Texas." Companies such as General Electric, Facebook, eBay, and Petco received these grants.[21] According to Perry, creating jobs "isn't rocket science. You keep the taxes relatively low, you have a regulatory climate that is fair."[22] In other words, applying conservative principles produces job growth, which provided Perry a winning issue on the campaign trail.

Of course, it is unclear how much effect Perry and his policies had on Texas's job growth. The most trenchant critique of Texas's job growth is that it is an artifact of the state's population growth.[23] The state's population grew in part due to high birthrates, especially among Hispanics, migration from other states, and immigration from Mexico and Central America.[24] While it is possible these migrants were attracted by the state's low taxes and lax regulatory environment, it is more likely that migrants came as part of the long term trend of migration toward warmer climates and the availability of real estate. Texas combines permissive zoning and land use regimes[25] with strict restrictions on home mortgages.[26] The combination kept the housing bubble away in the middle of the 2000s, and thus, the housing slump also stayed away during the most recent recession. Thus, strict regulations by the state government on mortgages helped Texas to avoid the worst of the housing-induced recession, which goes against the benefits of conservative *laissez-faire* economic policies that Perry liked to tout.

Overall, Perry claims more credit for the economic success of Texas than he deserves. But such a pattern is the norm in politics, and voters would of course give him a disproportionate share of the blame had the state's economy suffered during his term. Thus, the jobs issue was a clear advantage for Perry, and one he would exploit during the campaign.

Having jobs in 2012 was a clear advantage for Perry, but his record as Texas governor on other issues was mediocre at best. Perry has always suffered from the comparison to his predecessor George W. Bush. Perry's style has also contrasted with Bush's. While Bush reached across the partisan aisle in an effort to be a "uniter, not a divider, Perry seemed to prefer to be feared rather than loved. His signature moment as Governor was the Father's Day Massacre, when he vetoed 82 bills approved in his first legislative session as governor.[27] Texas journalist Paul Burka noted that as chief executive, Perry has been "dismissive of Democrats and fond of political maneuvers that put the heat on moderates within his own party."[28]

Perry's signature policy accomplishment as governor—a tort reform package passed in 2003—demonstrated his partisan and confrontational tendencies. The tort reform package, which went well beyond a set of reforms signed by Bush in 1995, were passed almost exclusively by Republicans in the state legislature over the opposition of not just Democrats, but even some moderate and establishment Republicans.[29] Perry never possessed a reputation as a strong, persuasive, or particularly effective governor. On key issues affecting the long-term health of the state (e.g., tax reform that would expand the tax base to stabilize state revenues, school funding and equalization), Perry's proposals went nowhere in the state legislature.[30] Perry often seemed to take a back seat to the cutthroat and partisan leadership style of House Speaker Tom Craddick.[31]

Overall, Perry had an impressive background for a Republican primary candidate. His rural biography, earned reputation as an effective and tough campaigner, and the growth in jobs during his term as Texas governor looked to be ideal for a candidate seeking the Republican nomination in 2012.

CAMPAIGN ORGANIZATION

Another Perry asset appeared to be his campaign organization. Recent presidential campaigns have been won not by veteran Washington-based operatives, but by consultants who had proven their capabilities at the statewide level, were well-versed in cutting edge techniques, and brought new energy and thinking to presidential races (e.g., David Plouffe, Karl Rove, and James Carville). Perry's team seemed to fit into this mold.

At the top of Perry's team was Dave Carney, who had worked for Perry since his 1998 run for Lieutenant Governor and whose relationship with Perry is described as "practically symbiotic."[32] Perry's victories in Texas, especially his defenestration of Hutchison in the 2010 primary, created an impressive reputation for Carney, and the rest of Perry's campaign team. Carney was known as both "innovative and nimble" and for being "tough-as-nails."[33] In his book *The Victory Lab*, journalist Sasha

Issenberg detailed how Carney hired four political scientists to rigorously study the effectiveness of various campaign techniques.[34] The scholars' conclusions: grassroots efforts were most effective at persuading and mobilizing voters; personal appearances in a media market boosted a candidate's approval ratings; television advertisements had an initial effect on voter perceptions, but one that would dissipate within a week; several common campaign techniques, such as robocalls and newspaper endorsements had no effect.[35] Carney followed the scholars' conclusions in 2010 against Hutchison, eschewing editorial boards and focusing on developing a grassroots organization to deliver Perry supporters to the polls.[36]

The rest of Perry's team was also well-steeped in Texas politics and had long experience with their candidate. Media consultant David Weeks was not only known as the top consultant in Texas, but had worked with Perry since his 1990 run for Agriculture Commissioner. Pollster Mike Baselice was similarly regarded as the top pollster in Texas and had worked with Perry since the 1990s. Perry's campaign manager, Rob Johnson, had served as his campaign manager in his successful 2010 gubernatorial re-election bid, and Denise Delisi, who had served previously as Perry's chief of staff, would serve as policy and strategy director.[37] Perry's team brought with it an intimate knowledge of their candidate, excellent reputations as political operatives in Texas, and the hunger to prove themselves on a bigger stage.

In addition, Perry would have plenty of what fellow Texas presidential candidate Phil Gramm called "most reliable friend you can have in American politics, and that's ready money."[38] Perry had developed an extensive fund raising network as the longest serving governor of the only solidly Republican state among the nation's largest states. Texas donors had proven their value (literally) not only to the two Bush presidents, but previous, though less successful, Texas presidential candidates Phil Gramm and John Connaly. Perry would be no different, and he raised over $17 million in his first seven weeks on the campaign trail.[39] Over half of that money ($9.7 million) came from Texas donors.[40] In addition, Perry's Super PAC, Make Us Great Again, could raise unlimited sums of money. It raised $5.5 million in 2011, mostly from Texas businessman and energy companies.[41]

The combination of his biography, record as governor, and political chops made Perry a formidable candidate. Further, as a three term governor of the nation's second largest state, no one could argue that Perry lacked the requisite experience to be president. This put Perry in a uniquely favorable position in 2012. The outsider candidates in the race (Michele Bachmann, Herman Cain, Newt Gingrich, and Ron Paul) could not match Perry when it came to political skill and success. The establishment candidates (Mitt Romney, Tim Pawlenty, and Jon Huntsman) could not match up to Perry's charisma or his conservative record. On paper,

Rick Perry looked like an ideal candidate. On August 13, 2011, Perry announced his candidacy for the presidency in front of a group of conservative bloggers in Charleston, South Carolina. His speech argued that President Obama's "spend-and-borrow agenda" had led to the first downgrade of the credit rating of the United States government, and calling for a focus on jobs via tax cuts and fewer regulations.[42] That week, polls of Republican primary voters nationally put Perry in the lead.

ISSUE STANCES

Like all the candidates in the 2012 Republican primary, Perry held standard conservative issue positions—taxes and government spending should both be cut, the Patient Protection and Affordable Care Act (Obamacare) should be repealed, the government should not implement a cap-and-trade program or other measures to curb global warming, and gays and lesbians should not be allowed to marry. Perry's tax plan would allow taxpayers to choose between their current tax payment or a 20 percent flat tax.[43] As the parties have become more internally homogeneous, fewer differences between primary election candidates are observed.[44] But as with all elections, campaigns need to distinguish themselves from their opponents. In a primary contest with few differences between the candidates, the differences are heightened and emphasized.

Perry and his campaign sought to emphasize two issue areas where his political record made him stand out positively from his fellow candidates. The first was jobs. As discussed, Texas grew greatly during Perry's term in office, with raw job and population growth higher than any other state in the 2000s. On the campaign trail, Perry claimed "I know how to create jobs."[45] According to Perry, Texas gained so many jobs "because we're all about smaller government; we're all about making government work. We're all about cutting taxes, cutting regulations and cutting litigation."[46]

A second issue that Perry emphasized was federalism. In 2011, Perry wrote a book titled *Fed Up: Our Fight to Save America from Washington*.[47] The book called for greatly reducing the size and role of the federal government, and called for most duties of the government to be performed at the state level. *Washington Post* columnist Ezra Klein wrote that Perry's book "can be summed up in one sentence: The federal government is unconstitutional. Not all of it, of course, just most of it. In particular, the parts that include Medicare, Medicaid, Social Security, education policy, banking regulations, environmental protection, gun control and a few other things I'm doubtlessly forgetting."[48]

In 2009 and 2010, Perry had made common cause with the Tea Party movement in Texas, using themes of federalism and returning power to the states as a way to make inroads as a long-serving elected official with the insurgent populist group.[49] It was at a Tea Party rally in April 2009 where Perry commented that "We've got a great union. There is absolutely no reason to dissolve it. But if Washington continues to thumb their nose at the American people, you know, who knows what may come out of that? But Texas is a very unique place and we're a pretty independent lot to boot."[50] Perry's comments created a national firestorm,[51] as many said Perry called for secession (read the words again, he does not advocate for secession; he opposes dissolving the union).[52] But the quote emphasized (and the national coverage magnified) Perry's support for federalism and his opposition to what he saw as the overreach of the federal government.

RHETORICAL BLUNDERS

For all of Perry's strengths as a candidate and his potentially effective message on jobs and federalism, Perry made a series of rhetorical blunders, starting from the opening days of his campaign, and lasting seemingly throughout his campaign.

In the opening week of his campaign, Perry told an audience at an Iowa house party, "If [Federal Reserve Chair Ben Bernanke] prints more money between now and the election, I dunno what y'all would do to him in Iowa, but we would treat him pretty ugly down in Texas. Printing more money to play politics at this particular time in American history is almost treasonous in my opinion."[53] Reaction to his comment was swift and universally negative, even from Republican opinion leaders. Former Bush White House and Treasury Department spokesman Tony Fratto called Perry's comments "inappropriate and unpresidential" and former Bush White House official Peter Wehner wrote that the comments were "the kind of blustering, unthinking comment that Perry's critics expect of him. Why he would play to stereotype is hard to fathom." Even Texan Karl Rove, top George W. Bush aide and Republican powerbroker, called Perry's remark "unfortunate. Governor Perry is going to have to fight the impression that he's a cowboy from Texas. This simply added to it."[54]

Perry's next bit of rhetorical excess was in New Hampshire. At a breakfast in Bedford, New Hampshire on August 17, he said that "there are a substantial number of scientists who have manipulated data [on global warming] so that they will have dollars rolling into their projects. I think we're seeing it almost weekly, or even daily, scientists who are coming forward and questioning the idea that man-made global warming is what is causing the climate to change."[55] The charge that scientists are manipulating data is outrageous at best, incorrect at worst. And the scientific consensus that global warming is caused by humans is strengthening, not weakening.[56] Then on August 18, Perry responded to a New Hampshire child's question about evolution by saying "[i]n Texas, we teach both creationism and evolution in our public schools—because I figure you're smart enough to figure out which one is right."[57] Perry may be right about the boy's intelligence, but he was not right about Texas public schools. Creationism is not part of the state's curriculum.[58]

In his first week on the campaign trail, Perry had stepped on his campaign message on three different occasions. One perspective was that Perry's bellicose rhetoric would appeal to conservative voters and donors. "This is the Pavlovian dinner bell for most Republicans—you know, global warming and creationism—and going after easy money," said political scientist Larry Sabato.[59] The other perspective was that Perry had damaged himself unnecessarily. Paul Burka called Perry's campaign "reckless" and asked "where is the message discipline." According to Burka, Perry needed to improve his campaign skills for the national environment. "Perry has had it easy for ten years . . . He didn't have to be on top of his game to win in Texas."[60] Burka also worried that Perry lacked "the instinct to understand where the majority of Americans stand on the conventional wisdom of the day. He has spent his entire career on the far right of the political spectrum, and sometimes he loses touch with what ordinary people who do not live in that neighborhood believe."[61]

DEBATE GAFFES

The 2012 Republican primary season featured a seemingly endless number of debates, and in these debates, Perry made a number of mistakes which were devastating to his nomination chances. While Perry's electoral record in Texas is impressive, his debate record and experience is less so. In 2010, Perry refused to debate Democratic nominee Bill White.[62] In 2006, Perry agreed to only one debate against his three challengers, and the Perry campaign strategically scheduled the debate on the Friday night before the Texas-Oklahoma football game, guaranteeing the least amount of exposure possible.[63]

Debates provided an opportunity for Perry's opponents to highlight two issues (quite possibly the only two issues) where Perry had deviated from orthodox conservative position while governor of Texas. Perry's inability to respond to these questions proved damaging to his campaign.

The first issue was immigration. Texas has long held a generally favorable impression of immigration, as the Rio Grande border has served as an entry point for Mexican immigrants to the state since the end of the Mexican-American War. The business community in Texas has long welcomed immigration as a means of attracting a low-cost workforce (and one that is unlikely to organize into a labor union).[64] But ever since nativist and nationalist elements in the conservative movement defeated a comprehensive immigration plan in 2007, Republican candidates have feared being called "soft" on immigration. Perry was on the wrong side of this issue. He was particularly vulnerable because as Governor, he signed a bill offering in-state tuition at Texas colleges and universities to undocumented students.

In the September 22 Fox News/Google debate, former Massachusetts Governor Mitt Romney criticized Perry for signing this law, calling it a "magnet that draws people into this country to get that education . . . That shouldn't be allowed. It makes no sense." Perry responded by saying "if you say that we should not educate children who have come into our state for no other reason than they've been brought there by no fault of their own, I don't think you have a heart."

Perry's response, which drew boos from the debate audience, was problematic for two reasons. First, Perry's response kept him on the wrong side of an important issue among Republican primary voters, and his defense of the program stoked fears of continuing unchecked immigration. Worse, his description of his opponents as not having a "heart" echoed liberal attacks on a broad array of conservative policy preferences.[65] Conservatives wanted to privatize the Social Security and Medicare programs in an effort to address the nation's long term budget issues, and needed to be able to withstand attacks that these changes in the program were "heartless." In other words, Perry damaged himself not only on immigration, but, by invoking emotional arguments in domestic policy, he raised questions about his ability to successfully argue for the bulk of the conservative domestic agenda. William Kristol, the influential editor of the *Weekly Standard*, wrote that Perry's debate performance "was close to a disqualifying two hours for him."[66] Shortly after this debate, Perry fell from the lead in polls of Republican primary voters, a lead he would never regain.

The second position where Perry deviated from conservative orthodoxy was on vaccines for the human papillomavirus (HPV). Medical research indicates that HPV is related to cervical cancer and that half of all sexually active men and women get the virus as some point in their lives.[67] The vaccine Gardisil inoculates recipients before their first sexual experience and lasts into adulthood. In 2007, Perry issued an executive order requiring the vaccine for 13 year old girls.[68] This set off a firestorm of controversy in the state, as social conservatives protested Perry's decision. Arguing that medical decisions were best left to parents and working under the presumption that their daughters would never have sex, conservatives pushed a bill through the state legislature to overturn Perry's decision. Rather than face a potential override of his veto, Perry allowed the bill to become law without his signature.[69]

In 2011, Perry's opponents saw this as an opportunity to attack him and to increase their standing with social conservative voters in Iowa. In a September 12, 2011 debate, Minnesota congresswoman Michele Bachmann made such an attack: "To have innocent 12-year girls be forced to have a government injection through an executive order is just flat-out wrong. [Cheers, applause.] That should never be done. That's a violation of a liberty interest." Former Pennsylvania Senator Rick Santorum piled on arguing that because HPV did not deal with a communicable disease "there is no government purpose served for having little girls inoculated at the force and—and compulsion of the government. This is big government run amok."[70]

Perry's response focused on the suggestion that he was influenced by a $5,000 donation made to his campaign by Merck, the maker of Gardisil:[71] "if you're saying that I can be bought for $5,000, I'm offended." [72] Perry's response was problematic not just because it implied there was a price above $5,000 at which he could be bought off, but also because it trivialized an issue that offended the social conservative base that was so key to his electoral chances. In addition, the HPV issue brought attention to Perry's affinity for "crony capitalism," the allegation that businesses close to Perry and donors to his campaigns won government contracts and favorable policy at the expense of fair and level market for all companies.[73] On HPV, Perry was lobbied on behalf of Merck by Mike Toomey, his former Chief of Staff,[74] and many thought Perry would not have given such a favorable hearing to someone he did not know well.

Of course, Perry's worse debate performance was still to come. In the November 9, 2011 debate, Perry discussed his plan to reduce the size of the federal government: "I will tell you, it is three agencies of government when I get there that are gone. Commerce, Education, and the—what's the third one there? Let's see." Mitt Romney tried to be helpful and added in "EPA"—the Environmental Protection Agency. Perry still could not identify the third department: "The third agency of government I would—I would do away with, Education, the…" One of the other candidates shouted out "Commerce." "Commerce, and let's see," Perry continued. "I can't. The third one, I can't. Sorry." And then Perry delivered the memorable *coup de grace* "Oops."

"Oops." This became a single one-word indictment of Rick Perry and his campaign. It is not clear what exactly the intellectual standards are for being president, but most Americans thought it included being able to count to three.[75] Perry's "oops" moment transcended the political press and provided an easily identifiable and understandable moment for the average voter to understand and reject Rick Perry. On the night of the "oops" debate, Bush advisor and Texas political strategist Mark McKinnon wrote that "we witnessed a political suicide live on national television . . . Perry is now a dead man walking. He'll go through the motions to save face, but . . . [o]nce they're laughing at you, you're finished."[76]

LAST THROES

Despite the embarrassment of his debate performances, Perry soldiered on toward the Iowa caucuses in January. He tried to make the best of his "oops" gaffe by joking about it.[77] Even before the "oops" gaffe, Perry brought on new campaign staff, and hired Joe Allbaugh, who had served as George W. Bush's campaign manager in 2000, as his new campaign manager.[78] Perry tried to re-seize the momentum as the anti-Washington candidate by releasing a government reform program which called for Congress to meet less often, reductions in Congressional pay and staffing budgets, and term limits for federal judges.[79] These efforts went nowhere among voters or Republican party leaders. Instead, they seemed to reinforce the negative impressions Perry had created, and it seemed that his campaign message changed from day to day.[80]

Perry still had money saved from the halcyon days after the announcement of his campaign, and more than all of his opponents save Mitt Romney. His campaign then bombarded Iowa airwaves with advertisements from Perry. Their strategy was to appeal to social conservatives, a vital group in the Iowa caucuses.[81] In the most prominent ad, Perry stood outside in a brown field jacket and declared that "I'm not ashamed to admit that I'm a Christian, but you don't need to be in the pew every Sunday to know there's something wrong in this country when gays can serve openly in the military but our kids can't openly celebrate Christmas or pray in school."[82] Perry's ad did move people, but unfortunately for him, those people were liberals and gay rights advocates. The ad garnered nearly 400,000 "dislikes" on YouTube in its first two days, more than the 255,000 dislikes garnered at that point for Rebecca Black's video "Friday."[83]

Many response videos were posted on YouTube condemning Perry's ad as anti-gay.[84] Further, a number of parodies were created, which not only mocked Perry as a homophobe, but noted the irony than his jacket made him look like Heath Ledger's character in the movie "Brokeback Mountain."[85]

Perry's campaign kept pouring more money into advertisements in Iowa. Yet, the ads seemed to have no effect on Iowa caucus-goers, and polling showed no movement in Perry's numbers. All the Texas campaign money in the world could not turn around perceptions of Perry as too dim and out-of-touch to be president.

Perry finished in 5th place in the Iowa caucuses, garnering only 10 percent of the vote.[86] The big question on caucus night for Perry is would he drop out of the race that night, or in the next few days.[87] When Perry announced on election night that he would return to Austin that night, rather than heading to campaign in New Hampshire or South Carolina, veteran political observers knew this was a tell that Perry would drop out in the next day or two.[88] But Perry threw these observers a curve, deciding to continue on,[89] sending out a Twitpic of him in jogging gear giving a "thumbs up" sign.[90] Nothing changed though for Perry. He received only 1,766 votes in New Hampshire (0.7 percent). Polls showed no momentum for him in South Carolina, and, on January 19, 2012, Perry finally put his campaign out of its misery, announcing that he was dropping out of the race.[91] In another demonstration of the leaden political touch he had demonstrated in national politics, Perry endorsed former House speaker Newt Gingrich, who was streaking to the top of South Carolina polls at that moment, only to crash and burn in the subsequent primaries.[92]

ANALYSIS

At the beginning of this chapter, I analogized Rick Perry to a highly touted college quarterback who turns out to be a bust in the NFL. He seemed to possess all the traits that would make him a successful candidate, yet when exposed to competition at the highest levels, he quickly proved to be out of his depth. So why? Why did Rick Perry fail to live up to expectations at the national level and prove to be a poor candidate?

The most common explanation for Perry's failure is that he was not, as *Vanity Fair* wrote, "the sharpest tool in the shed. After watching him march up the political ladder the last 20 years, few in Austin believe Perry possesses any genuine intellectual curiosity."[93] The job of president is of course difficult, requiring an individual to understand a wide range of issues, ranging from nuclear proliferation to budgetary issues, global warming to monetary policy. And on each of these issues, and the countless others that individual voters care about, presidential candidates are expected to possess an understanding of the issues and a sense of how he would direct the country's policy on this issue. Expert-level knowledge and a clear policy position on each policy issue are not required, but a candidate must give voters the sense that he will not be overwhelmed by the volume and difficulty of the decisions that face the President. Rick Perry never gave the impression that he possessed this knowledge. Sure, any of us can forget the third thing on a list, but that moment crystallized for voters the idea that Perry lacked the requisite brain power to be President.

The second reason for Perry's collapse was his terrible performance in the various debates throughout Fall 2011. Perry's lack of intellectual curiosity showed in these performances, where he seemed to lack understanding of many of the issues. The lack of preparation in the debates was easy for any observer to see.[94] Perry himself admitted that he "didn't have time to prepare for those debates. Obviously, it showed." Not knowing every policy detail is an easily forgivable sin among voters. The biggest damage to Perry came from his terrible debate answers to the two issues on which his record as Governor of Texas deviated from conservative orthodoxy—in-state tuition for illegal immigrants and the HPV vaccine requirement. These deviations were not fatal (the Republicans did nominate the godfather of Obamacare), but Perry's responses to questions on these issues demonstrated an inability to understand conservative positions on these issues. That he and his campaign seemed unprepared to answer these questions is a damning indictment of their political skills.

A third reason for Perry's campaign collapse is that he was not well prepared politically by his experience in Texas. Veteran Texas political journalist Paul Burka advanced this theory: "This has been a one-party state since [George] W. [Bush] defeated Ann [Richards] in 1994."[95] No Democrat has won a statewide election in Texas since 1994.[96] As a result, Perry "has never been in danger of losing a race" over the last decade.[97] He has used this security to avoid the press in Texas (he gave no interviews to newspaper editorial boards during the 2010 campaign)[98] and to slough off negative stories about him. And of course, the level of scrutiny offered by a state press corps always pales compared to the efforts of the national media. Burka speculated that "Perry has had it so easy . . . that I wonder if it has dulled his political acumen. . . . He hasn't had any big-league experience, and it shows. Sooner or later, he was bound to pay a price for not engaging in the give and take of a major political campaign."[99] Texas's conservative lean has allowed Perry to avoid tough opponents and tough questions, and thus, he has not learned how to use subtlety and tact in getting his message across to voters.

A final reason for, or really contributing factor, to Perry's failure was his physical condition. Perry had back surgery in June 2011, and in December, Perry suggested "I was pretty fatigued" in the first few debates.[100] Paul Burka noted after the September 11th debate (where Bachmann had attacked Perry on HPV) that Perry "looked uncomfortable, his face was strained, his combativeness was muted . . . He was low-energy and the feistiness wasn't there. That's why I'm wondering whether the back operation did not go well."[101] *Saturday Night Live* mocked Perry's debate performances with a sleeping Alec Baldwin.[102] While Perry's back surgery is not the reason that he bombed as a presidential candidate, it certainly did not help him.

Regardless of the reason, Rick Perry's 2012 presidential campaign will go down historically as a complete and total bust. Perry had what looked to be a strong résumé, message, and campaign operation entering the campaign. In a period of 72 hours, each of these strengths was called into question; within six weeks, they were all gone. Nothing in the rest of the campaign changed the impression that Perry had neither the intellectual candlepower, the fire in the belly, or the discipline to be a competent presidential candidate.

142   Chapter 7

In 1980, former Texas Governor John Connaly ran for President, and had "looks, money, leadership, and a can't-miss aura that left would-be opponents trembling in his wake."[103] Connally's campaign spent an impressive-for-its-time $11 million, but won but a single delegate (waggishly called the "$11 million delegate").[104] In 1996, Texas Senator Phil Gramm spent a then-impressive $21.1 million (Gramm wowed political observers by raising $4.1 million at a single Dallas dinner), yet also finished fifth in the Iowa caucuses.[105] These are the two most prominent examples of presidential campaigns with great resources but lousy results. Perry's campaign surpassed those of his fellow Texas Republicans. He rose to the top of the polls—which Connally and Gramm never did—before belly-flopping to a fifth place finish in Iowa. Unlike Connally, Perry did not win a single delegate. Perry's campaign became a national punchline, and that will likely serve as the legacy of his efforts in 2012.[106]

Where does this leave Perry moving forward? In Perry's mind, 2016 is the answer. In a April 2012 interview, Perry said that he would give running in 2016 "a good examination."[107] This is the point where people usually say "stranger things have happened in American politics;" they haven't. The combination of the remarkably negative impression he created in 2012 and a rising class of attractive Republican politicians (Paul Ryan, Chris Christie, Marco Rubio, Bobby Jindal, etc.) would make Perry the most extreme longshot imaginable in 2016 or 2020. 2012 was his moment to run nationally, and he failed at it.

In the state of Texas, Perry's political future is a more interesting topic. His run for president hurt Perry's standing within the state. A University of Texas/Texas Tribune poll from February 2012 shows Perry's approval rating in the state had dipped to 38 percent; disapproval had climbed to 45 percent. A majority of respondents (55 percent) thought Perry's run had "hurt Texas' image."[108] Despite these weaknesses, Perry has told insiders and funders that he would run again in 2014[109] (Texas does not have term limits). In April 2012, Perry said he was giving a fourth reelection bid "the appropriate consideration. My instincts are very positive towards it right now, but we'll wait until after the legislative session to make that announcement."[110] As the resources available to the state's sitting governor and the most experience wooing Texas voters, Perry would still be a formidable candidate.[111] On the other hand, many Texans feel that Perry embarrassed the state during his presidential run,[112] and in a state where all 27 statewide offices are held by Republicans, there is no shortage of serious potential candidates to challenge him in a 2014 Republican primary.[113] The smart money in the state is that Perry will not run for re-election in 2014, and his hint at a run that year is an attempt to avoid being seen as a lame duck and increase his leverage in the 2013 legislative session.[114]

Regardless of what happens to Perry in Texas, his national fate is sealed. He is a punchline, and will be remembered for years as the guy who could not count to three. In other words, Perry was a bust as presidential candidate. To be a bust, one needs a fabulous scouting report and a dreadful performance. The combination of Perry's electoral success and conservative record made him seem like an outstanding candidate for 2012. In reality, he was anything but.

NOTES

1. Mark Greenbaum, "Why is the GOP Presidential Field So Terrible? A Theory," *The New Republic* 2011, http://www.tnr.com/article/politics/88661/gingrich-paul-romney-huckabee-gop-presidential-field-terrible; Simon, Roger, "A Low Road through a Weak Field," *Politico* 2012, http://www.politico.com/news/stories/0112/72268.html.

2. Jay Root, "Update: Perry Announces 2012 Run, Attacks Obama," *Texas Tribune* 2011, "http://www.texastribune.org/texas-politics/2012-presidential-election/rick-perry-announces-president/"

3. Paul Burka, "Dear Yankee: Eight things you ought to know before you start writing stories about Rick Perry. You're welcome," *Texas Monthly*, August, 2011: 10.

4. Toby Harnden, "Rick Perry: the Paint Creek boy who would be king," *The Telegraph* 2011, "http://www.telegraph.co.uk/news/worldnews/northamerica/usa/8694278/Rick-Perry-the-Paint-Creek-boy-who-would-be-king.html"

5. Justin Elliot, "What I Learned About Rick Perry from Reading His Bizarre Book About the Boy Scouts," *The New Republic* 2011, "http://www.tnr.com/article/politics/94878/perry-boy-scouts-on-my-honor-aclu"

6. Chris Hooks, "Texas A&M Years Launched Perry—and a Rivalry," *Texas Tribune* 2011, "http://www.texastribune.org/texas-people/rick-perry/perry-aggie-years/"

7. Burka, "Dear Yankee."

8. Hooks, "Texas A&M Years Launched Perry."

9. Abby Livingston, "What is a yell leader?" *CNN* 2011, "http://politicalticker.blogs.cnn.com/2011/08/19/what-is-a-yell-leader/"

10. Sheryl Gay Stolberg, "For Perry, Life Was Broadened and Narrowed by the Military," *New York Times*, November 25, 2011, A1.

11. Seth C. McKee, *Republican Ascendancy in Southern U.S. House Elections* (Boulder, CO: Westview Press, 2010).

12. Justin Dehn and Thanh Tan, "Video: Analyzing 20 Years of Perry's Political Advertising," *Texas Tribune* 2001, "http://www.texastribune.org/texas-people/rick-perry/video-analyzing-20-years-of-perrys-political-ads/"

13. Hooks, "Texas A&M Years Launched Perry."

14. Lawrence Wright, "A Different Kind of Texan," *The New Yorker* 2011, "http://www.newyorker.com/talk/comment/2011/08/29/110829taco_talk_wright"

15. Office of the Secretary of State, "Race Summary Report," 1998, "http://elections.sos.state.tx.us/elchist.exe"

16. Daron Shaw and James Henson, "Texas Statewide Survey. Winter Instrument," Texas Department of Government 2009, "http://www.laits.utexas.edu/txp_media/html/poll/files/200903-summary.pdf"

17. Paul Burka, "Last Words About the Governor's Race," *Texas Monthly* 2010, "http://www.texasmonthly.com/blogs/burkablog/?p=6511"

18. Office of the Secretary of State, "Race Summary Report," 2010, "http://elections.sos.state.tx.us/elchist.exe"

19. Brad Plumer, "Breaking down Rick Perry's 'Texas Miracle,'" *Washington Post* 2011, "http://www.washingtonpost.com/blogs/ezra-klein/post/breaking-down-rick-perrys-texas-miracle/2011/08/15/gIQAzRHFHJ_blog.html"

20. Kurt Badenhausen, "Texas tops the list of the best states for jobs," *MSNBC* 2011, "http://www.msnbc.msn.com/id/45527495/ns/business-forbes.com/t/texas-tops-list-best-states-jobs/#.T0wVyvF8CtY."

21. Becca Aaronson, "Job Creation, Unemployment and the Texas Miracle," *Texas Tribune* 2011, "http://www.texastribune.org/texas-state-agencies/texas-workforce-commission/unemployment-miracle-texas/"

22. Wyatt Andrews, "How Rick Perry created the 'Texas Miracle'," *CBS News* 2011, "http://www.cbsnews.com/stories/2011/08/12/eveningnews/main20091874.shtml"

23. Paul Krugman, 2011, "The Texas Unmiracle," *New York Times*, August 14, 2011, A21.

24. Plumer, "Breaking down Rick Perry's 'Texas Miracle'."

25. Edward L. Glaeser and Kristina Tobio, "The Rise of the Sunbelt," Harvard Institute of Economic Research, Discussion Paper 2135, 2007. Available at "http://www.economics.harvard.edu/pub/hier/2007/HIER2135.pdf"

26. Alyssa Katz, "How Texas Escaped the Real Estate Crisis," *Washington Post* 2010, "http://www.washingtonpost.com/wp-dyn/content/article/2010/04/03/AR2010040304983.html"

27. Wright, "A Different Kind of Texan."

28. Burka, "Dear Yankee."

29. Rebecca Rodriguez, "Now It's Up to the Voters: Prop. 12, 21 other proposals on ballot today," *San Antonio Express News*, 2003, XX-YY.

30. Jane Elliott and R.G. Ratcliffe, "Perry blames lobbyists, lawmakers' lack of will: He won't call another special session, saying special interests ruled the last one," *Houston Chronicle* 2005 http://www.chron.com/news/article/Perry-blames-lobbyists-lawmakers-lack-of-will-1517491.php.

31. Dave Mann, "Fall of the House of Craddick: How did the formidable Republican lose his speakership?," *Texas Observer* 2009, http://www.texasobserver.org/archives/item/15551-2944-fall-of-the-house-of-craddick-how-did-the-formidable-republican-lose-his-speakership.

32. Abby Rapoport, "The Outsider: Can a camera-shy Dave Carney put Rick Perry in the White House?," *Texas Observer* 2011, http://www.texasobserver.org/cover-story/the-outsider.

33. Maria Recio, "Meet Dave Carney, Rick Perry's Karl Rove-like political guru," McClatchy Newspapers, 2011 "http://www.mcclatchydc.com/2011/09/29/125658/meet-dave-carney-rick-perrys-karl.html"

34. Sasha Issenberg, "Rick Perry and His Eggheads: Inside the Brainiest Political Operation in America," in *The Victory Lab* (Crown Books, 2011).

35. The four political scientists are Daron Shaw (University of Texas at Austin), Donald Green (Yale University), James Gimpel (University of Maryland), and Alan Gerber (Yale University). Much of their work from the Perry campaign has been published.

36. Rapoport, "The Outsider"; Recio, "Meet Dave Carney."

37. Philip Rucker, "Rick Perry staffs campaign with trusted Texas confidants," *Washington Post* 2011, http://www.washingtonpost.com/politics/rick-perry-staffs-campaign-with-trusted-texas-confidants/2011/09/02/gIQA4jm4wJ_story.html; Ross Ramsey, "Rick Perry's Brain Trust," *Texas Tribune* 2011 "http://www.texastribune.org/library/data/perrys-circle/"

38. Jason DeParle, "The First Primary," *New York Times Magazine*, 1995, p. 29.

39. Emily Ramshaw, "In Need of Good News, Perry Releases Fundraising Totals," *Texas Tribune* 2011, "http://www.texastribune.org/texas-politics/2012-presidential-election/need-good-news-perry-releases-fundraising-totals/"

40. Matt Stiles, "Mapping where GOP candidates raise their campaign donations," *The Daily Viz* 2011, "http://thedailyviz.com/post/11539284430/mapping-where-gop-candidates-raise-their-campaign"

41. Jason Embry, "A few top donors help pro-Perry super PAC raise $5.5 million," *Austin American-Statesman* 2012, http://www.statesman.com/news/texas-politics/a-few-top-donors-help-pro-perry-super-2139568.html.

42. Jay Root, "Updated: Perry Announced 2012 Run, Attacks Obama," *Texas Tribune* 2011, "http://www.texastribune.org/texas-politics/2012-presidential-election/rick-perry-announces-president/"

43. Kasie Hunt, "Texas Gov. Rick Perry calls for a flat tax," *Houston Chronicle* 2011, "http://www.chron.com/news/article/Texas-Gov-Rick-Perry-to-call-for-a-flat-tax-2226330.php"

44. David W. Rohde, *Parties and Leaders in the Postreform House* (Chicago: University of Chicago Press, 2011); Keith Poole, "An Update on Political Polarization (through 2011)," VoteView 2011, http://voteview.com/blog/?p=284.

45. Seema Mehta, "Rick Perry's Iowa pitch: 'I know how to create jobs'," *Los Angeles Times* 2011, http://articles.latimes.com/2011/aug/15/news/la-pn-perry-fair-20110815.

46. Jim Davenport, "Perry brings jobs message to high-unemployment SC," *Associated Press* 2011, http://www.omaha.com/article/20110819/AP06/308199856/1014.

47. Rick Perry, *Fed Up: Our Fight to Save America from Washington* (New York: Little, Brown Company, 2010).

48. Ezra Klein, "Perry's radical EU-style federalism," *Washington Post* 2011, "http://www.washingtonpost.com/business/economy/rick-perrys-radical-eu-style-federalism/2011/08/18/gIQArB7HOJ_story.html"

49. Andy Barr, "Rick Perry: Tea Party darling," *Politico* 2009, "http://www.politico.com/news/stories/0409/21295.html"; Paul Burka, "Rick Perry, teasip," *Texas Monthly* 2009, "http://www.texasmonthly.com/blogs/burkablog/?p=3457"

50. "What Perry Really Said About Secession," FactCheck.org 2011, "http://www.factcheck.org/2011/08/what-perry-really-said-about-secession/"

51. W. Gardner Selby and Jason Embry, "Perry Stands by Secession Comments: Governor says Texas is one state that could leave union, though he's not pushing it," *Austin American-Statesman* 2009, http://www.statesman.com/news/content/region/legislature/stories/04/17/0417gop.html.

52. Paul Burka, "Did Perry use the 's' word?," *Texas Monthly* 2011, "http://www.texasmonthly.com/blogs/burkablog/?p=11374"

53. Dan Amira, "Rick Perry Calls Ben Bernanke 'Almost Treasonous,' Not Sure About President Obama's Patriotism," *New York Magazine* 2011, "http://nymag.com/daily/intel/2011/08/rick_perry_accuses_ben_bernake.html"

54. Alexander Burns, "Bushies slam Rick Perry's Ben Bernanke comment," *Politico* 2011, "http://www.politico.com/news/stories/0811/61486.html"

55. Reston Maeva "Rick Perry calls global warming an unproven, costly theory," *Los Angeles Times* 2011, "http://articles.latimes.com/2011/aug/17/nation/la-na-0818-perry-global-warming-20110818"

56. Brad Plumer, "Despite Rick Perry, consensus on climate change keeps strengthening," *Washington Post* 2011, "http://www.washingtonpost.com/blogs/ezra-klein/post/despite-rick-perry-consensus-on-climate-change-keeps-strengthening/2011/08/23/gIQAMT3UZJ_blog.html"

57. Michael Falcone and Arlette Saenz, "NH Mother Uses Child as a Prop to Question Perry on Evolution," *ABC News* 2011, "http://abcnews.go.com/blogs/politics/2011/08/nh-mother-uses-child-as-a-prop-to-question-rick-perry-on-evolution/"

58. Paul Burka, "Perry on evolution/creationism," *Texas Monthly* 2011, "http://www.texasmonthly.com/blogs/burkablog/?p=11128"

59. Jay Root, "Perry Wrapping Up Extraordinary Week," *Texas Tribune* 2011, "http://www.texastribune.org/texas-politics/2012-presidential-election/perry-wrapping-extraordinary-week/"

60. Paul Burka, "The Perry campaign: Where is the message discipline?," *Texas Monthly* 2011, "http://www.texasmonthly.com/blogs/burkablog/?p=11120"

61. Paul Burka, "Perry, the EPA, and the normalcy compass," *Texas Monthly* 2011, "http://www.texasmonthly.com/blogs/burkablog/?p=11158"

62. Gromer Jeffers, Jr. and Wayne Slater, "Rick Perry still won't debate Bill White until tax records are released," *Dallas Morning-News* 2010, http://

www.dallasnews.com/news/politics/state-politics/20100914-Rick-Perry-still-won-t-debate-1143.ece.

63. Ralph Blumenthal, "Debate in Texas Race Focuses on Border, Crime, and Cigars," *New York Times* 2006, http://www.nytimes.com/2006/10/08/us/politics/08texas.html.

64. Ross Ramsey, "In Texas, Perry's Stance on In-State Tuition Isn't News," *Texas Tribune* 2011, "http://www.texastribune.org/texas-politics/2012-presidential-election/texas-sensibility-doesnt-travel-well/"

65. Paul Burka, "Blood and Irony," *Texas Monthly* 2011, "http://www.texasmonthly.com/blogs/burkablog/?p=11402"

66. William Kristol, "Special Editorial: Yikes," *Weekly Standard* 2011, "http://www.weeklystandard.com/blogs/special-editorial-yikes_594095.html"

67. Centers for Disease Control. "Genital HPV Infection—Fact Sheet," "http://www.cdc.gov/std/hpv/stdfact-hpv.htm"

68. Jay Root, "Under scrutiny, Perry walks back HPV decision," *Texas Tribune* 2011, "http://www.texastribune.org/texas-people/rick-perry/facing-new-scrutiny-perry-walks-back-hpv-decision/"

69. Janet Elliott, "Perry yields on HPV vaccines, chides lawmakers. Reluctant governor yields on HPV shots. Calling a veto useless, Perry chides legislators for opposing his vaccination order," *Houston Chronicle* 2007, "http://www.chron.com/news/article/Perry-yields-on-HPV-vaccines-chides-lawmakers-1830709.php"

70. The debate transcript is available at "http://www.nytimes.com/2011/09/13/us/politics/cnn-tea-party-republican-debate-in-tampa-fla.html?pagewanted=all"

71. Ryan Murphy, "On the Records: Perry Understated Merck Money," *Texas Tribune* 2011, http://www.texastribune.org/texas-newspaper/texas-news/records-fact-checking-perrys-merck-contributions/.

72. Again, this is from the debate transcript, available at "http://www.nytimes.com/2011/09/13/us/politics/cnn-tea-party-republican-debate-in-tampa-fla.html?pagewanted=all"

73. Charles Dameron, "Rick Perry's Crony Capitalism Problem: The presidential candidate's signature economic development initiative has raised questions among conservatives," *Wall Street Journal* 2011, "http://online.wsj.com/article/SB10001424052702304760604576428262897285614.html"; Richard S. Dunham, "Rick Perry battles charges of 'crony capitalism'," *San Francisco Chronicle*, September 15, 2011, A-11.

74. Matthew Yglesias, "Rick Perry, Merck, Gardisil, and How Lobbying Works," *Think Progress*, 2011, http://thinkprogress.org/yglesias/2011/09/13/318295/rick-perry-merck-gardasil-and-how-lobbying-works/.

75. Paul Begala, "The Stupid Party," *The Daily Beast* 2011, http://www.thedailybeast.com/newsweek/2011/11/13/rick-perry-shows-gop-dumbing-itself-down-to-be-our-stupid-party.html.

76. Mark McKinnon, "Last Rites for Rick Perry's Presidential Campaign After GOP Debate," *The Daily Beast* 2011, http://www.thedailybeast.com/articles/2011/11/09/last-rites-for-rick-perry-s-presidential-campaign-after-gop-debate.html.

77. Zeke Miller, "Rick Perry Fundraises Off OOPS! Gaffe," *Business Insider* 2011, http://articles.businessinsider.com/2011-11-10/politics/30381154_1_cnbc-debate-damage-control-federal-agencies.

78. Jay Root, "Joe Allbaugh, National Consultants Joining Perry," *Texas Tribune* 2011, http://www.texastribune.org/texas-politics/2012-presidential-election/joe-allbaugh-others-join-team-perry-sources/.

79. Rebecca Kaplan, "Perry Proposes Sweeping Government Reform," *National Journal* 2011, http://www.nationaljournal.com/2012-presidential-campaign/perry-proposes-sweeping-government-reform-20111115.

80. Paul Burka, "What is Perry's Message?," *Texas Monthly* 2011, http://www.texasmonthly.com/blogs/burkablog/?p=12084.

81. Michael O'Brien, "Perry bets the house on social conservatives," *MSNBC* 2011, http://firstread.msnbc.msn.com/_news/2011/12/08/9305940-perry-bets-the-house-on-social-conservatives.

82. Alexandra Petri, "Rick Perry's 'Strong' Ad—Obama Hates Christmas," *Washington Post* 2011, http://www.washingtonpost.com/blogs/compost/post/rick-perrys-strong-ad——obama-hates-christmas/2011/12/07/gIQAygSfdO_blog.html.

83. At the time of this writing, Perry's ad has 765,940 dislikes, still ahead of the 588,342 dislikes of "Friday." The most disliked video on YouTube is the video for Justin Beiber's song "Baby," which has over 2.4 million dislikes. Megan Gibson, "Rick Perry's 'Strong' Campaign Ad Gets the Web Angry—and Laughing," *Time* 2011, http://newsfeed.time.com/2011/12/09/rick-perrys-strong-campaign-ad-gets-the-web-angry-and-laughing/.

84. Susan Brooks Thistlewaite, "Parodies of Rick Perry's 'Strong' ad: the gift that keeps on giving," *Washington Post* 2011, http://www.washingtonpost.com/blogs/guest-voices/post/parodies-of-rick-perrys-strong-ad-the-gift-that-keeps-on-giving/2011/12/11/gIQA3jeipO_blog.html.

85. Lauren Kelley, "Hilarious: Rick Perry Wears Jacket from 'Brokeback Mountain' During Anti-Gay Ad," AlterNet.org 2011, http://www.alternet.org/newsandviews/article/745987/hilarious:_rick_perry_wears_jacket_from_ percent22brokeback_mountain percent22_during_anti-gay_ad/.

86. Iowa Caucus results are available online at http://iowacaucus.com/results/.

87. Amanda Terkel and Christina Wilkie, "Rick Perry Returning to Taxes After Disappointing Iowa Finish, Assessing Whether to Quit Race," *Huffington Post* 2012, http://www.huffingtonpost.com/2012/01/04/rick-perry-iowa-caucus-2012_n_1182583.html.

88. Peggy Fikac, "Perry returning to Texas to reassess his presidential campaign," *Houston Chronicle* 2012, http://blog.chron.com/rickperry/2012/01/perry-returning-to-texas-to-reassess-his-presidential-bid/.

89. Catalina Camia, "Morning jog helps Perry press on with White House bid," *USA Today* 2012, http://content.usatoday.com/communities/onpolitics/post/2012/01/reports-rick-perry-to-stay-in-presidential-race-/1#.T4RjoKtYuCM.

90. @GovernorPerry, https://twitter.com/#!/governorperry/statuses/154596463995912193.

91. Stephanie Condon, "Rick Perry drops his presidential bid," *CBS News* 2012, http://www.cbsnews.com/8301-503544_162-57361787-503544/rick-perry-drops-his-presidential-bid/.

92. Peter Hamby, "Perry drops out, endorses Gingrich," *CNN* 2012, http://articles.cnn.com/2012-01-19/politics/politics_perry-dropping-out_1_perry-campaign-gingrich-and-rick-santorum-press-conference?_s=PM:POLITICS.

93. Bryan Burrough, "Rick Perry Has Three Strikes Against Him: Pay-to-play cronyism. Roughshod, right-win politics. And…Oops, read on," *Vanity Fair* 2012, http://www.vanityfair.com/politics/2012/01/rick-perry-201201.

94. Byron York, "Perry locked, loaded for Thursday's debate," *Washington Examiner* 2011, http://campaign2012.washingtonexaminer.com/article/perry-locked-and-loaded-thursdays-debate.

95. Paul Burka, "The bush leagues," *Texas Monthly* 2011, http://www.texasmonthly.com/blogs/burkablog/?p=11350.

96. Texas Politics. "Increase in Republican Elected Officials, 1974-2002," University of Texas Liberal Arts Information Technology System, http://www.laits.utexas.edu/txp_media/html/part/features/0402_03/reprising.html.

97. Burka, "The bush leagues."

98. Jason Embry, "Perry will skip editorial boards," *Austin American-Statesman* 2010, http://www.statesman.com/blogs/content/shared-gen/blogs/austin/firstreading/entries/2010/08/12/perry_wont_meet_with_editorial.html.

99. Burka, "The bush leagues."

100. Kathie Obradovich, "Rick Perry 'a different candidate' in debates since recovery from surgery," *Des Moines Registrar* 2011, http://caucuses.desmoinesregister.com/2011/12/11/rick-perry-a-different-candidate-in-debates-since-recovery-from-surgery/.

101. Paul Burka, "Not Rick Perry's night," *Texas Monthly* 2011, http://www.texasmonthly.com/blogs/burkablog/?p=11333.

102. Matt Cherett, "Watch Alec Baldwin Play a Bumbling Rick Perry on SNL," *Gawker* 2011, http://gawker.com/5843612/watch-alec-baldwin-play-a-bumbling-rick-perry-on-snl.

103. Joe Holley, "Being from Texas might be a burden," *Houston Chronicle* 2012, http://blog.chron.com/rickperry/2012/01/being-from-texas-might-be-a-burden/.

104. John Stacks, "The Nation: Adieu, Big John," *Time* 1980, http://www.time.com/time/magazine/article/0,9171,921859,00.html.

105. . Sam Howe Verhovek, "Politics: Bowing Out; Big Budget, Early Start and the Candidate are Figured in the Collapse of Gramm Bid," *New York Times* 1996, http://www.nytimes.com/1996/02/15/us/politics-bowing-big-budget-early-start-candidate-are-figured-collapse-gramm-s.html?pagewanted=all&src=pm.

106. . Caroline Ward, "Tex Message: Rick Perry is the favorite punch line of the night at annual congressional dinner," *Houston Chronicle* 2012, http://blog.chron.com/txpotomac/2012/02/texmessage-rick-perry-is-the-favorite-punch-line-of-the-night-at-annual-congressional-dinner/.

107. Jack Fink, "Perry Interested in Another Run for President," CBSDFW.com 2012, http://dfw.cbslocal.com/2012/04/18/perry-will-give-another-run-for-president-a-good-examination/.

108. Texas Politics, "Assessments of Political Leaders (February, 2012)," University of Texas Liberal Arts Information Technology System, http://texaspolitics.laits.utexas.edu/11_3_0.html.

109. Jay Root, "Rick Perry Fuels Speculation About Re-election Bid," *Texas Tribune* 2012, http://www.texastribune.org/texas-politics/2014-statewide-elections/perry-fuels-speculation-about-re-elect-bid/.

110. Fink, "Perry Interested in Another Run for President."

111. Peggy Fikac, "Commentary: Perry would like you to think he'll seek re-election," *Houston Chronicle* 2012, http://blog.chron.com/txpotomac/2012/01/commentary-perry-would-like-you-to-think-he percentE2 percent80 percent99ll-seek-re-election/.

112. Bill Minutaglio, "Rick Perry's Fate in Texas, After the 2012 Presidential Race," *The Daily Beast* 2012, http://www.thedailybeast.com/newsweek/2012/01/21/rick-perry-s-fate-in-texas-after-the-2012-presidential-race.html.

113. Ross Ramsay, "Obstacles Exist on Path to the Top of the Org Chart," *Texas Tribune* 2012, http://www.texastribune.org/texas-politics/2014-statewide-elections/obstacles-top-org-chart/.

114. Paul Burka, "Perry 'leaning' toward running in 2014," *Texas Monthly* 2012, http://www.texasmonthly.com/blogs/burkablog/?p=12791.

EIGHT

Newt Gingrich: It Takes More than Ideas to Win a Nomination

Joshua P. Stockley

None of the Republican presidential candidates experienced a roller coaster ride quite like Newt Gingrich. His campaign started inauspiciously with botched campaign rollouts, verbal gaffes, staff problems, and a two-week long luxury vacation to the Mediterranean. Gingrich overcame these obstacles to become the frontrunner in the polls prior to the Iowa caucus, which was propelled by the combination of strong debate performances and mishaps by his opponents. Returning to the top of the polls came with a price—he became the focus of a relentless volley of negative campaign advertisements. Gingrich would lose in Iowa and New Hampshire before claiming his first victory in South Carolina. Alas, former Massachusetts Governor Mitt Romney's overwhelming financial advantage and former Pennsylvania Senator Rick Santorum's inexplicable conservative appeal deprived Gingrich of any substantial momentum heading into pivotal contests in Florida and on Super Tuesday. He lost Florida and won only one state on Super Tuesday—his home state of Georgia. Gingrich, the only Southern candidate after the withdrawal of Texas Governor Rick Perry, pinned his hopes of a third dramatic comeback on a Deep South strategy, but, again, came up short. The audacious architect of the first Republican House of Representatives in 50 years was unable to convert the skills that produced Republican majorities and a lucrative financial-political empire into a successful presidential nomination. Gingrich officially remained in the race until May 2, spending the latter days of his campaign criticizing Romney, attempting to retire campaign debts, advocating platform positions for the Republican National Convention, and disparaging President Barack Obama.

CANDIDATE BACKGROUND

Newton Leroy "Newt" Gingrich was born June 17, 1943 in Harrisburg, Pennsylvania. His adopted father served in the military, which entailed moving around for most of his childhood. In 1960, while in high school, his family moved to Georgia, where Gingrich would call home. Gingrich graduated from Baker High School in Columbus, Georgia before receiving a B.A. from Emory University in Atlanta, a M.S. from Tulane University in New Orleans, and a Ph.D. in modern European history from Tulane University.[1] He was a history professor at West Georgia College, now the University of West Georgia, when he ran unsuccessfully in 1974 and 1976 against incumbent Democrat Jack Flynt in Georgia's Sixth Congressional District.[2] Flynt retired in 1978 and Gingrich defeated State Senator Virginia Shapard to become Georgia's only Republican U.S. Representative.[3] It didn't take long for Gingrich to distinguish himself in Congress. First, he played a central role in bringing ethics charges against Speaker of the House Jim Wright (D-TX), which eventually led to Wright's resignation in 1988. Second, he surprisingly outmaneuvered veteran congressman Edward Rell Madigan (R-IL) to become House Minority Whip in 1989.[4] National fame arrived with the Republican wave of 1994, when he co-authored the "Contract with America"—the central campaign plank assisting in the election of 54 freshman Republican representatives resulting in the first Republican House majority in 50 years. In recognition of his leadership and efforts, Gingrich was elected Speaker of the House; however, the same combative and polarizing personality leading to his rise simultaneously contributed to his downfall. His tenure as Speaker was a bumpy one beset by a combative personality, ethics inquiries, government shutdowns, and, finally, an attempted leadership coup by his fellow Republicans. Perceived by his colleagues to be an increasing liability after Republicans lost seats in the 1998 midterm elections, Gingrich resigned both as Speaker and from Congress on November 6, 1998.[5]

Over the next decade, Gingrich maintained a national profile by reinventing himself as a policy wonk. He wrote several books, appeared as a paid contributor on Fox News, served as a senior fellow at the American Enterprise Institute, consultant for Pharmaceutical Research and Manufacturers of America and Freddie Mac, and founded a number of for-profit organizations – Gingrich Holdings and Gingrich Productions—and nonprofit organizations—Center for Health Transformation Foundation, Gingrich Foundation, American Solutions for Winning the Future, and Renewing American Leadership (ReAL).[6] In 2005, Gingrich's book tour,

"Winning the Future: A 21st Century Contract with America," featured stops in Iowa and New Hampshire and harsh criticisms of President Bush's foreign policy in Iraq. Insiders, pundits, and media interpreted these actions as an indication of potential presidential interest.

Gingrich appeared to be leaning against a run because the candidacy of former Tennessee Senator Fred Thompson spurred excitement among Republicans, particularly within the Southern elements of the party. When Thompson's campaign sputtered in September of 2007, Gingrich suddenly announced to supporters in Marietta, Georgia, that if they pledged at least $30 million to him, then he would compete for the Republican nomination.[7] Only two days later, he formally declared he would not run for president citing his inability to remain at the head of his successful political action committee—American Solutions for Winning the Future.[8] The decision not to run was made easier by his admissions months earlier of extramarital affairs with his first and second wife during an interview with Focus on the Family founder James Dobson; the latter occurring in the midst of the impeachment proceeding against President Clinton following revelations of an affair with intern Monica Lewinsky.[9] In the interview, Gingrich admitted to cheating on his first wife, Jackie Battley, before marrying his second wife Marianne Ginther; however, he testily disputed Battley's claim that he had discussed divorce terms with her while she was in the hospital recovering from cancer surgery. While leading the impeachment proceedings in 1998, Gingrich began an affair with Callista Bisek, a congressional aide in her twenties. He eventually divorced Marianne and married Callista in 2000.[10]

The extramarital revelations threatened Gingrich's relationships with the evangelical community, a significant voting bloc in the Republican nomination electorate that he had never been particularly close to while Speaker. To repair this relationship, Gingrich spent a significant portion of time in 2009 and 2010 cementing ties with the religious community. For example, via his non-profit organization Renewing American Leadership (ReAL), Gingrich channeled $150,000 to assist in the recall efforts against three Iowa Supreme Court justices who sided with gay marriage. He appeared at dozens of pastor meetings and pastoral conventions in Iowa, New Hampshire, and South Carolina, publicizing his "born again" conversion to Catholicism, opposing abortion and gay marriage, and decrying the perceived advancement of a secular America. He took steps to increase his appeal among pro-Israel Republicans by appearing on the cover of *Israeli Daily* and raising fears that Obama's foreign policy would lead to a "second holocaust." Gingrich used his books and Fox News appearances to build an identity as a culture-warrior conservative. Heading into 2011, he had developed a good rapport with evangelicals and more conservative elements of the Republican Party. Nevertheless, Gingrich was never able to effectively mute his thrice-married past, which deprived his campaign of the critical endorsements needed to obtain the unanimous support of the evangelical community and to prevent other conservatives from dipping into this base of voters.

Gingrich also spent considerable time and energy while out of office developing successful financial networks. From 2009-2011, his various for-profit organizations generated over $100 million in revenue; one non-profit organization, American Solutions for Winning the Future, generated $52 million in revenue.[11] American Solutions for Winning the Future maintained vast mailing and donor lists of several million names from a decade of selling memberships, books, videos, and other products. The group's donor base grew to include nearly 300,000 small contributors, those giving $200 or less, as well as wealthy benefactors, such as casino magnate and billionaire Sheldon Adelson. Adelson gave $6 million to the group from 2009-2010.[12] During this period, Gingrich's financial sums eclipsed the combined totals for the next three most prolific fundraisers eyeing presidential bids—former Massachusetts Governor Mitt Romney, former Alaska Governor Sarah Palin, and former Minnesota Governor Tim Pawlenty.[13]

Gingrich's PAC strategically contributed to local and state candidates and party committees in Iowa, New Hampshire, and South Carolina. American Solutions for Winning the Future allowed Gingrich to maintain a visible role in national elections and political discussions, but, just as importantly, maintained advertising, office space, polling, media, voter lists, contributor lists, and a 19-member staff—all necessary ingredients for a national campaign. These financial and political networks caused many strategists, insiders, and pundits to surmise that if Gingrich were to announce a run for president in 2012, then he, more so than any other candidate, would be best positioned to get off to a running start.

Alas, the campaign did not get off to a fast start. In January of 2011, Gingrich announced he would make a decision whether to run by the end of February and form a presidential exploratory committee by the first week of March.[14] On March 3, 2011, expecting a presidential announcement, Gingrich merely declared the creation of a website named NewtExplore2012. Ed Rollins, veteran GOP strategist, called the non-announcement a "disaster." David Yepsen, longtime *Des Moines Register* reporter, called the non-launch an "erratic" display of behavior not befitting of a serious presidential hopeful.[15] Gingrich was unable to form an exploratory committee because he had not yet severed ties with his financial conglomerates as legally required by federal campaign law. Also, he had not finalized the submission of a book manuscript and the completion of a film. Gingrich's inability to complete these tasks in a timely, discrete, and orderly fashion proved prescient. By May of 2011, it was not a matter of if Gingrich would run for president, but when his candidacy would become official.

CAMPAIGN

On Wednesday, May 11, 2011, Newt Gingrich formally launched his presidential campaign with an anti-climactic Twitter announcement—the first presidential candidate to declare with a tweet—with a link to a two-minute video on YouTube. Sadly, the attached link was broken, so it was several hours before anyone could view the online announcement.[16] Gingrich also posted his decision to run on Facebook and his campaign's official website. In his two-minute YouTube video, he said, "I'm announcing my candidacy for president of the United States because I believe we can return America to hope and opportunity, to full employment, to real security, to an American energy program, to a balanced budget . . . I worked with President Ronald Reagan in a very difficult period. We got jobs created again. Americans proud of America. And the Soviet Union disappeared." The campaign rollout signaled the issues and strategies Gingrich would use for his nomination run.

Issue Stances

In his announcement and subsequent speeches, Gingrich centered his campaign platform on the idea that he is cut from the same cloth as former President Ronald Reagan, a limited government conservative icon, while casting his opponents, particularly Romney, as moderates straying from Reagan's vision. To appeal to fiscal conservatives, Gingrich touted a supply-side economics strategy centered on the elimination of corporate taxes, capital gains taxes, and estate taxes. He pledged to implement a flat tax, keeping an option for charitable and home ownership deductions. Gingrich also promised to balance the budget and signed the Contract From America, placing himself in favorable position with Tea Party elements of the Republican electorate. To appeal to social conservatives, he constantly stressed his vehement opposition to gay marriage and abortion, claiming that secularism was on the rise and threatening the nation's Christian roots. These two themes featured prominently in his appearances and speeches throughout his campaign, regardless of geography and audience.

Also taking a major role was energy and national security, though these two issues evolved during the campaign. Gingrich began his campaign playing toward the fears of audiences familiar with photos of Obama bowing to dignitaries by stressing his refusal to bow to Saudi princes and pledging to expand oil and gas production in the Gulf of Mexico, Alaska, California, and other federal lands (the names of the federal land changed depending where he was speaking). Later in the campaign, as gasoline prices increased, Gingrich spoke more about his support for the Keystone XL Pipeline and promised to lower gasoline prices to $2.50. In some ways Gingrich appeared less hawkish than his fellow candidates by emphasizing a national security policy buttressed by a strong education system and strong military infrastructure. National security speeches frequently included references to increased investments in math and science as well as increased spending on military projects. He criticized Obama for being slow to respond to crises in Libya and Egypt, not stopping Iran's nuclear program, and withdrawing too slowly from Afghanistan. Gingrich claimed Obama was weakening the United States and was threatening the viability of a Jewish state.

While Gingrich touted an intense hostility to Obama's health care law, promising to repeal it in its entirety and to replace federal judges who voted to retain it, health care was not one of the more significant platforms in his campaign. Gingrich generally limited his health care discussions to calling Obamacare socialism, European socialism, or unconstitutional. Among older voters, he made a point to discuss his opposition to privatizing Medicare, putting him at odds with his opponents and many elected Republicans. Gingrich promised to create an optional private Social Security account and to lower unemployment to 4 percent, approximately the level when he was speaker of the House in the 1990s.

Finally, Gingrich frequently discussed immigration policy, though his position was somewhat more nuanced and complex than his opponents. At the very least, it signaled his desire to obtain the support of Latinos—a growing bloc in important states like Florida and Arizona. Gingrich advocated a more "humane" approach, supporting a pathway for legal citizenship for hardworking, churchgoing immigrants with families who had been here for a decade or more. He balanced his support for legal approaches to citizenship with calls for securing the U.S.-Mexican border, making English the official language, and creating local "citizen boards" to determine which immigrants stay.

Strategy

Gingrich opened his national campaign headquarters in Atlanta and hired individuals with extensive campaign experience. He first raided the staff of Texas Governor Rick Perry, also a rumored presidential candidate, by hiring Rob Johnson, Perry's campaign manager, to be his senior political adviser, and Dave Carney, Perry's top political adviser, to be his New Hampshire consultant. Gingrich tabbed Rick Tyler, senior adviser to Winning Our Future, to be his campaign spokesman; Sam Dawson, to be his campaign strategist; Katon Dawson, to be his consultant in South Carolina; and Craig Schoenfeld, to be his consultant in Iowa.[17] Gingrich assembled a veteran staff with a record of being able to fuse traditional campaign strategies—phone banking and canvassing—with newer, technological approaches—social networking and online fundraising. Gingrich signaled his desire to run an unorthodox campaign relying less on personal appearances and large personnel.[18]

Dave Carney tabbed the Gingrich campaign strategy as "leave no state behind," with a major focus of establishing a presence and actively campaigning in the first five states of Iowa, New Hampshire, South Carolina, Nevada, and Florida. Carney believed Gingrich's name recognition and visibility made him a national candidate, allowing him to forgo the strategy typically pursued by lesser-known and lesser-funded candidates—focusing on one or two of the first five contests in hopes the momentum from either a victory or strong showing translates into money, media attention, and organizational support in subsequent contests. By creating an organization in each of the first five states, the campaign could be better-positioned to absorb unpredictable events. Carney also eschewed the micro-targeting strategy popularized by Karl Rove in favor of a broader "right of center" approach primarily luring elderly, conservatives, evangelicals, and Tea Party supporters. Under the direction of Rob Johnson, the campaign was prepared to downplay traditional campaign tools—direct mail, phone calls, lawn signs, and newspaper ads—in favor of newer, electronic forms of voter outreach—social networking and online fundraising.[19] Gingrich envisioned a national structure and a nontraditional, national campaign. Outside of nontraditional, that did not happen.

Gingrich was set to launch a 17-stop tour of Iowa when disaster struck. It started with his May 15 appearance on *Meet the Press* with David Gregory when he referred to Representative Paul Ryan's (R-WI) Medicare proposal as "right-wing social engineering," saying "I don't think right-wing social engineering is any more desirable than left-wing social engineering. I don't think imposing radical change from the right or the left is a very good way for a free society to operate." Making matters worse, Gregory showed a clip from Gingrich's appearance on *Meet the Press* in 1993 where he made statements appearing to support the concept of an individual mandate. When asked to reconcile those statements with his present opposition to the individual mandate included in the Affordable Health Care for America Act, he confessed to previously supporting a "variation" of an individual mandate.[20] The campaign was immediately forced to play defense. Gingrich released a video on YouTube adamantly clarifying that he was "against any effort to impose a federal mandate on anyone because it is fundamentally wrong." The appearance of an evolving position on the individual mandate proved the least of his two problems. Republican officeholders and conservative pundits assailed Gingrich for criticizing Ryan's proposal, which was already under intense scrutiny by Democrats.

Conservative personalities Rush Limbaugh and Bill Bennett attacked Gingrich on the airwaves; House Republicans rushed to Ryan's defense and disparaged Gingrich for his lack of loyalty. Alex Castellanos penned a national editorial calling Gingrich, "the devil in a red dress, a temptress who would lead Republicans to ruin."[21] To make matters worse, video footage surfaced of a conservative Republican in Iowa, Russell Fuhrman, confronting Gingrich in a hotel, asking, "Why don't you get out before you make a bigger fool of yourself?"[22] Gingrich apologized to Representative Ryan and Republican leadership in a private caucus and to voters on YouTube, but the damage was done.

The month of May did not get any better. Another video emerged, this time of a man dumping a box full of confetti on Gingrich at a book signing in a Minneapolis, saying, "Feel the rainbow, Newt! Stop the hate! Stop anti-gay politics!"[23] Gingrich then had to defend allegations of a six-figure jewelry debt at Tiffany's, drawing comparisons to John Edwards's $400 haircut and becoming the subject of a round of late-night television jokes.[24] Media reports appeared claiming donors were deserting the Gingrich campaign, so Rick Tyler, Gingrich's campaign spokesman, sent out a scathing email accusing the media "literati" and "political elite" for purposefully sabotaging his presidential campaign.[25] The response, believed by many to have actually been penned by Gingrich and not Tyler, produced even more backlash and ridicule.

Less than a month later, Gingrich's staff resigned *en masse*. Rick Tyler, campaign spokesman, Rob Johnson, campaign manager, Dave Carney, new Hampshire operative, Katon Dawson, senior strategist, Sam Dawson, media consultant, Craig Schoenfeld, Iowa strategist, Walter Whetsell, South Carolina operative, and Scott Rials, Georgia operative, all stepped aside. Even former Governor of Georgia, Sonny Perdue, his national campaign co-chair, abandoned the campaign along with dozen of aides and staffers in Iowa, New Hampshire, and South Carolina. Publicly, the two sides cited a difference in campaign philosophy—Gingrich wanted a strategy centered on technology and debates; his staff wanted more appearances and more scheduled events.[26] Privately, senior staff felt Gingrich was undisciplined, Callista had too much input, he spent too little time campaigning (only 12 of his first 26 days), and he abruptly left for a two-week long Mediterranean excursion with his wife.[27]

Prior to the May debacle, polls showed solid support for Gingrich. During the spring of 2011, Romney's poll average was the highest of all the candidates, generally hovering in the mid- to upper-teens. Gingrich ranked second among the candidates in the low teens. They were the only two candidates receiving double-digit support in the polls in early 2011; however, after Gingrich's disastrous month, his poll numbers plummeted to an average 4.5 percent and would remain that way until September—good for sixth place behind Romney, Perry, Texas Congressman Ron Paul, Minnesota Representative Michele Bachmann, and former Godfather's Pizza CEO Herman Cain.[28]

With dwindling poll numbers, came dwindling financial support. Gingrich raised a paltry $2 million in the second quarter of 2011, reporting only $225,000 of cash on hand and $1 million of debt.[29] Former Minnesota Governor Tim Pawlenty and former Utah Governor Jon Huntsman raised more money in the second quarter, $4.2 million and $4.1 million respectively.[30] The third quarter proved even more disastrous, as Gingrich raised only $808,000, reporting $353,000 in the bank and $1.2 million of debt. The only candidate in worse financial shape was Huntsman, with $3 million in debt. The lack of funds forced Gingrich to abandon his "leave no state behind" strategy to open campaign headquarters and to install an organization in Iowa, New Hampshire, South Carolina, Nevada, and Florida. With the exception of Iowa, those plans were abandoned. Even then, the lack of resources forced Gingrich to forgo purchasing space at the famed Ames Straw Poll in August, choosing instead to mingle outside in the parking lot.[31] Unable to afford a staff, Gingrich spent the summer coordinating his own campaign, spending most of his time in Iowa, and participating in debates.

Debates

What salvaged the campaign were Gingrich's debate performances. The 2012 Republican nomination contest featured a record number of presidential debates—over 27 spread out from May of 2011 to March of 2012—watched by a record number of viewers—three to seven million viewers tuned into each debate (they were all televised). The debates showcased Gingrich's oratorical skills and grasp of ideas to a national audience—at no cost, the perfect prescription for a campaign with no money and no organization. While the other candidates struggled with consistency and moved up and down in the polls from June to December, Gingrich steadily rose in the polls and in the eyes of primary voters buoyed by commanding performances demarcated, in the early days, by a refusal to engage in personal criticisms of his fellow Republicans, repeatedly belittling the moderators and media, and providing clear, substantive answers on a wide range of foreign and domestic issues. One observer wrote, "Whatever happens to his campaign, Newt Gingrich certainly will be remembered in this campaign cycle for his razor-sharp tongue and for reeling off some of the best—and sharpest—debate lines of the 2012 contest."[32]

The earliest glimpse of Gingrich's ability to control a debate came during the third debate at Iowa State University in August, 2011. Chris Wallace asked Gingrich to respond to accusations that his campaign was faltering, to which Gingrich responded by asking him to "put aside the gotcha questions" and stop "playing Mickey Mouse games." Gingrich deflected the question by comparing his resignations to Ronald Reagan's resignation after being upset in New Hampshire in 1980 and urging participants to focus on ideas and Obama, not "campaign minutiae." His response drew a rousing applause by the audience and a positive reception by observers.[33] At the Palmetto Freedom Forum debate in Columbia, South Carolina on September 5, 2011, Gingrich displayed his intellectualism by giving precise answers to a wide range of questions, particularly on immigration, and avoiding attacks on his opponents. Several observers declared him the "winner" of the debate; one conservative pundit wrote, "it was easily the best 22 minutes of his campaign (The bar is admittedly not high). He thinks on his feet and he's smart."[34]

The Reagan Library debate in Simi Valley, California on September 7, 2011, is best known as the first debate featuring Perry as an official candidate, with Perry and Romney spending most of the time bickering with each other. In the meantime, Gingrich aimed his sharpest attacks for President Obama and the news media and accused the moderators of trying to instigate disagreements between the Republicans. Gingrich received a thunderous applause for referring to Obama as a practitioner of "class warfare" and "bureaucratic socialism."[35] At the Tea Party Express Debate in Tampa, Florida on September 12, he again avoided the fray between Perry and Romney to focus on Obama and the federal government. One person wrote, "I think he won the debate tonight. He got in a few good jokes, was able to shift the focus onto President Obama and even called the current economic situation the 'Obama Depression,' which resonates with many Americans."[36]

The Western Republican Leadership Debate in Las Vegas on October 18, was, perhaps, the feistiest debate and featured multiple exchanges between Perry, Cain, Romney, and Santorum. Gingrich saved his sharpest criticisms for President Obama and the moderator, CNN's Anderson Cooper. He discussed his faith, ridiculed Congress for wasteful spending, critiqued Cain's "9-9-9" plan, and pointed out, in a non-personal fashion, problems in Massachusetts related to the health care law passed while Romney was governor.[37] One analyst observed, "The former speaker was professorial, making historical references left and right and casting himself as an ideas man who is someone above the fray."[38] In this debate, watched by 5.5 million people, most pundits declared Gingrich the "winner."

Gingrich consistently delivered solid performances in the debates, sticking with the strategy of avoiding personal attacks of his opponents, attacking the media and moderators, and giving precise, technical answers to every issue. Voters and pundits alike took notice. The November 9 debate at Oakland University is best known for Perry's "Oops" moment. Lost in the hoopla surrounding Perry's mental lapse, one observer wrote, "Newt probably had the best line of the night when he said there's no way he could describe a health care solution in just thirty seconds. He's really showing the American people this is a difficult question, and a solution is not going to be easy."[39] At the November 12 Commander-in-Chief debate in Spartanburg, South Carolina, viewed by 5.5 million people, an analyst concluded, "Once again, the former House Speaker commanded the stage better than anyone else. He provided strong, substantive issues. Gingrich projects an aura that he knows the issues better than anyone else. Probably because he does know better. It was another very good performance."[40]

Some performances drew polarized reviews—praise from Republicans and condemnations from Democrats. In a December debate at Drake University, Gingrich called all Palestinians terrorists, "these people are terrorists. They teach terrorism in their schools. They have textbooks that say, if there are 13 Jews and nine Jews are killed, how many Jews are left? We pay for those textbooks through our aid money . . . It's fundamentally time for somebody to have the guts to stand up and say, enough lying about the Middle East."[41] The Drake University debate was the most-watched debate during the primaries, with 7,631,000 viewers. One pundit wrote, "Winner: Newt Gingrich: The former House Speaker seems to be adjusting nicely to his newfound frontrunner status. While he's long been one of the best natural debaters in the field, Gingrich seemed to be genuinely working to avoid coming off as a smarter-than-thou intellectual. He had his moments but overall the image he gave off was of a more approachable, kinder Newt . . . The best example? His well-rehearsed but nonetheless very well delivered response on whether his three marriages raised questions about his character. Gingrich was remorseful without being maudlin—striking just the right tone on a very tough question for him."[42]

Republicans found themselves stirred by Gingrich confronting moderators, dismantling President Obama, avoiding personal attacks, and giving articulate, precise answers to a wide range of questions. He simultaneously benefitted from catastrophic performances by Perry and Cain and the persistent bickering between Perry and Romney. Based exclusively on his debate performances, by early December Gingrich found himself at the top of the national polls, by a 35 percent to 22 percent margin over Romney, and at the top of the Iowa polls, by a 31 percent to 18 percent margin over Romney. A November poll conducted by the *New Hampshire Journal* showed Romney and Gingrich in a statistical dead heat—29 percent to 27 percent—which was a substantial improvement over the October poll showing Gingrich in third place with 10 percent to Romney's 41 percent.[43] In almost every state keeping polls, Gingrich found his support rising.

Surging poll numbers resulted in surging financial support. In the fourth quarter of 2011, Gingrich reported raising $10 million, with $2.1 million cash on hand and $1.2 million of debt.[44] Only Paul and Romney raised more money. With a drastically improved financial situation, Gingrich finally was able to open campaign offices and hire campaign staff. In November, he opened offices in New Hampshire and South Carolina and rehired two of his three Iowa consultants—Craig Schoenfeld, who had been state director, and Katie Koberg, who had been deputy director.[45] In December, Gingrich brought in Kevin Kellem, former Bush administration official and spokesman for Vice President Dick Cheney, to serve as senior adviser and Martin Baker, a well-regarded GOP consultant, to serve as political director.[46] He also hired former Representative Bob Walker of Pennsylvania to be his campaign manager, Michael Krull to be his deputy campaign manager, and R.C. Hammond to be his campaign spokesman along with established pollsters David Winston and Kellyanne Conway.[47] All of the momentum was on Gingrich's side, but it did not remain there for long.

OUTCOMES

At the Ames Straw Poll in August of 2011, Gingrich finished eighth (385 votes) behind Bachmann (4,823 votes), Paul (4,671), Pawlenty (2,293), Santorum (1,567), Cain (1,456), Perry (718), and Romney (567).[48] The straw poll came on the heels of his tumultuous summer, so an eighth place finish was not shocking. Nevertheless, Gingrich made a strategic decision to spend a disproportional amount of time—scheduling 134 events over 64 days—wooing evangelicals, 60 percent of Iowa's caucus electorate, and Tea Party supporters, 40 percent of Iowa's caucus electorate.[49] Gingrich used the themes of federal debt, tax burdens, government overreach, and Romney's extreme wealth to Tea Party audiences in Iowa. His populist appeal, combative tone, and intellectual rhetoric worked well with this group, though many remained skeptical by his tenure as a congressman (casting doubt on his claim of being anti-establishment) and position shifts (notably on global warming and the individual mandate).[50] A void of support emerged among Tea Party supporters with the collapse of Bachmann, Perry, and Cain. When their campaigns ended, Gingrich targeted their voters who had previously told volunteers they planned to vote for them; eighty-three percent of departing Cain voters indicated probable support for Gingrich.[51]

Gingrich targeted evangelicals by emphasizing his belief that life begins at conception, opposition to embryonic stem cells research, and opposition to gay marriage. He promoted a God-infused interpretation of American history at war with the encroaching secular media, academic, and legal elite. His infidelity was a source of concern for many evangelicals, which he attempted to deflect with themes of admission, penitence, forgiveness, and his "born-again" conversion to Catholicism. While Gingrich drew praise for not personally attacking his opponents during debates, at campaign stops he hammered Romney for having a "liberal past" as Governor of Massachusetts that included prior support for gay rights and abortion.

Gingrich was aided by the fact that evangelicals expressed greater anxiety over Romney's Mormon faith than Gingrich's infidelity; however, this infidelity prevented Gingrich from obtaining key endorsements in Iowa. For example, Family Leader CEO Bob Vander Plaats and fellow activist Chuck Hurley, two more influential figures in Iowa's evangelical community, endorsed Santorum over Gingrich.[52] Also, pamphlets appeared across the state, claiming to be authorized and funded by Iowans for Life, the largest and most powerful pro-life lobby in Iowa, attacking Gingrich as a "a pro-life fraud" and accusing Gingrich of campaigning for "pro-partial birth abortion candidates," urging "fellow Republicans to drop the pro-life issue because it was too divisive," and leaving the issue of abortion out of his book, Winning the Future."[53]

Alas, being the frontrunner came at a price. An analysis by Kantar Media's Campaign Media Analysis Group found that 45 percent of all the political ads in Iowa were attack spots against Gingrich, more than any other candidate. Only 6 percent of the ads were supportive of Gingrich.[54] Due to his slow start, Gingrich was only able to spend $431,760 on campaign advertisements and, sticking with his strategy of avoiding attacking his opponents, 83 percent of those ads were positive. Also problematic was the fact that Gingrich's first ad did not run until December 5, while his opponents began months earlier. All told, Gingrich was outspent by a 10 to 1 margin. The attack ads discussed how Gingrich was fined $300,000 for ethics violations while Speaker, took over $1.6 million in consulting fees from Freddie Mac just before the economic meltdown, supports amnesty for illegal immigrants, and teamed up with Nancy Pelosi and Al Gore on global warming. Attacks on Gingrich came beyond his opponents in Iowa.

One particularly damning criticism came courtesy of *National Review*, where he was caricatured on the cover as Marvin the Martian, an obvious stab at his Mars exploration positions. Inside, the editorial called him a "poor Speaker of the House" and attacked "his character flaws—his impulsiveness, his grandiosity, his weakness for half-baked (and not especially conservative) ideas" and his personal life "very few people with a personal history like his—two divorces, two marriages to former mistresses—have ever tried running for president." The editorial concluded his nomination would blow a historic opportunity and weaken the Republican chances of winning the White House.[55] Consequently, his poll numbers spiraled.

What also hurt was the fact that there were no debates between December 16 and January 3, providing a two and a half week dry spell for the best debater and depriving him a free counter-attack. Gingrich's last debate on December 16 was solid, but he found himself on the defensive during the entire debate having to respond to attacks about his role with Freddie Mac and votes for federal funding for Planned Parenthood. Some considered the debate his worst performance of the campaign, which was not the last impression he wanted to leave voters going into the debate moratorium.[56]

Just one month after sitting atop the polls in Iowa, Gingrich finished a distant fourth in the Iowa Caucus with only 13 percent of the vote.

Among Tea Party supporters, Santorum won 29 percent and Gingrich won only 15 percent behind Romney and Paul. Among evangelicals, Santorum won 32 percent and Gingrich won only 14 percent. The two groups he courted heavily abandoned him in favor of Santorum, the eventual Caucus winner. Gingrich failed to obtain a plurality of the vote among any demographic subgroup.

While his plunge was brought on by negative attacks from his opponents, his campaign organization offered no consistent message to rebut the most damaging claims, particularly those dealing with Freddie Mac, other than to complain about the negativity. Gingrich was unprepared for the attacks and he insisted on staying positive. Gingrich's organizational disunity manifested itself in other ways. Other failures included an incoherent grassroots mobilization and not hiring a day-to-day caucus organizer until a week before the election. He lacked the personnel to mobilize voters and to canvass neighborhoods, so he had nothing to fall back on when his momentum started to slip. He lacked the volunteers to maintain the phones for voter outreach when his public image was dimmed by the temporary cessation of debates.

The apex of his organizational ineptitude occurred when he left Iowa after the Sioux City debate on December 15 and did not return until December 27. One reason for his departure was that his campaign had neglected to obtain the number of signatures required by law to appear on the Virginia primary ballot. Gingrich was forced to campaign in Virginia to acquire signatures; however, the state Republican Party announced December 24 that he failed to acquire the 10,000 legal signatures. Adding insult to injury was a Quinnipiac University poll showing Gingrich with a 30 percent to 25 percent advantage over Romney in Virginia.[57] The other reason for his departure was his general disdain for spending time on the campaign trail and his brash assumption that his lead in the polls would hold up. Gingrich spent less time on the trail than his challengers, preferring to appear at book signings and private fundraisers.

New Hampshire

Gingrich chartered a late-night plane and arrived in New Hampshire before the final Iowa caucus results were even tallied. Before leaving, Gingrich blasted Romney for running a negative campaign, called Romney a liar, and vowed to run a more aggressive campaign in New Hampshire.[58] This would be difficult considering he got off to a late start. Gingrich closed his entire New Hampshire operation in June when his staff quit and funds dried up. With poll numbers rising and donations increasing after strong debates in November, he finally opened three offices, hired 15 staffers, and recruited volunteer captains for all 10 counties and the 20 largest cities. He hired New Hampshire Tea Party leader Andrew Hemingway to be his New Hampshire campaign director, a maneuver obviously designed to tap into the Tea Party network in an effort to make up ground quickly. By comparison, Romney had held 17 town hall meetings, visited 30 towns across all 10 counties, and organized an army of volunteers who had contacted 200,000 voters, knocked on 26,000 doors, distributed 15,000 yard signs, and blasted out 400 letters to local newspapers.[59] Romney had three television ads running; Gingrich's first ad did not appear until January 5.[60] Romney also managed to secure the endorsement of most of the state's GOP establishment; Gingrich only picked up the *New Hampshire Union Leader*.

While Romney had always been the heavy favorite and expected to win, Gingrich's campaign saw reasons for optimism in November and early December when polls showed their candidate increasing from 6 percent to 24 percent and Romney decreasing from 40 percent to 35 percent. In fact, a CNN poll in December showed Gingrich cutting Romney's lead to single-digits.[61] At the very least, a stronger than expected showing, even if it still entailed a second-place finish, could provide the campaign with some momentum heading the Southern portion of the nomination contest and Gingrich's backyard in South Carolina and Florida. Alas, it was not to be. The mid-December declining poll numbers observed in Iowa occurred simultaneously in New Hampshire for the same reasons—the break in the debate schedule and the overwhelming barrage of negative advertisements. By the time the campaign shifted to New Hampshire, Gingrich slipped to 13 percent in the polls behind Paul (19 percent) and Romney (41 percent).

The shift in the polls and barrage of negative advertisements affected Gingrich's rhetoric and debate performances. He gained notoriety early in the campaign for being calm, substantive, and above the fray; however, he became increasingly combative and confrontational. At a January 7 debate in Manchester, New Hampshire, the fourth-most watched debate in the campaign with 6,271,000 viewers, Gingrich repeatedly attacked Romney for his role at Bain Capital, accusing him of pillaging companies and cutting jobs to enrich himself and his colleagues. He compared Romney to two other presidential candidates from Massachusetts—former Governor Michael Dukakis and Senator John Kerry—and lambasted him for running negative ads claiming he supports federal funding for abortion. He also received a rousing applause for defiantly calling a gay rights question an example of "anti-Christian bigotry" and accusing Obama for conducting a "war on religion."[62] A day later in Concord, New Hampshire, Gingrich again fired repeated volleys at Romney, urging him to drop the "pious baloney" surrounding his political history and motivations. He also argued that the so-called "relatively timid Massachusetts moderate" would have a tough time running against President Obama because he does not present enough of a contrast from the president and could not be trusted to fight for important conservative principles.[63] The debates reflected a decision by Gingrich to stress new themes: one, Romney was not conservative enough; two, Romney profited as a corporate raider at Bain Capital.

The same factors that led to Gingrich's fourth-place collapse in Iowa resulted in a fourth-place finish in New Hampshire. First, there were financial factors. Romney's campaign spent $1 million in advertising, entirely negative, against Gingrich; Gingrich countered with a paltry $5,000 pro-Gingrich buy. The assault caused Gingrich to bitterly declare he had been "Romney-boated," an obvious reference to the damaging swift boat attacks ads against Kerry in 2004. Second, there were organizational factors. The Gingrich campaign failed to formulate an effective rebuttal to the Freddie Mac issue and lacked the manpower to canvass neighborhoods and to call voters to counter the attack ads. In the end, Gingrich finished with 9 percent of the vote, finishing behind Romney (39 percent), Paul (23 percent), and Huntsman (17 percent). The groups targeted by Gingrich in Iowa—conservative, Tea Party, evangelicals—divided their support for Romney and Santorum. It was a flawed electoral coalition from the beginning because very conservative voters and evangelical voters make up less than half of primary voters and 15 percent less of the Tea Party voters in New Hampshire as compared to Iowa.

South Carolina

Gingrich limped into the Palmetto State with 18 percent support in the polls, behind Romney (37 percent) and Santorum (19 percent); however, a substantial number of developments broke in Gingrich's favor and allowed him to convert a 20-point deficit into a 12-point margin of victory. First, billionaire casino magnate Sheldon Adelson came to the rescue with a $5 million contribution to the pro-Gingrich Super PAC, Winning the Future, including $3.4 million for advertising. The most significant was a 30-minute documentary, "King of Bain: When Mitt Romney Came to Town," describing Romney's role with Bain Capital as a corporate predator.[64] The Bain-centered campaign attempted to cast doubt upon Romney's primary argument—that as a successful executive in the private sector, he knew more than the other candidates about how to create jobs.[65] Other advertisements challenged Romney's assertion of being the best-positioned to defeat Obama and, for the first time, Romney found himself primarily on the defensive.[66] Gingrich had abandoned his prior strategy of refusing to negatively attack his rivals.

Second, Gingrich, for once, had a more extensive campaign organization than his opponents. In October of 2011, national coalition director Adam Waldeck moved to Charleston, bringing with him a list of donors, organizers, and voters. In November, the campaign opened a headquarters in Summerville and Greenville, with veteran Vince Haley in charge. South Carolina was one of the centers of the Tea Party movement, so the campaign made a concerted effort to tap into their support and network by hiring Allen Olson, founder of the Columbia Tea Party, Gerri McDaniel, Myrtle Beach Tea Party leader, Chris Horne, Charleston Tea Party leader, and Joanne Jones, Vice Chairman of the Charleston Tea Party. Also assisting in statewide efforts were Ruth Sherlock and Leslie Gaines, veteran South Carolina consultants and fundraisers.[67] In all, Gingrich had 12 paid staffers and five offices in the state, the only candidate with more than one office. Before the polls closed in New Hampshire, Gingrich physically moved his entire national operation to South Carolina.[68] Additionally, Gingrich received the endorsements of most of the political leaders in the state, with only Governor Nikki Haley endorsing Romney. While some organizational deficiencies remained, the existence of an extensive voter outreach organization allowed Gingrich to tap into voter support following watershed moments in the state's two debates.

Third, Gingrich received a significant boost from two televised debates on January 16 and January 19. During the January 16 debate in Myrtle Beach, Gingrich attacked Romney for refusing to release his tax returns. Romney was caught off-guard by the attack, stumbling over an incoherent answer failing to shed light over whether he would release his tax returns. Gingrich pounced on him for having something to hide. The second moment came in a racially charged exchange with Juan Williams, who suggested Gingrich's comments on food stamps and the lack of a work ethic in poor, black neighborhoods were racially insensitive. His response, a clip that became the heart of his final television ad in South Carolina, featured Gingrich jabbing his finger into the podium and lecturing Williams, "I believe every American of every background has been endowed by their creator with the right to pursue happiness. And if that makes liberals unhappy, I'm going to continue to find ways to help poor people learn how to get a job, learn how to get a better job, and learn some day to own the job." Gingrich received a standing ovation—purportedly the first standing ovation at a Republican debate since Ronald Reagan in 1980—a fact that did not escape unnoticed and would became a major talking point for the remainder of campaign in South Carolina.[69] Gingrich would also continue to refer to Obama as the "food stamp president" in his stumps speeches in South Carolina.

A mere three days later, it appeared Gingrich had another problem on his hands when his second wife, Marianne, gave a television interview claiming Gingrich had requested an open marriage in order to continue his affair with his now third-wife, Callista. CNN's John King opened the January 19 debate in Charleston by asking Gingrich about his ex-wife's claim. Gingrich fired back angrily, "Every person in here knows personal pain. Every person in here has had someone close to them go through painful things. To take an ex-wife and make it, two days before the primary, a significant question for a presidential campaign is as close to despicable as anything I can imagine." He received another rousing standing ovation and the energy from this one-liner assisted in another strong debate performance.[70] Gingrich received another break that same day when Perry abruptly quit the race and endorsed Gingrich.[71] This combined with earlier endorsements by Sarah and Todd Palin gave Tea Party supporters, conservatives, and evangelicals further reason to break for Gingrich.[72]

According to the exit polls, nearly two-thirds of South Carolina primary voters—65 percent—said the debates were one of the most important factors in deciding whom to support. Of those voters, 50 percent cast their ballot for Gingrich. Tea Party identifiers, 34 percent of the electorate, selected Gingrich over Romney 47 percent to 21 percent; evangelicals, 65 percent of the electorate, selected Gingrich over Santorum 44 percent to 21 percent.[73] Finally, conservatives, 36 percent of the voters, voted for Gingrich by a 48 percent to 23 percent margin over Santorum. The South Carolina Republican primary electorate contained a disproportionate amount of the key groups targeted by the Gingrich campaign—conservative, Tea Party, evangelicals—and Gingrich finally convinced those voters to support him over the other candidates en route to bulldozing the field. He won with 40 percent of the vote, besting Romney (28 percent) and Santorum (17 percent). Gingrich finally had a victory and momentum heading into a critical and potential game-changing primary in Florida.

Florida

When Gingrich surged in November, the effects were felt in Florida as well and he overtook Romney by an average 43 percent to 25 percent margin. Alas, when Gingrich collapsed in December, Romney regained the lead. Gingrich's upset victory in South Carolina provided the campaign with an overnight bump in the polls and a 15 percent Romney lead turned immediately into an 8 percent Gingrich lead. Gingrich placed his Florida operation in the hands of Jose Mallea, the individual who successfully engineered Senator Marco Rubio's victory in 2010. Like Iowa, New Hampshire, and South Carolina, Gingrich got off to a late start, not hiring Mallea until December 11 and not opening a headquarters until January 13.[74] Romney had opened a headquarters and hired a campaign staff in June. In December, while Gingrich was scrambling to attract signatures to appear on Virginia's ballot, Romney's campaign began targeting absentee voters. Restore Our Future, the Super PAC supporting Romney, started running attack ads January 3, the same day as the Iowa Caucus.[75]

The hiring of Mallea signaled a major effort by the Gingrich campaign to engage the Hispanic community. Four years earlier, Latinos opted for McCain over Romney by a 54 percent to 14 percent margin, playing a major role in ending Romney's 2008 presidential bid. Gingrich outlined a moderate immigration stance, saying the government should not expel immigrants if they have laid down roots here—for instance, if they have been here for a quarter of a century, raising a family, paying taxes, attending church, and obeying the law. Gingrich hoped this "more humane" approach, combined with themes of economic opportunity and prosperity, would resonate with Florida Latinos, generally more conservative than Latinos elsewhere. Gingrich also ran a controversial Spanish-language radio ad calling Romney "anti-immigrant."[76]

With Tea Party supporters, Gingrich railed against extravagant spending in Washington D.C. and Romney's extravagant wealth (juxtaposing the two), berated Romney's decision to hire former Charlie Crist staffers, and emphasized his balanced budgets as Speaker. He promised to eliminate Obama's czars and form a Tenth Amendment panel to be headed by Tea Party favorite Rick Perry.[77] He courted Tea Party leadership and received the endorsement of 42 Tea Party groups across the state. He stressed his self-proclaimed status as Ronald Reagan's heir and had Michael Reagan join him in appearances throughout the state.[78]

Gingrich's rhetoric became increasingly vapid, playing more on the fears and fantasies of various groups. With Latinos he promised Puerto Rican statehood and a "Cuban spring," with Jewish voters he stressed the threat posed by an Iranian nuclear weapon, at the Space Coast he made his infamous pledge to establish a lunar colony, and with religious voters argued stem-cell research was science justifying baby killing. He went so far as to accuse Romney of using his health care plan in Massachusetts to take kosher food away from elderly Jewish people. Gingrich repeatedly called Romney a "liar" and "liberal" at campaign appearances and during interviews.[79] His debate performances changed as well.

The first Florida debate in Tampa was the second-most watched debate of the presidential contest, with an audience of 7,125,000 people. To counter Gingrich's superior performances in South Carolina, Romney hired a debate coach prior to the debate.[80] And, it showed. Romney hammered Gingrich's record as Speaker, using the phrase "resign in disgrace" multiple times, and $1.6 million contract with Freddie Mac, asking Gingrich to release his contract to prove he was not lobbying for them.[81] In the second Florida debate in Jacksonville, Romney again went on the offensive, attacking Gingrich's proposal for a permanent American colony on the moon, reminding voters of his ethics fines as Speaker, and questioning his role with Freddie Mac and Fannie Mae (Florida had one of the highest foreclosure rates in the nation). Romney assailed Gingrich for running attack ads calling him anti-immigration. Gingrich tried to counter by turning the audience against the moderator and comparing Obamacare to Romneycare, but neither strategy worked.[82] Gingrich struggled and his bickering, something he had largely avoided all campaign, turned off voters.

While the Florida debates did not go well for Gingrich, they did not prove to be the difference. Romney, with support from his Super PAC, Restore Our Future, outspent Gingrich five-to-one across all ten major Florida media markets, over 90 percent of them being negative ads with the most damaging emphasizing Gingrich's ties to Freddie Mac. Gingrich would refer to the discrepancy as a "carpet bombing."[83]

Negative ads, financial superiority, improved debate performances, and superior organization allowed Romney to evaporate Gingrich's South Carolina momentum and to trounce Gingrich in the Sunshine State, 46 percent-32 percent. Among Latinos, Romney defeated Gingrich 54 percent-29 percent; among the Tea Party supporters and conservatives, Romney defeated Gingrich 41 percent-37 percent. Adding insult to injury, evangelicals split their votes evenly between the two candidates. Gingrich lost every significant constituency targeted by his campaign. The Florida loss seriously eroded Gingrich's presidential hopes, but he refused to withdraw from the race. The campaign made a conscious decision to focus time and resources on Nevada and the Southern portion of Super Tuesday—Georgia, Tennessee, and Oklahoma.

February

Gingrich mounted a late advance into Nevada, hoping the combination of Sheldon Adelson, Tea Party supporters, and conservatives could siphon delegates and momentum from Romney. The campaign opened offices in Las Vegas and Reno only a week before the caucus. Tiffany Ruegner, former organizer for the Tea Party Express, a group that played a critical role in Sharron Angle's upset victory over Sue Lowden, was hired to run the Nevada campaign. Employed since November, Gingrich hoped her Tea Party network could provide the volunteers, donors, and support needed to mobilize caucus goers; however, he was not aware of the fact that the Tea Party movement had largely fractured into disparate, unorganized groups after Angle's defeat to Harry Reid. Two events epitomized Gingrich's disarray in Nevada. One, Gingrich abruptly canceled a meeting with Nevada Governor Brian Sandoval after his campaign had arranged a photo opportunity with him, irking the governor and his staff with no reasons for the cancellation. Two, Gingrich scheduled a 1 p.m. rally in Reno, but volunteers put out word the event would be at noon before he showed up at 2 p.m. By then, most of his supporters left before he spoke.[84] Also, rather than barnstorming Nevada with public appearances and stump speeches, he spent most of his time fund raising and meeting with his closest advisers and supporters.[85]

The last-second push in Nevada was desperate from the beginning and Romney defeated Gingrich by a 50 percent to 21 percent margin with strong support from Mormons, his organization, and advertising. Romney and his allied Super PAC, Restore Our Future, spent $1 million on advertising; Gingrich spent none. The remnants of the Tea Party failed to deliver support for Gingrich, though he did beat Paul for second-place (he had campaigned in Nevada over a year and finished second there in 2008). Nevada was a waste of time and resources.

Publicly, the month of February provided a lull in the schedule—no debates were held between January 26 and February 22. Colorado, Minnesota, and Missouri all held events February 7, but Gingrich elected to skip these events. Strategically, these three states would not be awarding delegates, all three events being the first steps in a multi-tiered process to assign delegates. Missouri's primary was a non-binding "beauty contest" with no bearing on delegate allocation—they would be awarded March 17 at a caucus. Practically, Gingrich needed to reserve his resources for delegate-awarding contests with a high probability of winning or exceeding expectations. Gingrich and his Super PAC did not run any advertisements in Colorado, Minnesota, and Missouri; he did not even file to appear on the ballot for the Missouri primary.[86] Gingrich had only two staffers in Colorado and visited once, February 6, the day before the caucus, to make a speech at a Marriott and the Colorado School of Mines.[87] Gingrich appeared only once in Minnesota, addressing a ballroom of supporters in a Bloomington hotel.[88] Maine held a non-binding, week-long caucus from February 4-11; Gingrich had no staff, ran no commercials, and made no visits. Gingrich finished third in Colorado and fourth in Minnesota and Maine.

Gingrich also made the decision to skip the Arizona and Michigan primaries on February 28. He appeared once in Arizona to participate in a debate, but hired no staffers and spent no money advertising. Gingrich finished a distant third in Arizona and fourth in Michigan. Gingrich took a two-day tour of Washington, with a caucus on March 3, blaming Obama for high gasoline prices and criticizing gay marriage legislation recently signed into law by Governor Christine Gregoire.[89] Again, Gingrich spent no money on advertising and maintained no permanent campaign structure in the state, resulting in a fourth place finish and no delegates.

Accompanying the disappointing results was an erosion of public support, with Gingrich's poll average sliding from 30.3 percent, good for first, on the day of the Florida primary, January 31, to 14 percent, good for third behind Romney and Santorum, on the day of the Washington caucus on March 3.

On the one hand, investing little time and no resources on these February contests was necessary—Gingrich lacked cash and personnel. The decision to skip these states was justified because he had, at best, only a slim chance of winning and receiving delegates because he had ignored these states in 2011—again, due to the lack of resources. Nevertheless, skipping these events and the subsequent string of third and fourth place finishes had a damaging effect on his campaign. Publicly, media and voters began questioning the viability of his campaign and, combined with the rise of Santorum due to stronger than expected showings, began abandoning their previous support for his candidacy. Gingrich's February fundraising reflected this, as he raised just $2.6 million in the month of February. Unfortunately, he also spent $2.8 million, leaving him with just $1.5 million cash on hand and $1.6 million in debt. By comparison, Romney raised $12 million and Santorum brought in over $9 million. The only thing keeping the Gingrich candidacy financially afloat was the Super PAC Winning Our Future, which raised $5.7 million in February—$5 million courtesy of the Adelson family.[90] Gingrich vigorously courted the supporters of Perry and Cain, both of whom had endorsed Gingrich and had demonstrated financial success early in the campaign; however, this proved fruitless as their supporters and bundlers chose to stay neutral for the remainder of the nomination contest.

Gingrich spent the entire campaign relying upon strong debate performances and energetic stump speeches to overcome his organizational and financial deficiencies; however, the month of February featured only one debate. The last two debates of the campaign in Florida were his most disastrous and his least successful; unfortunately, they were the last national images left to voters participating in the February contests. The debate on February 22 in Mesa, Arizona was watched by only 4.7 million people, making it one of the least-viewed debates during the entire nomination contest. Gingrich had a fabulous performance, returning to the style that proved successful in the past—remaining above the fray, avoiding attacks on his opponents, attacking Obama and the moderators, and focusing on the issues of energy—complaining that Obama is bowing to foreign oil suppliers and promising $2.50 gas—and religious liberties—claiming Obama is at war with religion and assisting the rise of a secular state.[91] While it was a successful debate, it was not so momentous to result in a standing ovation or to halt the momentum of Santorum or Romney. It lacked a defining moment as achieved in South Carolina. Observers noted a marked change in the tone of his stump speeches, ceasing to mention his opponents almost entirely in favor of gas prices, energy policy, gay marriage, religious liberties, and states' rights. Gingrich's campaign increased the frequency of its usage of YouTube, Facebook, and Twitter in an effort to increase his outreach in a relatively inexpensive fashion.[92]

Super Tuesday

Gingrich had no momentum, was short on resources, and lacked a coherent organization, so he went South. His campaign staked any hopes of a comeback on a Southern strategy, concentrating all remaining resources, time, and personnel on the Super Tuesday states of Georgia, Oklahoma, and Tennessee, and the post-Super Tuesday states of Alabama and Mississippi. The campaign also committed to Ohio and Kansas. The Southern strategy offered promise. First, Gingrich was the only remaining Southerner in the field, a fact that could potentially sway voters looking to support the native son. One of those Southern states, Georgia, was his home state and the center of his political rise to power as Speaker. Gingrich made it a point to emphasize the non-Southern status of his opponents, calling Romney "Massachusetts moderate baloney" and Santorum "Pennsylvania big labor baloney."[93] Second, his only victory was a Southern state—South Carolina. He demonstrated success in the only Southern state he had competed in to date. Third, demographically the South offered a disproportionate amount of his targeted electoral constituency that had propelled him to victory in South Carolina—conservatives, evangelicals, Tea Party supporters—that had been absent in Arizona, Colorado, Maine, Michigan, Minnesota, and Washington. Fourth, polling data earlier in the race showed Gingrich running strong enough in these states, suggesting that victory was still a possibility. Gingrich believed a decisive victory in Georgia combined with wins in Oklahoma and Tennessee could restore relevancy and momentum.

Gingrich would have to conduct his Southern strategy with little organizational coherency. Outside of Georgia, the campaign had no headquarters or paid staff in Oklahoma or Tennessee. His February campaign stops to Oklahoma and Tennessee were his first appearances in these states during the entire campaign. Gingrich would have to win with little money and advertising. His advertisements did not appear until the week before Super Tuesday, but his opponents had started several weeks before and he would be outspent in every major media market in every state. Gingrich would have to win with only a handful of endorsements. Most of the established Republicans in the Super Tuesday states remained neutral; sensing that Romney's victory was likely, they did not want to alienate themselves from the possible future president. Gingrich employed surrogates on the campaign trail, with Herman Cain and Jackie Cushman, the daughter of the former speaker, making stops for him in Tennessee and Oklahoma.[94] Gingrich would have to win without any debates. A CNN debate scheduled for March 1 in Atlanta was cancelled; voters were only treated to a forum hosted by Mike Huckabee on Fox News. He would be deprived from an inexpensive national venue to make his final case with the voters. Gingrich spent considerably more time stressing his Southern credentials and discussing gasoline prices, hoping, at the very least, that voters in the "oil patch" would gravitate towards him over Santorum.

What Gingrich found in the South on Super Tuesday was no relevancy, no momentum, no renewal, and only one victory—his home state of Georgia. He finished a distant third in Oklahoma and Tennessee. In Ohio, a state to which he committed secondary resources, he also finished third. Outside of the South and inside of the South, Gingrich finished no better than third in any Super Tuesday state. Gingrich only won an estimated

74 delegates, good for third, behind Santorum (86) and Romney (212). Oklahoma offered one particular embarrassing case in point: Santorum and the Super PACs allied with his campaign spent no money on advertising in Oklahoma and he still finished ahead of Gingrich. Outside of Georgia, Gingrich won only a handful of counties and lost every key constituency—conservatives, evangelicals, Tea Party supporters. The Southern strategy had failed.

There was no hope for Gingrich after Super Tuesday. On March 10, Gingrich finished a disappointing third in Kansas, after spending more time and money in the state than any other candidate. On March 13, he finished second in Alabama and Mississippi. He spent more time campaigning in these two states than the other two candidates, though Romney's Restore Our Future blanketed both states with nearly $2 million in negative advertising. March 24, Gingrich finished third in Louisiana despite spending the entire week campaigning in the Pelican State. While his rivals competed in Illinois, Gingrich was stumping in Louisiana, working his way from Shreveport, the city in the most northwestern area of the state, to Port Fourchon at the state's southeastern tip.[95] It did not help. He won very few counties and lost conservatives, evangelicals, and Tea Party supporters to Santorum. The South had abandoned Gingrich in favor of two Yankees. Not only did the South reject Gingrich, but so too had the rest of the Republican electorate.

On March 27, Gingrich's campaign announced the cancellation of most of his campaign schedule, laid off about a third of full-time staff, and replaced his manager, Michael Krull with Vince Haley as part of what aides are calling a "big-choice convention" strategy. Publicly, this strategy featured two goals: one, continuing to emphasize that Gingrich is the most capable of defeating Obama by relying primarily on the issue of $2.50 gas; two, communicating directly to unpledged delegates in hopes of creating a brokered Republican National Convention in Tampa, Florida.[96] The latter would only be possible if Santorum and Paul remained in the race and siphoned enough delegates to prevent Romney from obtaining an outright majority. Mathematically, this possibility ended with Santorum's official withdrawal from the race on April 10 due to the illness of his daughter.[97] Privately, most people speculated that Gingrich remained in the race in order to retire campaign debts. His failed Southern strategy left the campaign with a $4.3 million debt and only $1.2 million cash on hand.[98] In the remaining contests, Gingrich finished between second or third—well behind Romney. The final stand was a disappointing and distant second-place finish in Delaware on April 24. On May 2, almost a year to the day that he entered the race, Gingrich announced the official suspension of his campaign.[99]

ANALYSIS

Newt Gingrich's failed presidential run illustrates the importance of money, strategy, and organization. Admittedly, he entered the campaign with serious flaws—arrogant and unlikable—and baggage—ethics violations, consulting contracts, and an adulterous past; however, he did extremely well in the debates when he showed mastery for policy details, from the budget to immigration, and an ability to challenge the news media, including debate moderators from the Fox News network. The debates kept Gingrich relevant, but, most importantly, they provided the campaign with free national exposure. Debates alone cannot sustain a campaign, especially when mistakes are made and opponents launch negative advertisements.

Gingrich made several critical mistakes. Some mistakes were minor, like his inability to restrain his legendary combativeness and anger when the attacks came in Florida. In his attempt to prove himself the ideas candidate, he sometimes expressed wild ideas—promising a moon colony. Several mistakes proved catastrophic, like calling Ryan's Medicare proposal "right-wing social engineering," refusing to spend more time on the campaign trail, and disagreeing with his staff over strategy. Gingrich wanted to wage an experimental campaign relying heavily on the internet and social networking; consequently, he failed to devote enough time to raising money, organizing his staff, and participating in retail, person-to-person politics. A personal vacation and book signings took precedent over campaigning.

Gingrich was outspent nearly four-to-one by Romney, with Romney's Super PAC, Restore Our Future, launching a highly destructive and effective air war. And, Gingrich never effectively created a coherent strategy to deal with the negative ads, especially when the attacks came about his consulting contract with Freddie Mac. Superior finances allowed Romney to establish an organizational presence in delegate-rich and early states several months in advance, while Gingrich, outside of Iowa and South Carolina, often launched his organization mere weeks in advance. A more effective organization could have allowed Gingrich to more effectively target voters and canvass precincts to counter the negative media assaults. At the very least, candidates cannot win a nomination without organizations in place beyond Iowa and New Hampshire. Gingrich relied too heavily on his Tea Party supporters, failing to realize how disconnected or extremely local these networks were. They could not be effectively counted upon to deliver mass number of voters across states, especially in caucus states.

In the end, the audacious architect of the first Republican House of Representatives in 50 years was unable to convert the skills that produced Republican majorities and a lucrative financial-political empire into a successful presidential nomination. Gingrich won only two states,

South Carolina and Georgia. He was relegated to merely being an individual, alongside Perry, Cain, and Santorum, who rose briefly to challenge Romney only to be cast aside by Romney's well-financed and traditionally-run organization. Romney had consistent messaging (fix the economy), superior fundraising, and effective negative advertising. Gingrich could not match him in any of those categories.

NOTES

1. "Gingrich, Newton Leroy," Directory of the United States Congress, http://bioguide.congress.gov/scripts/biodisplay.pl?index=G000225.
2. "Newt Gingrich," *Washington Post*, http://www.washingtonpost.com/politics/newt-gingrich/gIQAnmSt9O_topic.html.
3. Margaret Newkirk, "Gingrich Makes Last Stand in Must-Win Georgia as Hopes Sputter," *Bloomberg* 2012, http://www.bloomberg.com/news/2012-03-01/gingrich-has-last-stand-in-must-win-georgia-as-presidential-hopes-sputter.html.
4. Guy Gugliotta and Juliet Eilperin, "Gingrich Steps Down in Face of Rebellion, "*Washington Post* 1998, http://www.washingtonpost.com/wp-srv/politics/govt/leadership/stories/gingrich110798.htm.
5. Gugliotta and Eilperin, "Gingrich Steps Down."
6. "The house that Newt built," *Washington Post* 2012, http://www.washingtonpost.com/politics/the-house-that-newt-built/2011/11/26/gIQAqxpazN_graphic.html.
7. "Gingrich rules out run for president," *CNN* 2007, http://articles.cnn.com/2007-09-29/politics/gingrich_1_gingrich-supporters-first-republican-speaker-house-speaker-newt-gingrich?_s=PM:POLITICS.
8. Sarah Wheaton, "Gingrich Won't Run in 2008," *New York Times* 2007, http://thecaucus.blogs.nytimes.com/2007/09/29/gingrich-wont-run-in-2008.
9. Quaid, "Gingrich decides against 2008 run for the White House, spokesman says," *Seattle Times* 2007, http://seattletimes.nwsource.com/html/nationworld/2003912714_webgingrich29.html.
10. "Gingrich Admits to Affair During Clinton Impeachment," *ABC News* 2007, http://abcnews.go.com/Politics/story?id=2937633&page=2#.T5w1NlLNn5w.
11. "Newt Gingrich Inc.: How the GOP hopeful went from political flameout to fortune," *Washington Post* 2011, http://www.washingtonpost.com/politics/newt-gingrich-and-how-he-got-rich/2011/11/21/gIQAftOglN_story_4.html.
12. Dan Eggen, "Newt Gingrich's financial empire shows his fundraising prowess," *Washington Post* 2011, http://www.washingtonpost.com/wp-dyn/content/article/2011/02/15/AR2011021506344_2.html?sid=ST2011030304317.
13. Kenneth P. Vogel, "Newt Gingrich haul far outpaces other 2012 hopefuls," *Politico* 2011, http://www.politico.com/news/stories/0211/48864.html.
14. Alexander Burns, "2012 kickoff could come as early as February," *Politico* 2011, http://www.politico.com/news/stories/0111/48410.html.
15. Alexander Burns, "Newt Gingrich's rough week," *Politico* 2011, http://www.politico.com/news/stories/0311/50648.html.
16. Doug Mataconis, "Newt Gingrich Announces He's Running For President," *Outside the Beltway* 2011, http://www.outsidethebeltway.com/newt-gingrich-announces-hes-running-for-president/.
17. Molly Ball, "N.H. insider Dave Carney will support Gingrich," *Politico* 2011, http://www.politico.com/news/stories/0511/54484.html#ixzz1tRj3Gb5W; Jason Embry, "Top Perry aide takes senior job with Gingrich," *Austin Statesman* 2011, http://www.statesman.com/blogs/content/shared-gen/blogs/austin/politics/entries/2011/03/23/top_perry_aide_takes_senior_jo.html; Jeff Zelleny and Trip Gabriel, "Gingrich's

Senior Campaign Staff Resigns," *New York Times* 2011, http://thecaucus.blogs.nytimes.com/2011/06/09/gingrich-senior-campaign-staff-resigns/.

18. Alex Brandon, "Gingrich primes White House announcement, opens HQ," *MSNBC* 2012, http://www.msnbc.msn.com/id/42912877/ns/politics-decision_2012/#.T51r8FLNn5w.

19. Jonathan Martin, "Newt Gingrich's route: Leave no state behind," *Politico* 2011, http://www.politico.com/news/stories/0511/54709.html.

20. Kendra Marr, "Newt Gingrich's rough roll-out," *Politico 2011,* http://www.politico.com/news/stories/0511/55082.html#ixzz1tRt3trZ9.

21. Alex Castellanos, "Newt Gingrich is the devil in a red dress," *Daily Caller* 2011, http://dailycaller.com/2011/05/17/newt-gingrich-femme-fatale/.

22. Jason Clayworth, "Iowan to Gingrich: Get out now before you make a bigger fool of yourself," *Des Moines Register* 2011, http://blogs.desmoinesregister.com/dmr/index.php/2011/05/16/iowan-to-gingrich-get-out-now-before-you-make-a-bigger-fool-of-yourself/.

23. Brian Bakst, "Gingrich Doused with Glitter, Told to 'Stop the Hate'," *Associated Press* 2011, http://www.edgeboston.com/news/national///119738/gingrich_doused_with_glitter,_told_to_ percentE2 percent80 percent99stop_the_hate percentE2 percent80 percent99.

24. Sheryl Gay Stolberg, "All That Glitters May Redefine Run by Gingrich," *New York Times* 2011, http://www.nytimes.com/2011/05/25/us/politics/25gingrich.html.

25. Jon Ward, "GOP Donors Deserting Newt Gingrich," *Huffington Post* 2011, http://www.huffingtonpost.com/2011/05/18/gop-donors-deserting-newt-gingrich_n_863910.html.

26. Jonathan Martin and Maggie Haberman, "Newt Gingrich advisers resign en masse," *Huffington Post* 2011, http://www.politico.com/news/stories/0611/56631.html.

27. Chris Cillizza and Karen Tumulty, "Gingrich presidential campaign implodes," *Washington Post* 2011, http://www.washingtonpost.com/blogs/the-fix/post/gingrich-senior-aides-resign/2011/06/09/AGN77VNH_blog.html.

28. "2012 Republican Presidential Nomination," *Real Clear Politics*, http://www.realclearpolitics.com/epolls/2012/president/us/republican_presidential_nomination-1452.html#polls.

29. James Oliphant and Tom Hamburger, "Gingrich to report weak second-quarter fundraising haul," *Los Angeles Times* 2011, http://articles.latimes.com/2011/jul/06/news/la-pn-gingrich-fundraising-20110706.

30. Alexis Levinson, "Pawlenty campaigns raises $4.2 million in second quarter," *Daily Caller* 2011, http://dailycaller.com/2011/07/01/pawlenty-campaigns-raises-4-2-million-in-second-quarter/.

31. Kevin Hall, "Gingrich's Wild Roller Coaster Ride Finally Ending, Set to Endorse Romney," *Iowa Republican* 2012, http://theiowarepublican.com/2012/gingrich percentE2 percent80 percent99s-wild-roller-coaster-ride-finally-ending-set-to-endorse-romney/.

32. Kevin Robillard, "Newt Gingrich's 5 best debate zingers," *Politico* 2012, http://www.politico.com/news/stories/0112/71592.html.

33. Tommy Christopher, "Newt Gingrich Brawls With Fox News' Chris Wallace Over Debate 'Gotcha' Question," *Media-ite* 2011,http://www.mediaite.com/tv/newt-gingrich-brawls-with-fox-news-chris-wallace-over-debate-gotcha-question/.

34. Will Cain, "Winners and Losers of SC Debate: Best 22 Minutes of Newt's Campaign. Bachmann Fumbles on Federalism," *The Blaze* 2011, http://www.theblaze.com/blog/2011/09/06/winners-and-losers-of-sc-debate-best-22-minutes-of-newts-campaign-bachmann-fumbles-on-federalism/.

35. Frank James, "Perry, Romney Rivalry Still Defines GOP Race After Debate," *NPR* 2011, http://www.npr.org/blogs/itsallpolitics/2011/09/08/140276754/perry-romney-still-owned-race-after-reagan-library-debate.

36. Katie Pavlich, "CNN/Tea Party Express Debate: Winners and Losers," *Town Hall* 2011, http://townhall.com/tipsheet/katiepavlich/2011/09/12/cnntea_party_express_debate_winners_and_losers

37. Peter Grier, "Is New Gingrich the GOP's Next Flavor of the Month?," *Christian Science Monitor* 2011, http://www.csmonitor.com/U.S.A/Politics/The-Vote/2011/1019/Is-Newt-Gingrich-the-GOP-s-next-flavor-of-the-month.

38. Brian Montopoli, Corbett B. Daly, and Lucy Madison, "GOP debate in Vegas: Winners and losers," *CBS News* 2011, http://www.cbsnews.com/8301-503544_162-20122333-503544.html?tag=cbsContent;carouselBar.

39. Jonathan Oosting, "Who stood out at GOP debate? Oakland University faculty, students weigh in," *MLive* 2011, http://www.mlive.com/news/detroit/index.ssf/2011/11/who_stood_out_at_the_gop_debat.html.

40. Kevin Hal, "'Commander-in-Chief' Debate Recap, Winners and Losers," *Iowa Republican* 2011, http://theiowarepublican.com/2011/ percentE2 percent80 percent9Ccommander-in-chief percentE2 percent80 percent9D-debate-recap-winners-and-losers/.

41. Phoebe Greenwood, "Newt Gingrich condemned for calling Palestinians 'terrorists'," *The Guardian* 2011, http://www.guardian.co.uk/world/2011/dec/11/newt-gingrich-palestinian-comments-criticised.

42. Chris Cillizza, "Iowa Republican debate: Winners and losers," *Washington Post* 2011, http://www.washingtonpost.com/blogs/the-fix/post/iowa-republican-debate-winners-and-losers/2011/12/10/gIQA5E2wlO_blog.html.

43. Shawn Millerickm "Poll: Romney, Gingrich in Statistical Dead Heat," *New Hampshire Journal* 2011, http://nhjournal.com/2011/11/18/poll-romney-gingrich-in-statistical-dead-heat-in-n-h/.

44. Nicholas Confessore, "In Last Quarter of 2011, Gingrich Rakes In Nearly $10 Million," *New York Times* 2012, http://thecaucus.blogs.nytimes.com/2012/01/31/in-last-quarter-of-2011-gingrich-rakes-in-nearly-10-million/.

45. Trip Gabriel, "Gingrich Staffers Who Quit in June Return to Campaign," *New York Times* 2011, http://thecaucus.blogs.nytimes.com/2011/11/17/gingrich-staffers-who-quit-in-june-return-to-campaign/.

46. Katharine Q. Seelye, "Gingrich Hires a Political Director and Announces an Endorsement," *New York Times* 2011, http://thecaucus.blogs.nytimes.com/2011/12/19/gingrich-hires-a-political-director-and-announces-an-endorsement/.

47. Jonathan Martin, "Gingrich hires veteran operative," *Politico* 2011, http://www.politico.com/blogs/burns-haberman/2011/12/gingrich-hires-veteran-operative-107941.html.

48. Chris Cillizza, "Michele Bachmann Wins the Ames Straw Poll," *Washington Post* 2011, http://www.washingtonpost.com/blogs/the-fix/post/michele-bachmann-wins-the-ames-straw-poll/2011/08/13/gIQApgnoDJ_blog.html.

49. James E. Wilkerson and Craig Johnsn, "Candidate Visits to Iowa," *Des Moines Registrar* 2011, http://caucuses.desmoinesregister.com/data/iowa-caucus/candidate-tracker/.

50. Tracy Jan, "Tea Party members get behind Gingrich," *Boston Globe* 2011, http://articles.boston.com/2011-12-08/news/30491205_1_newt-gingrich-house-tea-party-caucus-tea-partiers.

51. John Dickerson, "Why Gingrich is surging in Iowa," *CBS News* 2011, http://www.cbsnews.com/8301-503544_162-57337487-503544/why-gingrich-is-surging-in-iowa/.

52. Jennifer Jacobs, "Two Iowa conservative leaders pick Rick Santorum, ask other candidates to merge," *Des Moines Register* 2011, http://caucuses.desmoinesregister.com/2011/12/20/rick-santorum-gets-endorsement-from-bob-vander-plaats-and-chuck-hurley/.

53. "Newt Gingrich Courts Iowa Conservatives as Critics Label Him a 'Pro-Life Fraud'," *ABC News* 2011, http://abcnews.go.com/blogs/politics/2011/12/newt-gingrich-courts-iowa-conservatives-as-critics-label-him-a-pro-life-fraud/.

54. Kevin Liptak, "Nearly half of Iowa ads attack Gingrich," *CNN* 2011, http://politicalticker.blogs.cnn.com/2011/12/30/nearly-half-of-iowa-ads-attack-gingrich/.

55. Sarah Maslin Nir, "National Review Makes Its Case Against Gingrich," *New Yotk Times* 2011, http://thecaucus.blogs.nytimes.com/2011/12/14/the-national-review-makes-its-case-against-gingrich/.

56. Kevin Hall, "Sioux City Presidential Debate Recap, Winners and Losers," *Iowa Republican* 2011, http://theiowarepublican.com/2011/sioux-city-presidential-debate-recap-winners-and-losers/.

57. Jonathan Martin, "How Newt Gingrich Blew It: An Iowa Roadmap," *Politico* 2012, http://www.politico.com/news/stories/0112/71014.html.

58. Jason Clayworth, "Gingrich comes out swinging in New Hampshire," *Des Moines Register* 2012, http://caucuses.desmoinesregister.com/2012/01/04/gingrich-comes-out-swinging-in-new-hampshire/.

59. Michael Levenson, "Gingrich hastens to build a network," *Boston Globe* 2011, http://articles.boston.com/2011-12-12/news/30507920_1_newt-gingrich-campaign-mitt-romney-new-hampshire/2.

60. Trip Gabriel, "Gingrich Takes On Romney," *New York Times* 2012, http://thecaucus.blogs.nytimes.com/2012/01/05/gingrich-takes-on-romney/.

61. Stephen Shepard, "Gingrich Leads in Three of Four New Early-State Polls," *National Journal* 2011, http://www.nationaljournal.com/2012-presidential-campaign/gingrich-leads-in-three-of-four-new-early-state-polls-20111207.

62. Jamie Weinstein, "Gingrich blasts 'anti-Christian bigotry', Perry promises to end 'war on religion'," *Daily Caller* 2012, http://dailycaller.com/2012/01/07/gingrich-blasts-anti-christian-bigotry-perry-promises-to-end-war-on-religion/.

63. Lucy Madison, "Gingrich to Romney: Drop the 'pious baloney'," *CBS News* 2012, http://www.cbsnews.com/8301-503544_162-57354657-503544/gingrich-to-romney-drop-the-pious-baloney/.

64. . "Newt Gingrich wins South Carolina primary ," *Washington Post* 2012, http://www.washingtonpost.com/politics/newt-gingrich-wins-south-carolina-primary/2012/01/21/gIQAKTxBHQ_story_1.html.

65. Trip Gabriel and Nicolas Confessore, "PAC Ads to Attack Romney as Predatory Capitalist," *New York Times* 2012, http://www.nytimes.com/2012/01/09/us/politics/pro-gingrich-pac-plans-tv-ads-against-romney.html?pagewanted=all.

66. http://www.foxnews.com/us/2012/01/22/extraordinary-gingrich-comeback-also-vindication/

67. "Gingrich Campaign Adds Staff in South Carolina," *FitsNews* 2011, http://www.fitsnews.com/2011/11/07/gingrich-campaign-adds-staff-in-sc/.

68. Molly Ball, "Newt's Secret Campaign: How Gingrich Really Won S.C.," *The Atlantic*, http://www.theatlantic.com/politics/archive/2012/01/newts-secret-campaign-how-gingrich-really-won-sc/251783/.

69. Trip Gabriel, "Gingrich Feels Heat From Romney, and Welcomes It," *New York Times* 2012, http://thecaucus.blogs.nytimes.com/2012/01/18/gingrich-feels-heat-from-romney-and-welcomes-it/.

70. "Extraordinary Gingrich comeback also vindication," *Fox News* 2012, http://www.foxnews.com/us/2012/01/22/extraordinary-gingrich-comeback-also-vindication/.

71. Mark Memmott, "Rick Perry Quits GOP Presidential Race, Endorses Gingrich," *NPR* 2012, http://www.npr.org/blogs/thetwo-way/2012/01/19/145446676/reports-rick-perry-to-drop-out-of-gop-presidential-race.

72. Tony Lee, "How Newt Gingrich won South Carolina," *Humane Events* 2012, http://www.humanevents.com/article.php?id=48980.

73. Samuel J. Best, "How Newt Gingrich won the South Carolina primary," *CBS News* 2012, http://www.cbsnews.com/8301-503544_162-57363403-503544/how-newt-gingrich-won-the-south-carolina-primary/.

74. "How Newt Gingrich won the South Carolina primary," *Orlando Sentinel* 2012, http://www.orlandosentinel.com/news/politics/os-pictures-newt-gingrich-opens-orlando-campaign-office,0,6817041.photogallery.

75. Michael Falcone, "How Newt Gingrich won the South Carolina primary," *ABC News* 2012, http://abcnews.go.com/blogs/politics/2012/01/inside-mitt-romneys-florida-war-room-aides-see-six-months-of-preparation-paying-off/.

76. "Gingrich hires former Rubio campaign chief Jose Mallea," *Miami Herald* 2012, http://www.freerepublic.com/focus/f-news/2819301/posts.

77. Huma Khan, "Newt Gingrich's 'Beating the Pavement' Appeals to Florida Tea Partiers," *ABC News* 2012, http://abcnews.go.com/blogs/politics/2012/01/newt-gingrichs-beating-the-pavement-appeals-to-florida-tea-partiers/.

78. Amy Gardner and Rosalind S. Helderman, "Newt Gingrich using energy, power of tea party movement," *Washington Post* 2012, http://www.washingtonpost.com/politics/newt-gingrich-using-energy-power-of-tea-party-movement/2012/01/24/gIQAs7WnOQ_story.html.

79. Alex Altman, "Outstumped and Outspent, Newt Gingrich Flounders in Florida," *Time* 2012, http://swampland.time.com/2012/01/30/out-stumped-and-out-spent-newt-gingrich-flounders-in-florida/.

80. Michael D. Shear, "Romney Adds a Top Debate Coach," *New York Times* 2012, http://thecaucus.blogs.nytimes.com/2012/01/23/romney-adds-a-top-debate-coach/.

81. Chris Cillizza, "Florida Republican debate: Winners and losers," *Washington Post* 2012, http://www.washingtonpost.com/blogs/the-fix/post/florida-republican-debate-winners-and-losers/2012/01/24/gIQAAHrONQ_blog.html.

82. Doug Mataconis, "Romney Fights, Gingrich Falters In Final Florida Debate," *Outside the Beltway* 2012, http://www.outsidethebeltway.com/romney-fights-gingrich-falters-in-final-florida-debate/.

83. Thomas Beaumont, "Gingrich bemoans Romney's Florida 'carpet-bombing'," *Associated Press* 2012, http://news.yahoo.com/gingrich-bemoans-romneys-florida-carpet-bombing-160236545.html.

84. "Romney, Paul Hold the Cards in Nevada," *Wall Street Journal* 2012, http://online.wsj.com/article/SB10001424052970203920204577195304143272164.html.

85. "Gingrich Says He'll Battle On," *Wall Street Journal* 2012, http://online.wsj.com/article/SB10001424052970203937509977204112096354148.html.

86. Alexander Burns, "Newt Gingrich missing candidate from Missouri primary ballot," *Politico* 2012, http://www.politico.com/news/stories/1211/69861.html.

87. Sara Burnett, "Romney, Gingrich, Santorum to campaign in Colorado today in advance of GOP caucus," *Denver Post* 2012, http://www.denverpost.com/breakingnews/ci_19903640

88. "Republican presidential hopefuls Gingrich, Santorum and Paul visit Minnesota," *Pioneer Press* 2012, http://www.twincities.com/ci_19907297.

89. Jeff Rhodes, "Gingrich tells Washington voters Obama likes high gas prices," *The Olympia Report* 2012, http://theolympiareport.com/gingrich-tells-washington-state-obama-wants-higher-gas-prices/.

90. Holly Bailey, "Mitt Romney outdoes rivals in February fundraising, as Gingrich faces major debts," *Yahoo* 2012, http://news.yahoo.com/blogs/ticket/mitt-romney-outdoes-rivals-february-fundraising-gingrich-faces-151203820.html.

91. Ginger Gibson, "Newt Gingrich back on his game," *Politico* 2012, http://www.politico.com/news/stories/0212/73188.html.

92. Shawna Shepherd, "Gingrich pins hopes on hashtags," *CNN* 2012, http://articles.cnn.com/2012-03-10/politics/politics_gingrich-social-media_1_newt-gingrich-social-media-hash-tag?_s=PM:POLITICS.

93. William Douglas and David Lightman, "Gingrich pursues Southern strategy to break back into 2-man race," *McClatchy* 2012, http://www.mcclatchydc.com/2012/03/01/140557/gingrich-pursues-southern-strategy.html.

94. "Super Tuesday: Newt Gingrich makes Tennessee primary pitch," *Politico* 2012, http://www.politico.com/news/stories/0312/73647_Page2.html.

95. Ginger Gibson, "Newt Gingrich may come up empty in Louisiana," *Politico* 2012, http://www.politico.com/news/stories/0312/74412.html.

96. Mike Allen and Ginger Gibson, "Newt Gingrich cuts staff, aims for Tampa," *Politico* 2012, http://www.politico.com/news/stories/0312/74569.html.

97. Katharine Q Seelye and Jim Rutenberg, "Santorum Quits Race, Clearing a Path for Romney," *New York Times* 2012, http://www.nytimes.com/2012/04/11/us/politics/rick-santorum-withdraws-from-republican-race.html?pagewanted=all.

98. Anna Sale, "Through Debt And Derision, Gingrich Keeps Running," *NPR* 2012, http://www.npr.org/2012/04/24/151285343/through-debt-and-derision-gingrich-keeps-running.

99. John Helton and Alyssa McClendon, "Gingrich's 2012 campaign leaves him with mixed legacy," *CNN* 2012, http://www.cnn.com/2012/04/25/politics/gingrich-campaign-obit/index.html.

NINE

Ron Paul: Establishment Outsider or Radical Insider?

Jeremy D. Walling

Modern campaigns expend untold time, energy, and resources manipulating the fringes of the candidate's image. Whether through targeted polling or paid image consultants, candidates' hairstyles, wardrobes, vernacular, and accents all seem to be subject to the whims of the electorate or the expert wisdom of the paid consultant. The "science" of campaigning tells a candidate to wear the flannel shirt at the rural pancake house and the open-collared Oxford shirt with rolled-up sleeves while touring the auto parts factory. Candidates present tailored iterations of their basic message to different audiences, depending on the presence of senior citizens, blue-collar union workers, or Catholics in the crowd. With stakes often so high, the public images of contemporary candidates are increasingly manipulated and constantly micromanaged. With his receding white hair, crisp, conservative suit, and endless refrains of ending The Fed, Congressman Ron Paul is the exception to countless rules of the campaign game that so many consider sacrosanct. What other 77-year-old former obstetrician stirs up such fervor and commitment among college-aged audiences with references to Austrian economics and devolution?

At a time when only two of 535 members of Congress do not represent the major parties, brand identity is as critical to candidates as it is to Coca-Cola or Disney. However, the candidate who stands at the fringes of the national party can represent the median voter in a House district. In a party with rhetoric commonly peppered with general references to states rights and limited government, Ron Paul would unequivocally defer to the states on most issues and is ever eager to provide specific departments and agencies that should be abolished. Championed as an outsider, Paul is certainly a nonmainstream Republican on many policy issues. Nevertheless, Ron Paul has served as a Republican for two stints in the U.S. House for a total of 11 terms. In two of his three presidential campaigns Paul ran as a Republican, running as a Libertarian Party candidate in only 1988. With a mix of clear libertarian ideology and adherence to the Republican Party label, Ron Paul is an outsider-insider. As a Republican, he claimed a spot on the primary debate stage, forcing issues and generally acting as a pest to the more mainstream candidates. His early successes, including a third place finish in Iowa and a (distant) second place finish in New Hampshire, proved to be anomalies. This chapter seeks to make sense of Ron Paul's 2012 presidential candidacy and analyze its deceptively significant impact on the overall campaign.

CANDIDATE BACKGROUND

Born in Pittsburgh, Pennsylvania, Ron Paul attended Gettysburg College and earned his medical degree from Duke University. Following medical school, Paul was drafted and spent the mid to late 1960s as a flight surgeon in the United States Air Force before settling in Texas and establishing an obstetrics/gynecology practice. Paul's official House website boasts that he has delivered "more than 4000 babies!" Paul concedes that his work as an obstetrician contributed to his views on the abortion issue. Paul states: "It was pretty dramatic for me, to see a two-and-a-half-pound baby taken out crying and breathing and put in a bucket."[1] Although his stance on the issue places Ron Paul at odds with fellow libertarians who would consider a pro-life position to be inconsistent with libertarianism, Paul argues that his views are congruent. Ron Paul's experience led him to consider the liberty of the unborn as the central concern in the abortion debate. Furthermore, despite his clearly pro-life personal views, Ron Paul argues that the abortion policy decision should be made at the state level.

Despite this potential minor divergence from libertarian ideology, Ron Paul arguably exhibits more ideological purity than the other 2012 Republican presidential candidates. It was as a medical resident in the 1960s that Paul began to explore libertarianism and the Austrian school of economics. George Will famously observed that while most members of Congress line their office walls with photos of celebrities and dignitaries, Ron Paul's wall is proudly adorned with photos of Hayek and von Mises.[2] Ron Paul's exposure to Murray Rothbard, Friedrich Hayek, and Ludwig von Mises clearly informed his "sound money" economic principles, influencing his familiar calls for a return to the gold standard. In fact, it was Nixon's policies regarding gold that influenced Paul to become involved in politics. Paul states:

I remember the day very clearly. Nixon closed the gold window, which meant admitting that we could no longer meet our commitments and that there would be no more backing of the dollar. After that day, all money would be political money rather than money of real value. I was astounded.[3]

In 1974, Ron Paul competed for the Republican nomination for Texas' 22nd House seat and was defeated in the primary. The winner of the seat later resigned, allowing Paul to win a special election in 1976. Later that year, Paul headed into the campaign the incumbent, losing the general election by fewer than 300 votes. Paul then regained the seat in 1978, winning reelection in 1980 and again in 1982. Ron Paul declined to seek reelection in 1984, choosing instead to run for the U.S. Senate. Paul lost the Republican primary to Phil Gramm. Ron Paul's vacated House seat was filled by Tom DeLay.

Despite his inconsistent early political performances, Ron Paul's legislative behavior during his first continuous tenure in Congress exhibited the ideological consistency and policy stands that would become his trademark. Paul utilized his position as a member of the House Banking Committee to criticize the Federal Reserve Board and federal government banking policies for contributing to the economic maladies of the time. He alienated constituents by voting against pork projects, including the NASA Manned Spacecraft Center.[4] Paul also famously introduced bills that would reduce congressional pay and would institute term limits in Congress. The lone Republican to vote against the 1981 defense budget was Ron Paul.[5] Ron Paul's early legislative behavior, far more trustee than delegate, demonstrated extreme adherence to principle, often at the expense of popularity both inside the beltway and back home in his district. Following his 1984 Senate primary loss, Ron Paul returned to private life.

In 1987, Paul aligned his partisanship with his ideology and resigned the Republican Party for the Libertarian Party. The next year, Paul sought and won the Libertarian nomination for President of the United States. Covering Paul's 1988 presidential campaign, the *Los Angeles Times* noted: "In his more candid moments, Paul admits that he cannot win."[6] Paul campaigned to the younger generation, focusing heavily on college campuses. During the 1988 campaign he told the *New York Times*: "These kids will vote eventually, and maybe, just maybe they'll go home and talk to their parents."[7] Thus, Paul's strategy combined ideological seed-planting and viral, word-of-mouth components. On the ballot in 46 states, Ron Paul finished a distant third with 423,179 votes, which amounted to around 0.5 percent of the popular vote.

Ron Paul returned to the Republican Party in 1996 to campaign for Texas' 14th U.S. House district. Although Paul's primary opponent, incumbent Republican Greg Laughlin, received the party endorsement,

Paul received help from the somewhat motley crew of retired pitcher Nolan Ryan and presidential candidates Steve Forbes and Pat Buchanan. Paul won the general election with 51.1 percent of the vote. Ron Paul's district popularity and incumbency advantage are evident in his subsequent general election results: 1998, 55.3; 2000: 59.7; 2002, 68.1; 2004, unopposed; 2006, 60.2; 2008, unopposed; and 2010, 76.0. During his third stint in the House, Paul has served on the Committee on Foreign Affairs and the Committee on Financial Services. Perhaps fittingly, Ron Paul is the chairman of the Subcommittee on Domestic Monetary Policy and Technology. During the better part of twelve terms in the U.S. House, Ron Paul has sponsored over 600 bills. In his eleventh term, Paul sponsored a bill that would allow a Galveston, Texas, customhouse to be sold to the Galveston Historical Foundation. The bill passed the House via voice vote and the Senate by unanimous consent. Although Ron Paul's amendments to other bills have shaped legislation, H.R. 2121 is Ron Paul's only sponsored bill to become public law. When asked by George Will whether other House Republicans agree with him, Paul replied: "Every one of them at times. But none of them all the time."[8] Will refers to Paul's legislative approach as "philosophical eccentricity."[9]

In 2008 Ron Paul ran for President of the United States for a second time, this time as a Republican. Despite seeking the nomination from within the party, Paul maintained the outsider strategy of his Libertarian Party campaign in 1988. He was immensely popular with college students and many supporters created their own cardboard signs to show their support. In 2007, Paul organized a grassroots campaign, successfully utilizing social media. With his low national name recognition, he surprised pundits by out-fundraising all Republican candidates in the final quarter of 2007. The *New York Times* famously reported that his supporters consisted of "largely iconoclastic white men."[10] Ron Paul came in fifth in both the Iowa Caucuses and the New Hampshire Primary. He placed second in the Nevada Caucuses, but subsequently came in only as high as fourth or fifth place in virtually every state. Senator John McCain locked up the Republican nomination by March. At a campaign speech in March, Paul acknowledged that "victory in the conventional political sense is not available in the presidential race."[11] When asked by *Newsweek* why he decided to stick around, Paul responded: "How long should I do this?—I would feel badly. I would feel as though I let them down."[12] Despite earning only a mere handful of delegates, Ron Paul refused to concede the nomination until June. Once he did drop out, Ron Paul refused to endorse McCain, stating that McCain "doesn't represent anything I've talked about for 30 years."[13] Instead, Ron Paul expressed vague support for an array of top third-party candidates. Following the campaign, Ron Paul returned to the House and continued advancing his ideological and often quixotic legislative agenda.

ISSUE STANCES

Among candidates in the 2012 Republican presidential field, Ron Paul's ideological consistency is particularly notable. In fact, many of Ron Paul's 2012 positions were firmly established in his farewell address to the House as he prepared to leave Congress the first time. In an address to the House on September 19, 1984, Paul outlined "the problems our nation faces and the actions needed to correct them."[14] Remarkably, the issues Paul champions nearly 30 years later are virtually identical to the items detailed in the speech. Of himself, Paul states: "Some have said my approach is not practical, but most concede 'At least he's consistent'."[15] Much of Paul's lengthy speech dealt with problems observed in Congress itself, noting frequent partisan pettiness and "grandstanding." The balance of the speech consisted of Paul's observations of domestic and global politics of the time, characterizing government policy decisions as "contradictions."

The Economy

Minimal government is a core libertarian issue and Ron Paul reports in the 1984 speech that he voted against 99 percent of spending, which he equates with "voting with the taxpayer 99 percent of the time."[16] He subsequently concedes that although he would likely endorse as much as 20 percent of spending programs, his negative voting behavior is intended to counteract the supportive votes of other members. Paul's speech, given in the midst of President Reagan's first term, argues that deficits reveal "power gravitating in the hands of a centralized authority" and a resulting loss of individual liberty.[17] Paul also decries the existence of corporate welfare, the term itself of more contemporary vintage, stating that businesses "demand the rigors of the free market for their competitors and socialism/fascism for themselves."[18] Government intervention in the economy, which Paul describes "as a philosophy in itself and not a compromise with anything," leads to contradictions such as support for both free trade and protectionist policies, promises of tax cuts canceled out by spending hikes, and agriculture policies that create surpluses only to be followed with government purchase of the surplus.

Limited government is the common denominator of much of Ron Paul's issue positions, although calls for minimal or nonexistent government often emerge. Paul has advocated abolition of the Federal Emergency Management Agency, citing mismanagement, waste, and flawed underlying assumptions as the major reasons. In a post on his House website, Paul says: "The establishment of FEMA is symptomatic of a blind belief in big government's ability to do anything and everything for anyone and everyone." Naturally, Paul's position is unpopular with victims of natural and unnatural disasters. However, it should be noted that

Paul's own House district is situated within a possible hurricane zone. In advance of his 2012 presidential campaign, Ron Paul released his "Plan to Restore America." To cut $1 trillion, Paul would, among other reductions and absolute cuts, completely eliminate the Departments of Energy, Housing and Urban Development, Commerce, Interior, and Education, all of which he considers beyond the scope of national government authority and a threat to individual liberty and property rights. In keeping with that perspective, Paul's plan would also cut the Transportation Safety Administration. Finally, the 2009 book *End the Fed* outlines Paul's perceptions of the ill effects of the Federal Reserve Board's policy decisions and regulations, namely monetary inflation. Once again, Paul's objection is tempered with an acknowledgement of reality. In the case of the Federal Reserve, it is the fact that it is congruent with the adoption of fiat currency.

National Security and Foreign Policy

To Paul, the failures of government intervention in the economy were rivaled only by intervention into international affairs. Paul's assessment is that American foreign policy had "given us nearly a century of war."[19] His contemporary stance on the Middle East is reflected in the 1984 address, when he states: "Loyally standing by our ally Israel is in conflict with satisfying the Arab interests that are always represented by big business in each administration."[20] This leads to a "guarantee that the American taxpayer will be funding both sides of any armed conflict."[21] According to Ron Paul, the major consequence of American intervention into global affairs is the detrimental effect on the U.S. military. He argues that "we continuously sacrifice ourselves to the world by assuming the role of world policeman, which precipitates international crises on a regular basis, all while neglecting our own defenses."[22] By the early years of the Reagan administration, Ron Paul had firmly established his view that the United States should look after itself and spend less time meddling in the affairs of other states. In 2007, fully in the midst of post-September 11 policy decisions, Paul told the *Washington Post*: "Here we are, so intimidated and so insecure and we're acting like such bullies that we have to attack third-world nations that have no military and have no weapon."[23] Paul's policy of noninterventionism leads him to advocate withdrawal from Afghanistan and Iraq and to support Israel by leaving it alone.

The Proper Role of Government

Contemporary supporters of Ron Paul would hardly be surprised to find that his stances on social issues are revealed in the 1984 address. Paul's positions on forced busing, eminent domain, drug policy, and gun control are virtually identical to his 2012 positions. In the 1984 address,

Paul states: "Careless disregard for liberty allows the government to violate the basic premise of a free society; there shall be no initiation by force by anyone, particularly government."[24] Ron Paul opposed both the initial adoption and the reauthorization of the PATRIOT ACT, federally derived identification standards through the REAL ID Act, and domestic surveillance by the National Security Administration. According to Paul, public education and the definition of marriage should be the domain of states, arguing that the Constitution provides no role for the national government. A physician by trade, Paul opposes the notion that citizens have a "right to health care," voting against the Medicare prescription drug plan in 2003, the State Children's Health Insurance Program (SCHIP), and insurance plans that require coverage for people with preexisting conditions.

Fundamentally, his view of the role of government and its relationship to the individual is the cornerstone of his ideology and informs all of his political stances. Such radical consistency is rare in American politics, and to many, it is an admirable trait. However, it is the nuances of his positions that invite intraparty opposition and underscore that, in fact, Ron Paul is a libertarian wearing a Republican uniform. While many in his party supported war in Iraq, Paul's opposition to the initiation of force leads to his position as Republican Party pariah. While pro-choice advocates define the important individual in the abortion issue as the pregnant woman, Paul argues that it is the unborn individual who deserves protection. The former position alienates Paul from many Republicans who see Iraq as an unfortunate but justifiable military action. The latter stance alienates Paul from pro-choice Democrats and many Libertarians who define the role of the individual differently.

THE CAMPAIGN

The 2010 edition of the annual Conservative Political Action Conference (CPAC) Straw Poll produced a somewhat surprising result. Ron Paul was victorious with 31 percent of the vote, nearly 10 points ahead of second place finisher Mitt Romney. CNN reported that Paul's win "drew a volley of loud boos from the CPAC audience."[25] It was notable that 54 percent of the 2010 CPAC attendees were in the 18-to-25-year-old age group. Paul repeated the performance in 2011, gaining 30 percent of the vote. CPAC chairman David Keene observed: "I'm not a Ron Paul supporter, but he energized kids."[26] Unsurprisingly, Paul followed his CPAC performance with a commanding victory in the Tea Party Patriots poll, beating Herman Cain and Sarah Palin. With vocal support among Republican conservatives and Tea Party movement, Ron Paul formally declared his third candidacy for President of the United States in May of 2011, his second as a Republican. Two months later, Paul announced that he would not campaign for his House seat in order to focus on his presidential campaign. Paul's campaign strategy consisted of a focus on performing well in caucus states, a continuation of his role as the archetypal ideological candidate, and an effort to cultivate his support among younger citizens by emphasizing the intergenerational damage done by government.

Early Success: Debates and Straw Polls

Ron Paul's performance at the June 13, 2011, Republican debate at New Hampshire's St. Anselm College set the tone for his campaign. Paul introduced himself to the audience by informing them that he delivered 4,000 babies, but that he would "like to be known and defend the title that I am the champion of liberty and I defend the Constitution."[27] Paul used his limited speaking time to express his unwavering support for a free market economy, criticize the Fed and the U.S. monetary system, and to continue to decry rampant domestic and military spending.[28] Subsequently, Paul won the Southern Republican Leadership Conference Straw Poll by 19 points and the Clay County Iowa Straw Poll by 13 points. In August, Michele Bachmann defeated Paul in the celebrated Ames Straw Poll by a mere 152 votes. Paul faced another narrow loss to Herman Cain in Cain's home state Republican Party straw poll, but demolished all challengers in the New Hampshire Young Republican's Straw Poll. Paul gained 45 percent of the vote, 35 points over second place Mitt Romney. These early victories reflect two facets of Paul's campaign strategy. First, Ron Paul was clearly viewed by straw poll participants as the ideological candidate. While other candidates may occasionally exhibit vague or slippery points of view, Paul's consistency was appealing to early participants in the "invisible primary" stage of the 2012 Republican nomination process. Furthermore, Paul's early victories are indicative of his support among young voters.

In September of 2011, Ron Paul participated in two debates to mixed acclaim. At a September 5 debate in South Carolina, Paul responded to Senator Jim DeMint's question about which programs he would advocate cutting by saying that it would be easier and shorter to provide a list of programs that should be kept.[29] In his speaking time, Paul once again criticized the Fed, referring to them as "counterfeiters" at one point, and Keynesian economics.[30] Paul's remarks, all of which revolving around limited government and the Constitution, were greeted by the audience with appropriate laughter and applause. Ron Paul's performance at the September 12, 2011, Tea Party Debate was hardly as favorably received. Paul received the expected applause at comments regarding Social Security reform, as well as his claim that the Departments of Education and Energy be cut.[31] Rick Santorum asked Paul a pointed question about a statement on Paul's website regarding the motivations behind the September 11 attacks. As Paul essentially confirmed the statement on the website, which essentially suggested that U.S. presence in the Middle East and our relations with the Palestinians contributed to the motive for the attacks, the audience audibly booed. Paul attempted to clarify, stating that the United States had been bombing Iraq for 10 years. He closed with the defensive: "Would you be annoyed? If you're not annoyed, then there's some problem."[32] At another point in the debate, moderator Wolf Blitzer engaged Paul in a discussion of mandatory health insurance. Blitzer asked whether someone who voluntarily refuses to buy insurance should be "left to die."[33] Yahoo News reported that the question alone prompted "several loud cheers of 'yeah!'" from the audience.[34] Paul immediately responded that in his years practicing medicine in a Catholic hospital, no one who needed care was turned way, a statement that drew broad support from the audience. In an attempt at damage control over the audience reaction at the Tea Party Debate, Paul claimed that "The Media took it and twisted it . . . I think they were cheering self-reliance."[35] Despite mixed results in debate performances in August, Ron Paul continued to win straw polls. Paul posted enormous victories in the California, Ohio, and North Carolina straw polls. Although he finished fifth in a Florida straw poll, Paul received 82 percent of the vote in the National Federation of Republican Assemblies Straw Poll in Iowa.

Campaign Finance

Frank Davies of Mercury News reported in 2008: "Ron Paul, the libertarian contrarian of the GOP, did not use the Internet to find his fervent band of followers and donors. They found him—and set records in the process."[36] Davies attributes the origin of the now common term "moneybomb," a one-day grassroots fundraising event, to Ron Paul supporters.[37] The initial moneybomb event, November 5, 2007, raised $4.3 million from more than 35,000 supporters. Just a few weeks later, on December 16, Paul's campaign bested this initial result by raising an astonishing $6.1 million in one day. The moneybomb strategy was so successfully utilized in the 2008 presidential election, Paul supporters revived it for the 2012 campaign. Like 2007-2008, the moneybomb events were often tied to a historical event, such as the anniversary of the Boston Tea Party or Constitution Day. The June 5, 2011, moneybomb event was titled "Revolution v. Romneycare" and was scheduled to commemorate the date the gold standard was abandoned in 1933. The event was tremendously successful, raising $1.1 million. Other events referenced Paul himself, such as moneybomb on his birthday, or characteristics of the campaign. Following a claim by Paul that he did not speak at all during a 40 minute span in a CNN-sponsored, Anderson Cooper-moderated debate, supporters organized the "Black This Out" moneybomb to combat the alleged media blackout of Paul's campaign. Cooper later defensively argued that 19 minutes, 16 seconds was the longest stretch without a statement by Paul.[38] Nevertheless, Paul's supporters perceived a coordinated media blackout and responded generously, generating $2.75 million in a couple of days.

The Paul campaign once again benefitted greatly from the moneybomb strategy, raising an astounding amount of money in small donations via the Internet. However, Ron Paul faced a formidable challenger in Mitt Romney, a candidate who was successful at raising money from more traditional sources. By the second quarter of 2011, Paul's $4.5 million was a distant second to Mitt Romney's $18.25 million. Despite the massive success of the Paul moneybomb events, Romney was reported to have raised $10.25 million in a May 16, 2011, phone bank fundraising event.[39] To be sure, Paul's supporters were passionate, but the very reason many of them were so attracted to Paul, repelled many others. Despite offering clear, stable, ideological positions, Paul's ability to win was always in question. In contrast, Romney seemed destined to win, if not the presidency, the GOP nomination. The massive disparity in fundraising certainly reflects Paul's intense popularity among a smaller segment of citizens. In the end, Ron Paul raised over $41 million in the campaign cycle, good for a distant second to Mitt Romney.

Media Blackout?

As the title of the Paul moneybomb "Black This Out" indicates, supporters perceived that the media was at best diminishing Ron Paul's role in the nomination process. To some it was a coordinated effort to marginalize his candidacy and jeopardize his potential success by refusing to cover him. In the wake of Paul's narrow loss to Michele Bachmann in the Ames Straw Poll, on an August 14, 2011, episode of CNN's Reliable Sources, z*Politico*'s Roger Simon accused the media of ignoring Ron Paul, stating: "The media doesn't believe Ron Paul has a hoot in hell's chance of winning the Iowa Caucuses, winning the Republican nomination, or winning the presidency." Subsequently, Simon took his case to *Politico*, arguing that Paul was getting "shafted" and referred to the candidate as "media poison."[40] Jon Stewart echoed similar ponderings on *The Daily Show*.[41] Salon's Steve Kornacki agreed that Paul received little to no coverage, but stated: "Paul didn't actually do anything to change the prevailing perception of his campaign and its appeal."[42] In other words, Kornacki merely restated Simon's original point. The media did not believe Paul could win and that his success at straw polls was yet another indication of the activity of his small following fervent true believers.

Paul Mulshine of *The Star Ledger* trumpeted *New York Times*' Public Editor Arthur Brisbane's public admission of an editorial decision to minimize coverage of both Paul and Rick Santorum, citing lack of a "coherent narrative."[43] Mulshine's assessment of the *Times*' decision was more accusatory, stating: "If (a) candidate also proposes ending a whole passel of programs deemed untouchable by the *Times*, well that's all the more reason not to let readers hear about the guy."[44] Mulshine's column confirmed the impression held by many Paul supporters. Paul was not being suppressed by the media simply because he lacked "narrative" or was unlikely to win, but because his ideas threatened the ideals championed by the media. Whether the reason was insignificance or ideological opposition, Pew Research Center empirically demonstrated that Paul received less coverage in 2011. From January through August of 2011, Paul was the "dominant newsmaker" in only 27 campaign stories despite strong debate performances and straw poll victories.[45] Romney, Bachmann, and Newt Gingrich were the dominant newsmakers in over 100 stories each, while incumbent president Barack Obama was dominant in 221 stories.[46] The Pew study's title was "Are The Media Ignoring Ron Paul?" Whatever the justification, the results of the study suggest the answer is affirmative.

Election Results

January 3, 2012, marked the official beginning of the nomination process with the Iowa caucuses. Santorum won by 3/100ths of a percentage point over Romney, with Paul coming in third. However, the nonbinding character of the caucus meant the results did not determine pledged delegates. As a result, Paul walked away from the Iowa caucuses with 22 of 28 delegates. This result was reflective of Paul's strategy of performing well in caucus states. In the aftermath of the Iowa caucuses, ABC News hosted a particularly contentious Republican debate in which Paul referred to Santorum as "a big-government conservative" and Santorum replied "You vote against everything. I don't vote against everything."[47] Notably, Paul narrowed his attack to Santorum, leaving Romney to the other candidates. The outcome of the New Hampshire primary suggested why Paul's campaign adopted such a strategy. Romney won the primary handily, capturing 7 delegates to Paul's 3. Prior to the New Hampshire primary, Paul was asked about his approach to campaigning in Florida. He replied: "We don't have a big campaign planned there but they'll know we're there and we have the caucus states that we'll be paying more attention to."[48] The Paul campaign's premonition in the futility of expending scarce resources in Florida proved wise, as Ron Paul received no delegates in either the Florida or South Carolina primaries.

The results of the February nominating events challenged Paul's caucus strategy. Paul finished second in the Minnesota caucuses and fourth in both the Nevada and Colorado caucuses, resulting in Paul receiving only a handful of delegates. Paul finished second in Maine, but gained 20 delegates due to a two-stage delegate process. Paul's lackluster showing continued in the Michigan and Arizona primaries, coming in third and fourth respectively. Prior to Super Tuesday, Paul had 72 delegates to Romney's 155. On Super Tuesday, Paul came in second in North Dakota, Vermont, and Virginia, and no higher in any other state. Paul earned a single delegate by winning the caucuses of the U.S. Virgin Islands. In the nominating events following Super Tuesday, Paul picked up only 35 delegates. As Romney surged ahead, Santorum and Gingrich dropped out, leaving Paul as Romney's lone challenger. By virtue of longevity, Paul was considered runner-up in the nomination, 154 delegates to Romney's towering 1,489.

According to Republican Party rules, a candidate must earn plurality of delegates in 5 states to earn an official spot as a nominee at the national convention. Paul had done so in 4 states: Iowa, Louisiana, Maine, and Minnesota. In July, Nebraska's GOP convention represented Ron Paul's last chance to appear on the Republican National Convention Stage outside of an invited speaking spot. Paul earned only 2 delegates, leading ABC News to report that Paul's "delegate insurgency has come to an end."[49] In response, Paul supporters planned a rally outside the Tampa convention center. Former Constitution Party presidential candidate and Paul rally attendee Chuck Baldwin exclaimed: ""I believe that Ron Paul has ignited something in our hearts that God put there and that many men have been trying to squash for a number of decades."[50] Buzzfeed's Rosie Gray interviewed attendees regarding their willingness to vote for Romney, to which one responded "Hell no."[51] In an hour-and-seven-minute long speech to the rally, Ron Paul poked and prodded the Romney campaign and continued to champion the cause of liberty, arguing: "When it returns, once again you'll be able to drink raw milk. You'll be able to make rope out of hemp."[52] Small issues for most, but to Ron Paul these are indicative of the sort of busybody, invasive policies constantly espoused by the U.S. government. Paul continued to court young Americans, stating: "We have an open tent, we want new people to come in, we want to appeal to young people."[53] To the end, Ron Paul championed liberty and the cause of future generations that will inherit contemporary problems. Rosie Gray notes that Senator Rand Paul, Ron Paul's son, is a candidate to replace his father and "become the tent."[54] However, Rand Paul's endorsement of Romney alienated many of the Ron Paul faithful.[55] Thus, the future of the Ron Paul movement faces serious uncertainty.

ANALYSIS AND CONCLUSION

Ron Paul's third presidential campaign ended as many expected. Like his campaign in 2008, Ron Paul surprised observers with the ability to raise large sums of money in disparate spurts and to make primary debates more interesting. Also like the 2008 campaign, Paul lost the nomination.

During that 2008 run, Paul conceded that the likelihood of his nomination was minimal. Nevertheless, his ultimate purpose, to act as party contrarian and champion small government and liberty, was intact. Paul's campaign strategy was to focus on and perform well in caucus states, to present a consistent ideological choice to voters, and to court younger voters. Clearly, the Paul campaign exhibited laser-like focus on caucus states. Paul utilized resources strategically and stayed away from primary states, like Florida, that promised minimal gain. However, Paul's straw poll success was not repeated once the delegate selection process began. The initial plank of Paul's strategy was ultimately unsuccessful. Paul did provide Republican voters with a consistent ideological candidate. Paul's debate performances and appearances were all reminiscent of his 1984 farewell address to Congress. His contemporary calls for liberty, limited government, revised monetary policy, and contracted foreign policy are virtually identical to his 1980s issue positions. Finally, Paul's concern for the intergenerational impact of contemporary economic and domestic policy decisions clearly resonated with young citizens. Ever popular on university campuses, Paul's public appearances were replete with college aged supporters.

Ron Paul's electability was always in doubt, in large part for the reasons that his supporters adored him. Rick Santorum's debate claim that Paul voted against everything, while Santorum did not is reflective of this issue. Santorum's argument that government solutions and government spending are sometimes appropriate is shared by many citizens, even some conservative voters. Paul's role in Congress was to act as contrarian, whether or not it meant being the only "no" vote on an issue. However, Paul admitted in his 1984 farewell speech to Congress that he actually supported some of the policies against which he voted. This presents the problematic dichotomy of Ron Paul. In an elected assembly, Paul adopted the role of the one who pushes against the tide, even if he was the only member pushing. He conceded that he might also push against an issue he supports. Many of his supporters admire this about Paul, as demonstrated by the fact that his House district reelected him repeatedly. At least someone is saying "no." To be sure, this strategy attracts some voters while repelling others. Furthermore, this type of issue underscores a critical difference between serving as a member of the House of Representatives and being President of the United States. While House constituents may admire a representative who stands up in a bold, ideological way, they recognize that this is one person out of 435. It is difficult to determine whether Americans would accept a president who behaves in such a bold, contrarian fashion. Much was made of the media's treatment of Paul. Certainly the mainstream media either ignored or suppressed Paul's campaign. Although supporters cried out that this harmed the potential success of the campaign, Ron Paul's road to the Republican nomination was troubled from the beginning. Beyond the quirks of

Paul's personality or the media's unfair treatment of his campaign, it is hard to ignore the formidable challenge of Mitt Romney's broad appeal and fundraising ability.

Overall, Ron Paul's 2012 presidential campaign was moderately successful. In absolute terms, he outperformed his 2008 campaign. On the debate stage, he reprised his congressional role as resident troublemaker. Furthermore, he demonstrated successful alternative fundraising capabilities. Fundamentally, Ron Paul provides an example of an ideological outsider attempting to enact change from within. The longtime libertarian put on a Republican uniform to participate in the discussion and attempt to alter the direction of the party. Surely a calculated move, as an outsider's potential is limited, never setting foot on the debate platform. Certainly Ron Paul could have sought and won the Libertarian Party nomination. Instead, he chose to champion libertarian ideals and attempt to shape the Republican Party. To the end, Paul argued to supporters that the Republican platform was "a very libertarian, conservative document."[56] Despite two decades of service in Congress, a feat that surely establishes one as a fixture of the government, Ron Paul's status as an outsider never wavered.

NOTES

1. Christopher Caldwell, "The Antiwar, Anti-Abortion, Anti-Drug-Enforcement-Administration, Anti-Medicare Candidacy of Dr. Ron Paul," *New York Times* 2007, http://www.nytimes.com/2007/07/22/magazine/22Paul-t.html?_r=3&pagewanted=print& (accessed March 13, 2012).

2. George F. Will, "A Cheerful Anachronism," *BuzzFeed* 2007, http://www.thedailybeast.com/newsweek/2007/02/25/a-cheerful-anachronism.html (accessed February 1, 2011).

3. S. C. Gwynne, "Dr. No," *Texas Monthly* 2001, http://www.texasmonthly.com/content/dr-no (accessed January 18, 2012).

4. John H. Fund, "The Libertarian Congressman is Back," *Wall Street Journal* 1997, http://www.seedship.com/politics/ronpaul1.html (accessed January 14, 2012).

5. Michael Kennedy, "Hopeless Presidential Race : Libertarian Plods On --Alone and Unheard," *Los Angeles Times* 1988, http://articles.latimes.com/1988-05-10/news/mn-2480_1_libertarian-party (accessed February 14, 2011).

6. Kennedy, "Hopeless Presidential Race."

7. Andrew Rosenthal, "Now for a Real Underdog: Ron Paul, Libertarian, for President," *New York Times* 1988, http://www.nytimes.com/1988/10/17/us/now-for-a-real-underdog-ron-paul-libertarian-for-president.html (accessed March 11, 2011).

8. Will, "A Cheerful Anachronism."

9. Will, "A Cheerful Anachronism."

10. Katherine Q. Seelye and Leslie Wayne, "The Web Takes Ron Paul for a Ride," *New York Times* 2007, http://www.nytimes.com/2007/11/11/us/politics/11paul.html?_r=1 (accessed January 13, 2011).

11. Sarah Elkins, "'I Feel Badly About Just Quitting'," *The Daily Beast* 2008, http://www.thedailybeast.com/newsweek/2008/03/19/i-feel-badly-about-just-quitting.html (accessed April 14, 2011).

12. . Elkins, "'I Feel Badly'."

13. "Paul says he's still in the race 'to influence ideas'," *CNN* 2008, http://edition.cnn.com/2008/POLITICS/03/10/paul.campaign/index.html (accessed January 2, 2011).

14. Ron Paul, "Some Observations on Four Terms in Congress," Speech before the U.S. House, September 19, 1984, http://www.lewrockwell.com/paul/paul433.html (accessed January 2, 2011).

15. Paul, "Some Observations."
16. Paul, "Some Observations."
17. Paul, "Some Observations."
18. Paul, "Some Observations."
19. Paul, "Some Observations."
20. Paul, "Some Observations."
21. Paul, "Some Observations."
22. Paul, "Some Observations."

23. Michael D. Shear, "Ron Paul: Give Peace a Chance," *Washington Post* 2007, http://www.washingtonpost.com/wp-dyn/content/article/2007/10/11/AR2007101101555.html (accessed March 11, 2011).

24. Paul, "Some Observations."

25. Peter Hamby, "Rep. Ron Paul surprise winner of CPAC presidential straw poll," *CNN* 2010, http://www.cnn.com/2010/POLITICS/02/20/conservatives.meeting/index.html (accessed January 1, 2011).

26. Stephanie Condon, "Ron Paul Wins CPAC Straw Poll," *CBS News* 2011, http://www.cbsnews.com/8301-503544_162-20031660-503544.html (accessed March 8, 2011).

27. "Republican Debate Transcript—June 13, 2011," *CNN* 2011, http://transcripts.cnn.com/TRANSCRIPTS/1106/13/se.02.html (accessed June 14, 2011).

28. "Republican Debate Transcript—June 13, 2011."

29. "GOP Presidential Forum Transcript—September 5, 2011," *CNN* 2011, http://transcripts.cnn.com/TRANSCRIPTS/1109/05/se.01.html (accessed September 14, 2011).

30. "GOP Presidential Forum Transcript—September 5, 2011."

31. "CNN-Tea Party Republican Debate Transcript—September 12, 2011," *CNN* 2011, http://transcripts.cnn.com/TRANSCRIPTS/1109/12/se.06.html (accessed September 15, 2011).

32. "CNN-Tea Party Republican Debate Transcript—September 12, 2011."

33. "CNN-Tea Party Republican Debate Transcript—September 12, 2011."

34. Rachel Rose Hartman, "Audience at tea party debate cheers leaving uninsured to die," *Yahoo* 2011, http://news.yahoo.com/blogs/ticket/audience-tea-party-debate-cheers-leaving-uninsured-die-163216817.html (accessed October 4, 2011).

35. Carla Maranucci, "Ron Paul says media misreported Tea Party cheering on uninsured," *Texas on the Potomac* 2011, http://blog.chron.com/txpotomac/2011/09/ron-paul-says-media-misreported-tea-party-cheering-on-uninsured-with-video/ (accessed October 1, 2011).

36. Frank Davies, "Primary preview: Ron Paul's anti-war bid powered by Net activists," *Mercury News* 2008, http://www.mercurynews.com/elections/ci_8025814 (accessed June 30, 2010).

37. Davies, "Primary preview."

38. Rebecca Stewart, "Texas Rep. Ron Paul drops a bomb," *CNN* 2011, http://politicalticker.blogs.cnn.com/2011/10/24/texas-rep-ron-paul-drops-a-bomb/ (accessed December 14, 2011).

39. Christina Silva, "Romney raises $10 million in one day of phone calls," *CNN* 2011, http://articles.washingtonpost.com/2011-05-17/politics/35232779_1_mitt-romney-phone-bank-fundraiser-gop-nomination (accessed June 1, 2011).

40. Roger Simon, "Ron Paul remains media poison," *Politico* 2011, http://www.politico.com/news/stories/0811/61412.html (accessed September 3, 2011).

41. Matt Cherette, "Jon Stewart: Why Is the Media Ignoring Ron Paul?," *Gawker* 2011, http://gawker.com/5831167/jon-stewart-why-is-the-media-ignoring-ron-paul (accessed April 14, 2012).

42. Steve Kornacki, "No, Ron Paul is not getting screwed," *Salon* 2011, http://www.salon.com/2011/08/16/ron_paul_2012_4/ (accessed September 13, 2012).

43. Arthur Brisbane, "News Narratives for 2012," *New York Times* 2012, http://www.nytimes.com/2012/01/08/opinion/sunday/news-narratives-for-2012.html?_r=0 (accessed April 14, 2012).

44. Paul Mulshine, "The Times admits it deep-sixed Ron Paul," *Independent Press* 2012, http://blog.nj.com/njv_paul_mulshine/2012/01/the_times_admits_it_deep-sixed.html (accessed February 2, 2012).

45. "Are the Media Ignoring Ron Paul?," *Pew* 2011, http://www.journalism.org/numbers_report/are_media_ignoring_ron_paul (accessed March 1, 2012).

46. "Are the Media Ignoring Ron Paul?"

47. "Republican primary debate—January 7, 2012," *Washington Post* 2012, http://www.washingtonpost.com/wp-srv/politics/2012-presidential-debates/republican-primary-debate-january-7-2012/ (accessed January 8, 2012).

48. Dana Bash, "Paul not focusing resources on Florida," *CNN* 2012, http://politicalticker.blogs.cnn.com/2012/01/09/paul-not-focusing-resources-on-florida/ (accessed February 2, 2012).

49. Chris Good, "Ron Paul's Delegate Insurgency Ends in Nebraska," *ABC News* 2012, http://abcnews.go.com/blogs/politics/2012/07/ron-pauls-delegate-insurgency-ends-in-nebraska/ (accessed July 1, 2012).

50. Rosie Gray, "Bitter Paul Supporters Talk Mutiny In Tampa," *BuzzFeed* 2012, http://www.buzzfeed.com/rosiegray/bitter-paul-supporters-talk-mutiny-in-tampa (accessed August 27, 2012).

51. Gray, "Bitter Paul Supporters."

52. Rosie Gray, "Ron Paul Takes An Unapologetic Final Bow," *BuzzFeed* 2012, http://www.buzzfeed.com/rosiegray/ron-paul-takes-an-unapologetic-final-bow (accessed August 28, 2012).

53. Gray, "Ron Paul Takes."

54. Gray, "Ron Paul Takes."

55. James Hohman and Manu Raju, "Ron Paul movement not ready to pass torch to Rand Paul," *Politico* 2012, http://www.politico.com/news/stories/0812/80307.html (accessed September 3, 2012).

56. Hohman and Rahu, "Ron Paul movement not ready."

TEN

Of Sweater Vests and Broken Dreams: Santorum's Almost Win

Daniel J. Coffey and Terrence M. O'Sullivan

Rick Santorum's journey in the 2012 Republican nomination is perhaps the most quixotic of all of the contestants. As this chapter will review, there are multiple interpretations for Santorum's defeat. In the language of social science, Santorum's' defeat was over-determined. He was outspent, but probably wasn't a strong enough candidate to win in the first place, and he was too far to the right of many primary voters who doubted he had a chance to win in a general election. To a large degree—and ironically, in retrospect—Santorum's path most closely followed that of Mitt Romney in 2008.

For political observers, however, Santorum represents a potential view of the future of the Republican Party. In a year with especially poor socially conservative candidates, Santorum may be seen as representing (or cementing the representation of) a new kind of Republican: working class social conservatives. Yet, while many in the media have been quick to identify fault lines within the GOP and Santorum as the vehicle representing these fault lines (particularly class), Santorum and his rivals were unable to knock the "moderate" Mitt Romney off of his pedestal, just as previous nomination struggles failed to defeat other GOP front-runners. It remains to be seen, then, whether the Santorum campaign represents a prototype of a new Republican Party or a rehash of the Patrick Buchanan campaign of 1992.

From Iowa on through until he bowed out of his Republican presidential nomination run on April 10, 2012, Rick Santorum had been exploiting two main advantages among Republicans: A far right, social conservative favorite among evangelical Christians and Tea Party members, and as a kind of counter-establishment, populist "not-Romney." By the time he ran out of money and suspended his run, announced in his home state, at Gettysburg, Rick Santorum had won 11 states, and meaningfully moved the GOP primary debate appreciably to the political right. Despite his continued relative popularity among the Party's conservative religious right, key Republican funding had dried up in the wake of February 28th Michigan and April 3rd Wisconsin primary losses.[1] Despite being far outspent by the Romney campaign, at the time of his withdrawal, Santorum was acknowledged to have run a canny, comparatively effective run as the main alternative to his massively well-funded, better-organized, and Republican establishment-supported opponent, Mitt Romney.[2] All along, he had based his run on appealing to Republican conservatives unhappy with the history, ideological flexibility, and lack of social conservative credentials of the GOP establishment's anointed candidate, Romney.

Regardless, though Santorum had been far outspent by then, he had arguably ideologically hemmed in Mitt Romney, and made the general election playing field against Barack Obama all-the-more difficult for the soon-to-be Republican nominee. Santorum had also likely revived his own moribund political career, potentially setting the stage for a serious future presidential run in 2016 or after.

CANDIDATE BACKGROUND

Santorum was born in 1952 and raised in Winchester, Virginia. The family apparently was nominal Catholics. Santorum spent most of his youth in the suburbs outside Pittsburgh and then attended Penn State. Santorum earned a MBA from the University of Pittsburgh and a law degree from Dickinson. He married his wife while working at a law firm; together they had seven children.[3]

Santorum's political career began in 1990, when he successfully defeated a long time Democratic incumbent in the Pittsburgh suburbs and then leapfrogged into the Senate in the year of the "Republican Revolution" in 1994.

Santorum was a staunch conservative from the start. He attained some degree of notoriety when he played a leading role in the effort to stop Terri Schiavo from being removed from life support by her husband, stating he was "defending a disabled person from being executed."[4] Santorum had also earlier compared homosexual relationships to bestiality. These comments earned Santorum one of the first "Google bombs" when his surname was given a vulgar, but fake, definition.

By personality Santorum was genuinely perceived as genuine even by his opponents. At the same time, he had a reputation for being aggressive and politically tone-deaf. Byron York stated that Santorum "often struck people as arrogant and headstrong, preachy and judgmental." [5] Indeed, many analysts claimed that Santorum's personal flaws were a primary cause for his defeat in the primaries. In fact, there were several moments when Santorum's campaign seemed to be taking off when the candidate made a number of puzzling statements that undermined his stature as a front-runner.

Six years earlier, Rick Santorum's political life had seemed seriously in doubt when he lost, by an 18-point landslide, his 2006 Pennsylvania Senate reelection race to Democrat Bob Casey.[6] Democrats made major gains in the House and Senate in 2006, retaking both from the Republicans, an event believed to have been heavily reliant on voter disaffection with conservative Republican policies during the administration of George W. Bush. Yet Santorum's defeat was seen as a severe repudiation of his particular brand of conservatism and his defeat was the worst suffered by an incumbent in the state since 1980.

PRESIDENTIAL RUN

Santorum nevertheless kept a relatively high profile afterwards among conservatives, aided by a post-defeat media-related career as a Fox News analyst.[7] With Mitt Romney the clear frontrunner and Mike Huckabee declining to run, the GOP race did not appear to have a clear favorite among social conservatives.

Yet, Santorum was dismissed with figurative "eye rolls" by many political analysts and was seen as a quixotic fringe candidate.[8] During the primary, Donald Trump, who became a Santorum supporter after himself dropping his own primary run, seemed, with grudging admiration, to sum up the collective disbelief in Santorum's success, saying, "Rick Santorum was a sitting senator who, in re-election, lost by 19 points . . . Then he goes out and says, 'Oh, OK, I just lost by the biggest margin in history, now I'm going to run for president.' Tell me, how does that work?"[9]

Santorum's main strategy was to press forward with a "consistently conservative" view. In this sense, Santorum was mainly competing against Rick Perry and Michele Bachmann to be the alternative to Romney. Santorum's campaign recognized it would have little trouble with the candidate's socially conservative credentials, but neither of his two main rivals had clearly identifiable problems and his fundraising and poll numbers trailed badly behind throughout most of 2011.

The Invisible Primary

Rick Santorum's run for the Republican primary was a "dark horse" one from the start. Yet Santorum was, in many regards, the ideal candidate for the Tea Party wing of the GOP. As one journalist noted when Santorum was exploring joining the race in 2010, "few have so gleefully ransacked the established order or shown such contempt for its protocols."[10]

Yet, in the lead-up to the Republican primary voting, Rick Santorum was faced with the challenge of lacking credibility as a presidential candidate and Bachmann and Perry were still garnering significant attention from the party's socially conservative base. Perry, as an incumbent governor of a large southern state, was hailed early on as just what the party needed to challenge Obama in the general election. The Republican debates would become a proving ground for many of these candidates, including Santorum. As the season progressed, Santorum's stump speech increasingly framed Obama's reelection prospects in near-apocalyptic terms: "Democracy and freedom will disappear."[11]

The race for the nomination was greatly affected by the large number of nationally televised debates in 2011. In many ways, the debates served Santorum but not necessarily because of his strong performance. Some early debates had failed to knock Romney from his perch, but it was the third, in August in Ames, Iowa, where the race arguably began to heat up, with vigorous sparring among the candidates.[12] On September 7th, Rick Perry took part in his first debate, and was stealing much of the far right attention from others such as Santorum, with popular assertions such as "Social Security is a Ponzi scheme."[13] The statement drew considerable attention, but raised some doubts about Perry as a candidate with broad appeal.

It was the infamous September 22nd, 2011 Florida Fox News/Google-sponsored debate, the third after Rick Perry—then still ahead in the Republican primary polling—had entered the race, where Santorum began to gain traction as Perry faded. That evening Santorum was aggressive, Perry confused and self-contradictory.[14] In one example, Santorum was shown and asked his opinion about a YouTube video by Stephen Hill, a soldier in Iraq who, until repeal of the Pentagon's Don't Ask, Don't Tell policy had been forced to "lie about who [he] was" in order to serve in the military. The audience loudly booed the soldier, and Santorum drew cheers when he insisted that repeal of the policy introduced "social engineering" into the military, and that he would revert to the original policy if he were president.[15]

Santorum played the aggressor in each debate while Perry stumbled badly and Bachmann failed to stir much more attention after her initial rise. For example, on October 18 in Las Vegas, Nevada, Santorum attacked Romney about his health care reform initiative in Massachusetts:

"You just don't have credibility . . . your consultants helped Obama craft Obamacare." Romney replied "the Massachusetts plan . . . was something crafted for a state . . . if I'm president of the United States, I will repeal [Obamacare] for the American people."[16] Santorum would maintain his aggressive posture and this may have helped place him in an advantageous position to seize the opportunity when it would arise in the lead up to Iowa. November's debates saw poor debate performances, and the slow implosion of Rick Perry as the "not-Romney" front-runner.

Santorum did not benefit right away. As late as November 11, Herman Cain still was polling around 20 percent, and when he dropped out, much of his support seemed to go directly to Newt Gingrich. Perry and Bachmann never consistently polled more than 10 percent in the polls after November. Once Newt Gingrich emerged as a top candidate to challenge Romney, he became a target for all the other primary challengers.[17] By mid-December, Santorum's poll numbers began to creep up.

The Primaries Begin

By the time the Republican Primary season kicked off, Santorum's candidacy was still not viewed by mainstream pundits and political analysts as more than a symbolic run from the Party's far right, given the financial strength of the Romney campaign.

Iowa

Santorum placed a big bet on Iowa, but in a manner that was different than many of his rivals. Due to the high number of debates and the condensed schedule, many of the Republican candidates focused attention on national media outlets with relatively little attention to the traditional grassroots campaigning that usually are keys to winning in Iowa. Santorum, in contrast, had 189 caucus captains in place in 50 Iowa counties by October.[18] Santorum also appear to have engaged in what was labeled a "ring of fire" strategy of yielding the population centers and amassing support specifically targeted in the outer edges and rural areas.[19] The first evidence that this strategy was paying off occurred in August when Santorum finished third in the Ames Straw Poll. Santorum had been quietly building a ground game. Santorum had made 266 visits to the state, more than any of his other rivals.

This was important; the political science research has been clear that grassroots mobilization can be more effective than mass media contact and Santorum's ground game emphasis compared to his rivals allowed him to capitalize on the springboard that Iowa often can be. Yet, just days before the Iowa caucuses, Santorum's support surged. While Santorum had never polled more than 6 percent prior to December 10th, numerous polls between December 11 and December 27 registered support hovering around 16 percent. In the next week, Santorum was twice shown with 18 percent. Helping his cause was the Super PAC Red, White and Blue Fund which spent nearly $700,000 on his behalf.[20]

Moreover, Iowa, like many states, has a strong and vocal evangelical movement. As the first state, it was ideal for Santorum and a crucial test for Santorum's socially conservative rivals. Bachmann's poor performance in her native state along with Perry's weak finish amplified the importance of his first place finish. The national media had not covered Santorum and his victory caught many by surprise. Just as Iowa often can be a ticket to national stature, Santorum benefitted greatly and was instantly seen as Romney's main rival. Nearly all of the information about Santorum glowed about his "surprise" win and for primary voters just tuning into the dynamics of the contest, this information stream would weigh heavily on their consideration of the remaining candidates. Santorum won 32 percent of the state's evangelical voters, more than twice what any of his rivals won.

Nonetheless, Santorum was believed initially to have lost the Iowa Caucuses by a whisper-thin eight votes, giving an early boost to Mitt Romney. But two weeks later, the final certified GOP tally was reported to have accounted for lost and miscounted ballots, and showed Santorum winning by 34 votes out of almost 30,000 cast. As predicted, Santorum ran strongly among his Party's most right wing members: the very conservative (35 percent of total Caucus voters), evangelical Christians (32 percent), and Tea Party-associated (29 percent) primary Caucus-goers— groups among whom Romney fared relatively poorly.[21] Michele Bachmann, national Tea Party favorite who had won Iowa's August Ames Straw Poll, and staked her fate on winning in the state, was badly beaten, and soon pulled out of the race. The other main contender for Santorum's main support base, Rick Perry, who also fared poorly in Iowa, chose to skip New Hampshire to concentrate on South Carolina.

New Hampshire

In contrast to Iowa, New Hampshire was never seen as competitive for the Santorum campaign. Mitt Romney held an early lead in polls heading into New Hampshire's primary, and won big, while Ron Paul took second in the libertarian-leaning state. Santorum tied for fourth place (with Newt Gingrich), at just-fewer than 10 percent.[22]

South Carolina

Two days ahead of the South Carolina primary, Rick Perry, another major competitor for the GOP far right "not-Romney" vote, dropped out of the race. But instead of throwing his support to fellow social conservative, Santorum, Perry endorsed Newt Gingrich—who went on to win his first primary there, based in part on his strong GOP primary debate performances.[23]

South Carolina was a setback for the Santorum campaign, as he did not win a single county and finished third with 17 percent of the vote. Santorum had made more visits than any other candidate (64 to Gingrich's 58), but Gingrich had made more stops in the lead up to the primary. Moreover, Super PAC spending and advertising placed Santorum at a disadvantage. Santorum ($500,000) was outspent individually by Romney ($1.4 million) and Gingrich ($600,000). Santorum's Super PAC, the Red, White and Blue Fund spent about $800,000. but it was largely a side act to the nearly $8 million ad-war between Gingrich and Romney.[24]

Newt Gingrich revitalized his campaign and took the state's "true conservative" (and anti-Romney) mantle and revived his campaign prospects with his big come-from-behind (40 percent) win over Romney. Gingrich appealed both to conservatives anxious for a viable alternative to Romney, but also to Republican moderates, taking almost as high a percentage of them as Romney did.[25] Gingrich was supported by large percentages of the state's social conservatives, Tea partiers, and evangelical Christians—all still ostensibly searching for a viable alternative to Romney.

Florida

By Florida's January 31st primary, Gingrich had seemingly become Romney's—and of course Santorum's—main competition, but the three other principal challengers were overwhelmed by the weight of Mitt Romney's superior funding, which financed massive numbers of negative campaign ads primarily aimed at crippling Gingrich's billionaire/Super PAC fueled campaign. Romney out-spent Gingrich by over 5 to 1, pumping over $15 million into ads in Florida in a successful effort to stop Gingrich's momentum coming out of South Carolina. The lesson, as one political analyst noted, was that well-organized negative campaigning works: "You can't launch a giant, massive, negative, evil campaign like this without having all the other operational apparatus in place. It takes money and organization . . . There is no substitute for nuking the ever-loving shit out of the other guy."[26]

The negative ad campaign paid off, and the front-runner won with 46 percent, to Gingrich's 32 percent and Santorum's also-ran 12 percent showing.[27] The effects of Santorum's early fundraising weakness were becoming manifest; again, he did not win a single county and was third behind Gingrich and Romney in visits to the state. Just before the primary, his campaign calculated he had no chance of winning and pulled out of any meaningful campaign activity.[28]

In the race for the not-Romney second place, Gingrich once again won more of the social conservatives' and "very conservatives'" votes than

Santorum—by an 11 percent margin in both instances. Gingrich attempted to spin his loss on the evening of the primary in a positive way, asserting that Santorum and Ron Paul were now irrelevant: "It is now clear that this will be a two-man race between the conservative leader, Newt Gingrich, and the Massachusetts moderate, Mitt Romney."[29] Nevertheless, Romney's tsunami of negative advertising dealt a significant blow to Gingrich going into the following week, and contributed to Santorum's resurgence.

Nevada, Colorado, Minnesota, Missouri, and Maine

Santorum's campaign relied on a strategy of carefully selecting states and regions for advertising and voter targeting. This was essential given the campaign's fundraising problems. Despite another win for Romney in the February 4th Nevada caucuses, on Tuesday, February 7th, weeks before the critical Michigan and March "Super Tuesday" primaries, Rick Santorum revived his campaign, and arguably took the "true conservative" challenger mantle back from Gingrich, with big wins in Colorado and Minnesota caucuses and the non-binding Missouri primary. Thus began Santorum's big, if short-lived "surge" against frontrunner Romney.

The victories were the product of several factors. None of the states were particularly, large or contained expensive media markets. Spending in the three states for all candidates and PACs was only about half a million dollars, perfect for a campaign trailing in fundraising.[30] In addition, the candidates were largely focused on other upcoming states, such as Michigan, and one, Missouri, did not even really count and Gingrich and Paul were not on the ballot. Santorum's socially conservative views, his campaign's focus on visits and grassroots campaigning and the absence of major competition aligned with a quirk of the calendar to contribute to a major night for Santorum.

Colorado was the main prize for the night. Romney had easily won in 2008 and Santorum had caught nearly everyone off-guard with his win. He had the most visits of any candidates (11). Santorum won 44 counties, nearly all in the eastern part of the state and 40 percent of the vote to Romney's 35 percent, and Gingrich a distant third at 13 percent (and Ron Paul 12 percent).[31]

In Minnesota, Santorum dominated winning all but four counties in the state. Like Iowa, it contained a vocal evangelical wing and ranks among the most conservative of Republican state parties. Santorum visited 9 times compared to only 2 visits for Romney and Gingrich. Santorum won 45 percent, Ron Paul 27 percent, and Romney and Gingrich trailing at 17 percent and 11 percent, respectively.

In Missouri, Santorum was the only candidate really competing since the state legislature had failed to move the state primary and so the state party settled on a later caucus in March. Still, Santorum's decision to try to win the meaningless primary was timed perfectly and set off a media firestorm as he "swept" the night's contests. Once again, Romney's ability to sew up the Republican nomination, and attract the GOP's conservative base, was called into question. Santorum said to jubilant supporters the night of the victories, "I don't stand here and claim to be the conservative alternative to Mitt Romney. I stand here to be the conservative alternative to Barack Obama."[32] National media quickly proclaimed Santorum to again be the main challenger to Romney. Santorum's fundraising and poll support surged. Santorum had not cracked the 20 percent barrier in any national poll, and would poll above 30 percent for the rest of February and lead Romney most of the month.[33]

THE LEAD UP TO SUPER-TUESDAY AND AFTER

Romney responded by challenging Santorum's conservative credentials. The attacks were particularly acute on Santorum's record in the Senate. At a debate in Arizona shortly before that state's February 28 primary, Ron Paul joined in with Romney in attacking Santorum. Santorum was unable to effectively defend his record of voting for No Child Left Behind, funding for Planned Parenthood, and earmarks for his home state. *The New York Times* concluded, "It was Mr. Santorum's first time in the cross hairs as a leading candidate . . . by the end of the night, the scrutiny seemed to wear on Mr. Santorum, who was taunted with boos when he said he had voted for the education program even though 'it was against the principles I believed in'."[34]

Santorum shot back at an event at which both Romney and Santorum appeared on the eve of the Michigan primary, a crucial Midwestern battleground in which Santorum was believed to have a chance to turn the race in his favor. Santorum charged, "we have a Republican running for president who's campaigning as an Occupy Wall Streeter" in reference to Romney's plan to reduce taxes but limit deductions for the top 1 percent.[35]

Analysts simultaneously wondered if Santorum would be competitive over the long primary calendar when the race shifted to more large states with primaries. Ed Rollins was quoted as saying if Santorum won on Super Tuesday, the party simply would not go along with supporting him. John Heilemann opined that a Santorum nomination would be an electoral disaster and would strengthen the hand of party moderates:

> A Santorum nomination would be seen by many liberals as a scary and retrograde proposition. And no doubt it would make for a wild ride, with enough talk of Satan, abortifacients, and sweater vests to drive any sane man bonkers. But in the long run, it might do a world of good, compelling Republicans to return to their senses-and forge ahead into

the 21st century. Which is why all people of common sense and goodwill might consider, in the days ahead, adopting a slogan that may strike them as odd, perverse, or even demented: Go, Rick, go.[36]

Yet, approaching Michigan the Santorum campaign had reason to believe it could win. Santorum appealed to Michigan's famous blue-collar Reagan Democrats and Romney was on record as having opposed the auto-bailout that saved General Motors and Chrysler and was quite popular in the state. It would prove to be the beginning of the end for Santorum's bid. Once again, the dominance of Romney's organization and finances were enough to hold off a challenge. Romney held onto Michigan (one of Romney's "home states") primary, with 41 percent to Santorum's 38 percent. Santorum won well over a majority of counties, but mostly in rural areas. Santorum also won evangelical voters, but lost badly among all ideological groups except self-identified "very conservative voters." Nearly ninety percent of voters labeled the economy or the deficit as the most important issues and Santorum lost both groups, winning only those voters who felt abortion was the most important issue.

As Marty Cohen and his colleagues point out in their study of presidential nominations in *The Party Decides*, party elites still largely control the nomination process.[37] Santorum's claims to a broad support base were weakened and Romney's electability was confirmed. As the primaries continued, not only would Santorum face a financial disadvantage, but Romney's victories were evidence to the party elite he merited their endorsements and Romney's camp slowly accumulated the political capital of the endorsees. Further breaking Santorum's momentum was Romney victories in the Arizona caucus, and then in the Washington and Alaska caucuses a few days later.

Super Tuesday on March 6 represented a chance for Santorum to recapture his momentum. In addition to the largest share of delegates on any one night, many of the states on Super Tuesday had larger than average evangelical populations.

The Super Tuesday primary in Ohio was considered by some to be the ultimate show-down between Romney and Santorum—a litmus test for which candidate might be the strongest against Obama in November. Ohio, like Michigan, contained a large number of evangelical voters but also had a large population of blue-collar white voters disgruntled with the state of the economy. While Ohio had voted for Obama in 2008, it was repeatedly pointed out that no Republican had ever won the White House without also winning Ohio. Early polls heightened the intrigue as some polls showed Santorum with a commanding lead, but a lead that was weakening as the election progressed. Ominously for Santorum, almost none of the state's elite backed him. In contrast in 2008, the state Democratic Party had come out heavily in favor of Hillary Clinton, propelling her to victory. Romney had the backing of respected Senator Rob Portman, who had previously considered his own run for the presidency.

Despite Santorum's wins in Tennessee, Oklahoma, and Kansas (social conservative, evangelical, and Tea Party bastions), Romney eked-out the win in Ohio, and this set the final stage for the Republican primary. Romney won nearly every population center in the state, and Romney held a 3-1 advertising advantage. Moreover, Santorum had failed to qualify for 18 of the state's 66 delegates, again due to the campaign's early organizational problems.[38] Santorum lost suburban voters (40 to 38) and urban voters (44 to 30). Tellingly, as in Michigan, voters who supported a "true conservative" backed Santorum (51 to 13) but only 17 percent of voters labeled this as their main concern; the plurality of voters (41 percent) selected "defeating Barack Obama" and Romney easily won this group (52 to 27).

While doubts still remained about Romney's inevitability as the GOP nominee,[39] his close win in another key swing state was still a major step toward assuring GOP donors that he could indeed win in the general election. Splitting the Super Tuesday narrative was Gingrich's victory in Georgia while Santorum had also failed to qualify for the Virginia ballot, a state that increasingly appears important for the general election.[40]

Santorum's hope for a last-ditch upset was in Wisconsin's April 3rd primary, but Romney won that contest by seven points, 44 to 37 over Santorum.[41] Santorum took a break from the campaign for a number of days, ostensibly to tend to the illness of his daughter, Bella, with the promise to campaign in his home state, Pennsylvania, for the April 24th primary there. But his daughter's illness appears to have been less of a factor than having run out of money, Romney's overwhelming delegate lead, and polls that showed him possibly losing his home state, given trends in early April.[42]

When he "suspended" his campaign on April 10th, Rick Santorum notably did not endorse Mitt Romney then. He asserted in a speech in Gettysburg that "We made a decision to get into this race at our kitchen table, against all the odds, and we made a decision over the weekend that while this presidential race is over for me, and we will suspend our campaign effective today, we are not done fighting."[43] His subsequent, reluctant, qualified endorsement of Mitt Romney highlights the continued ambivalence about Romney's candidacy among the GOP base. Santorum's website had a letter to his followers that listed his problems with the front-runner, before endorsing him in paragraph 13.

UNDERSTANDING THE SANTORUM CAMPAIGN

The main question to come out of Santorum's run was what it meant for the GOP in the future. Santorum clearly appealed to social conservatives within the Republican Party. Some mentions were periodically made to "catalyzing" events that may have spurred interest in a socially conservative candidate, but the reality is that social conservatives form a significant bloc of the Republican electorate and since Romney is often seen as a moderate, it stood to reason that at least one or more opponents would be in line to win these votes. In previous elections, Patrick Buchanan and Mike Huckabee had played this role. It is a different claim altogether that Santorum's success represents an irreparable and growing fault line within the party along not just social ideology but economic and demographic lines as well.

Santorum's messages and advertisements played to social conservatives. In Michigan, Santorum ran a series of ads emphasizing his conservatism, with Sarah Palin stating in one Rick Santorum has been "consistent protecting the sanctity of life."[44] It is not clear his campaign was reaching out to social conservatives any more than the logic of the situation would have dictated, however.

It is the case that in January evangelical pastors in Texas met and decided to endorse Santorum but the endorsement was hardly a reflection of a consensus. Perry, after all, had endorsed mandatory HPV vaccines in Texas, Bachmann had already dropped out, and Gingrich had a personal record that did not fit well with the beliefs of most evangelicals. The group also decided not to urge any of the remaining conservatives to drop out and organizational and financial support did not clearly change after this endorsement.[45]

Exit polls were not taken for all states and so we have a limited ability to understand exactly how Santorum's support varied across states. The relationships are, of course, not one for one. This is, after all, a primary in which ideological differences between candidates are muted and voters are simultaneously weighting policy fidelity and electability. Nevertheless, some patterns were fairly clear. In states in which there were more religious conservatives, Santorum did well. While he was in the race, Santorum won an average of 35 percent of the evangelical vote. This may underestimate his support; exit polls were not available in many states Santorum won such as Iowa and Minnesota. He also won an average of 37 percent of the most conservative voters in each state where an exit poll was conducted and 31 percent of those who most strongly supported the Tea Party.

An analysis by Michael Tesler for YouGov confirms that moral conservatives moved towards Santorum as the primary season went on. From January to February, the proportion of moral conservatives (defined as respondents who oppose gay marriage and think abortion should be illegal in all circumstances) in the poll that supported Santorum nearly tripled (from 20 percent to over 50 percent), without a similar surge among socially moderate or liberal Republicans.[46]

The most plausible account is that Santorum largely benefitted from the consolidation of the conservative bloc and not really as any change in the candidate's own issue positions. As social conservatives dropped out of the race, particularly Rick Perry and Michele Bachmann, conservatives rallied to Santorum. It is possible a better candidate or campaign might have been able to do a better job converting social votes. A Santorum campaign field director from Georgia was quoted as saying, "The church-going population is pretty much ours anyway" when asked why the candidate was not reaching out to evangelicals in the same way as the other Republican candidates.[47] Santorum never won more than half of all evangelical voters in any one state with the exception of Michigan.

Santorum's campaign was also often seen as representing an increasingly fractured party along class lines. Internal class divisions are quite rare within the party, but observers have wondered since the Reagan Democrats appeared in the 1980s whether the party can successfully maintain a coalition of working-class or rural voters and wealthy voters. While many claims about the shift in poor or working class whites to the GOP have been overstated (see, for example Franks' *What's the Matter with Kansas?*), it is apparent that there is a least a sizable contingent of non-wealthy voters in the Republican Party.

Many analysts claim that Santorum's appeal and his resurgence were due to the increasing importance of these divisions. John Heilemann claimed, for example:

> As the party has grown whiter, less well schooled, more blue-collar, and more hair-curlingly populist. The result has been a party divided along the lines of culture and class: Establishment versus grassroots, secular versus religious, upscale versus downscale, highfalutin versus hoi polloi. And with those divisions have arisen the competing electoral coalitions-shirts versus skins, regulars versus red-hots-represented by Romney and Santorum, which are now increasingly likely to duke it out all spring.[48]

A study by the *Wall Street Journal* noted that across states, Santorum dominated in counties with incomes below the state median (46 to 15 percent), while Romney was favored by counties with income levels above state medians (46 percent to 39 percent).[49]

The division is not hard to understand. Given the candidate backgrounds, Romney would be expected to have an appeal to what has been the traditional backbone of the party, moderate to conservative upper-class voters and often in states along the East and West Coast. Santorum, in contrast, consistently won rural counties. Santorum often played up his background and targeted these rural voters.

It is harder to detect a clear pattern in the exit polls, however. In many states, middle income voters were the plurality of voters. Among middle-income voters, Santorum tended to outperform Romney who did especially well among upper income voters. For example, in Ohio, Santorum won lower income (37-34) and middle-income voters (43-32) while Romney won upper-income voters (46-33). Yet, in Wisconsin, Santorum lost among all groups, even though he was more competitive among lower-income (36-39) and middle income voters (40-42) compared to upper-income voters (33-53). Across all states, there was a statistically significant and positive relationship between the percentage of the vote Santorum won and the percentage of voters who reported making below $50,000 per year, while there was a statistically significant but negative relationship between the percentage of voters in a primary reporting making more than $100,000 per year.[50] As such, Santorum does appear to have tapped into an important divide within the GOP. Overall, in the contested states, for voters with incomes below $50,000 Santorum won one-quarter of these voters and won approximately 40 percent of these voters in later primaries. Yet, low-income voters made up only about one in three primary voters and Santorum never won a majority of these voters in any state.

A third line of explanation about Santorum's failure to unseat Romney lies on the candidate himself. As noted above, he had a reputation for being combative and difficult to work with, even by his aides and supporters.

Santorum's tendencies were manifested several times during the campaign. As his poll numbers were rising, Santorum, emphasizing his support for a greater role for religion in the public sphere, challenged then-presidential candidate John F. Kennedy's defense of the separate role of a politician's religious beliefs and their role as an elected official. Santorum, appearing on ABC News program "This Week," stated, "What kind of country do we live in that says only people of nonfaith can come into the public square and make their case? That makes me throw up"[51]

The statement did not go over well and Santorum was on the defensive as the Michigan primary approached. As noted the state was a huge one for Santorum, but it is unclear what effect this had on the final outcome. While Santorum had led in most polls, Romney had caught Santorum a week before the Catholic comments. Moreover, while Santorum lost Catholic voters (44 to 30), his support among Catholics is hard to gauge as many of the early primary states either did not have exit polls or Santorum performed poorly where exit polls were taken. In Florida, for example, Santorum won only 10 percent of Catholics while Romney won 56 percent, and in Nevada Santorum was defeated among Catholics 48 to 13 percent.

Social identity is complex; many social identities have a fluid political relevance. Santorum never identified himself as the "Catholic" candidate and none of his positions clearly stood out as "Catholic" as opposed to ordinary social conservatism. In addition, many Catholics are not Republicans and so to speak of the Republican Catholic vote is to more or less discuss voters are more or less identical in issue positions to other non-Catholic social conservatives. Consequently, the Kennedy statements notwithstanding, Santorum had performed relatively poorly among Catholics but considerably better among evangelicals. In the end, probably most damaging for Santorum in the long run was a concern that he was not "presidential" material and primary voters, as studies have shown time and again, weigh policy fidelity and electability. Romney's advantage in this regard was reinforced as a result.

About the same time, Santorum then made further news when he stated:

> Some people have incredible gifts with their hands. Some people have incredible gifts and . . . want to work out there making things. President Obama once said he wants everybody in America to go to college. What a snob. There are good decent men and women who go out and work hard every day and put their skills to test that aren't taught by some liberal college professor trying to indoctrinate them. Oh, I understand why he wants you to go to college. He wants to remake you in his image. I want to create jobs so people can remake their children into their image, not his.

Santorum was speaking at a Tea Party group and was clearly courting voters among the powerful wing of the GOP that tends to mistrust social and political institutions. There were almost no divisions by education despite many claims Santorum had also tapped into a new and growing division within the party. For example, Santorum lost both non-college graduates (43 to 37) and college graduates (46 to 36) in Wisconsin. He generally did better among non-college graduates, but this is highly correlated with income and so it is unclear if his statements did anything to heighten the division.

Once again, however the comment called into question Santorum's legitimacy as a candidate. As Republican and respected Virginia Governor Robert F. McDonnell said of Santorum, "when you look at what's going on in other countries, China, India, the premium they put on higher education — we've got to do better if we still want to be the global leader we are."[52] Santorum, while briefly leading Romney in early to mid-February, relinquished the lead and never reestablished it. These comments were not all that was at work in this shift, but it is clear that Santorum the candidate was judged by primary voters to lack the ability to defeat Barack Obama and did not have the right experience to be president.

CAMPAIGN FINANCE

In many ways finance was a double edged sword for Santorum. His campaign never raised the necessary funds to compete and he certainly was not the fundraiser Rick Perry, Ron Paul, or Mitt Romney were. Yet, his campaign operated early on without substantial debt and seemed to draw from a wider base than either Romney or Perry. In addition, while Santorum's grassroots efforts were largely a survival mechanism, they that paid off in the short run.

Santorum began 2012 facing a $55 million disadvantage against Romney. He raised only $2.2 million in all of 2011, placing him ninth amongst the candidates (but safely ahead of Thaddeus Cotter and Gary Johnson). The impact of this fundraising disadvantage would be felt for the duration of the primaries. Although his better funded rivals stumbled and Santorum's fundraising picked up, Santorum lacked a strong organization that could quickly move operations from state to state when the primary schedule kicked into high gear. In fact, in two crucial states, the lack of funds early on meant that he was not eligible to compete fully in two crucial states, Virginia and Ohio.

Ultimately Santorum raised just over $20 million mostly from individual contributions. Of his contributions, small donors accounted for just over half (51 percent) which compared well to Romney (11 percent), Perry (5 percent), although it was in line with Herman Cain (54 percent) and Gingrich (48 percent) and Ron Paul (45 percent).

As with many candidates, Santorum's fundraising closely matched his chances in the eyes of donors. From his announcement in June that he was seeking the presidency, he never broke a million dollars in fundraising in any quarter, but as the Iowa primary approached, his fundraising took off. In February, after wins in Iowa and then the "sweep" in the first week of the month, Santorum raised over $9 million compared to just $2.6 million for Gingrich and $3.3 million for prolific fundraiser Ron Paul, but still behind Romney's $11.5 million. Sweater vests were even used as a fundraising vehicle.[53]

The primary outside group supporting Santorum was the Red, White and Blue Super PAC which donated the largest share of outside spending on his behalf. The groups had three main donors; Foster Friess, Dr. John Templeton Jr., a born-again Christian who runs the John Templeton Foundation, and Frank Hanna III, who supports Catholic philanthropic causes. Friess was motivated as he put it because, "The faith component that Rick and I share is that we know that we're here to be a channel of God's love to others, his hands and feet in a hurting world, and to be a blessing to every person he puts in our path."[54]

Yet as the campaign wore on it became increasingly apparent Santorum would not be able to keep pace with his rival. In March he spent nearly a million more than he raised ($5.8 to $5.0). The primary calendar was not favorable; including the fact that many states were populated by moderates, Santorum also would have to compete in media rich states where advertising would be more expensive and necessary to compete. The moment Santorum dropped out he was facing a number of expensive and moderate states such that is difficult to see how he would have continued to compete meaningful.

The primary calendar this year, as in other years, favored the party nominee. Moreover, as the campaign wore on, organization advertising would become increasingly valuable as the focus of the campaign shifted to larger media rich states like Illinois, Pennsylvania, and New York. Not coincidentally, these states were primaries states with more moderate electorates than the smaller caucus states Santorum competed in early on. One is reminded of Paul Tsongas; he quit just before the New York primary stating the following about the campaign:

> And it was obvious that to go into New York defenseless in terms of financial resources, being unable to get up on the air in the Buffalos, Schenectadys, etc., would have meant that we could not compete, and the danger was and the great agony was that the message--if I had gone down in that way, that the message would have been so damaged, that all that we have endured for would have been hurt.[55]

CONCLUSION

Santorum's rise and fall highlight the difficulties insurgent campaigns have running in national presidential primaries. Romney was the established front-runner, as were Bob Dole and John McCain. As Cohen et al. note in the *Party Decides*, "parties resist candidates who are unacceptable to important members of the coalition, even when those candidates are popular with voters." Santorum's loss, along with those of Huckabee and Buchanan before him, strongly suggests that social conservatives remain an important but not unchallenged wing of the party. In order to win a nomination party elites, especially relative moderates, are necessary while social conservatives and Tea Partiers are not.

Many comparisons were made between this primary fight and the famous battle between Reagan and Ford in 1976. In that election, the party still had a large contingent of Northeastern and Midwestern liberals. Reagan was seen as too conservative but many also doubted his character and fitness for the presidency. In this sense, many believe Santorum suffered from the same problems and that this election represents a similar moment in party history. Either Romney's win represents continued dominance of the party moderates (relatively speaking) or the last election for the old order and the rise of a new anti-establishment, populist form of conservatism.

It seems that the former explanation makes more sense. Nate Silver noted Santorum's support was less impressive since the competition was not stellar and some of Mr. Santorum's support came by virtue of being an "anti-Romney" candidate.[56] Had Perry been a better debater, it is likely Santorum would not have had such a rise to prominence, but it is not clear Perry would have been better able to fight off Romney at the grassroots level since both men depended heavily on elite support. Certainly, social conservatives can successfully back a candidate, but as was the case with George W. Bush in 2000, the support of the party establishment is also necessary and the party continues to back relatively moderate candidates.

NOTES

1. Rebecca Kaplan, "Santorum: I left GOP race because money dried up," *CBS News* 2012, http://www.cbsnews.com/8301-503544_162-57413143-503544/santorum-i-left-gop-race-because-money-dried-up/.
2. Kaplan, "Santorum: I left." The Washington Post ranked Santorum's campaign as second only to Romney's, among the many Republican presidential aspirants.
3. "Rick Santorum Biography," *Bio*, http://www.biography.com/people/rick-santorum-20688005.
4. Katharine Q. Seelye, "A Passionate Persona Forged in a Brutal Defeat," *New York Times*, March 17, 2012, 1.
5. Byron York, "Why did Santorum lose in 2006?," *Washington Examiner* 2012, http://washingtonexaminer.com/why-did-santorum-lose-in-2006/article/1126896.
6. "Rick Santorum," *Washington Post* 2012, http://www.washingtonpost.com/rick-santorum-2012-presidential-candidate/gIQA61AHdO_topic.html.
7. Nonetheless, Santorum was highly critical of his former employers toward the end of the campaign, accusing Fox News of bias against him, and "shilling" in favor of GOP leadership favorite, Romney (a charge also leveled by Newt Gingrich). This relationship deteriorated to the point of rancor toward the end of Santorum's primary run. Justin Sink, "Santorum: Fox News is 'shilling' for Mitt Romney," *The Hill* 2012, http://thehill.com/blogs/blog-briefing-room/news/215737-santorum-fox-news-is-schilling-for-mitt-romney.
8. Chris Cillazza, "Ranking the Republican presidential candidates: The best and worst," *Washington Post* 2012, http://www.washingtonpost.com/blogs/the-fix/post/ranking-the-republican-presidential-candidates-the-best-and-worst/2012/04/13/gIQA6HOEFT_blog.html.
9. Byron York, "York: Why did Santorum lose his seat by 18 points," *Washington Examiner* 2012, http://campaign2012.washingtonexaminer.com/article/york-why-did-santorum-lose-his-sen-seat-18-pt/379616.
10. Karen Tumulty, "Santorum: A 2012 long shot tests the water," *Washington Post* 2010, http://www.washingtonpost.com/wp-dyn/content/article/2010/12/06/AR2010120606175.html?sid=ST2010120905856
11. Tumulty, Santorum: A 2012 long shot."
12. "Candidates hit hard in testy GOP debate," *MSNBC*, 2011). http://today.msnbc.msn.com/id/44110355/ns/today-today_news/t/its-debate-night-gop-iowa/.
13. "The Republican Debate at the Reagan Library," *New York Times*, 2011, http://www.nytimes.com/2011/09/08/us/politics/08republican-debate-text.html?_r=3&pagewanted=all.
14. Jennifer Rubin, "Orlando GOP debate: A strong night for Santorum as Perry fades," *Washington Post*, 2011, http://www.washingtonpost.com/blogs/right-turn/post/orlando-gop-debate-a-strong-night-for-santorum-as-perry-fades/2011/03/29/gIQA-HuXJpK_blog.html.
15. Jason Linkins, "Republican Debate Audience Boos Gay Soldier Stephen Hill After DADT Repeal Question (VIDEO)," *Huffington Post* 2011, http://www.huffingtonpost.com/2011/09/22/republican-debate-dadt-repeal-rick-santorum_n_977105.html.

16. Paul Steinhauser and Peter Hamby, "Five things we learned from Tuesday's GOP debate," *CNN* 2011, http://articles.cnn.com/2011-10-19/politics/politics_five-things-learned-gop-debate_1_herman-cain-romneycare-godfather-s-pizza-ceo?_s=PM:POLITICS.

17. Stephanie Condon, "Gingrich hammered for Freddie Mac ties," *CBS News* 2011, http://www.cbsnews.com/8301-503544_162-57343988-503544/newt-gingrich-hammered-for-freddie-mac-ties/.

18. Dan Hirschhorn, "Santorum in for long haul in Iowa," *Politico* 2011, http://www.politico.com/news/stories/1011/66575.html.

19. Hirschhornn, "Santorum in for."

20. Paul Blumenthal, "Newt Gingrich South Carolina Surge Boosted By Super PAC Spending Spree," *Huffington Post* 2012, http://www.huffingtonpost.com/2012/01/20/newt-gingrich-south-carolina-super-pac-spending_n_1219093.html.

21. "Campaign 2012: Republican Primary Tracker: Iowa," *Washington Post* 2011, http://www.washingtonpost.com/wp-srv/special/politics/primary-tracker/Iowa/.

22. "Campaign 2012: Republican Primary Tracker: New Hampshire," *Washington Post* 2011, http://www.washingtonpost.com/wp-srv/special/politics/primary-tracker/New-Hampshire/.

23. "Rick Perry Drops Out Of 2012 Presidential Race Ahead Of South Carolina Primary," *Huffington Post* 2012, http://www.huffingtonpost.com/2012/01/19/rick-perry-drops-out-2012-_n_1214032.html.

24. Blumenthal, "Newt Gingrich South Carolina."

25. "Campaign 2012: Republican Primary Tracker: South Carolina," *Washington Post* 2011, http://www.washingtonpost.com/wp-srv/special/politics/primary-tracker/South-Carolina/.

26. John Avlon, "Romney Ramps Up Attack Ads Against Gingrich to Unprecedented Levels,"*Daily Beast* 2012, http://www.thedailybeast.com/articles/2012/01/31/romney-ramps-up-attack-ads-against-gingrich-to-unprecedented-levels.html.

27. "Campaign 2012: Republican Primary Tracker: Florida," *Washington Post* 2011, http://www.washingtonpost.com/wp-s rv/special/politics/primary-tracker/Florida/.

28. "Campaign 2012: Republican Primary Tracker: Florida."

29. Stephen Stromberg, "After Mitt Romney's win in the Florida Republican primary, will Santorum surge?," *Washington Post* 2012, http://www.washingtonpost.com/blogs/post-partisan/post/after-mitt-romneys-win-in-the-florida-republican-primary-will-santorum-surge/2012/01/31/gIQAmpmdgQ_blog.html.

30. Michael D. Shear, "In Santorum's Sweep, Sign of G.O.P. Unease With Romney," *New York Times* 2012, http://www.nytimes.com/2012/02/09/us/politics/santorum-sweep-sets-stage-for-new-battle-in-republican-race.html?pagewanted=all&_r=0.

31. Philip Rucker and Nia-Malika Henderson, "Santorum revives campaign with wins in Colorado, Missouri and Minnesota," *Washington Post* 2012, http://www.washingtonpost.com/politics/santorum-poised-for-breakthrough-in-three-states-contests/2012/02/07/gIQAoE3bxQ_story.html.

32. Tom Cohen, "Santorum jolts GOP presidential race with 3-state sweep," *CNN* 2012, http://www.cnn.com/2012/02/07/politics/gop-tuesday-contests/index.html.

33. Dan Balz, "Can Santorum become more than 'not Romney'?," *Washington Post* http://www.washingtonpost.com/politics/can-rick-santorum-become-more-than-not-mitt/2012/02/14/gIQA4jw9DR_story.html; Dalia Sussman, "Santorum Catches Up With Romney in New Poll," *New York Times* 2012, http://thecaucus.blogs.nytimes.com/2012/02/14/santorum-is-tied-with-romney-in-new-poll/?hp.

34. Katharine Q. Seelye, "Specter Denies Deal With Santorum," *New York Times* 2012, http://thecaucus.blogs.nytimes.com/2012/02/23/specter-disputes-santorums-account-of-deal-on-judges/.

35. Seema Mehta, "Battling to be the conservative," *Los Angeles Times*, February 26, 2012, A13.

36. John Heilemann, "The Lost Party," *New York Magazine* 2012, http://nymag.com/news/features/gop-primary-heilemann-2012-3/index6.html.

37. Marty Cohen, David Karol, Hans Noel, and John Zaller, *The Party Decides: Presidential Nominations Before and After Reform* (Chicago, University of Chicago Press, 2008).

38. Katharine Q. Seelye, "Romney and Santorum Fight It Out in Ohio With Much at Stake," *New York Times*, March 7, 2012, A18.

39. Jim Rutenberg, "Romney Appears the Ohio Winner; Santorum Strong," *New York Times* 2012, http://www.nytimes.com/2012/03/07/us/politics/super-tuesday-republican-primary-results.html?pagewanted=all.

40. Paul Steinhauser and Tom Cohen, "Super Tuesday: Romney wins 4 states, Santorum 3; Gingrich nabs Georgia," *CNN* 2012, http://articles.cnn.com/2012-03-06/politics/politics_super-tuesday_1_romney-and-santorum-newt-gingrich-rick-santorum-three?_s=PM:POLITICS.

41. Arlette Saenz, "Santorum Hopeful He'll Pull Off a Wisconsin Upset," *ABC News* 2012, http://abcnews.go.com/blogs/politics/2012/04/santorum-hopeful-hell-pull-off-a-wisconsin-upset/.

42. "Santorum Leads Romney In Pennsylvania GOP Primary, Quinnipiac University Poll Finds," Quinnipiac University 2012, http://www.quinnipiac.edu/institutes-and-centers/polling-institute/pennsylvania/release-detail?ReleaseID=1731.

43. Sam Stein, "Rick Santorum Drops Out: GOP Presidential Candidate Suspends 2012 Campaign," *Huffington Post* 2012, http://www.huffingtonpost.com/2012/04/10/rick-santorum-drops-out-2012-race_n_1415372.html.

44. Shushannah Walshe, "Rick Santorum Campaign Goes on the Air With Ads in Michigan," *ABC News* 2012, http://abcnews.go.com/blogs/politics/2012/02/rick-santorum-campaign-goes-on-the-air-with-ads-in-michigan/.

45. Felicia Sonmez, "Santorum wins support of evangelical leaders at Texas meeting," *Washington Post* 2012, http://www.washingtonpost.com/blogs/post-politics/post/santorum-wins-support-of-texas-evangelical-leaders/2012/01/14/gIQAP8BpyP_blog.html.

46. Michael Tesler, "Moral Conservatives Spark the Santorum Surge," *YouGov* 2012, http://today.yougov.com/news/2012/02/21/moral-conservatives-spark-santorum-surge/.

47. Krissah Thompson, "'Perfect candidate' eludes evangelical voters," *Washington Post*, March 3, 2012, A07.

48. John Heilemann, "The Lost Party: The strangest primary season in memory reveals a GOP that's tearing itself apart," *New York Magazine* 2012, http://nymag.com/news/features/gop-primary-heilemann-2012-3/.

49. Harold Meyerson, "The GOP's class war," *Washington Post*, February 17, 2012, A17.

50. The correlation between Santorum's overall voter and the percentage he won among various income subgroups is usually significant and positive for all income categories. This is because if Santorum (or any candidate) did well in a particular state, he would do well among all groups, and in states where he did poorly, he would win a smaller share of the votes for all groups. It is more insightful, then to compare his percentage of the vote to the percent of the primary electorate within each category, rather than how well he performed within each category.

51. Michael Barbaro, "Santorum Makes Case for Religion in Public Sphere," *New York Times* 2012, http://www.nytimes.com/2012/02/27/us/politics/santorum-makes-case-for-religion-in-public-sphere.html?pagewanted=all.

52. Sandhya Somashekhar and David Nakamura, "Rick Santorum takes heat for 'snob' comment against President Obama," *Washington Post* 2012, http://www.washingtonpost.com/politics/rick-santorum-takes-heat-for-snob-comment-against-president-obama/2012/02/27/gIQADiXteR_story.html.

53. Felicia Sonmez, "Rick Santorum's sweater vests become a fundraising incentive ahead of the New Hampshire primary," *Washington Post* 2012, http://www.washingtonpost.com/blogs/election-2012/post/rick-santorums-sweater-vests-be-

come-a-fundraising-incentive-ahead-of-new-hampshire-primary/2012/01/10/gIQAiPx-EoP_blog.html.

54. Matea Gold and Melanie Mason, "The religious right bankrolls Santorum; Evangelical Christians and conservative Catholics have given heavily to a 'super PAC' backing him," *Los Angeles Times*, February 12, 2012, A15.

55. Robin Toner, "Tsongas Abandons Campaign, Leaving Clinton a Clear Path toward Showdown with Bush," *New York Times* 1992, http://www.nytimes.com/1992/03/20/us/1992-campaign-primaries-tsongas-abandons-campaign-leaving-clinton-clear-path.html?pagewanted=all&src=pm.

56. Nate Silver, "What Does Santorum's Future Hold?," *New York Times* 2012, http://fivethirtyeight.blogs.nytimes.com/2012/01/10/what-does-santorums-future-hold/.

ELEVEN

Mitt Romney—The Republican Choice: Inevitability, Electability, and Lack of Enthusiasm

Sean D. Foreman

Inevitability. That is the image that Mitt Romney and his supporters sought to portray throughout the 2012 Republican nomination campaign. Electability. That is the trait that Republican voters were seeking in their quest to beat President Barack Obama. Lack of enthusiasm. That is the term that many analysts and Republican Party voters used to describe Romney's candidacy. Ultimately, Romney was able to survive a rancorous, contested primary by projecting inevitability and proving the case that he was the most electable Republican for the general election to overcome the lack of enthusiasm for his candidacy and secure his party's nomination for president.

Romney entered the 2012 presidential campaign as the perceived frontrunner for the Republican Party. One reason for that is that he basically never stopped campaigning after losing the GOP nomination to John McCain in 2008. Another reason is the financial advantage Romney enjoyed both with vast personal wealth and the ability to fundraise from top political donors. Moreover, Romney "looks the part," appearing, acting, and sounding presidential on a stage compared to the variety of challengers who vied for the Republican nomination in 2012.

An old adage goes that "Democrats fall in love, Republicans fall in line" when it comes to presidential candidates.[1] Jimmy Carter in 1976, Bill Clinton in 1992, and Obama in 2008 were examples of Democratic candidates who endeared themselves to caucus goers and primary voters even as they lacked a national reputation or following prior to their presidential runs. Meanwhile, four of the last five Republican candidates for president (Ronald Reagan, George H.W. Bush, Bob Dole, and John McCain) had run at least once before they won their party's approval.[2] Given that trend, Romney entered the race as a strong favorite to win the GOP nomination. But he still had to prove it to Republican primary voters who constantly questioned his conservative credentials.

Romney came in second in both the 2008 Iowa caucus to Mike Huckabee and New Hampshire primary to John McCain. Romney then won the primary in Michigan, where his father served as governor, and Nevada caucus. But John McCain's victory in the Florida primary propelled him to a significant set of victories on Super Tuesday on February 5, 2008. Two days later at the Conservative Political Action Conference (CPAC) convention Romney gave a rousing speech where he announced that he would end his campaign. The early exit by Romney in 2008 allowed him to curry favor with the party base and to retreat from the public spotlight to regroup for another run in 2012.

Romney wrote a book, *No Apology: The Case for American Greatness* that was published in 2010 and went on a speaking tour.[3] It was clear that he would again seek the Republican nomination in 2012 and he was one of the frontrunners heading into the campaign season. The book and talking points foreshadowed Romney's 2012 campaign theme "Believe in America" in a not-so-subtle comparison to President Obama whom many Republicans saw as apologizing for the United States around the world.

Romney announced his 2012 presidential campaign in Stratham, New Hampshire, at Doug and Stella Scamman's Bittersweet Farm. While he was an immediate leader in a crowded field, many conservative voters and commentators sought a conservative alternative to the "Massachusetts moderate" as former House Speaker Newt Gingrich and others came to call Romney. In polls from August 2011 through the time he essentially clinched the nomination in April 2012 Romney faced significant challenges from a number of contenders who tried to carry the "anti-Mitt" label and rally conservative voters to their cause. Ultimately Romney survived the challenges and clinched the GOP nomination to carry the Republican mantle in the battle to beat President Obama.

CANDIDATE BACKGROUND: WHO IS MITT?

Willard Mitt Romney was born March 12, 1947 in Detroit, Michigan.[4] His father, George Romney, emerged from humble beginnings. George, who was born to parents on a Mormon mission in Mexico, apprenticed as a lath and plaster carpenter and sold aluminum paint before a career in the automotive industry. George rose to be chief executive of American Motors, then Governor of Michigan, and Secretary of Housing and Urban Development in the Nixon Administration.[5] His mother, Lenore, abandoned an acting career to marry George. Both of Romney's parents are descendants of prominent leaders in the Mormon Church of Jesus Christ of Latter-day Saints.[6]

Mitt was the youngest of four children, with two older sisters and a brother. Mitt was referred to as being a "miracle child" in the Romney household.[7] Mitt greatly admired and respected both of his parents. His father, who was quite proud of his youngest son, was a professional role model. From his mother, Mitt inherited diplomatic and smooth interpersonal skills.

Romney attended public elementary school and then enrolled in the prestigious preparatory Cranbrook School in Bloomfield Hills, Michigan. Romney did not excel in academics or athletics—he briefly ran cross country—but was social and showed leadership qualities.[8] He found his niche when his father was elected governor during his sophomore year. Mitt played a role in the campaign and did some work in the governor's office.

During his senior year at Cranbrook Romney met his future wife, Ann Davies, who was two years younger, and they started dating. When Romney graduated from high school in 1965 the two made an agreement to someday marry.[9]

Romney attended Stanford University for a year. He worked nights as a security guard and used the money he earned to fund trips home to see Ann. While many students were involved in protests against the war in Vietnam, Romney prominently led counter-protests against the protesters.

After that year at Stanford he did a two-and-a-half-year Mormon mission in France. During this time Romney began to develop along the path to becoming a leader in his church. He also had a brush with a tragic event that would shape his life in young adulthood. Romney was driving a car cautiously on a rainy night that was hit by a Catholic priest in a truck along a narrow road. The leader of the Mormon mission in France and his wife rode in the front seat with Mitt while three other passengers were in the back seat. The head-on collision crushed the front of their car. The mission leader's wife was killed. Romney was knocked unconscious and had to be pried from the car by rescuers. With injuries that initially appeared more severe than they were, Romney was actually pronounced dead by a French police officer.[10] After a brief time in a coma, Romney recovered from a head injury, broken arm, and a bunch of bruises.

Romney returned from France to enroll in Brigham Young University in Provo, Utah, where Ann was a student and many young Mormon men attended after their missions. Romney joined the honors program and quickly got engaged to Ann. Mitt and Ann married in March 1969. He was 22 and she was 19 years old. A year later their first son was born. In 1971, Romney graduated with high honors and a degree in English Literature and was selected to give a speech at his class's BYU graduation.

With a lifelong goal of attending Harvard, something his father did not have the opportunity to do, Romney headed to Boston for professional training. He was selected for a newly created joint J.D. and MBA program. The program was rigorous and Romney excelled even as he was starting a new family.[11]

Having completed the prestigious Harvard dual program, Romney was sought after with job opportunities. He began his professional career working with the Boston Consulting Group. Then he went to work for Bill Bain at Bain & Company, working his way to a vice president position in 1978. When Bain wanted to start a new venture capital firm in 1984 he looked to then 36-year old Mitt Romney to lead the efforts. The goal was to invest in new companies or to take over struggling companies and make them more competitive, or more attractive to other investors. One of Romney's most notable successes with Bain Capital was investing in a start-up company called Staples designed to sell office supplies in bulk to small- and medium-sized companies.[12] There are also examples of investments that did not work out as well for Bain and its investors. Ultimately with many companies that were bought, restructured or sold, in a process termed as creative destruction and wealth creation, tens of thousands of jobs were both created and lost in companies around the world.

During his time at Bain Capital Romney acquired great personal wealth. Estimates put Romney's wealth at around $250 million.[13] There are reports that some of his money is sheltered in offshore accounts in Bermuda and the Cayman Islands.[14] Romney's tax returns show he earned $21.7 million in 2010 and $29.9 million in 2011, mostly in profits from dividends or investment interest.[15]

A question arose during one of the Republican debates in January 2012 as to whether Romney had benefited from his family's wealth in building his business career when he responded, "I didn't inherit money from my parents."[16] Romney clearly had support from his family throughout college and graduate school. His parents bought him and Ann a car as a wedding gift and helped the couple buy a house in Massachusetts when he attended Harvard. The question of whether Mitt Romney inherited money from his father, and how much, was asked in a C-SPAN interview in 2005. Romney said that he received some money when his father died but that the money was donated to an endowment at BYU to support the George W. Romney Institute of Public Management.[17] When asked about it in subsequent interviews Romney downplays the significance of the donation.

ISSUE STANCES

Business Background

Romney made his fortune as a venture capitalist. But his tenure with Bain Capital turned out to be an issue in the primary from unlikely corners, such as his conservative opponents. Rick Perry called it "vulture capitalism" while Newt Gingrich criticized how Romney made his money through creative destruction. Libertarian Ron Paul, a fierce advocate of free markets, refused to pile on this issue. Romney countered the attacks by saying that he expected Democrats to attack him but not fellow Republicans. He also defended his record for overall net job creation.

Bain Capital was in the business of either investing in start-up companies or in buying troubled companies, reorganizing them, and then selling them off either in part or in whole to other companies. Romney himself is known for his management consulting background and his ability to analyze a deal. He was not the person who came up with investment ideas or courted new deals. But he could see the advantages and disadvantages of deals and make the financial assessment that was good for Bain and its investors.[18]

The issue of Romney releasing his tax returns became controversial during the primaries. Romney's father had set a strong example by releasing 12 years of tax returns when he ran in 1968.[19] While presidential candidates are not legally required to release their tax records Romney promised to make documents public and then dragged his feet. Eventually he released returns for 2010 and 2011 showing he earned $21.7 and $29.9 million, respectively, mostly in capital gains. Since the money was earned as returns on investments Romney paid fifteen percent taxes on it under IRS guidelines.[20]

While Romney supported the bank bailout he had a documented position against the auto bailout.[21] Romney famously opposed the idea of bailing out General Motors, Ford, or Chrysler in an opinion piece that ran in the *New York Times* in October 2008.[22] In the article titled "Let Detroit Go Bankrupt" Romney made the case for managed bankruptcy rather than a bailout. "The federal government should provide guarantees for post-bankruptcy financing and assure car buyers that their warranties are not at risk. In a managed bankruptcy, the federal government would propel newly competitive and viable automakers, rather than seal their fate with a bailout check," Romney wrote. Romney's position was not popular in Michigan, where his father once managed a car company, but it appealed to fiscal conservatives and Tea Party-types. In May 2012, Romney took heat for making the case that his idea worked. The headline of the article made it sound like he wanted the American auto industry to perish.[23] Instead he was arguing for what in fact ultimately happened: allow the companies to file for Chapter 11 bankruptcy and then come in with federal loans to guarantee their recovery. It should be noted that Romney did not choose the title of the editorial.

Before that happened, Romney claimed, labor unions benefited from the bailout in what Romney called 'crony capitalism' in another op-ed in the *Detroit News* on Valentine's Day 2012. Romney wrote that he was a 'son of Detroit' who grew up with American cars in his bones. While had advocated for managed bankruptcy, as painful as that process might be for a company and its employees, what instead happened with the bailouts of General Motors and Chrysler, according to Romney was that union bosses that supported the Democratic Party were rewarded despite their inefficient agreements at the expense of taxpayers.[24] Romney tried to stake out ground that he supported aiding American auto manufacturers while not backing the federal bailout program. It was a way that he could play to his strength as being an expert in managing capitalism as "creative destruction."[25]

Romney's role in running the 2002 Olympic Games in Salt Lake City is touted as part of his business background and success. Romney was the president and CEO of the games and is credited for saving them from funding scandals. He wrote a book about his involvement called *Turnaround: Crisis, Leadership and the Olympic Games* and highlighted his experience in his 2002 gubernatorial campaign. The Salt Lake Games garnered $1.3 billion in federal aid, more than double the 1996 Atlanta Games as well as millions of dollars in Utah state aid. Romney was registered as a lobbyist and led efforts to secure that money for Olympic projects.[26]

The Economy

Romney launched a 59-point plan for dealing with the economy in September 2011.[27] Lengthy and cumbersome, it did not lend to easy explanation to the American people and he soon abandoned the '59' part in his speeches. As the campaign progressed he focused on a few key ideas to highlight his agenda if elected president.

A popular talking point with Romney during the debates was support for the "cut, cap, and balance." This phrase became prevalent among Republicans, particularly in the House of Representatives, in August 2011 during the debate over raising the U.S. debt ceiling. The concept calls for cutting federal budget spending, capping new spending, and having a balanced budget. Romney signed a pledge to support a balanced budget amendment. He also called for cutting federal spending and capping it at 20 percent of GDP.

Romney called for an extension of the so-called Bush tax cuts for middle and upper income earners. That tax reduction was actually renewed under Obama during the 2010 lame duck session of Congress and was set to expire at the end of 2012. Romney's full economic plan calls for an across the board 20 percent cut in marginal rates. He also calls for cutting the corporate tax rate to 25 percent. It would take congressional approval to implement these ideas and they would presumably be met with significant cuts in spending.[28]

Romney also talked about reducing the federal workforce and restructuring the federal government though he did not put forward specific plans for making this happen. When asked at an early debate in New Hampshire in June 2011, he said, "Instead of thinking in the federal budget, what we should cut—we should ask ourselves the opposite question. What should we keep?"[29] In the wake of tornadoes and flooding in the Midwest Romney even indicated that spending on FEMA and disaster relief could be cut in order to restore fiscal responsibility.

A sticking point for Romney was his record as governor of Massachusetts. He claimed a record of job growth while Democrats pointed to the anemic employment growth under his watch. A common talking point of Romney's opponents was that Massachusetts was ranked 47th in job creation during his four years as governor. The Romney team rebuttal is that, in fact, including Washington, D.C. in the mix, Massachusetts was 51st in job creation during Romney's first year in office. His administration managed to move the commonwealth up to 30th by 2006, his final year in office.[30]

Out of Touch Comments

Romney ran a largely controlled campaign on big picture themes that would help him win the nomination. He was mostly disciplined in the debates as he dodged attacks and deflected attention to his criticisms of President Obama. He raised money and ran ads to tear down his opponents while ferociously defending his own record. Meanwhile he kept his interviews with national press and on talk shows to a minimum. Romney was shielded from press scrutiny by not granting too many interviews and selectively speaking with reporters.

Some comments by Romney, however, showed he may be out of touch with average American voters. In a GOP debate on December 10, Romney tried to bet Rick Perry $10,000 over a comment Perry made about Romney's support for an individual health care mandate.[31] The claim made by Perry that Romney showed support for a federal individual mandate in his first edition hard cover book, and then removed it from the second edition paperback copy, was found to be "mostly false" by Factcheck.org.[32] More coverage was devoted to the size of the attempted bet than the issue at hand as people largely noticed that Romney picked that figure out of his head seemingly without much thought.

During an interview with CNN on January 31, Romney made a comment that was seized upon by his critics. Romney said, "I'm not concerned about the very poor. We have a safety net there. If it needs a repair, I'll fix it. I'm not concerned about the very rich; they're doing just fine." Romney was attempting to highlight his campaign's concern for the middle class. He also used the occasion to reiterate his position in support of increases in the federal minimum wage tied to the rate of inflation in opposition to his party. But the "I'm not concerned about the very poor" comment became the sound bite of the week and was used as an example that Romney, who has a net worth estimated at more than $200 million does not understand the plight of poor Americans.[33]

These comments were on top of joking with a group of unemployed Floridians that he was "also unemployed," telling some New Hampshire voters that he once received a "pink slip," calling his speaking fees in 2011 of $347,327 "not very much," his argument with attendees at an Iowa rally that "corporations are people," and that his wife has "a couple of Cadillacs" during an event in Detroit did not help his image as understanding the feelings of average Americans during the economic downturn.

RomneyCare

The albatross around Romney's campaign was the Massachusetts health care law enacted in 2006 while Romney was governor. Referred to by critics as "RomneyCare" the wide-sweeping state-based health care law contained a provision mandating that all residents of the commonwealth buy health insurance or else be subject to a tax penalty and it was supposed to control costs.

Romney supported the individual mandate and while he vetoed eight provisions of the bill, the vetoes were all eventually overridden by the legislature. When he launched his campaign for president in 2008 he initially said the health care law would be an advantage for him over the Democrats because he was able to get passed what they were not able to do under President Bill Clinton in the 1990s. But as the campaign progressed Romney distanced himself from his health care policy accomplishment.[34]

The Massachusetts law was seen by many, including those who worked on both bills, as a model for the national health care law passed in April 2010.[35] Often called "ObamaCare" after the Affordable Care Act was passed by a Democratically-controlled Congress and signed into law by President Obama, the national law included a controversial individual mandate provision which was upheld by the U.S. Supreme Court in 2012. Romney in several interviews and speeches claimed that the Massachusetts law was a model for the nation. He even wrote an op-ed in July 2009 suggesting that the president look to Massachusetts as an example.[36] When he became a candidate for president in 2012, Romney repeatedly vowed to work to repeal the national law. He cited the 10th Amendment and said that states should decide solutions that best fit their specific circumstances rather than having a uniform federal policy.

The desire to repeal ObamaCare was a central part of the Tea Party movement and message in 2010. The Republican-led House voted to repeal the law in early 2011 but it was mostly a symbolic vote as the Democrats still controlled the Senate and Obama would veto any attempt to repeal his signature health care policy. The promise to repeal ObamaCare became a type of litmus test for 2012 presidential candidates. In most of the presidential debates and in campaign speeches it was a popular applause line to promise to repeal ObamaCare if the candidate were elected.

Romney's credibility on health care was constantly questioned due to his history. Tim Pawlenty called it "ObamneyCare" combining the two names in reference to the two plans being essentially the same. Michele Bachmann further popularized that criticism. Rick Santorum called Romney "the worst Republican in the country" to run against Obama and that he was "uniquely disqualified" to carry the party's voice on the health care issue.[37] Santorum noted that the Republicans would have to concede their opposition to the health care law with Romney as the party's nominee.

On June 28, the Supreme Court by a 5-4 decision upheld the Affordable Care Act. In a controversial, and unanticipated, decision, Chief Justice Roberts wrote the Court's opinion upholding the individual mandate as a constitutional taxing power by Congress but struck down the rationale that it was a legitimate use of the commerce clause. Within an hour of the Court's decision, Romney gave a speech where he echoed a key phrase for Republicans in Justice Robert's decision. He said that it was bad policy and that if the American people did not like it then they should vote for elected officials who would overturn it. Buoyed by conservative discontent with the decision the Romney campaign reported raising more than $4.5 million in campaign contributions in the 24 hours following the Court's decision.[38]

Ideology

A major theme throughout the campaign was whether Romney was conservative enough to win the Republican nomination. In 2008 he positioned himself as being more conservative than John McCain but was not as conservative as former Arkansas governor and pastor, Mike Huckabee. The road to the Republican nomination was seen by many as running through the base of the party, made up of social conservatives and Christian evangelicals. The fiscal conservatives and Tea Party supporters would play a role but conventional wisdom states that Republican candidates have to appeal to the social right wing. Romney had an easier time convincing the fiscal conservatives due to his background as a private equity capitalist—although he supported the bank bailout in 2008—than he would have satisfying the social conservatives seen as the party's foundational voters especially in the south.

At the 2012 Conservative Political Action Conference (CPAC) Romney said "I fought against long odds in a deep blue state, but I was a severely conservative Republican governor" and used some variation on the words "conservative" and "conservatism" 24 times in his prepared remarks.[39] The "severely conservative" comment left people wondering what he meant. Romney cited his beliefs and upbringing in religious liberty and economic opportunity.[40] In later explaining the comment Romney mentioned his enforcement of immigration laws, his support of English immersion programs in schools, and his support of religious liberty for the Catholic Church. Romney also added that he managed the Salt Lake City Olympics conservatively though that happened before he was governor.[41]

The event was a micro view of the Romney narrative that was shaped as early as in the 2008 campaign. He is a pragmatic businessman but wants to paint himself as a conservative icon. As one conservative writer put it, Romney desperately tried to impersonate a conservative Republican. "That persona—angry, simple-minded, xenophobic, jingoistic—is exactly what Romney (who is himself cultured, content, and cosmopolitan) imagines the average GOP voter to be."[42]

There was also a concern that Romney lacks authenticity. It seems that he would say whatever he needed to say to win voters. Romney's positions were more liberal in his run for the U.S. Senate in Massachusetts in 1994. He said at the time he would be better for gays in the state than the popular liberal Senator Edward Kennedy. Romney said he would not try to change the abortion laws in the commonwealth. While he was running to represent one of the most liberal states in the country Romney was much more in tune with the popular opinions of Massachusetts and New England than he was with conservatives and evangelicals in the U.S. heartland and south. His ideological inconsistency raised questions from Republican primary voters in 2012. It led Gingrich and others to label him as a "Massachusetts moderate" as Romney tried to position himself to the right of his former positions.

Immigration

Romney was especially conservative on immigration issues during the nomination campaign. Perry criticized him in a debate for having hired a company that hired illegal aliens on his lawn. It was a story that first arose in 2006 and Romney addressed it in the 2008 campaign. Romney dismissed that as old news and said that "I don't think I've ever hired an illegal immigrant in my life."[43] Romney went further to call for a national e-verify system to combat the hiring of illegal immigrants.

During the campaign Romney called for veto of the DREAM ACT, which would provide a pathway to citizenship for people in the country illegally, called the Arizona immigration law a model for the country, and said that people in the country illegally should "self deport" to their home countries. He also sought the endorsement of former California governor Pete Wilson, an immigration hard-liner, and named Wilson an honorary co-chair of Romney's California campaign.[44]

These positions appeal to the traditional Republican base but seemed to be at odds with the objective of increasing support from Hispanic voters. Favoring the Arizona law made Romney a hard-liner on the issue in the context of current policy debates. The U.S. Supreme Court invalidated several parts of the Arizona law SB 1070 on June 25 while upholding the most controversial part allowing law enforcement officials to ask people for proof of citizenship. Romney was caught flat footed in his response to the Court decision. President Obama had issued an executive order the previous week calling for a two-year deferral in deportations for people under 30 years old here illegally if they served in the military or attended college. Romney followed the lead of Florida Senator Marco Rubio, a leading Hispanic Republican voice, saying that Obama's move was a short term fix for a long term problem. The Republicans also criticized the president for usurping Congress' authority on immigration policy.[45]

The Mormon Issue

The "elephant in the room" for some conservatives with Romney's run for president is his religion. Mitt Romney comes from a prominent Mormon family. His lineage is rooted in the fathers of the Church of Jesus Christ of Latter Day Saints.[46] Romney himself has held important leadership positions serving as leader of the Cambridge ward, then bishop of the Belmont ward, and eventually stake president, which made him the leader of the Mormon congregation, in the greater Boston area.[47]

During the 2008 campaign Romney gave a speech about religion. He talked about his belief in Christ but did not get into details about Mormonism. Questions were raised in 2008 and again leading into 2012 that evangelical Protestants and conservative Catholics would not support Romney as many of them view LDS as a cult. Yet Romney's faith did not become a detrimental issue for him. He often referred to his experiences in his church as building character and leadership skills without getting into specific discussions about religion or spirituality. "I'm—without question—I'm a member of the Church of Jesus Christ of Latter-day Saints. I'm proud of that," Romney said in an interview with NBC News on July 25. "Some call that the Mormon Church, that's fine with me. I'll talk about my experiences in the church. There's no question they've helped shape my perspective."[48]

Despite some calls for him to address the issue again Romney remained largely silent on religion during the 2012 campaign. The issue appeared to wither away from the political radar rather than intensify when Romney clinched the Republican nomination. As the Republican convention approached a poll released by Pew Research Center's Forum on Religion and Public Life found that sixty percent of registered voters knew that Romney was a member of the Church of Ladder Day Saints. Of those surveyed eighty percent said that Romney's religion would not negatively impact their vote, with sixty percent saying that they were comfortable with his religion and twenty one percent saying it did not matter to them.[49]

CAMPAIGN

Strategy

Romney's strategy throughout the campaign appeared to be to look beyond the caucuses and primaries and focus on the general election campaign. Romney ran against Obama from the start of the Republican nomination campaign rather than focusing on his intraparty opponents. The strategy worked as he ultimately won the nomination despite having less than half of his party's support in any contests where he had competition and months of jockeying between supposedly more conservative candidates vying to be the alternative to Romney.

Romney had to avoid prolonged discussions on the health care issue due to his championing of universal coverage in Massachusetts. He continually said that it was a state-based solution for a specific set of issues in his state but that it was not appropriate for a national program. Indeed Romney signed on to the "repeal ObamaCare" line of thinking early in the campaign and stuck to it saying that the Democrat passed health plan would be expensive and be a job killer.

The main impetus of Romney's campaign was to talk about the economy and to establish his bona fides from the business world. As long as Romney kept the discussion on the state of the economy and off of social issues he was comfortable with the tone of the campaign. Romney had to defend his record from attacks that he profited mightily at the expense of some weaker companies. He used his background at Bain as an avenue to say that he understood how the economy worked and how to create jobs and grow opportunities as industries and fundamentals shift.

What Romney did not talk much about was his religion. Questions about whether evangelicals would vote for a Mormon candidate were part of a whisper campaign by other candidates and were material for discussion by pundits on talk shows. But discussion about religion was largely muted during the campaign and despite calls by critics for Romney to address the issue like he did in 2008, he did not.

Also the history of "flip-flopping" by Romney on abortion policy, gay rights, and gun laws in the past left Romney vulnerable. But Romney put forward a strong social conservative front in debates and forums and was able to hold off serious concerns about his views by sticking to a script of how his views had evolved over the years.

A gaffe by a senior aide made conservatives wary just as Romney had essentially clinched the nomination. Eric Fehrnstrom, a trusted communications specialist, said in a CNN interview that the general campaign would be 'almost like an Etch-A-Sketch. You can kind of shake it up and restart all over again.'[50] The comment drew immediate reaction from Democrats and from Republican rivals Gingrich and Santorum who were still not mathematically eliminated yet, as they each showed up at campaign appearances donning the popular children's toy in which pictures are not permanent and are constantly redrawn.

Financing

Romney dominated his opponents in fundraising. Through the January 31 reporting period his campaign raised $63.7 million and far outpaced his opponents ($31.1 million for Ron Paul, $18.3 for Newt Gingrich and $6.7 for Santorum). Meanwhile President Obama had $151.4 million reported. But most of Romney's donors were the large money supporters and few were from grass-roots supporters. Only ten percent of his contributions, $6.4 million, were under $200 while nearly half of his opponents' funds came from smaller donations.[51] The fact that he had tapped out large donors posed a challenge to the Romney campaign that they needed to find more small donors. Add to that the lack of enthusiasm for the candidate, the lack of any unexpected primary wins to show his electability, and the perception that he was so wealthy that many usual contributors hesitated to donate to his campaign.[52]

By the end of May, Romney had raised $120.6 million for his campaign while Obama had raised $255.2 million. Individuals donated $112.7 million and PACs put in another $766,553 to Romney. Of the individual donors $71 million came in contributions of $2000 and more while $19 million came in contributions of $200 and under. A challenge for the Romney campaign is that they had spent $105 million and had just under $17 million cash on hand. (The Obama campaign had $109.7 million cash on hand) Not surprisingly, Romney's largest hauls came from California ($12.3 million), New York ($10.8 million), Florida ($9.4 million), Texas ($7.4 million), and Massachusetts ($4.8 million).[53]

But individual contributions were not the most important factor to watch in 2012. It was the Political Action Committees (PACs) and specifically the unlimited contributions to "Super PACs" thanks in part to the *Citizens United v. FEC* (2010) decision. The pro-Romney Super PAC Restore Our Future, Inc. raised $43 million as of the end of February. Restore Our Future was largely responsible for Romney's success in Iowa, Florida, Ohio, Michigan, and elsewhere where the committee significantly outspent rival groups and blanketed the air with negative ads against Gingrich and Santorum. Restore Our Future took in contributions totaling $61.4 million by the end of May including $8.6 million in April when Romney clinched the GOP nomination. By contrast, the pro-Obama Super PAC Priorities USA Action had raised about $6.5 million through February and nearly $14.3 million by the end of May.

The spending by the pro-Romney Super PAC helped him to defeat Gingrich and Santorum and win the nomination. The regulations do not allow for any coordination between the candidate's campaign and the actions by the "independent" committees. There was concern during the primaries that people who worked for Restore Our Future were former Romney staffers. Restore Our Future ran negative ads in key primary states and was particularly harsh against Gingrich. When Gingrich called on Romney to denounce the committee's ads Romney claimed that he did not see the ads nor did he have any control over their content. This pattern is likely to persist in the general election campaign.

Debates

Romney essentially played it safe in the debates. He did not particularly stand out in the debates while Gingrich had some stellar performances that helped propel him to the top of the field. Conversely, Rick Perry's campaign suffered from some comments he made in debates.

Romney was often the focus of attacks from each of his competitors.[54] He basically deflected those criticisms and while he sometimes counterattacked he usually focused his remarks on the Obama administration. Being a front-running candidate he was usually in the center of the stage, had more questions addressed to him, and had more time to speak.

Romney had largely steady performances. His best performance came in Florida after he lost the South Carolina primary to Gingrich. Romney came out swinging and shed his passive-aggressive style for more of an aggressor stance. His answers on the economy and immigration helped to secure his position and win the Florida primary.

The lowlight for Romney in the debates is when he offered a $10,000 bet to Texas Gov. Perry over an accusation about Romney's position on health care. While fact checkers determined that Romney would have won the bet, the perception of the situation was far worse for Romney as his ease at putting $10,000 at stake appeared elitist to middle class Americans.[55]

At the February 22nd debate in Arizona the gloves came off and Romney and Santorum had a series of testy exchanges that attacked each other professionally and personally.[56] Santorum criticized Romney for supporting the Wall Street bailout for wealthy bankers but not the one for the auto industry and working class Americans. In the spirit of the double-team effort that had emerged Gingrich also hammered at Romney's record for attacking Santorum on support of Congressional earmarks while defending his acceptance of public funding in support of the Salt Lake City Olympic Games.

Endorsements

Romney netted many big name endorsements on his way to the nomination. Some came early in the process and others happened around the time specific states held their primaries. Former Minnesota Governor Tim Pawlenty, himself an early front running candidate, dropped out after the Iowa straw poll in August 2011 and backed Romney. Pawlenty was a frequent surrogate on the television talk shows and on the short list for Romney's vice presidential nominee.

New Jersey Governor Chris Christie, Mississippi Governor Haley Barbour, businessman Donald Trump, Arizona Governor Jan Brewer, Arizona Senator John McCain, Oklahoma Senator Tom Coburn, House Majority Leader Eric Cantor, former New Hampshire Governor John Sununu, and former first lady Barbara Bush were some of the notable names to endorse Romney's run.

On March 21, former Florida Governor Jeb Bush endorsed Romney. The timing, a day after the Illinois primary, seemed strange as it was not aimed at influencing the vote in any particular primary. Bush went on to say that Romney should pick Marco Rubio, a U.S. Senator from Florida and Bush protégé, as his running mate. In the last week of March, Rubio gave his own endorsement of Romney. This was followed by a press conference with former president George H.W. Bush and Barbara Bush where the former president gave his official endorsement.

Wisconsin Representative Paul Ryan, chair of the House Budget Committee, provided a key endorsement prior to his state's primary. The Ryan endorsement the week before the primary was seen as significant since he represents a district in southern Wisconsin which is more working class and could have supported Santorum. Conversely, in Ohio, Attorney General Mike DeWine initially endorsed Romney and then switched to supporting Santorum. DeWine, who served in the Senate with Santorum, cited Romney's divisive and negative campaign as the reason for his change of heart.

OUTCOME

Romney averaged first or second in public opinion polls throughout 2011. One of the interesting features of the race was that other candidates who were seen as being more conservative than Romney jumped to the top of the polls and then fell almost as quickly as they rose (for example, Bachmann, Perry, Cain, Gingrich, and Santorum). Each was viewed as the "anti-Romney" around which conservatives might rally. Each was found to have flaws in their message or in their personal life that led voters to abandon them (see other chapters).

One conservative who never rose in the pre-primary polls was Rick Santorum, a former U.S. Senator from Pennsylvania who lost his 2006 reelection bid by 18 points. Santorum's campaign did not take off until his surprising finish in the Iowa caucus that made him a player in the nomination fight.

The Iowa Caucus was held on January 3. Team Romney played down expectations in Iowa. Having come in second in 2008 behind Mike Huckabee and spending a lot of time there in the following years, Romney initially expected to do well. But in summer 2011 there appeared to be a change in strategy. Romney spent less time and attention in Iowa; he chose not to campaign for the Ames Straw Poll. Bachmann, a hometown favorite, won the Ames Straw Poll on August 13 to propel her candidacy. Romney came in seventh behind Rick Perry who was a write-in candidate and announced his candidacy on the same day in South Carolina. Tim Pawlenty finished second and, lacking money, dropped out of the race soon after and endorsed Romney. By the end of 2011 the Romney team started to push the narrative that they would not do well in Iowa and even diverted the candidate away from appearing at too many events in Iowa.

Romney was declared the winner of the Iowa caucus on election night by eight votes over Santorum. There were questions about the vote count around the state and specifically the totals for Romney, Santorum, and Ron Paul. Finally, two weeks later, Iowa officials stated that Santorum had won the caucus by 34 votes. For Romney it was not a major setback. He already exceeded expectations in Iowa and went to New Hampshire looking like the inevitable nominee. For Santorum it was a great victory but one that was tamped down by losing out on the big momentum and fundraising advantages he could have garnered from his underdog triumph.

The Romney campaign waltzed into New Hampshire on January 10 as the heavy favorite. Being the former governor of the neighboring Massachusetts and having a home in the Granite State, the question was not whether Romney would win but by how much. He won 39.3 percent of the vote compared to 22.9 percent for Ron Paul and 16.9 percent for Jon Huntsman. Romney earned eight of the twelve delegates. Disappointed with the result, Huntsman dropped out of the race.

The Iowa and New Hampshire victories propelled Romney on to South Carolina with a chance to sweep the first three states and all but clinch the nomination. But Gingrich had other plans and went on the attack. Gingrich won among more conservative South Carolina voters with 40.4 percent of the vote to Romney's 27.8 percent. Nearly all categories of voters by age, income, and ideology favored Gingrich over Romney. In a closed primary with a significant portion of evangelicals, questions immediately reemerged as to whether Romney could win Christian conservative base voters in the Republican Party.

A turning point came in Florida. Romney was the early favorite in Florida from the time the Sunshine State decided to front load their primary to January 31 in an attempt to be the kingmaker. Romney placed second on Florida in 2008 behind McCain. The importance of Florida was understood by the various campaigns. It is the fourth largest state, the largest swing state, and it contains significant Hispanic and Jewish populations. Romney was the favorite because he had an organization in place, he had money to spend on Florida's 10 major media markets, and he had people on the ground to gather absentee ballots, an important part of winning in Florida.

He racked up key endorsements including from Cuban-American members of Congress Ileana Ros-Lehtinen, Mario Diaz-Balart, and former congressman Lincoln Diaz-Balart, as well as Congressman Connie Mack IV, the frontrunner for the Republican nomination for U.S. Senate. Romney had campaigned for Marco Rubio during his Senate race in 2010 and tried to tie his campaign to the popular first term Senator. Rubio did not endorse in the race and neither did former governor Jeb Bush. (George H.W. Bush did not endorse but said during this time he preferred Romney).[57] Romney did well in the two Florida debates and Gingrich sunk partially on his immigration stance and his extended discussion of establishing a moon colony. When Gingrich's Super PAC ran an ad criticizing Romney as being "anti-immigrant" Rubio defended Romney and condemned the ad.[58] Having an advantage in absentee and early voting and a strong money advantage, Romney won a significant victory in Florida with 46 percent to Gingrich's 32 percent and 13 percent for Santorum to regain control of the race.

Then Romney hit a minor bump in the road. Santorum won Missouri, Minnesota, and Colorado on February 7. Although Missouri was a nonbinding "beauty contest" and Gingrich was not on the ballot, the 50 percent win by Santorum again led to questions of whether Romney could win the heartland and among the average Republican voters.

On February 11, Romney righted his campaign with two small but significant victories. First, he won the Maine caucuses by 39 percent to 36 percent over Ron Paul. The northeastern state was an expected victory for Romney. The close second for Paul was a credit to him as he worked hard in Maine and was generally strong in caucus states.

The other victory came in a straw poll at the Conservative Political Action Conference (CPAC) among the core of the country's conservatives. Four years prior Romney gave a rousing speech to CPAC that impressed many conservatives. However, that was Romney's concession speech as he stepped out of the 2008 race. Four years later he was left with the criticism that he was not conservative enough for the stalwart conservatives. His straw poll victory at their significant convention was notable.

Then Romney straightened his campaign's ship on February 28 with victories in Arizona and Michigan. Arizona was not suspenseful as he led in the polls throughout the campaign. The endorsement of Arizona Senator and 2008 Republican Presidential nominee John McCain during the New Hampshire primary gave him a popular and tireless supporter in Arizona. Then two days before the vote, Arizona Governor Jan Brewer endorsed Romney citing his immigration policy and his electability.

The big test was Romney's native state of Michigan. The state where Romney was born and raised, where his father was a three-term governor, and a swing state that would be a test of a candidate's electability, it would have been devastating for Romney to lose there. Santorum pulled ahead in several polls and by as much as nine points in the week leading up to the primary due to slips in Romney's campaign.[59] Santorum put out a "robocall" to Democrats that called for them to go out and vote for him in Michigan's open primary. Exit polls showed that some of them did vote and they preferred Santorum. Romney got the endorsement of Governor Rick Snyder, a businessman who in his first term was enjoying popularity among Republicans. Romney pulled out a 41 percent-38 percent victory.

That set the stage for Super Tuesday on March 6. Romney regained his frontrunner status and left Santorum and Gingrich searching for ways to get back into the race while Ron Paul continued to appeal to his core voters. A turning point on the Sunday before Super Tuesday occurred during a forum on *Huckabee*, a show hosted by the former Arkansas governor and 2008 presidential candidate. On the forum televised on Fox News, Romney was asked a direct question from a small business owner whose son was injured in combat. Romney's answer exhibited emotions and showed his humanity as opposed to perceptions of him as being robotic. The minor incident played a major role in the news cycle leading into the biggest day of primary elections in the 2012 campaign.

On Super Tuesday, Romney won six out of ten contests including the biggest prize, Ohio. He also won Alaska, Idaho, Massachusetts, Vermont, and Virginia. Virginia was a 60-40 win for Romney over Ron Paul. Neither Gingrich nor Santorum qualified under the stringent Virginia election rules even though it was both of their home states at the time. Romney's Virginia win over his two main competitors granted him an extra advantage in delegates. But the 40 percent of the vote that Paul garnered was seen as a protest and a collection of the anti-Romney sentiment in the electorate. Meanwhile Santorum won Tennessee, Oklahoma, and North Dakota, and Gingrich won Georgia, where he had served as a Congressman and Speaker of the House. Those outcomes showed that Romney was having trouble winning in the south, but his second place finish in

Georgia, Tennessee, and Oklahoma showed that he was strong enough to beat back his other competitors.[60]

Santorum went on to win Kansas, Alabama, Mississippi, three reliable Republican states. Still, Romney's lead in the delegate count was insurmountable and his fundraising advantage was formidable. Santorum's wins did not translate into large donations and through the end he and Gingrich continued to split the anti-Romney vote. With conservatives divided, and a stronger campaign apparatus than his opponents, Romney was able to hold off the challengers.

On March 18, Romney won Puerto Rico's delegates with the help of the endorsement of Governor Luis Fortuño, who was then mentioned as a vice presidential candidate.[61] As a U.S. territory, Puerto Rico does not have any electoral votes in the presidential election—though its residents do vote in presidential primaries—and the issue of potential statehood is controversial.

March 20 in Illinois was a turning point. The see-saw battle between Romney and his more conservative opponents broke in Romney's favor when he won the Illinois primary by 47 percent to 35 percent against Santorum. In President Obama's home state, Romney and the pro-Romney Super PAC outspent Santorum by seven to one.[62] Romney won moderates but he also won more conservative voters. He won voters who support the Tea Party as well as those that oppose it. He won Catholic voters and he closed the gap with evangelical voters. Romney won folks earning $50,000-$100,000, which Santorum had won in several other states, while winning the upper income voters. It was a nearly complete victory that sealed the nomination for the former Massachusetts governor.

Romney's speech that evening showed a tired candidate who made several slips. But the message was as clear as it had been during the primaries. He continued to attack the president and compared his vision with that of the man in the White House.

> And three years of Barack Obama have brought us fewer jobs and shrinking paychecks, but many of us believed we were in danger of losing something even more than the value of our homes and our 401(k)s. After years of too many apologies and not enough jobs, historic drops in income and historic highs in gas prices, a president who doesn't hesitate to use all the means necessary to force through Obamacare on the American public, but leads from behind in the world. It's time to say these words, this word: enough. We've had enough … You and I know something the president still hasn't learned. Even after three years and hundreds of billions of dollars of spending and borrowing, it is not the government that creates our prosperity. The prosperity of America is the product of free markets and free people, and they must be protected and nurtured … I'm offering a real choice and a

new beginning. I'm running for president because I have the experience and the vision to get us out of this mess.[63]

Santorum and Gingrich both said they would stay in the race but it was just a matter of time before they would be forced out. Santorum won Louisiana on March 24 continuing his dominance in the south and with evangelical voters.

On April 3, Romney won in Wisconsin 44 percent to 37 percent for Santorum as well as a 49-29 percent margin in Maryland and a commanding 70 percent win in Washington, D.C. Santorum announced on April 10, two weeks before the Pennsylvania primary that he would quit the race saying he needed to spend more time with his family. A lack of funding, polls showing Romney ahead in the state Santorum once represented in the Senate, and an ill daughter at home sealed Santorum's campaign and ensured that Romney would be the Republican nominee.

Romney won the rest of the primary contests and officially secured the 1,144 delegates needed to clinch the nomination with a victory in Texas on May 29. Romney was in Las Vegas that evening at a fundraiser with Donald Trump. Newt Gingrich also joined the presumptive nominee on the night Romney secured the necessary delegates which under proportional allocation rules for some time seemed unreachable. Gingrich released his supporters, most prominently casino magnate Sheldon Adelson, to donate to Romney's campaign and the pro-Romney Super PAC Restore Our Future, Inc.

At one point in the thick of the contests it appeared that the race would run through all 50 states as it did between Democratic candidates Barack Obama and Hillary Clinton in 2008. But Romney was able to run a largely disciplined campaign, raise money, stay on message, and split the conservative vote between his rivals. There were five contests on June 5 but by then Romney was already the presumptive Republican nominee and had pivoted to fully focus on the battle to beat President Obama.

ANALYSIS

Romney started the nomination campaign as a strong front runner though not the clear favorite. He struggled to get more than 25 percent to 30 percent in the pre-primary polls and then to get above 40 percent in many of the primaries and caucuses. A series of "anti-Romney" candidates rose and fell (Bachmann, Perry, Cain, Gingrich, and Santorum) as rank-and-file conservative Republicans yearned for someone to better represent their views than the party establishment-favored Romney. Ultimately, due to a financial advantage, the lack of a clear alternative for conservative voters, and a relatively disciplined campaign, Romney prevailed.

For a period of time it was popular to talk about the possibility of a brokered national convention in Tampa, Florida, from August 27-30, something that had not happened since 1952. If Gingrich or Santorum or both stayed in the race along with Ron Paul then maybe they could have split the delegates and denied Romney the clear majority needed to win the nomination. Talk of a new candidate jumping in the race even as late as February showed that Romney lacked the confidence of many Republicans.[64] Ultimately, Romney outlasted his opponents and won the nomination outright.

As veteran political commentator E.J. Dionne put it during the campaign:

> Mitt Romney is grinding his way to the Republican presidential nomination not by winning hearts but by imposing his will on a party that keeps resisting him. He is assembling the peripheral elements of the GOP as his rivals divide the votes of the passionate believers. His campaign is part John McCain, part Michael Dukakis and part Richard Nixon. In its way, Romney's achievement is impressive. He is neither a natural politician nor a comfortable spokesman for an increasingly ideological, evangelical, Southern and enraged political coalition. Romney is a man of flexible views from the Northeast, a Mormon who wins votes from the least religious sectors of his party, a rather satisfied man who has to announce that he's angry because he doesn't look it.[65]

Romney endured the nomination campaign despite his failure to earn large support from evangelical voters. In each primary where evangelicals were a minority of the overall voters Romney won and where evangelicals were the majority of voters Romney lost either to Santorum or Gingrich.[66]

A number of factors contributed to Romney's nomination: his financial advantage, the relatively weak field of competitors, the perception among the mainstream that his competitors were too conservative for the country as a whole, his support from the party establishment, and his largely disciplined and simple campaign message. Romney benefited from the perception that he would be the best candidate to handle the economy. He kept the criticism on the Obama administration and ran a campaign that made a plurality of voters believe that he had the best chances of beating the president.

Romney survived the rough primary campaign relatively unscathed. He was attacked by his rivals for being a "vulture capitalist" and for getting wealthy at Bain Capital while thousands of people lost their jobs at companies that Bain either sold or closed down through restructuring. When Romney clinched the nomination the Obama campaign started to attack. But Democrats like Newark Mayor Cory Booker, Massachusetts Governor Duval Patrick, and Former President Bill Clinton essentially defended Romney's record at Bain Capital.

The issue of Romney releasing more than two years of tax returns became more vexing during the summer months. Calls from Republican rivals were to be expected during the primary process. But once Romney became the Republican standard bearer then Democrats and the mainstream media started to demand more transparency and more information about his financial background. Then conservative columnists like William Kristol and George Will put more pressure on Romney with further calls for him to release more tax returns and put the issue behind him. Still Romney, who had provided the McCain campaign with 23 years of tax returns when he was vetted for the vice presidential spot in 2008, stuck to his decision to only release two years to the public.[67]

It was clear for many months leading into the campaign that the economy would be the dominant issue. With unemployment nationally over eight percent, gas and food prices rising, a lingering housing crisis, and the cost and supply of energy resources dominating the economic concerns, the candidate that could articulate a stronger vision for economic recovery and growth would have the advantage. In 1992, the phrase "It's the economy, stupid" dominated the campaign. Twenty years later the same theme resonated heavily as the United States was still struggling to emerge from a financial downturn that began prior to the 2008 election.

In late July many national polls showed Romney and Obama in a statistical dead heat. Several polls showed Romney with a slight lead while others gave the edge to the president. A significant development was that more Americans believed that Romney would be stronger on the economy even as more people seemed to personally like Obama better than the Republican challenger.[68]

Throughout the campaign, Romney was critiqued on his history of various positions and statements on health care, abortion, gay rights, guns, and immigration. Romney was able to deflect criticism, defeat several challengers, and devote his attention to positioning himself to battle President Obama for the presidency on November 6, 2012.

NOTES

1. James Walcott. "Looking for Love in All the Right Places," *Vanity Fair* 2011, "http://www.vanityfair.com/politics/features/2011/06/james-wolcott-republicans2012-201106"

2. The fifth, George W. Bush, son of George H.W. Bush, won the nomination on his first attempt.

3. Alex Altman, "Mitt Romney's *No Apology*," *Time* 2010,"http://www.time.com/time/politics/article/0,8599,1969266,00.html"

4. Romney was named for J. Willard Marriot, the hotel magnate, a close friend of his father, and Milton 'Mitt' Romney, a relative who played for the NFL's Chicago Bears. According to Romney's brother, he was called Bill as a child until in kindergarten he started calling himself Mitt (Harvard Crimson).

5. 'About Mitt,' "http://mittromney.com/learn/mitt" (accessed February 15, 2012).

6. Michael Kranish and Scott Helman, *The Real Romney* (New York: HarperCollins, 2012); R.B. Scott. *Mitt Romney: An Inside Look at the Man and His Politics* (Guilford, CT: Lyons Press: 2012).

7. Romney's parents wanted a fourth child but were told by doctors for five years that it was not possible, then Lenore became pregnant with Mitt.

8. Jeffrey N. Gell, "Romney Gains Momentum As He Keeps On Running," *The Harvard Crimson* 1994, "http://www.thecrimson.com/article/1994/10/21/romney-gains-momentum-as-he-keeps/" (accessed February 22, 2012).

9. Kranish and Helman, *The Real Romney*.

10. Kranish and Helman, *The Real Romney*.

11. Gell, "Romney Gains Momentum," Kranish and Helman, *The Real Romney*.

12. Gell, "Romney Gains Momentum," Kranish and Helman, *The Real Romney*.

13. Robert Frank, "Romney is the Richest Candidate in a Decade," *Wall Street Journal* 2012, "http://blogs.wsj.com/wealth/2012/01/03/romney-is-richest-candidate-in-a-decade/" (accessed June 20, 2012).

14. Nicholas Shaxson, "Where the Money Lives," *Vanity Fair* 2012, "http://www.vanityfair.com/politics/2012/08/investigating-mitt-romney-offshore-accounts"

15. Lori Montgomery, Jia Lynn Yang, and Philip Rucker, "Mitt Romney's tax returns shed some light on his investment wealth," *Washington Post* 2012, "http://www.washingtonpost.com/politics/2012/01/23/gI-QAj5bUMQ_story.html?wpisrc=al_comboNP" (accessed July 18, 2012).

16. "Mitt Romney says he didn't inherit money from his parents," *Politifact* 2012, "http://www.politifact.com/truth-o-meter/statements/2012/jan/20/mitt-romney/mitt-romney-says-he-didnt-inherit-money-his-parent/" (accessed March 1, 2012).

17. Kranish and Helman, *The Real Romney*; Politifact, "Mitt Romney says."

18. Kranish and Helman, *The Real Romney*.

19. Alicia Cohn, "Romney's tax return headache," *The Hill*, January 17, 2012.

20. Montgomery, Yang, and Rucker, "Mitt Romney's tax returns."

21. Frederick E. Allen, "Romney: I like Bank Bailouts, Just Not Auto Bailout," *Forbes* 2012, http://www.forbes.com/sites/frederickallen/2012/03/22/romney-i-like-bank-bail-outs-just-not-auto-bailouts/" (accessed June 15, 2012).; Jackie Kucinich, "Romney seems unscathed over support for TARP," *USA Today* 2012, "http://www.usatoday.com/news/politics/story/2012-03-26/romney-TARP-bank-bailout/53794680/1"

22. Mitt Romney, "Let Detroit Go Bankrupt," *New York Times* 2008, "http://www.nytimes.com/2008/11/19/opinion/19iht-edromney.1.17959143.html?_r=1" (accessed March 1, 2012).

23. Headlines are almost never written by the author of an article or column.

24. Mitt Romney, "U.S. autos bailout was 'crony capitalism on a grand scale'," *The Detroit News* 2012, "http://www.detroitnews.com/article/20120214/OPINION01/202140336" (accessed March 15, 2012).

25. Kranish and Helman, *The Real Romney*.

26. Jason Cherkis, "Mitt Romney Registered as Lobbyist for Salt Lake City Olympics," *Huffington Post* 2012, http://www.huffingtonpost.com/2012/07/26/mitt-romney-olympics_n_1704261.html

27. "Believe in America: Mitt Romney's plan for jobs and economic growth," "http://www.mittromney.com/blogs/mitts-view/2011/09/believe-america-mitt-romneys-plan-jobs-and-economic-growth (accessed June 29, 2012).

28. "Mitt Romney's Plan for Jobs and Economic Growth," "http://www.mittromney.com/issues/tax"

29. "On the Issues: Mitt Romney on Budget & Economy," "http://www.issues2000.org/2012/Mitt_Romney_Budget_+_Economy.htm"

30. Katrina Trinko, "Romney Advisor: Romney took Massachusetts from last in job creation to 30th," *National Review* 2012, "http://www.nationalreview.com/corner/301652/romney-adviser-romney-took-massachusetts-last-job-creation-30th-katrina-trinko"(accessed June 15, 2012).

31. Matt DeLong, "Mitt Romney challenges Rick Perry to $10,000 bet in GOP debate," *Washington Post* 2011, "http://www.washingtonpost.com/blogs/election-2012/post/mitt-romney-challenges-rick-perry-to-10000-bet-in-gop-debate/2011/12/11/gIQAudrBnO_blog.html" (accessed April 25, 2012)

32. Becky Bowers, "Rick Perry says Mitt Romney's book deleted line that Mass. health care law should be the model for the country," *Politifact* 2011, "http://www.politifact.com/truth-o-meter/statements/2011/dec/11/rick-perry/rick-perry-says-mitt-romneys-book-deleted-line-mas/"(accessed April 25, 2012)

33. Ashley Parker, "'Poor' Quote by Romney Joins a List Critics Love," *New York Times* 2012, "http://www.nytimes.com/2012/02/02/us/politics/poor-quote-by-romney-seized-on-by-his-critics.html" (accessed April 25, 2012).

34. Michael Tanner, "Lessons from the Fall of RomneyCare," *Cato Institute* 2008, "http://www.cato.org/pubs/policy_report/v30n1/cpr30n1-1.html"

35. Josh Dzieza, "Romneycare and Obamacare differ only in inconsequential ways," *The Daily Beast* 2012, "http://www.thedailybeast.com/articles/2012/03/06/romneycare-and-obamacare-differ-only-in-inconsequential-ways.html" (accessed April 30, 2012); Elise Foley, 'Obama Campaign celebrates 'Romneycare' Anniversary,' *Huffington Post*, "http://www.huffingtonpost.com/2012/04/12/obama-campaign-romney-care_n_1420184.html"

36. Mitt Romney, "Mr. President, what's the rush?," *USA Today* 2009, "http://www.usatoday.com/printedition/news/20090730/column30_st.art.htm" (accessed March 30, 2012).

37. Phillip Elliott, "Rick Santorum: Mitt Romney 'worst Republican' to face Obama," *Huffington Post* 2012, "http://www.huffingtonpost.com/2012/03/25/rick-santorum-mitt-romney-worst-republican_n_1378713.html"(accessed March 30, 2012).

38. Kristen A. Lee, "Romney campaign donations hit $4.6 million following health care decision," *New York Daily News* 2012, "http://www.nydailynews.com/news/election-2012/romney-campaign-donations-hit-4-6-million-health-care-decision-article-1.1104716" (accessed July 1, 2012).

39. Michael O'Brien, "Romney boasts of 'severely conservative' record in CPAC speech," *MSNBC* 2012, "http://nbcpolitics.nbcnews.msn.com/_news/2012/02/10/10375038-romney-boasts-of-severely-conservative-record-in-cpac-speech?lite" (accessed March 8, 2012).

40. Julie Hirschfird Davis, "Romney Calls Himself 'Severely Conservative' as Rivals Make Case," *Bloomberg Businessweek* 2012, "http://www.businessweek.com/news/2012-02-12/romney-calls-himself-severely-conservative-as-rivals-make-case.html" (accessed April 25, 2012)

41. "Romney defends himself as 'severely conservative'," *Boston Globe* 2012, "http://www.boston.com/news/politics/articles/2012/02/22/romney_defends_himself_as_severely_conservative/"

42. Christopher Orr, "Mitt Romney as Tarantino's Superman," *The New Republic* 2008, "http://www.tnr.com/blog/the-plank/mitt-romney-tarantinos-superman" ; Eric Ericson, "A severe conservative speaks at CPAC," *Red State* 2011, "http://www.redstate.com/erick/2012/02/10/a-severe-conservative-speaks-at-cpac/" (accessed May 1, 2012).

43. Julia Preston, Binyamin Appelbaum, and Trip Gabriel, "Romney's Lawn Care History and the Fight Over Immigration," *New York Times* 2011, http://www.nytimes.com/2011/10/19/us/politics/illegal-immigration-and-romneys-lawn-care-debated.html (accessed May 14, 2012).

44. Elizabeth Llorente, "Former Gov. Pete Wilson, Immigration Hardliner, Named Honorary Romney Campaign Chair," *Fox News Latino* 2012. "http://latino.foxnews.com/latino/politics/2012/02/06/mitt-romney-names-former-gov-pete-wilson-immigration-hardliner-as-honorary" (accessed May 14, 2012).

45. Tom Cohen, "Obama administration to stop deporting some young illegal immigrants," *CNN* 2012, "http://www.cnn.com/2012/06/15/politics/immigration/index.html" (accessed June 25, 2012).

46. Kranish and Helman, *The Real Romney*.
47. Kranish and Helman, *The Real Romney*.
48. "Poll: Qualms about Mormonism widespread, but may not impact Romney's run for the presidency," *Washington Post* 2012, "http://www.washingtonpost.com/politics/poll-qualms-about-mormonism-widespread-but-may-not-impact-romneys-run-for-the-presidency/2012/07/26/gJQAqZYmBX_story.html" (accessed July 26, 2012).
49. "Poll: Qualms about Mormonism."
50. Michael D. Shear, "For Romney's Trusted Advisor, 'Etch-A-Sketch' Comment is a Rare Misstep," *New York Times* 2012, "http://www.nytimes.com/2012/03/22/us/politics/etch-a-sketch-remark-a-rare-misstep-for-romney-adviser.html"
51. "Candidate support from small donors," *New York Times* 2012, "http://www.nytimes.com/interactive/2012/03/08/us/politics/small-donor-support.html?ref=politics" (accessed March 8, 2012).
52. Nicholas Confessore and Ashley Parker, "Romney Lags in Small Donors as Big Givers Hit Limits," *New York Times*, 2012, "http://www.nytimes.com/2012/03/08/us/politics/romney-lags-in-gop-grass-roots-fund-raising.html?_r=1&ref=todayspaper" (accessed March 8, 2012).
53. Federal Election Commission, "2012 Presidential Campaign Finance," "http://www.fec.gov/disclosurep/pnational.do" (accessed June 28, 2012).
54. Jeff Zeleny and Jim Rutenberg, "Romney is Opponents' Main Target in G.O.P. Debate," *New York Times*, January 16, 2012. "http://www.nytimes.com/2012/01/17/us/politics/forceful-attack-against-romney-in-republican-debate.html?pagewanted=all" (accessed June 25, 2012).
55. Bowers, "Rick Perry says Mitt Romney's book."
56. Alexander Burns, "Republican debate: Mitt Romney and Rick Santorum get personal in Arizona," *Politico* 2012, "http://www.politico.com/news/stories/0212/73185.html" (accessed June 25, 2012).
57. Both Rubio and Jeb Bush later endorsed Romney.
58. "Rubio defends Romney's immigration record," *CBS Miami* 2012, "http://miami.cbslocal.com/2012/01/25/rubio-defends-romneys-immigration-record/" (accessed January 30, 2012).
59. These included a small audience for a campaign rally at Ford Field and the comment about his wife having 'a couple of Cadillacs.'
60. "State-by-State Primary Results," *New York Times* 2012, "http://elections.nytimes.com/2012/primaries/calendar" (accessed June 22, 2012).
61. Daniel Strauss, "GOP strategists: Puerto Rico Gov. Fortuno is sleeper vice presidential pick," *The Hill* 2012, "http://thehill.com/blogs/ballot-box/presidential-races/221497-gop-strategists-puerto-rico-gov-fortuno-is-a-sleeper-vp-pick" (accessed June 28, 2012).
62. "Lopsided Illinois Primary: Santorum Faces 7-to-1 Spending Disadvantage Against Romney Forces," *ABC News* 2012, "http://abcnews.go.com/blogs/politics/2012/03/lopsided-illinois-primary-santorum-faces-7-to-1-spending-imbalance-against-romney-forces/" (accessed March 25, 2012).
63. "Mitt Romney's Illinois Victory Speech," *Real Clear Politics* 2012, "http://www.realclearpolitics.com/articles/2012/03/20/mitt_romneys_illinois_victory_speech_113565.html" (accessed June 15, 2012).
64. Jeb Bush, Chris Christie, and Mitch Daniels were consistently suggested as candidates to get in the race.
65. E. J. Dionne, "Mitt Romney, Winning votes but not love," *Washington Post* 2012, "http://www.washingtonpost.com/opinions/mitt-romney-winning-votes-not-love/2012/03/07/gIQADLiExR_story.html" (accessed March 8, 2012).
66. E. J. Dionne, "Romney's challenge to sway evangelical voters," *Washington Post* 2012, "http://www.washingtonpost.com/opinions/religion-continues-to-play-a-strong-role-in-the-gop-campaign/2012/03/21/gIQAgGIJSS_story.html" (accessed March 25, 2012).

67. Justin Sink, "Former McCain advisor: Romney taxes complex but not 'disqualifying'," *The Hill* 2012, "http://thehill.com/blogs/blog-briefing-room/news/239367-mccain-adviser-romneys-tax-returns-do-not-look-anything-like-the-average-american" (accessed July 27, 2012).

68. Michael O'Brien, "Romney fights to retain economy as trump card," *MSNBC* 2012, "http://nbcpolitics.msnbc.msn.com/_news/2012/07/25/12951184-romney-fights-to-retain-economy-as-trump-card?lite" (accessed July 27, 2012); Susan Page, "Poll: Romney preferred over Obama to handle the economy," *USA Today* 2012, "http://www.usatoday.com/news/politics/story/2012-07-23/poll-romney-obama-economy/56439758/1" (accessed July 27, 2012); Danny Yadron, "WSJ/NBC Poll: Romney Leads on the Economy, Trails Elsewhere," *The Wall Street Journal* 2012, "http://blogs.wsj.com/washwire/2012/07/24/wsjnbc-poll-romney-leads-on-the-economy-trails-elsewhere/" (accessed July 27, 2012).

TWELVE
The Victor's Reward and the Future of the GOP

William J. Miller

If one wished to summarize the 2012 elections, they could do so with the following two statements: 1) Given the economic situation, Republicans should have won in 2012; 2) Instead, the GOP snatched defeat from the jaws of victory.[1] As Paul Krugman told America prior to the election, it is simply not an easy time to be a Republican candidate. To win a nomination, you must manage to appeal to business leaders, evangelical Christians, and those who are opposed to taxes and big government all at the same time. So preach government interference on social issues and laissez-faire policies economically. Then assure America that President Obama (who gave us a Republican-designed healthcare reform and assured the killing of Osama bin Laden) is a socialist looking to obliterate everything sacred in the United States. To do this—as Krugman notes—one must be cynical or clueless.[2] In the case of Mitt Romney, this is even more difficult because by being a cynic, one is forced to act clueless in order to appeal to certain facets of the Republican base. But unfortunately, his acting was too obvious and as a result, a series of clueless challengers routinely came up and attempted to unseat him without success. Dog after dog kept trying to catch the proverbial car, only to end up being run over.[3] The sheer volume of challengers, however, showed the overall discontent with a Romney candidacy.

James Carville was as direct as to ask, "Why does this thing that appears to have so much value have so many low bidders?"[4] Further, he explains that the GOP nomination became "the political equivalent of the Hope Diamond going for $99.99."[5] The fact is that there was too much misinformation, unworkable solutions (such as electrifying border fences to solve the illegal immigration issue), and right-wing pandering that moderate Republicans realized there was no point in even entering the fray. It came down to the well-known adage "Do not deal with stupid. They drag you down to their level and then beat you with experience." And it is not that I am aiming to label any Republican voters or candidates stupid, but their actions have led to serious questions and harmed the party. Herman Cain did not know China has nuclear weapons. Michele Bachmann did not know there was an American embassy in Iran. Rick Perry still contests evolution and did not know 18 year olds could vote for him. Republicans watching debates live chose to boo a gay soldier and cheer the idea of Americans dying without health insurance. Watching from the outside, one would be worried about any of the individuals on stage being identified as the right person to lead the backbone of the free world.

Mitt Romney was the rock. While every other Republican candidate succumbed to some fatal flaw, Romney stood strong in the storm and ultimately claimed victory. Yet for many Republicans, he was not worthy of a ringing endorsement. He emerged from the storm too battered to rally complete support. Instead, it seemed that more than a few GOP supporters supported Romney simply because he survived. And as soon as he finished winning the nomination, an ever more difficult fight waited just around the corner.

ROMNEY AGAINST OBAMA

After everything Romney went through and survived to win the Republican nomination, his prize was to face another battle—one being played at an even higher level with a far greater prize to be won. And in the end, Romney was unable to carry the torch all the way to the finish, losing the general election to Obama and only faring moderately better than John McCain had done in 2008. The narrative one could use to describe the 2012 presidential race is quite simple: Romney experienced a prolonged primary battle in which he had to bring together a fractured party while Obama utilized momentum from his historic 2008 victory coupled with successful legislative efforts and policy decisions to overcome lagging approval numbers and debatable economic gains.

The general election campaign got going with Obama launching television ads in swing states that were designed to paint Romney as an elitist, incapable of understanding the issues facing Middle America. Romney knew foreign policy would be a noted weakness on his resume and consequently he took off for Europe. Unlike Obama's rock star tour in 2007, Romney's was full of gaffes. As the campaign went on, Bill Clinton began actively campaigning for Obama. His appearances corresponded with an Obama surge in national public opinion polls. Then Romney was videotaped at a Republican fundraiser in Florida stating that he had little concern for the 47 percent of Americans "who are dependent on government" and "will vote for this president (Obama) no matter what." After that became publicized, Obama seemed to have a clear path to victory.[6]

Then he took the stage in Denver for the first presidential debate. Whether it was because he failed to take Romney seriously or was simply over-confident, President Obama delivered a deflating performance, opening the door for his Republican challenger to regain some momentum. While Obama was able to regain his debate mastery from 2008 in the subsequent presidential debates, his empathetic response to Hurricane Sandy really seemed to resonate with voters. While pundits and pollsters seemed to think the race would be close on Election Day, Obama's targeted effort was able to guarantee him a second presidential term. His performance was strikingly similar to 2008, with only North Carolina and Indiana switching from blue to red (which was largely expected given the surprise of both states' leanings four years prior).

There is no denying the 2008 election was a historic occurrence. Between the significance of Obama being the first African-American president and his utilization of new technologies better than any campaign before, 2008 will be a year election scholars look back on for all of time. But 2012 may actually be more meaningful when we consider long-term trends. 2008 suggested that the American electorate was fundamentally changing; 2012 confirmed it. As Chuck Warren—a Republican strategist—suggested following the 2012 results, "we're a Mad Men party in a Modern Family world."[7] If the GOP chooses to serve as a regionalized party largely consisting of older white evangelical males, there is only a limited opportunity for success moving forward. Everyone knew that some key demographic groups would come into play during 2012, but not even most Democrats thought Romney would fare so poorly with Latinos, young voters, women, and suburbanites.

Once the results from Florida came in roughly a week after the polls closed, Obama won the Electoral College 332-206 (slightly worse than his 365-173 win over McCain in 2008). But the popular vote was actually much closer with Obama only ahead by approximately 2.5 million votes (more than seven million less than in 2008). So while Obama actually fared worse nationwide, he was successful with the Electoral College by winning each of the pre-identified swing states within the entire electorate. In 2012, the nine identified swing states were Colorado, Florida, Iowa, Nevada, New Hampshire, North Carolina, Ohio, Virginia, and Wisconsin (with Colorado, Florida, Ohio, and Virginia being identified as the most competitive). While these statewide results demonstrate how Obama won, what matters for Republicans moving forward is how key voting blocs within key states ultimately swung the election to Obama.

What the 2012 election demonstrates best is exactly how demographics are guiding voters toward particular candidates more than ever. If only white men could vote, Romney would have won 45 states. If only men could vote, Romney would have won 34 states. If only white voters could participate electorally, Romney would have claimed 39 states. Even if voters only over age 24 could have voted, Romney would have been successful in 27 states (including flipping Ohio and Florida). But with the modern electorate, Romney only won in 24 states. As the electorate expands, Romney's performance weakens significantly. The 2010 Census results showed that minorities could be a political force if they came out to vote. Despite Obama's efforts to appeal to these voters through federal support for education, housing, and medical care, he still was not sure whether they would actually be out to cast ballots. Brookings created three pre-election simulations to predict how minorities could impact the 2012 election.[8] In the initial scenario, Brookings took 2008 turnouts and margins and applied them to the 2010 Census population. With those parameters in place, Obama won 358-180, including ten states solely due to minority votes. In the second iteration, Brookings instead applied 2004 turnouts and margins for all voters to the 2010 Census figures. Here, Romney won the Electoral College, but Obama claimed 11 states solely due to minority votes. And in the last scenario, Brookings used 2004 turnouts and margins for whites and 2008 for minorities. Obama won this iteration 292-246, with 14 states being propelled to the Democrat thanks to minority votes.

The demographic changes in 2012 that propelled Obama to victory were labeled as tectonic by some and have the potential to alter the political landscape far into the future.[9] Working-class, Caucasian voters that tend to be older have voluntarily become Republicans while being joined by rural and small-town Depression-era individuals. In the other direction, cities and large suburbs with rapidly expanding minority bases are the new Democratic strongholds. To describe the entire 2012 election in one sentence, we could state that while Romney did slightly better for almost every demographic (gender, racial, ethnic, almost all income and education categories) than McCain did in 2008, his key constituencies (the less-educated and whites) did not turn out to vote like they were expected to and Obama did much better with two groups, Hispanics and Asian-Americans.

In the 2012 presidential election, CNN chose six swing voters in six swing states and followed their decision-making process. They had a millennial from New Hampshire, a Catholic residing in Ohio, a long-term unemployed male from Nevada, a Latino in Florida, a single woman in Virginia, and an evangelical male in Iowa. And the ultimate vote decision of these six largely reflected the nation as a whole with five out of six indicating that Obama was their candidate of choice come Election Day.[10] Romney simply needed white males to turn out. Bill McIntruff claimed early in the campaign that the white/nonwhite divide would be the most important measure for Romney on Election Day. If the number dropped below 73 percent, odds were that Obama would have a fairly easy win.[11] Even with Romney doing four points better than McCain had with white voters, it did not matter when they were two percent less of the vote share. Obama—on the other hand—did best with what was referred to as the "coalition of the ascendant."[12] Young people, minorities, college-educated, and blue-collar women formed the backbone of his core electorate. And they were turning out at high volumes.

It was difficult to pinpoint exactly what group was most important to Obama's re-election. But many would argue it was actually white America, which failed to turn out in the requisite numbers to lead Romney to the White House. A week after the election, Dick Morris explained, "the mainstream media is pushing the story that a massive turnout among minorities and the young drowned the white male vote as America changes its demography. But the real reason is that the whites who supported Romney didn't turn out to vote."[13] Morris highlighted Ohio as an example. Romney lost Ohio by approximately 110,000 votes; but he also received nearly 100,000 less votes in the Buckeye State than McCain had in 2008.

What we saw in 2012 was evidence of a pivot election in which the electorate makes a lasting shift. If we consider the pro-Obama (and likely pro-Democrat) changes from 2012, 70 percent of Latinos, 73 percent of Asian-Americans, more than 90 percent of African-Americans, 60 percent of Americans under 30, and approximately 60 percent of unmarried women supported Barack Obama in the 2012 election. And most importantly, all of these groups made up a larger share of the electorate in 2012 than they had in 2008.[14] It may well be that as we see the partitioning of the country based on demographic peculiarities that Republicans can remain competitive in House districts (as based on 2010 and 2012 results) but be at a disadvantage in national elections.

WHERE DO THEY GO FROM HERE?

For individual Republican voters, the question entering 2016 is what their ultimate goal is. If individual voters want to vote for the candidate that best fits their individual values and beliefs, there will likely be another crowded, possibly drawn out nomination battle. On the other hand, if their version of success is assuring that the GOP takes back the White House by defeating Hillary Clinton, Andrew Cuomo, Joe Biden, or whichever Democrat they face, there should be a more streamlined, less combative environment. But as we know, voters are finicky. Asking someone to sacrifice their desired vote for the good of the party is not an easy task—particularly when the Republican Party exists in as extreme silos as it does today. When we point to differences within party believers today, we are mixing individuals who consider transvaginal ultrasounds, corporate tax rates, and individual liberty to be priority issues.

Democrats used to be accused of being the big tent party; they accepted any opinion and view and were willing to somehow fit it into the party platform. Whereas Republicans were identified by either being small government, pro-business, or social conservatives, Democrats were known as anyone not a Republican for simplicity's sake. In the past, this led to many arguing it was difficult to be a Democratic candidate because you had to appeal to so many different factions. But today, it is becoming increasingly clear that it is actually easier to be a Democratic candidate since that party's various factions have become increasingly more accepting of their differences than Republican counterparts. In 2008, President Obama was able to run on the slogans of Hope and Change; in 2012, he successfully followed up with the theme of Forward. While admittedly simplistic, the themes worked so well because they encompassed the desires of all party identifiers (along with many non-Democrats). For a national-level Republican candidate, the task of finding a one-word vision would be a Sisyphean task.

But what do Republicans expect? When a large sector of your base is made up of evangelical Christian farmers who publicly denounce welfare programs but protest when farm subsidies are cut, it is hard to rely on or even expect rational, educated decision-making when choosing a candidate that optimizes odds in a general election. So what do Republicans need to do between today and 2016? First, they need to focus on internal dynamics by identifying candidates that could potentially appeal to all three factions--the business-backers, Tea Partiers, and evangelical Christians. And once these individuals have been identified, they need to make sure they do more to build up the possible candidates rather than bringing them center stage to be tarred and feathered as they seemingly did to Romney. If instead the party chooses to cannibalize presumptive favorites who have the best chances at defeating their opponents, it could be a long time before a Republican takes back the White House.

The problem for Republicans, of course, is that their strongest demographic supporters are quickly perishing. As former Minnesota Senator Norm Coleman stated after the election, "What worries me is that the GOP is about to become the WOP—the White Old Party."[15] Likewise, another pundit predicted, "any candidate that wants to run a campaign only at whites is going to lose . . . [Republican] voters are white, aging, and dying off."[16] Higher levels of turnout do not mean much when the group is quickly shrinking in terms of electoral percentage. And Republicans have not taken this news necessarily well. November 14th, Romney met with supporters on a conference call and stated that Obama had followed the "old playbook" of targeting specific initiatives to swing voters—"especially the African-American community, the Hispanic community and young people . . . In each case, they were very generous in what they gave to those groups."[17] Romney discussed forgiving college loan interest and certain Obamacare provisions as examples of reaching out to young voters, for example. With regards to Hispanics, Romney stated, "free health care was a big plus. But in addition with regards to Hispanic voters, the amnesty for children of illegals, the so-called DREAM Act kids, was a huge plus for that voting group."[18]

While Romney's reaction seemed to be that of a sore loser coming to grips with the outcome of a hard-fought race, those of Main Republican Chairman Charlie Webster were even more alarming. Webster claimed, "in some parts of rural Maine, there were dozens, dozens of black people who came in and voted on Election Day. Everybody has a right to vote, but nobody in town knows anyone who's black. How did that happen? I don't know. We're going to find out."[19] Webster seems to be in complete denial. Demographically, he must face the same two realizations that all Republicans need to. First, and foremost, the Republicans have a Latino problem. They have not been within 20 points of the Democratic nominee with this demographic since George W. Bush lost by 18 points to John Kerry amongst Hispanics in 2004. And it will take more than rolling out Hispanic Republicans such as Marco Rubio, Ted Cruz, Susana Martinez, or Brian Sandoval once every four years at the Republican Convention to close that gap. As Republican strategist Ana Navarro explained, "If we don't do better with Hispanics, we'll be out of the White House forever."[20] And second, the white vote is shrinking and will likely not rebound unless the GOP takes critical steps to better reach out to voters of all walks of life and improve their ground game.

So who are the 2016 options? For Tea Party supporters, Marco Rubio (Senator from Florida) and Rand Paul (Senator from Kentucky) would both be appealing. Paul, especially, has advocated the Tea Party message at the national level since joining Congress. He has even worked to expand the Tea Party focus to include all constitutional issues—as evidenced by his famous drone filibuster. And Rubio ran a Tea Party campaign but has failed to officially join the subsequent caucus in the Senate. Both, however, have negatives that could be exploited by social conservatives. Many Christians question Paul's Aqua Buddha controversy from college while Rubio spent time in the Mormon Church in his pre-teen years. Plus Rubio needs to remember to keep water at the podium to prevent potential embarrassment.

Paul Ryan could be an option. He withstood the test well as a vice presidential nominee in 2012 and holds many of the pro-business and anti-government ideals that two factions of the Republican Party support. But he is Catholic (which likely would cause a degree of angst with evangelical Christians—especially in the South). And he did not succeed in getting Romney the excitement bump he needed to win the White House. Evangelical Christians would likely support seeing Rick Santorum run again. But his story is old now. The same issues that prevented him from winning in 2012 would likely re-emerge in 2016. He is simply too polarizing. Mike Huckabee would be an acceptable alternative. Yet would he give up a comfortable life as a popular commentator to enter the ring and have to fight for his views and beliefs again? And then there are the three governors. Chris Christie is still immensely popular with the GOP due to his union-busting, no-holds-barred approach to politics. Yet his positive sentiment toward Obama in the immediate lead-up to the 2012 elections during the aftermath of Hurricane Sandy has led to some Republicans souring on him. Bobby Jindal was the golden child of the GOP only a few years ago. Then he gave the Republican Response to the State of the Union Address in 2009. His robotic, rambling message turned off supporters and led to his disappearance from the national political discussion for quite a while. Maybe the 2016 Republican race will call out another member of a legacy family—with attention focused on former Florida Governor Jed Bush. He is friendly with Hispanics and speaks the language well. He was a popular, moderate governor who had few major controversies directly tied back to him during his term (except the Terri Schiavo case and the 2000 election nightmare). But his last name is Bush and that may eliminate him from contention. Or that could be the fault of his moderate reputation. Regardless, it is highly doubtful that both Bush and Rubio would stay in the race at the same time for long given the potential for splitting the Florida vote and costing both of them the chance to win the nomination.

Who will be the Republican savior? It is too early to tell for sure. But the qualifications for the position are more demanding now than at any point in recent memory. First, the candidate will have to unite business leaders, Tea Party patriots, and evangelical Christians under one banner. Then, the nominee will need to assure that the GOP reaches out to new potential supporters—especially Hispanics and younger voters. But the efforts to reach these targeted populations will need to be genuine. Paying lip service to concerns and ideas will simply not cut it. In fact, it will likely backfire and harm the party moving forward. And did I mention that this savior candidate will need to be basically bulletproof? Before he or she ever sees a general election, fellow Republicans will make sure the world knows about every possible negative they possess. Assuming they heed the warning, the 2012 nomination should have reminded Republicans that there is no benefit to doing all of the opposition research for their Democratic opponents. With friends like the ones who took the stage more than twenty times with him throughout 2011 and 2012, why would Mitt Romney need to be concerned with enemies?

NOTES

1. Paul Krugman, "Send in the Clowns," *New York Times* 2011, http://www.nytimes.com/2011/12/05/opinion/send-in-the-clueless.html?partner=rssnyt&emc=rss&_r=0 (accessed January 2, 2012).
2. Krugman, "Send in the Clowns."
3. Chris Cillizza, "What Herman Cain meant," *Washington Post* 2011, http://www.washingtonpost.com/blogs/the-fix/post/what-herman-cain-meant/2011/12/03/gIQArl07OO_blog.html (accessed March 4, 2012).
4. James Carville, "Why the GOP Field is So Weak," *CNN* 2011, http://www.cnn.com/2011/12/08/opinion/carville-gop-field/index.html?hpt=hp_c3 (accessed December 29, 2011).
5. Carville, "Why the GOP Field is So Weak."
6. Lucy Madison, "Fact-checking Romney's '47 percent' comment," *CBS News* 2011, http://www.cbsnews.com/8301-503544_162-57515033-503544/fact-checking-romneys-47-percent-comment/ (accessed December 24, 2012).
7. Laura Chapin, "The GOP now a 'Mad Men' party in a 'Modern Family' world," *Denver Post* 2012, http://blogs.denverpost.com/opinion/2012/11/07/gop-mad-men-party-modern-family-world/28232/ (accessed February 11, 2013).
8. William H. Frey, "Why Minorities Will Decide the 2012 U.S. Election," *Brookings Institute* 2012, http://www.brookings.edu/research/opinions/2012/05/01-race-elections-frey.
9. Neil King, Jr., "Vote Data Show Changing Nation," *Wall Street Journal* 2012, http://online.wsj.com/article/SB10001424127887324073504578105360833569352.html (accessed March 11, 2013).
10. "The Undecided: Have they made up their minds?," *CNN* 2012, http://www.cnn.com/2012/11/05/politics/undecided-voters-decisions/index.html (accessed March 1, 2013).
11. "What to watch for on Election Night," *CNN* 2012, http://www.cnn.com/2012/11/06/politics/what-to-watch-election/index.html (accessed November 22, 2012).
12. Ronald Brownstein, "Why Obama is Leading in Swing States," *National Journal* 2012 http://www.nationaljournal.com/2012-presidential-campaign/why-obama-is-leading-in-swing-states-20121001 (accessed October 15, 2012).
13. Dick Morris, "The Real Reason We Lost," Dick Morris.com 2012, http://www.dickmorris.com/the-real-reason-we-lost/ (accessed December 21, 2012).
14. David, Lauter, "Nonwhite voters and cultural shifts make 2012 election pivotal," *Los Angeles Times* 2012, http://articles.latimes.com/2012/nov/10/nation/la-na-election-20121111 (accessed December 1, 2012).
15. King, Jr., "Vote Data Show Changing Nation."
16. Halimah Abdullah, "With their big political win, the new American electorate has arrived," *CNN* 2012, http://www.cnn.com/2012/11/09/politics/demographic-political-power/index.html (accessed December 5, 2012).
17. Ashley Parker, "Romney Blames Loss on Obama's 'Gifts' to Minorities and Young Voters," *New York Times* 2012, http://thecaucus.blogs.nytimes.com/2012/11/14/romney-blames-loss-on-obamas-gifts-to-minorities-and-young-voters (accessed February 4, 2013).
18. Parker, "Romney Blames Loss on Obama's 'Gifts' to Minorities and Young Voters."
19. Kevin Robillard, "GOP chief: Mystery black voters," *Politico* 2012, http://www.politico.com/news/stories/1112/83895.html (accessed February 2, 2013).
20. Paul Steinhauser, "Five things we learned on Election Night," *CNN* 2012, http://www.cnn.com/2012/11/07/politics/5-things-election-night/index.html (accessed February 2, 2013).

About the Editor

William J. Miller is the director of institutional research and effectiveness at Flagler College in St. Augustine, Florida. He received his doctorate in 2010 in public administration and urban studies from The University of Akron along with a master's degree in applied politics (campaign management and polling). He had previously earned his B.A. from the Ohio University Honors Tutorial College and an M.A. in political science also from Ohio. He is the editor of *Tea Party Effects on 2010 U.S. Senate Elections: Stuck in the Middle to Lose* , *Taking Sides: Clashing Views on Public Administration and Policy*, *The Political Battle over Congressional Redistricting* , *The Tea Party in Government: Does the Party Roll On?*, and *Handbook on Teaching and Learning in Political Science and International Relations*. His research appears in *Journal of Political Science Education*, *Journal of Political Marketing*, *Studies in Conflict and Terrorism*, *International Studies Quarterly*, *Nonproliferation Review*, *Afro-Americans in New York Life and History*, *Journal of South Asian and Middle Eastern Studies*, *American Behavioral Scientist*, *PS: Political Science and Politics*, *e-Journal of Public Affairs*, *Political Science Quarterly*, and *Journal of Common Market Studies*.

About the Contributors

Brian Arbour is an assistant professor of political science at John Jay College, City University of New York. His research focuses on campaign message strategy and ethnic voting in American elections. He received his Ph.D. from the University of Texas at Austin, where he got to see the political strengths and weaknesses of Rick Perry from an up close perspective. Professor Arbour also works on the Decision Desk for Fox News Channel, the election night group that analyzes exit poll results and calls races for the network.

Daniel J. Coffey is an associate professor of political science at the University of Akron and a research fellow in the Ray C. Bliss Institute of Applied Politics. His research interests include political parties, state politics, campaigns and elections, and political psychology. He has published articles in *State Politics and Policy Quarterly*, *PS: Political Science*, and the *Journal of Political Science Education*. He is also the lead author of *Buckeye Battleground: Ohio, Campaigns, and Elections in the Twenty-First Century*, along with John C. Green, David B. Cohen, and Stephen C. Brooks, and co-editor (with John C. Green) of *The State of the Parties* (5th and 6th editions).

William Cunion is an associate professor of political science and an associate academic dean at the University of Mount Union in Alliance, Ohio. He teaches a variety of courses in American Government, and has written a number of book chapters and articles on the presidency. He also spends a tremendous amount of time in meetings that would surely be better spent with his family in Shaker Heights, Ohio.

David F. Damore is an associate professor of political science at the University of Nevada, Las Vegas, a Nonresident Senior Fellow in Governance Studies at the Brookings Institution, and a contributing analyst for Latino Decisions. His primary research interests are the study of campaigns and elections and policy making at the state and federal levels. He is presently working on a book length manuscript examining the political and economic consequences of Nevada's geography. Dr. Damore's research has been published in academic outlets such as the *Journal of Politics*, *Political Behavior*, *Political Research Quarterly*, *State Politics and Policy Quarterly*, and *American Politics Quarterly*.

Sean D. Foreman is an associate professor of political science at Barry University. He is co-editor of The *Roads to Congress 2010* where he wrote the Introduction and about Marco Rubio's election to the U.S. Senate, and co-editor of *The Roads to Congress 2012* in which he wrote the Introduction and about Florida District 26. He authored chapters about Florida Districts 21 and 25 U.S. Congressional elections for *The Roads to Congress 2008* and "Marco Rubio in Florida: The First Tea Party Senator—Or Not?" in *Stuck in the Middle to Lose: Tea Party Effects on 2010 U.S. Senate Elections*. His article "Top 10 Reasons Why Barack Obama Won the Presidency in 2008 and What It Means in the 2012 Election," was published in the *Florida Political Chronicle*. Foreman served as president of the Florida Political Science Association in 2012-13. Foreman hosts a weekly radio show called *World of Politics* on Barry's WBRY radio station that streams on the Internet at www.barry.edu/radiostation, is a guest on talk radio and television programs in Florida and around the world, and is quoted in many publications on Florida and national elections.

Brandy Kennedy is an assistant professor of political science and public administration at Georgia College and State University. She received her Ph.D. from the University of Oklahoma. Her dissertation, "Representative Bureaucracy: An Exploratory Analysis Using Role Perception" uses mixed methodology to explore bureaucratic role perceptions. Her research and teaching interests include representation, political behavior, and public opinion.

Terrence M. O'Sullivan is an associate director of the Center for Emergency Management and Homeland Security Policy Research, assistant professor of political science, and adjunct professor in the Consortium of Eastern Ohio Master of Public Health (CEOMPH) Program at the University of Akron. Before joining the faculty at Akron, he was a research associate at the Center for Risk and Economic Analysis of Terrorism Events (CREATE) at the University of Southern California–the first Department of Homeland Security Center of Excellence. His research includes examination of domestic U.S. politics and policy, especially around areas of natural disaster, public health, and terrorism risk.

Andrew L. Pieper is an assistant professor of political science at Kennesaw State University in metro Atlanta. He teaches courses in American politics, including the U.S. Presidency, U.S. Congress, political behavior, and research methods. His research interests revolve around the intersection of religion and American politics, particularly in the culture wars between the American left and right. He has published in numerous outlets, including the *New England Journal of Public Policy* and *American*

Politics Research. His current research focuses on religion and the environmental movement.

Joshua T. Putnam is a visiting assistant professor of political science at Davidson College, having received his Ph.D. from the University of Georgia. Most of his research explores the ways in which national party delegate selection rules impact state-level decision-making in response as well as the subsequent process of nominating presidential candidates. His blog Frontloading HQ has garnered national attention from the media, national and state parties, and campaigns by highlighting the intricacies of these rules and placing their impact in their proper context within the presidential primary and caucus system.

Kenneth J. Retzl is a doctoral student at the University of Nevada, Las Vegas. His research focuses on various aspects of public opinion, both in the United States and abroad.

Jason Rich is an assistant professor of political science at Georgia College. His research interests include U.S. foreign policy, international security, and U.S. electoral studies. He has published articles and chapters on coercion theory, paradiplomacy, as well as U.S. and Canadian foreign policy. During the 2012 election cycle he conducted a series of student-centered focus groups on the presidential debates and provided regular commentary and analysis for the local media. Currently his research focuses on the balancing behavior of the United States as well as international cooperation in response to HIV/AIDS.

Joshua P. Stockley (Ph.D., University of Oklahoma, 2005) is an associate professor of political science and director of the honors program at the University of Louisiana at Monroe. His teaching and research cover American government, state and local politics, campaigns and elections, political parties, Southern politics, culture and politics, public policy, and public administration. He has published articles and book chapters that have appeared in the journals *Race, Class, and Gender*, *Southern Political Report*, and *Louisiana Progress Journal*, as well as edited volumes *Mediated Images of the South* and *The Roads to Congress*. He writes a regular column for the *News-Star* and is a frequent media contributor to newspapers, radio stations, and television stations in the state and nation.

Jeremy D. Walling is an associate professor of political science at Southeast Missouri State University. He received his Ph.D. in 2005 from the University of Kansas and his M.P.A. from Missouri State University in 1998. He studies American national institutions, state politics, intergovernmental relations, and public administration ethics and accountability. He was co-editor (with William J. Miller) of *Tea Party Effects on*

2010 U.S. Senate Elections: Stuck in the Middle to Lose and *Taking Sides: Clashing Views in Public Administration and Policy*. Book chapters have been published in *The Battle to Face Obama: The 2012 Republican Nomination* , *Teaching Politics Beyond the Book,* and *The Constitutionalism of American States*. His work has also appeared in *The Handbook of Administrative Ethics* and *Public Personnel Management,* both with H. George Frederickson.

Index

Adelson, Sheldon, 14, 31, 152, 164, 168, 170, 238
Akin, Todd, 96
Allred, Gloria, 114
Ames Straw Poll, 9, 11, 12, 77, 88, 89, 94, 157, 160, 188, 190, 201, 202, 234
Anderson, Bob, 80
Angle, Sharron, 168

Bachmann, Michele, ix, 9, 9–10, 12, 15, 38, 39, 68, 77–96, 103, 104, 133, 137, 160, 188, 190, 199, 209, 246
Bailek, Sharon, 114
Bain Capital, 4, 13, 16, 163, 164, 222, 223–224, 230, 239–240
Baker, Martin, 160
Baldwin, Chuck, 192
Barbour, Haley, 11, 43–44, 48, 233
Bartlett, Bruch, 107
Battley, Jackie, 151
Bell, Chris, 130
Bennett, Bill, 155
Bernanke, Ben, 7, 135
Biden, Joe, 249
bin Laden, Osama, 2, 245
Bisek, Callista, 151
Block, Mark, 8, 110, 117
Boehner, John, 48, 86
Bolton, John, 46, 47, 48
Booker, Corey, 239
Brazil, Jamie, 111
Brewer, Jan, 233, 236
Brisbane, Arthur, 190
Brown, Scott, 41, 42
Buchanan, Pat, 184, 207, 213
Burka, Paul, 136, 141
Bush, Barbara, 233
Bush, George W., 29, 43, 46, 54, 64, 68, 79, 119, 120, 130, 132, 135, 139, 141, 199, 214, 251

Bush, Jeb, 11, 35, 44, 233, 235, 252
Cain, Herman, ix, 8–9, 12, 15, 38, 39, 68, 71, 91, 92, 95, 103–121, 133, 156, 159, 160, 170, 174, 187, 201, 246
Cantor, Eric, 233
Carey, Ron, 89
Carney, Dave, 132–133, 154–155, 156
Carter, Jimmy, 78, 219
Carville, James, 132, 245
Casey, Bob, 199
Castellanos, Alex, 155
Cato Institute, 64
Cavuto, Neil, 109
Chaffetz, Jason, 65
Cheney, Dick, 46, 79, 159
Chocola, Chrtis, 64
Christie, Chris, 11, 35, 52–53, 54, 73, 142, 233, 252
Citizens United v. FEC, 3, 231
Clar, Tarryl, 80
Clark, Wesley, 54
Clinton, Bill, 6, 151, 219, 226, 240, 246
Clinton, Hillary, 206, 238, 249
Coburn, Tom, 233
Colbert, Stephen, 69
Coleman, Norm, 250
Colmes, Alan, 5
Connaly, John, 133, 142
Conway, Kellyanne, 160
Cooper, Anderson, 158, 189
Corker, Bob, 42
Crist, Charlie, 49, 167
Cruz, Ted, 251
Cuomo, Andrew, 249
Cuomo, Mario, 43

Daniels, Mitch, 11, 35, 51–52, 73
Daschle, Tom, 40
Davis, Fred, 66

Dawson, Katon, 154, 156
Dawson, Sam, 154, 156
Dean, Matt, 79
Defense of Marriage Act, 82
DeLay, Tom, 183
Delisi, Denise, 133
DeMint, Jim, 41, 48, 188
Democratic Change Commission, 23
Democratic National Committee, 23, 26
DeWine, Mike, 233
Diaz-Balart, Mario, 235
Dickerson, John, 92
Dionne, E.J., 239
Dobson, James, 151
Dodd-Frank Act, 67
Dole, Bob, 50, 213, 220
Don't Ask, Don't Tell, 82, 200
DREAM ACT, 7, 16, 228
Dukakis, Michael, 163, 239
Dyke, Jim, 90

Eisenhower, Dwight, 45
Erickson, Erick, 118

Fannie Mae, 92, 167
Fehrnstrom, Eric, 231
Fischer, Bryan, 109
Fleetwood, Susannah, 3
Flynt, Jack, 150
Forbes, Steve, 110, 184
Ford, Gerald, 213
Ford, Jr., Harol, 42
Fortuno, Luis, 43, 237
Frank, T.A., 120
Fratto, Tony, 135
Freddie Mac, 12, 92, 150, 161, 162, 164, 167, 168, 173
Friedman, Kinky, 130
Friess, Foster, 14, 31, 212

Gacy, John Wayne, 15, 87
Gaddafi, Muammar, 2, 91, 115
Gaines, Leslie, 165
Garfield, James, 54
General Motors, 4, 206, 223–224
Gingrich, Newt, ix, 6–7, 12–15, 15, 16, 30, 31, 36, 37, 38, 39, 40, 55, 92, 113, 115, 116, 133, 140, 149–174, 192, 201, 203, 208, 220, 223, 228, 231–232, 236

Giuliani, Rudy, 94
Godfather's Pizza, 8, 104, 156
Goldberg, Bernard, 47
Gordon, J.D., 115
Gore, Al, 29, 161
Gramm, Phill, 133, 142, 183
Gray, Rosie, 192
Gregory, David, 155

Haley, Nikki, 165
Haley, Vince, 164, 172
Hammond, R.C., 160
Hanna III, Frank, 212
Hannity, Sean, 114
Harding, Warren G., 54, 55
Hastert, Dennis, 79
Hayek, Friedrich, 182
Healthcare reform, 2, 11, 38, 48, 81, 83, 84, 86, 107, 134, 141, 154, 155, 158, 167, 189, 200–201, 226–227, 230
Heilemann, John, 205
Hemingway, Andrew, 163
Hightower, Jim, 129
Hill, Stephen, 200
Horne, Chris, 165
HPV, 7, 9, 15, 16, 90, 128, 137–138, 141, 208
Huckabee, Mike, 11, 42, 50–51, 85, 93, 111, 171, 199, 208, 213, 227, 234, 236, 252
Huntsman, Jon, ix, 10, 11, 14, 15, 38, 61–73, 92, 106, 113, 129, 133, 156–157, 164
Hurley, Chuck, 161
Hutchison, Kay Bailey, 130, 131, 132–133

InTrade, 3
Issenberg, Sasha, 133

Jacobs, Larry, 85, 87
Jindal, Bobby, 35, 48, 49, 50, 142, 252
Johnson, Gary, 11, 212
Johnson, Rob, 133, 154–155, 156
Jones, Joanne, 165

Kasich, John, 3
Keene, David, 187
Kellem, Kevin, 159

Kennedy, John F., 2, 5, 15, 210, 211
Kennedy, Mark, 79
Kennedy, Edward, 41, 228
Kerry, John, 29, 163–164, 251
King Jr., Martin Luther, 6
King, John, 165
Klein, Ezra, 134
Koberg, Katie, 159
Kraushaar, Karen, 114
Krauthammer, Charles, 51
Kristol, William, 137, 240
Krugman, Paul, 245
Krull, Michael, 160, 172

Laffer, Arthur, 106
Laidig, Gary, 78
Laughlin, Greg, 183
Lee, Mike, 2
Libya, 8, 9, 15, 82, 87, 91, 115, 118, 118–119, 154
Limbaugh, Rush, 155
Lowden, Sue, 168
Lowrie, Rich, 110
Lowry, Kevin, 118–119

Madigan, Edward, 150
Mallea, Jose, 166
Marianne Ginther, 151
Martinez, Susana, 251
Matthews, Chris, 80
McCain, John, 5, 29, 50, 63, 66, 71, 93, 112, 166, 184, 213, 219, 220, 227, 233, 235, 236, 239, 240, 246, 247, 248, 249
McConnell, Mitch, 40
McCormack, John, 117
McDaniel, Gerri, 165
McDonnell, Bob, 45, 211
McGovern-Fraser Commission, 21, 32n1
McIntruff, Bill, 248
McKinnon, Mark, 89, 138
Medicare, 10, 87, 90, 134, 137, 154, 155, 173, 187
Medved, Michael, 121
Merck, 90, 138
Morgan, Piers, 108
Morris, Dick, 249
Mourdock, Richard, 96
Mulshire, Paul, 190

National Restaurant Association, 8, 9, 113
Nixon, Richard, 61, 62, 182–183, 220, 239
No Child Left Behind, 205
Noonan, Peggy, 118–119
Norquist, Grover, 43
Norris, Chuck, 50
Norwick, Yale, 79
Noyes, Rich, 69

Obama, Barack, ix, 2, 3, 4, 5, 7, 8, 9, 10, 12, 13, 16, 21, 30, 35, 36, 40, 41, 42, 44, 49, 55, 62, 65, 67, 85, 87, 93, 105, 119, 129, 134, 150, 153, 158, 159, 165, 170, 198, 200, 207, 211, 219, 231, 237–238, 240, 245, 246–249
O'Brien, Soledad, 37
Occupy Wall Streetr, 45, 205
Olson, Allen, 165
O'Malley, Martin, 169
Otto, Rebecca, 79

Palin, Sarah, 14, 42, 51, 55, 80, 85, 93, 94, 152, 166, 187, 208
Pataki, George, 43, 44
Patrick, Duval, 240
PATRIOT ACT, 187
Paul, Rand, 2, 41, 192, 251
Paul, Ron, ix, 5–6, 13, 16, 38, 39, 40, 92, 133, 156, 181–194, 202, 205, 212, 223, 231, 234
Pawlenty, Tim, 11, 15, 38, 133, 152, 156, 160, 227, 233, 234
Pelosi, Nancy, 79, 161
Pence, Mike, 42
Perdue, Sonny, 156
Perot, Ross, 110
Perry, Rick, ix, 7–8, 11–12, 15, 16, 37, 38, 39, 54, 68, 89, 90, 91, 94, 95, 104, 113, 114, 119, 127–142, 149, 154, 156, 158, 159, 160, 167, 174, 199, 200, 202, 208, 209, 212, 213, 223, 225, 232, 246
Petraeus, David, 45–46, 48
Plouffe, David, 132
Polk, James, 54
Polyansky, Don, 89

Reagan, Ronald, 6, 42–43, 50, 63, 66, 85, 153, 157, 165, 167, 185, 186, 209, 213, 220
REAL ID Act, 187
Reid, Harry, 168
Republican National Committee, 11, 23–24, 26, 28–29, 80, 90
Republican Temporary Delegate Selection Committee, 22, 23
Rice, Condoleezza, 46
Richards, Ann, 141
Roberts, John, 227
Roemer, Buddy, 11
Rollins, Ed, 85, 89, 152, 205
Romney, Ann, 220
Romney, Mitt, ix, 1, 4, 11–12, 12–13, 14–15, 16, 16–17, 29, 29–30, 31, 36–37, 38, 39, 40, 42, 48, 50–51, 55, 61, 63, 67, 68, 70, 71, 72, 73, 77, 86, 90, 91, 93, 95, 104, 112, 113, 115, 121, 129, 133, 137, 138, 149, 153, 158, 160, 162–163, 168, 173, 187, 190, 192, 199, 202, 203, 204–205, 206, 209, 212, 213, 219–240, 245, 246–249
Roosevelt, Franklin Delano, 2
Ros-Lehtinen, Ileana, 235
Rothbard, Murray, 182
Rove, Karl, 79, 132, 135
Rubio, Marco, 2, 11, 41, 48, 49–50, 58n46, 142, 166, 229, 233, 235, 243n57, 251–252
Ryan, Nolan, 184
Ryan, Paul, 10, 35, 48–49, 50, 54, 122n13, 142, 155–156, 173, 233, 251

Sabato, Larry, 136
Sanchez, Tony, 130
Sandoval, Brian, 73, 168, 251
Santorum, Rick, ix, 5, 12–13, 14–15, 15, 16, 30, 31, 38, 39, 40, 55, 138, 149, 161, 162, 170, 172, 174, 191–192, 193, 197–214, 227, 231–232, 234, 236, 251
Savage, Dan, 5
Schiavo, Terri, 198
SCHIP, 187
Schoenfield, Craig, 154, 156, 159
Scott, Rick, 45
Searcy, Nick, 117
Sharp, John, 130

Sherlock, Ruth, 165
Sherman, William, 45
Simon, Roger, 190
Snowe, Olympia, 41
Snyder, Rick, 236
Sorensen, Kent, 92
Stephanopoulos, George, 65
Stewart, Jon, 190
Strayhorn, Carol Keaton, 130
Sullivan, Lyno, 78, 79
Sununu, John, 233
Super PAC, 3, 12, 13, 14, 30–31, 32, 70, 133, 152, 164, 166, 168, 168–169, 170, 172, 173, 202, 203, 212, 231–232, 235, 237, 238
Superdelegates, 22

Tea Party, ix, 1, 2, 6, 10, 11, 17, 39, 40, 45, 49, 51, 61, 77, 80, 81, 82–83, 84, 86, 89, 92, 93, 95–96, 103, 105, 134, 153, 155, 160, 162, 162–166, 167, 168, 171, 173, 187, 188–189, 202, 207, 211, 223, 227, 237, 251, 252
Templeton, Jr., John, 212
Tesler, Michael, 208
Thompson, Fred, 54, 151
Thompson, Ted, 78–79
Thune, John, 11, 40–41
Tinklenberg, Elwin, 80
Toomey, Mike, 138
Toomey, Scott, 110
Trump, Donald, 11, 12, 15, 47, 48, 103, 199, 233, 238
Tsongas, Paul, 213
Tyler, Rick, 154, 156

Vander Plaats, Bob, 160
von Mises, Ludwig, 182

Waldeck, Adam, 164
Walker, Bob, 160
Walker, Scott, 3, 45, 108
Warren, Chuck, 247
Wayne, John, 15, 87
Weaver, John, 66
Webster, Charlie, 251
Weeks, David, 133
Wehner, Peter, 135
Welch, David, 90

Wetterling, Patty, 79
Whetsell, Walter, 156
White, Bill, 131, 136
White, Ginger, 115, 116, 121
Will, George, 182, 184, 240
Williams, Juan, 7, 165
Williamson, Kevin, 107
Wilson, Pete, 229

Winston, David, 160
Wood, L. Lin, 115
Woodruff, Judy, 114
Wright, Jim, 150

Yepsen, David, 152
York, Byron, 199